The BCS Glossary of ICT and COMPUTING TERMS

Eleventh Edition

Edited by

**The British Computer Society Schools Expert Panel
Glossary Working Party**

Members of the Working Party
ARNOLD BURDETT
DIANA BURKHARDT
ALINE CUMMING
HAZEL CURTIS
ALAN HUNTER
FRANK HURVID
JOHN JAWORSKI
THOMAS NG
JOHN SOUTHALL

Former members of the Working Party

(whose work is included in this edition)
BRIAN JACKSON
LAURIE KELLER
GRAHAM ROGERS
TIM REEVE

PEARSON
Prentice
Hall

in association with The British Computer Society

Harlow, England • London • New York • Boston • San Francisco • Toronto • Sydney • Singapore • Hong Kong
Tokyo • Seoul • Taipei • New Delhi • Cape Town • Madrid • Mexico City • Amsterdam • Munich • Paris • Milan

Pearson Education Limited
Edinburgh Gate
Harlow
Essex CM20 2JE
England

and Associated Companies throughout the world

Visit us on the World Wide Web at:
www.pearsoned.co.uk

First published by the British Computer Society 1977
Fourth, fifth and sixth editions published by Cambridge University Press
Seventh edition published by Pitman Publishing 1991
Eighth edition published by Longman Group Ltd. 1995
Ninth edition published by Addison Wesley Longman 1988
Tenth edition published by Pearson Education Ltd. 2002
This edition published 2005

ISBN 0131 479571

British Library Cataloguing-in-Publication Data
A catalogue record for this book is available from the British Library

Library of Congress Cataloging-in-Publication Data
The BCS glossary of IT and computing terms / edited by the British Computer Society
  Schools Expert Panel Glossary Working Party.—11th ed.
    p.   cm.
  Rev. ed. of: A glossary of computing terms. Addison-Wesley, 2002.
  Includes index.
  ISBN 0-13-147957-1 (pbk.)
    1. Electronic data processing—Dictionaries.   2. Computers—Dictionaries.
  3. Information technology—Dictionaries.   I. British Computer Society. Glossary
Working Party.   II. Title: Glossary of computing terms.

QA76.15.G59 2004
004′.014—dc22   2004054680

10 9 8 7 6 5 4 3 2 1
09 08 07 06 05

Typeset in 10/12pt Times by 35
Printed in Great Britain by Henry Ling Ltd., at the Dorset Press, Dorchester, Dorset

The publisher's policy is to use paper manufactured from sustainable forests.

22399

The BCS Glossary of ICT and Computing Terms

We work with leading authors to develop the strongest
educational materials in computing, bringing cutting-edge
thinking and best learning practice to a global market.

Under a range of well-known imprints, including
Prentice Hall, we craft high-quality print and electronic
publications which help readers to understand and apply
their content, whether studying or at work.

To find out more about the complete range of our
publishing, please visit us on the World Wide Web at:
www.pearsoned.co.uk

Contents

Part D   How Computers Work

Part E   Appendices

Tables and Figures

Tables

Figures

How to use this glossary

This glossary is not a dictionary; nor is it intended to be used as a text book. The only place you will find a full alphabetical list of all the terms covered is in the index at the back of the book.

For example, looking up 'virus checking' in the index leads you to page 153. You will need to scan the page for '*Virus checking*'. You will find it as part of the definition of 'Anti-virus software', which is reproduced below.

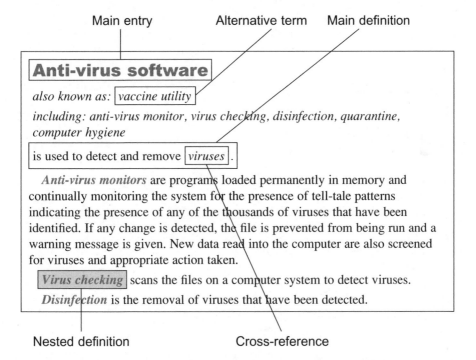

An alternative way of finding the appropriate entry is to examine the lines in *italics* immediately after the main entry. These provide a list of terms covered in that definition.

Each section begins with some background information (see, for example, pages 141–142) and you may like to read this as well.

There are, of course, other ways of using this glossary. Related terms occur together, and you may find it helpful to read through a complete section or subsection.

Tim Reeve

This glossary is dedicated to the memory of Tim Reeve. He was a founder member of the Glossary Working Party in 1974. In 1991 he became its Chair and at his untimely death in October 2000 he was working on the final draft of the tenth edition.

Introduction

This glossary, which contains over 3000 terms, provides not only a comprehensive definition of each term but also sufficient additional material to enable the reader to understand the importance of the term, how to use it appropriately and its relation to other terms used in the same area of computing. To this end, terms are gathered into parts, describing how computer systems are used, what they are made of, how they are developed and how computers work. As you would expect in an authoritative volume, there are also copious appendices.

Each part is divided into sections defining terms on a particular topic; large sections are subdivided further. It is hoped that readers will take advantage of this structure to browse within sections; to assist in this, each section has a general introduction providing additional information that puts the terms into context.

The glossary has as one of its principal aims to meet the needs of students following courses leading to examinations at school and college level. It is often a definitive reference source, specified in examination board syllabuses. The content has increasingly found wide acceptance in universities and colleges as well as in support of induction sessions and training courses, including the European Computer Driving Licence (ECDL), within government departments and industry generally. The glossary has also proved popular with home-based computer users.

As well as a continued monitoring of new terms entering this area, which are added when the Working Party feels they have become sufficiently established and widespread, there has been an attempt to ensure that the glossary reflects developments in the National Curriculum for England and Wales, GCSE, AS level and A level specification, the Scottish Curriculum and the Northern Ireland system (as well as vocational and other courses at a variety of levels). The KS3 ICT strategy has involved a broader community of teachers who seek definitions, and the sections on general computing terms and using your computer have been extended to match their needs.

The Working Party is conscious of the need to provide definitions that cover the use of terms in the context of large computer systems as well as the world of microcomputers. Although for many school and college students large computer systems may be outside their practical experience, they are likely to encounter consequences of the use of such systems in their future in the outside world.

Decisions about which terms to rewrite, include or delete must again trust their justification to time. Some terms have been considered but not included since it was judged either that their use in schools and colleges was not yet apparent or that the terms themselves lacked consistency in use. Some terms used in a special environment such as mathematics or sound belong to the terminology of those environments and are not defined here. A minority of such terms have a distinct meaning in a computing environment so do need to be defined and are included.

The origins of the glossary – over 30 years ago – have been instrumental in determining its development from a tiny listing to the 3000+ terms in the publication today. In 1974, a conference of the Regional Examining Boards for the Certificate of Secondary Education invited the British Computer Society to produce a standardised list of terms for use in computer studies courses and examination syllabuses. The Society's Schools Committee set up a Working Party with a remit to produce what was thought to be a 'once-off' document containing about 100 terms. At the time, there was only one A level computing examination and a small number of computing examinations for 16-year-olds. Those schools involved in computer studies relied on batch processing using punched cards to be sent off to university computing centres or, for a few fortunates, an on-line terminal connecting them to the local-authority computer. Microcomputers were just beginning to appear but were rare in schools.

This list of terms had a very limited distribution, being available only to the examiners of those Regional Examining Boards. Teachers preparing pupils for these examinations protested that this was unfair, since it was impractical to try to prepare pupils to deal with terms that were known only to those examiners with access to copies of the list.

At the end of 1974, work therefore began on the first 'public' edition of the glossary. It was decided to include a simple and concise definition of each of the terms that were unique to computing and to indicate which were preferred terms – at a time when almost all sources of computing expertise were inventing their own vocabulary. When this first real edition appeared in 1977, it contained some 430 terms, of which 260 were defined. Given that the target audience was the 14–16-year-old pupil, it was decided that, as far as possible without compromising technical accuracy, basic English should be used in the explanation of the term – an objective still retained wherever possible.

The popularity of the first edition was such that, following several reprints, further editions were demanded. They included those new terms that, appearing almost daily, were required to keep pace both with the rapid development of the technology and with the increasing use of computers in education. It is the policy to update the glossary every three years or so.

Acknowledgements

The Working Party has appreciated the help it received from those members of the BCS Schools Expert Panel (formerly Schools Committee) who made comments and suggestions about material to include in this edition.

We would like to mention Ian Utting from the University of Kent, Percy Mett from the Open University and Alfred Vella who commented on Section C9 Programming Languages. Simon Chalton of Bird & Bird and Les Fraser contributed significantly to the computer security and data protection references in Section A18.

Finally, George Cumming has applied his 'Engineer's eyes' to the checking and proof-reading. Any mistakes that slipped through are ours, however.

The Working Party also welcomes offers from teachers willing to involve their students in a review of this edition and would like to express its thanks to all who have commented, criticised and made helpful suggestions on the 10th edition. Where possible, these have been taken into account in preparing this 11th edition.

By post to: K. Allen, The British Computer Society, 1 Sanford Street, Swindon, Wiltshire SN1 1HJ
By email: glossary@hq.bcs.org.uk
Internet: www.bcs.org.uk

Alternatively, contact any member of the Working Party through the BCS.

Disclaimer

Neither the BCS nor contributors to the glossary shall have any responsibility for loss suffered as a result of reliance on the glossary, and readers should take their own legal advice on the application of the terms covered, particularly in Section A18, which is intended as an aid to understanding computer security. The glossary is not a definitive statement of the meaning of terms.

Publisher's Acknowledgement

Windows screenshots reprinted by permission from Microsoft Corporation.

Part

A How Computer Systems are Used

This section contains terms that may be met by any computer user working with applications in any of the areas covered. Some sections in Part A are concerned with general issues and others with well-defined areas of computer use. Some sections contain terms that might have been placed in Part B or even in Part C or Part D, but they were kept with other related terms for completeness; this is particularly true of the sections covering the Internet, sound and user interfaces, which have become more prominent aspects of computer use since the previous editions were published. Some terms have references to terms in Part B, Part C or Part D, which will provide readers with pointers to other associated terms and concepts.

General Computing Terms

When approaching computing for the first time, we meet a range of terms that people involved in the industry take for granted. These terms are often vague generalisations and may mean different things to different people. They are also applied to a wide range of situations within computing, and their precise meaning may vary between contexts.

Most jargon we meet when using a computer is related to the task we are doing. The **software** used to perform the task is called the **application**. Examples of these applications include **word processing**, **computer art** and using a **database**. However, there is some jargon that relates to running the computer itself, i.e. how we control or operate a computer.

This section provides general definitions of some of the more common computing terms that are either used in a general context or apply across many areas of computing.

Information Processing

Information processing

is the organisation, manipulation and distribution of information. As these activities are central to almost every use of computers, the term is in common use to mean almost the same as 'computing'. See also *Data* and *information*, page 306.

Information Technology (IT)

including: ICT (Information and Communication Technology)
is the application of appropriate (enabling) technologies to information processing. The current interest centres on computing, telecommunications and digital electronics. In the UK schools sector, the preferred term is *ICT (Information and Communication Technology)*.

Telecommunications

is a general term describing the communication of information over a distance. The method of communication is normally via a cable, wire or *fibre optic* (see page 209) or electromagnetic radiation. See also *wireless communication*, page 208.

Computer

is a machine that processes data. It takes data, in digital form, which are processed automatically before being output in some way. It is programmable, so that the rules used to process the data can be changed. It is an automatic, programmable, digital data processor. These ideas are expanded in the introduction to Section B1, page 165. The definition excludes the *analog computer* (page 166).

Computer system

including: configuration
is the complete collection of components (hardware, software, peripherals, power supplies, communications links) making up a single computer installation. The particular choice of components is known as the *configuration* – different systems may or may not have the same configuration.

Embedded system

is the use of a computer system built into a machine of some sort, usually to provide a means of control. The computer system is generally small, often a single micro-processor with very limited functions. The user may not realise that instructions are being carried out by a computer but simply that there are controls to operate the machine. Examples are electronic washing machines, video recorders, burglar alarms and car engine management systems.

Media

is the collective name for materials (tape, disk, paper, cards, etc.) used to hold data.

Parts of the Computer

Hardware

is the physical part of a computer system – the processor(s), storage, input and out-put peripherals, etc. This is in contrast to the *software* (see below), which includes application packages, and the data in the storage.

Peripheral

also known as: device
including: input device, output device, input/output device (I/O device), storage device
is a piece of equipment (or hardware) that can be connected to the central process-ing unit. It is used to provide input, output and backing storage for the computer system. No particular peripheral is required by a computer, but every computer must have some method of input and output (for example, a washing machine may simply have push buttons for input and *actuators* (see page 130) for output. They are often referred to as follows:

Input device is a peripheral unit that can accept data, presented in the appropriate
   machine-readable form, decode the data and transmit them as electrical pulses
   to the central processing unit.

Output device is a peripheral unit that translates signals from the computer into a
   human-readable form or into a form suitable for re-processing by the computer
   at a later stage.

Input/output device (I/O device) is a peripheral unit that can be used both as an input
   device and as an output device. In some instances, 'input/output device' may be
   two separate devices housed in the same cabinet.

Storage device is a peripheral unit that allows the user to store data in an electronic
   form for a longer period of time and when the computer is switched off. The
   data can only be read by the computer and are not in human-readable form.

Software

including: applications program, applications package, generic software, product-ivity tool, content free software, framework program
consists of programs, routines and procedures (together with their associated docu-mentation) that can be run on a computer system.

An *applications program* is a computer information system designed to carry out a task (such as keeping accounts or editing text) that would need to be carried out even if computers did not exist.

An *applications package* is a complete set of applications programs together with the associated documentation (see *user documentation*, page 69). Where the applica-tion is appropriate to many areas, it is usual to describe it as *generic software* or as a *productivity tool*. For example, *word processing* (see page 22) can be used in personal correspondence, the production of business 'form letters', academic research, compilation of glossaries, writing books, etc.

Content-free software, or *framework programs*, can be adapted by a user for a range of unrelated tasks. For example, a program to provide help facilities may also be used to provide an index or may be used independently to provide a simple elec-tronic book. The software does not start with any data, but is a tool to present data to the user's requirements.

See also *systems software*, page 336.

Integrated package

also known as: integrated program
is a single piece of software that provides a user with basic information processing functions. It usually provides for word processing, spreadsheets and small databases and may include additional facilities such as charts, a diary and communications. It is designed so that data can be moved easily between the various parts, enabling complex tasks to be performed easily.

Tutorial

is a program that helps a user to learn about a new application. The tutorial will include a simple explanation of how to use the new system, diagrams and possibly examples that the user can try whilst the tutorial program monitors the user's progress.

Facsimile transmission (fax)

including: fax machine, fax groups, fax modem
is the use of regular voice-quality telephone lines to send copies of documents, which may include drawings as well as text.

A *fax machine* is connected to the telephone system in order to send and receive copies of the transmitted documents. The sender inserts the document into their fax machine and dials the number of the receiving machine. The sending machine scans the paper on a line-by-line basis and transmits the resulting information to the receiving machine. The receiving machine re-creates the document using photocopier technology (for this reason, many fax machines can also operate as photocopiers).

The two fax machines need to be able to communicate with each other. In order to simplify the process of identifying compatibility, fax machines are classified into *fax groups* with different technical specifications. The two machines need to belong to compatible groups.

A *fax modem* is a special type of *modem* (see page 207) that allows a computer connected to a telephone line to send faxes directly. It does not need to produce a paper copy first, and when a fax is received the computer operator can process it.

Computer bureau

including: data processor
is an organisation that offers a range of computing services for hire (for example, data preparation, payroll processing). Bureaux usually offer two types of service: they provide computing facilities for organisations that do not have any of their own and they also offer specialist services covering vital common operations (for example, payroll) to organisations that do not have the appropriate piece of applications software.

Data processor is the name used in the *Data Protection Act 1998* (see page 143) for a computer bureau.

Outsourcing

is the purchase of services from outside contractors rather than employing staff to do the tasks. Traditionally, large computer organisations have employed many staff such as *systems analysts* and *programmers* (see page 138). It may be more economic to contract another organisation to provide these services and not have the expense and complication of direct employment of staff.

Facilities management

also known as: managed services
is the contracting of the computer operations to an outside organisation. The facilities management company employs the staff, runs the operation and often owns the computer hardware. The contract for this kind of service will specify what the computer system must provide for the fee charged.

PART A

Using Your Computer

Other related terms may be found in A1 General Computing Terms; for fuller definitions, see D1 Systems Software.

There are important similarities between the way we use motor vehicles and the way we use computers. In both cases, the majority of users are completely unconcerned about the internal workings of the machine but are nonetheless capable of becoming skilled in its use. Anyone studying this glossary is likely to be seeking an understanding of what goes on 'under the bonnet', but in this section we look at the terms and definitions that are to do with the general use of computers. The parallel with motorcars continues to be instructive – while most drivers are unaware of the technicalities of the car, they must be acquainted with some features that are not just to do with steering it in the direction they want to go – the need for petrol and oil, and the ways in which a flat battery may be avoided. The explanations in this section are the equivalent for the computer.

Computer tasks can be divided into two broad categories. There are those that have been made necessary only by the existence of the computer – the handling of printers, the storage of data on disks, the location of documents, and so forth. These tasks are performed by **systems software**, and we would not need to undertake these tasks if computers did not exist. However, there is a much more important category of task. These are the things that we would want to do even if computers did not exist; they are generally known as **applications** and are carried out by **applications software**. It is in this second category that we find word processing, where the computer enhances our ability to create, edit and lay out text. Letters were written and books published long before there were computers. Similarly with spreadsheets: accountants tallied columns of figures and derived calculations from numerical data even before the mechanical calculator.

In operating a computer, users may find themselves performing the same types of actions in different applications, or even when interacting with systems software. These common operations are collected in this section. The subsection The Size of Things may seem to be technical, but the terms described below, **bit**, **byte** and **word**, are often used to describe the size or capacity of a computer.

The power of the computer is so great that it is tempting to believe that it has created new applications – things we were unable to do before the computer. However, while the computer may have made some tasks practicable and feasible, in general a little reflection will reveal the possibility (if not the widespread practice) of most applications before the advent of the computer. It is worth remembering that photographers were retouching pictures before digital manipulation of images became commonplace, that librarians maintained card indexes before databases, that letters were sent before e-mails, and that musicians were creating electronic music before computers.

Perhaps the most likely candidate for a truly new application is in the use of the Internet, and especially the World Wide Web. It is hard to see which human activity in pre-computer days parallels the creation of the personal statements of interests and activities that appear on Web pages, much less the growth of e-commerce. That is, until we remember letters, newsletters, magazines and mail-order catalogues!

System Software

Operating system

is the name given to the collection of systems software that manages the computer. It is usually supplied with the computer. The most common operating systems today are Windows and Linux (for the PC), MacOS (for the Macintosh) and UNIX (for larger computers). The operating system gives the computer its 'look and feel' and generates great passion between advocates of alternative systems. See also Section D1.

Driver

is a piece of systems software supplied with a peripheral (such as a printer, a mouse, a display screen or a keyboard). It bridges the gap between the operating system and the peripheral and converts commands from one into instructions that the other can obey. In this way, applications software such as a word processor can, for example, issue a 'print' instruction to the operating system in a standard way, without needing to know the details of the particular printer being used. The casual user may meet drivers when he or she installs or upgrades a peripheral.

Filter

including: graphics filter
is a piece of software, used in conjunction with an application, that allows data stored in one format to be accessed by an application that uses another format. For example, a word-processing application, such as Microsoft Word, will provide filters for documents created in its major competitors, such as WordPerfect. In this way, users will not be dissuaded from buying Microsoft Word because all their previous work was created in WordPerfect. Even between software created by the same

manufacturer, a filter may be necessary, for example to import a spreadsheet into a database package. It may not always be possible to convert every feature supported by one format into another format. The user is unlikely to be aware of a filter unless he or she encounters an error message reporting the failure or absence of an appropriate one.

A *graphics filter* is a particularly common form of filter. There are many alternative formats for the storage of graphical data, not necessarily associated with any one commercial package. To be able to work with these formats, *graphics packages* (see page 26) must provide appropriate graphics filters to allow images to be loaded or saved.

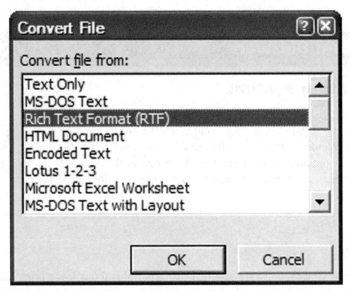

The options in this dialogue box are all filters that enable data to be imported into a word-processing program.

Figure A2.1 Filters

Organising Data

File

also known as: document
including: filename
is a collection of data items stored in the computer and handled as a single unit. How and where the data are stored will be organised by the *operating system* (see page 9 and page 336). Files are given *filenames* (see below), so that the user can later access

the correct one. Systems software also creates files in order to keep track of the operation of the computer. As the word 'file' is largely a technical one, most applications software refers to its files as *documents*, even though these may be spreadsheets, databases or images as well as text-based files.

File type

including: filename extension, file associations
is the type of data that are held in a file. This might be an executable program or data structured for a particular application.

To assist the user in recognising the appropriate file, many computer systems use a short three- or four-character *filename extension* added to the name to identify the file type. Thus, the file 'timetable.doc' is seen to be a word-processing document, 'message.txt' a text file, 'barbecue.bmp' a bitmap graphic, and so on. Table A2.1 lists some common extensions; a more complete table can be found on page 410.

As well as assisting the user, *file associations* may be created, so that all files with a given extension will be linked to a given application. With appropriate associations set up, it is possible for the user to simply double-click on (say) the file 'barbecue.bmp', and this action will launch the chosen image-processing program and load the graphic file for editing or printing. In this way, the user is encouraged to focus on the data rather than on the programs that process them.

Folder

also known as: directory
including: nested folders, subfolders, sub-directories
is the name given to a collection of files for organisational purposes. By keeping related files in the same folder, the user can select from the files he or she is working on without being distracted by files to do with other work. Folders are also known as *directories*. A well-thought-out directory system can make computer use easier. To this end, the user can create *nested folders* with one or more folders stored in another. For example, a folder of word-processing documents can contain *subfolders* (*sub-directories*) for letters, for research, for diaries, and so on.

The Size of Things

Bit (BInary digiT)

is a single digit in a binary number; it is either a 0 or a 1. It is the smallest unit of storage, since all data are stored as binary codes. Many computers are described as '16-bit', '32-bit', and so on; this usage is explained under *word*, page 14.

Table A2.1 Common filename extensions

File type	Filename extension	Comments
Document (word processor)	.doc	A word-processor file typically will contain formatting and layout information as well as the text
Text file	.txt	A text file has no formatting information and is accessible by many applications without needing processing. It is much smaller than a word-processor file
Web page	.htm, .html	A text file, but one that uses 'tags' that will enable it to be displayed properly in a Web browser (see *HTML*, page 303, and *browser*, page 101)
Program	.exe	A file containing a program. Double-clicking on an .exe file will normally cause it to execute rather than to open in an associated application
Portable document format	.pdf	A PDF file is specific to the Acrobat system. Although a commercial product, the Adobe Systems' Acrobat *reader* is widely and freely available, enabling documents prepared using a variety of applications to be accessed by users who may not own the original application. The software for *creating* .pdf files, however, is a paid-for product
Still images	.bmp, .gif, .tif, .jpg	Various still-image graphics formats (see Table A4.1, page 28)
Video	.avi, .mov, .wmv	Various moving video formats (see Table A4.1, page 28)
Audio	.wav, .mp3, .aiff, .wma	Various sound formats (see Table A5.1, page 49)

Transfer format	.csv, .tsv	A text file used for transferring data between spreadsheets or databases. Use of these extensions guarantees that the file is formatted with distinct data items separated by commas (.csv, comma-separated variables) or by tab characters (.tsv, tab-separated variables). Empty or missing items would be recorded as successive commas or tabs
Rich text format	.rtf	This is a text file generated by an application such as a word processor that allows users to choose different fonts and text effects, such as italics, underlining, etc. The .rtf file simply contains the text mixed with special 'tags' similar to HTML (see page 303) that allow the formatting to be re-created when the file is opened in an application with an appropriate filter (see above)
Temporary	.tmp	A temporary file that may be deleted safely. Most users only see .tmp files when an application crashes or the computer fails and temporary files that would normally have been deleted when no longer required are left occupying space on the user's disk
Compressed	.zip, .hqa	A file that has been compressed to save space and that must be decompressed before the contents can be accessed
Back-up	.bak	A back-up file; an exact copy of another file
Initial data	.ini	Many applications use initial data files to store data used in customising an application, so that it can open each time looking as the user last saw it
Data	.dat	A general-purpose data file
Library	.dll	A dynamic link library file (specific to Windows). Such files contain common software routines used by several applications, or 'plug-ins' (see page 000) that extend the capability of an existing application

PART A

Byte

including: kilobytes, megabytes, gigabytes, terabytes
is a group of bits, typically eight, representing a single character. This is normally the smallest grouping used by computers, which rarely need to access single bits. The capacity of a computer and of its peripherals is measured in bytes – or, more conveniently, in multiples such as *kilobytes*, *megabytes*, *gigabytes* or *terabytes* (see *Units*, page 409). Thus, a computer may have 512 megabytes of memory and an 80-gigabyte hard disk.

A single byte may also be used to represent a small number, either less than 256 or between -127 and $+128$.

Word

including: word length
is a group of bits that can be addressed, transferred and manipulated as a single unit by the central processor. The size of a word, the *word length*, is determined by the width of the data pathways within the computer and is usually larger than a *byte* (see above), possibly consisting of 16, 24, 36 or even 64 bits. Large word sizes mean that a computer can transfer data in larger groups than a computer with a smaller word size, and this generally means faster operation.

Operation

Customise

including workspace
is to tailor an application or even a whole computer system to the preferences of a specific user. Usually, the user can make cosmetic as well as operational changes. The colours and layout of the desktop might be customised, as might the sounds that the computer generates to signal (for example) an error. The sizes of text and icons may be changed, as may the language in which messages are displayed. The operation of an application may also be tuned to suit the user's preferences. Shortcut keys can be defined to carry out operations that the user has frequent need for, the space left for margins may be defined or the number of decimal places used in displaying a number can be specified. The changes made to the basic operation of the application are saved when the application is closed, so that it will reopen with the same customisation as before. Sometimes, it is possible for different users to save their own customisation, known as a *workspace*, and to call up their own preferences subsequently. In this way, different users of the same computer can still benefit from an application tailored to their own needs.

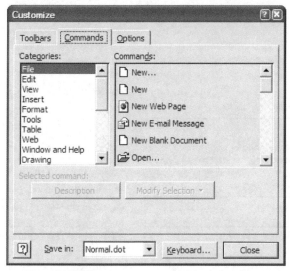

The upper dialogue box allows the user to select which word-processor functions will be marked by special characters on the screen. The lower dialogue box allows the user to add or delete commands on the menus.

Figure A2.2 Two examples of customising

Default

including: default option, default value

is an assumption made by computer software in the absence of explicit instructions to the contrary. This may be a *default option* – your files are listed in alphabetical order unless you request date or size order – or a *default value* – the computer prints one copy of a document unless you request multiple copies. A common default option is seen in the Print command in a word processor. Pressing the Print button on the toolbar normally prints one copy of the entire document on the default printer nominated by the user. To access another printer, to print multiple copies, or to print selected pages, the user must select the more complicated Print dialogue box (see Figure A2.3).

The best software is designed so that the most frequently used options are all available as defaults, meaning that users are not troubled by the need to continually specify such values. It is often possible for users to customise software by selecting their own choice of defaults.

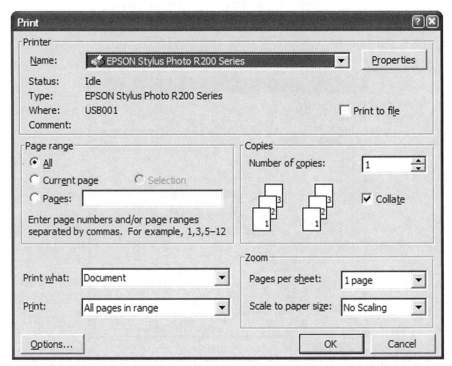

Pressing the Print button (fifth from left) on the toolbar shown at the top causes the same effect as the options shown in the full Print dialogue box below (one collated copy of the entire document on the Epson Stylus printer). However, in the dialogue box, none of these is assumed, and any or all of them may be changed.

Figure A2.3 Default options

Object linking and embedding (OLE)

including: embedded object, linked object
is the insertion of data items in one format into data in another format, for example a picture in a text file. Information such as the location and the format of the data may be included as links to the data, or the data may be embedded in the file. A program using the data can load the right program to edit that particular type of data without the user having to export the data, edit it and later import it back again (see page 21). Each item is an *object* (see page 242).

Embedded objects are inserted as part of the data and saved with them. Later changes made to the original do not appear in the copy.

Linked objects are stored separately and loaded only when they are needed; the location (usually a filename) is stored in the main data. Changes made to the linked object automatically apply to the main data.

Operational mode

including: batch processing, transaction processing, multi-access, time-sharing, real-time system, interactive processing, remote access, tele-processing, off-line processing, on-line processing
is the way a computer system is used and operated. Decisions about operational modes are made during systems design. Often the operating system (see page 336) manages the functioning of the operational modes in use.

The terms in this section are not necessarily mutually exclusive, and more than one might be applicable to any particular computer system.

In *batch processing*, all the data to be input are collected together before being processed as a single efficient operation. This method is also used when computer users submit individual *jobs* (see page 344) that are processed together as a batch.

Transaction processing deals with each set of data from a user as it is submitted. This is normally used in commercial systems where a transaction may be a booking, an order or an invoice. Each transaction is completed before the next is begun.

Multi-access systems allow several users apparently to have individual control of the computer at the same time. One method of implementing a multi-access system is by allocating a period of time to each user; this is called *time-sharing*. See also *time slice*, page 208.

A *real-time system* is one that can react fast enough to influence behaviour in the outside world; for example, this is necessary in air-traffic control systems and desirable in on-line reservation systems.

Interactive processing provides the user with direct, immediate responses from the system. There is often some kind of dialogue with the system. Examples include the booking of airline tickets and requesting information about a bank account through a cash-dispensing machine.

Remote access or *tele-processing* is the use of a geographically remote computer system via communications links. See also *remote job entry*, page 344.

PART A

Off-line processing occurs when computer devices are not under the immediate control of the main computer, for example data entry to disk or tape storage.

On-line processing allows the user to interact directly with the main computer.

Channel

including: channel number, handle, port, port number
is any physical path along which data may be transmitted between two points. The physical path may be a separate wire, a group of wires or shared with other channels on a single wire (see *multiplexor*, page 207).

The data that a channel carries may be a radio or TV signal, communications between two computer devices (for example, music systems), or communications between a computer and its peripherals. Although different devices work totally differently, they are simply sending or receiving data, but along different physical routes.

A *channel number* is given to each channel. A device can select the data being received (or where they are sent to) simply by altering the channel number and allowing the electronics to redirect the data stream.

An example is a music system, where a generated tune could be saved to a suitable disk or played by a variety of output devices. Each output device can be linked to a separate output channel of a *MIDI interface* (see page 50) that switches the output to one or more devices simply by setting and altering channel numbers.

Within a computer system, channels identify which peripherals data are being sent to or received from, particularly between a central processing unit and a peripheral device or, by extension, between the user's program and a file on the backing store. The channel number acts as a shortcut and avoids the need to initialise the peripheral each time data are sent or received. It allows great flexibility in switching between peripherals and adding peripherals to the system.

A *handle* is similar to a channel number but used within a computer program to identify a resource. For example, a file handle will identify a file currently available for access by the program.

A *port* identifies where a channel enters or leaves a computer system. These are physical locations where peripherals or other components can be plugged in and often include an interface to convert the data into the appropriate form. For examples, see *interface board*, page 363. Within the computer system, each port may be given a *port number*, which allows the computer to select peripherals easily.

Overtype

sometimes: overwrite
including: insert
is to replace text on a screen with other text entered from the keyboard (or possibly read from a file) during the process of entering or editing a document. When

overtyping, new characters replace those already on the screen. It is possible to *insert* text, when existing text moves to make space for the new characters.

Cut & paste

including: clipboard, notepad

is the technique of transferring a section of data (text in a word processor, or diagrams and text in a page make-up package) from one part of a document to another part of the same document, or to another document. The data are first selected (highlighted) and the user then 'cuts' them from the document (it is usually possible to copy rather than necessarily cut out the data). The cursor is moved to the new position, and the data are 'pasted' in place. In most applications, the data are held in a temporary storage area called the *clipboard* or *notepad*. Data held in these storage areas will normally remain there until overwritten by new data, so allowing one exact copy of the original to be pasted in more than one place.

Justification

including: left justification, right justification, full justification, centring

is the arrangement of characters so that they align with margins. This may occur on the screen or on a printer, or it may be required when setting out data in columns or as forms (see Figure A2.4).

Left justification is the normal method of aligning continuous text, with an even left-hand margin. This often leaves an uneven right-hand margin, since each printed line is likely to contain characters (for example words, spaces and punctuation marks) that occupy different lengths of line.

Right justification is normal for columns of numbers, although it is sometimes seen in text. Here, an even right-hand margin is created. This may well result in a ragged left-hand margin, since each printed line is likely to contain characters (for example words, spaces and punctuation) that occupy different lengths of line.

Full justification (sometimes simply referred to as **justification**) has even margins at both left-hand and right-hand ends of the line. It is created by the (automatic) insertion of extra spaces (soft spaces) between words once a line of approximately the correct length has been entered.

Centring,
which is often used for headings
and
similar displays,
places the characters symmetrically between the
margins.

Figure A2.4   Justification

PART A

WYSIWYG (What You See Is What You Get)

(pronounced 'wizzy-wig') refers to a screen display that matches the eventual printed output in layout, highlighting, underlining, font, etc. Such displays are particularly helpful in applications such as *desktop publishing* (see page 160) and *spreadsheets* (see Section A9, page 83).

Dictionary

is the list of allowable words that can be used in a particular application. Although most applications contain a standard dictionary, sometimes there is a facility to allow an individual user to create a separate personal dictionary, which is then referred to if a particular word entered by that user is not found in the standard dictionary.

Thesaurus

is a dictionary arranged by meaning instead of spelling. A computer-based thesaurus used in conjunction with a word processor allows a user to select a word in the text, and to be offered a range of words with similar or related meanings. Using one of these instead of the original word can enhance the writer's prose style.

Spelling checker

also known as: spellchecker
including: grammar checker
is a program that is normally used with a word processor or desktop publishing system to check the spelling in a document. Each word in the document is checked against the dictionary (see above). If it does not appear in the dictionary, the user is told this. The word may be correct (but not in the dictionary) or it may be spelled wrongly. Some programs can check the spelling as the document is typed or correct frequent misspellings automatically.

   With faster computers, it is possible for there to be a *grammar checker*, which attempts to identify poor use of language in a document. As 'correct' language is much more to personal taste, a grammar checker usually flags fragments of the text for more consideration (see Figure A2.5).

Spelling checker

also known as: spellchecker

including: grammar checker

is a program which is normally used with a word processor or desk-top publishing system to check the spelling in a document. Each word in the document is checked against the dictionary (see above). If it does not appear in the dictionary, the user is told this. The word may be correct (but not in the dictionary) or it may be wrongly spelled. Some programs can check the spelling as the document is typed, or correct frequent misspellings automatically.

With faster computers, it is possible for there to be a ***grammar checker***, which attempts to identify poor use of language in a document. As 'correct' language is much more to personal taste, a grammer checker usually flags fragments of the text for more consideration. See Figure A2.5 below.

The above definition as it appeared on the screen while typing. The grammar checker is suggesting that the first three lines should begin with capital letters, while the spelling checker is indicating that it does not know the (deliberately misspelled) word 'grammer'. Pop-up boxes would offer the user guidance in each case.

Figure A2.5　Spelling and grammar checking

Export

including: import

is to create a data file using one piece of software so that it can be read by a different piece of software. *Import* is the corresponding read process to accept a file produced by some other software.

Often there is a specific version of a particular package whose file and data formats are chosen by its manufacturer to be the standard version for exporting from and importing into that package. Using these formats reduces the problems of data transfer between different software applications. See also *filter* on page 9.

Word Processing and Text Manipulation

For details of printing and display devices used in word- and document-processing applications, see B4 Output. See also Specialised Computer Applications in A19.

Computers are used for the production of typed documents such as letters and reports. The application (program) carrying this out is usually known as a **word processor**. The advantages are quick storage and recovery, ease of editing, and the ability to alter and update documents without having to retype the whole document. Document formatting, the arrangement of text on the page, is carried out by the application.

More complex operations such as the integration of non-textual characters into the document are known as **document processing**. Preparing multimedia documents for web sites is carried out by specialist software.

A number of terms have become general, and it is helpful to understand and use the correct terms for each task.

Word processing

Including: word processor
is the application of computing to the production, editing and formatting of typed letters and documents, including the addition of stored text (for example, for personalised circulars). A system dedicated to this application is often referred to as a *word processor*. An alternative to a word processor when only limited formatting is needed is a *text editor* (see below).

Text editor

is a program for creating and amending text. It is designed to be used for preparing the source text of programs and for editing text files. It can have similar editing functions to a word processor but requires a more formal approach than is usual in word processing if formatting is to be retained. See also D1 *Systems Software* (page 335).

Document processing

is an extension of the formatting functions that have been common to word processing packages for some years, in order to allow the integration of non-textual characters into the layout. Associated with this extension has been the use of bitmapping or pixel mapping to take advantage of the ability of extremely high-definition monitors and of laser-printer techniques to produce fine lines, graduated density and (where necessary) apparently continuous spectrum colour.

Typical document production will include diagrams, graphic characters, numerical items, picture representation and symbols as well as text. The software associated with document processing needs to be able to manipulate areas of the document as if it were a single entity – analogous to alphanumeric character manipulation in text processing.

A general requirement of computers that run document-processing systems is an abundance of memory and a fast processor.

Mailmerge

is the process of combining a document (often a letter) and a data file (often a list of names and addresses) in such a way that copies of the document for different people are suitably different. In its simplest form, this is merely ensuring that letters have the correct style and title for the addressee and that the address is inserted into the appropriate place. More complex uses can include inserting whole paragraphs into standard letters or documents. The process remains the same for all applications; a document is set up that has marked places within it at which data from other files are inserted.

Line break

is the place where a line of printed text ends. Word processors normally break lines only between words or, if sufficiently sophisticated, by inserting hyphens at appropriate places.

Word wrap

is a facility available in many word processing packages that breaks lines automatically between words. When the text being typed on the line reaches beyond the right-hand margin, the whole of the last word is transferred to the beginning of the next line, and the typing then continues on the new line.

Hard space

including: soft space

is an intended space that the user has explicitly typed (such as the space between two adjacent words). A *soft space* is inserted by software to even out the look of a line in order to create justified text. These 'extra' spaces must be remembered by the software, so that they can be removed where necessary if the user alters the formatting later. Reformatting justified text does not remove the hard spaces.

Non-breaking space

including: pad character

is the type of space that occurs between words that should not appear on separate lines (such as that in 'Henry IV'). Many word processors allow the user to type a special combination of keys to insert such a character, sometimes called a *pad character*, which will print as a space but will not be allowed as a line break.

Micro-spacing

is a feature available on some printers to print fully justified text by inserting small amounts of *soft space* (see above) in order to spread the total amount of added space evenly across a line. This ability is particularly necessary when proportional fonts (where characters occupy different widths of printed space) are being used and fully justified text is still required.

Subheading

including: side heading

is a heading or title applied to a section of the document. It is usually placed to the left-hand side of the line and is sometimes termed a *side heading*.

Template

also known as: style sheet

is the basic structure for a document and contains a collection of document settings such as page layout, special formatting and styles. The use of a template ensures the uniform look and feel of a group of documents.

Style

is a collection of formatting characteristics that may be applied to text in a document to quickly change its appearance. When a style is applied to a piece of text, then a whole group of formats is applied in one simple task.

Rule

is simply any straight line on a document. It may be vertical to separate columns or horizontal to separate sections of text.

Body text

is the basic style of the text in a document.

Case

including: upper case, lower case
is a description of the appearance of a character in a font. It may be in CAPITAL LETTERS, when it would be called *upper case*, or in small letters (like this text), when it would be called *lower case*.

White space

including: river
is the blank areas on a page. Sometimes the white space will give the appearance of a white line, or white lines, running down through the text – white spaces like these are called *rivers*.

Typeface

is the design of the characters in a collection of characters. A typeface may be a **bold** one or an *italic* one. Care needs to be taken not to confuse this with *font* (see below).

Font

is the set of characters and symbols available for use when typing a document. There are many different designs of fonts available; some may have some fancy curves added to the more usual form of the letters/symbols, whilst others may be very plain.

A word processor usually has a collection of fonts available for use. When selecting your font, care should be exercised: it should be appropriate for the document. As a general guide, it is normally good practice to use no more than two fonts in any one document. See also page 195.

Graphics, Design and Digital Imaging

Other related terms may be found in B2 Input.

Computers are very well suited to producing and editing digital images, pictures and other graphics. These images may be created entirely within the computer (using a **painting** or **drawing** package), or they may be loaded into the computer from an increasing number of suitable electronic devices, such as a digital camera, an image scanner or a video camera.

There are much more data in a picture than in other forms of data, such as a text document. A typical still picture may use as much as 3 Mb of storage, while a four-minute video sequence may use as much as 1 Gb. Storing and processing such images have always been possible on larger computers and are now possible on PCs as adequate storage media and processor speeds are available. Many people now regularly use digital cameras and download the images to improve, retouch or edit them on the computer before sharing them with friends by e-mail, CD, DVD or the Web.

Other packages use graphics as part of the design process for books and other printed matter – adding illustrations or decorative borders. In some cases, a photograph (or even 'live-action' video) can be retouched electronically to add, remove or recolour some elements of the picture. Many TV graphics are now generated purely electronically.

In other applications, such as **computer aided design** (CAD) (see Section A19), the processing power of the computer is used for calculation as well as for the pure drawing.

The use of the **Internet** (see Section A12) has made the technical details of graphics (especially image compression, see below) particularly important. Web site designers must make appropriate choices of format in order to reduce the time taken to download a Web page without compromising quality.

Image Data Formats

Image compression

including: compress, redundancy, lossless, lossy, JPEG, MPEG, delta compression
is to reduce the size of an image data file, i.e. *compress* it, so that it may be stored

more economically or transmitted faster. This is particularly important where video sequences are played on a screen or recorded on to video tape, as a failure to transmit the data at a steady (high) speed will cause the images to distort. There are many storage and compression schemes for graphical data, optimised for different characteristics of images, and some common ones are listed in Table A4.1.

Redundancy is repeated data describing the same element of an image. A common technique in compression schemes is the identification of redundancy. For example, in an image with a solid background colour, it can be more efficient to store the information that the next 500 pixels are all the same, rather than repeating the pixel data 500 times.

Lossless compression schemes are those that allow the original images to be recreated; others are *lossy* and generally involve a loss of resolution in parts of the image where experience shows that it will be least noticed.

The *JPEG* format (defined by the Joint Photographic Expert Group) is used for still images. It works by identifying areas of the image that are similar – an arrangement of pixels that is repeated elsewhere in the image, perhaps after a scaling or a rotation. It is more efficient to store information about these similarities than it is to repeat the data.

The *MPEG* formats (defined by the Motion Picture Experts Group) are used for moving images, such as video, and work by a method known as *delta compression*. In order to cope with the high demands of TV standard pictures (25 separate frames transmitted every second in the UK), a full picture is sent only occasionally (typically five times a second); between these frames, information concerning only changes to the image is transmitted. This uses much less data, particularly where the picture is relatively static, as with a title or caption. See also *data compression*, page 329.

Render

including: wire frame, texture, light sources

is to prepare a complete, full-resolution version of an image that previously existed only in a draft form. Many image-manipulation programs and video-editing systems offer the user an inferior version of the image while it is being worked on, which must be rendered before it appears in its final form. For example, a 3D drawing package may represent solid objects in *wire frame* form, showing only the outlines. When the user is satisfied with the arrangement of the objects, the image will be rendered to incorporate surface texture, illumination and shadows (see below). Similarly, a complex transition applied to a video sequence, such as a 'page turn' to introduce a new image, will be ignored or presented at low resolution until the user is satisfied with the timing, after which it must be rendered before it can be viewed as intended. Video rendering for even modest sequences can take an appreciable length of time, possibly several hours.

Texture can usually be added to images of solid objects when rendering, giving the surface the appearance of being created from a 'real' material such as stone or wood.

PART A

Table A4.1 Image-compression formats

Type	File extension	Lossless?	Type	Comments
Windows bitmap (PC)	.bmp	Yes	Still-image bitmap	Uncompressed data; one of the standard formats. See also page 329
Tagged Image File Format	.tif, .tiff	Yes	Still-image bitmap	Compressed data, one of the standard formats
Graphics Interchange Format	.gif	Yes	Still-image bitmap	Good for images with large areas of solid colour. As 8 bits are used, only 256 distinct colours can be represented. A simple 'animated' version is available, suited to Web graphics
Portable Network Graphics	.png	Yes	Still-image bitmap	Good for images with large areas of solid colour. PNG uses 24 bits and can represent millions of distinct colours
Joint Photographic Experts Group	.jpeg, .jpg, .jpe	No	Still image	Good for photographic images
Vector	.wmf, .dxf	Yes	Still-image vector	The industry-standard CAD format
QuickTime	.mov	See comments	Video	Although storage as a .mov file is lossless, the data being stored are probably already held using lossy compression
Audio-video interleaved	.avi	See comments	Video	Although storage as an .avi file is lossless, the data being stored are probably already held using lossy compression
MPEG-1	.mpg	No	Video	Suited to small, low-resolution sequences on CD
MPEG-2	.m2v, .mpg, .mp2	No	Video	Suited to full-screen high-resolution sequences on DVD
Digital video (DV)	.avi	See comments	Video	DV data are already compressed in the camera. This format does not compress further
Windows Media Player	.wmv	No	Video	Proprietary format for Microsoft's Windows Media Player. The accompanying audio, if any, is stored in .wma format

Light sources can also be specified when rendering. The position and colour of the lights illuminating an object will affect where reflections and shadows fall in the finished image.

Colour correction

including: white balance, colour channel, alpha channel
is to adjust the colour information in an image. This may be done for effect or to correct an error when the image was captured. Cameras see colours in a different way to humans. For example, sunlight is generally bluer than indoor lighting, which has a red cast. When viewing a scene, the human brain compensates for this, and we are generally unaware of the effect. In 'ordinary' photography, corrections are made when the photograph is printed. Digital devices can compensate, provided they 'know' which colour in the scene is intended to be white. This can be done automatically (but may be fooled by, for example, a very red sunset) or manually, by pointing the camera at a white object and making the camera perform a *white balance*.

When a scene has been captured incorrectly (the camera has been told it's indoors when really the scene is lit by sunlight), it is possible to adjust the colours after the picture has been downloaded into a computer. Often, separate controls to manipulate separately red, green and blue are provided; these are known as the *colour channels*, and are similar in principle to methods of printing where each colour is applied separately. See also *colour model*, page 193. A further channel, known as the *alpha channel*, is sometimes provided, which allows the user to specify which areas of the picture are to be transparent and allow a background image to show through.

Streaming video

including: streaming audio
is a technique used to allow moving video to be displayed on a Web site, without an excessive delay while a (potentially massive) data file is downloaded. The opening seconds of the video must be downloaded before playback can begin, to provide a buffer. The player software starts to play this video to the user and keeps the buffer filled by downloading the next images while the first are playing. If transmission delays over the Internet cause the buffer to become dangerously low, the quality of the new images is reduced to allow more of them to be transmitted, in order to catch up. One characteristic of this method of delivery is that once playback is completed, the user has no permanent copy of the video on their computer. This can be an advantage, for example where a film company wishes to show extracts from a popular film but not allow these extracts to remain in other hands.

Similar *streaming audio* techniques can be used for sound files.

PART A

Graphic Design Applications

Computer graphics

is the use of the computer to display pictorial information. This can be as simple as a line drawing or chart, or as complicated as an animated sequence of pictures. The output might be shown on the computer screen, printed out as hard copy, or transferred directly to videotape.

Vector graphics

including: line art
is a method of creating images where the instructions for drawing certain basic shapes, such as lines, rectangles, circles and so forth, rather than the picture itself, are stored. These basic shapes, or 'objects', can easily be moved around the drawing or laid on top of other objects. Because of the way they are constructed, they do not interfere with one another, and they can be thought of as existing in separate 'layers'; text in drawings would be stored as shapes – each letter being a separate object. Most *line art* of this sort tends to have only a few elements, so there is a considerable advantage in that less storage is needed, as compared with bitmapped graphics (see below). Scaling the picture up or down in size would not alter the clarity of the drawing.

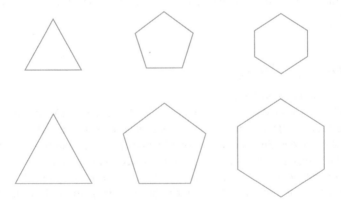

Figure A4.1   Vector graphics at two scalings

Graphics tablet

also known as: graphics pad
including: stylus

is a device used to input drawings into a computer, mimicking the use of a pen or a paintbrush. The user draws with a stylus on a flat pad or tablet (sometimes called a *graphics pad*), either copying a drawing or working freehand.

Stylus is the name for devices used for drawing on a graphics tablet. The movement of the stylus is detected by the tablet and its software in one of a variety of ways, for example through the use of a wire matrix in the pad or by sensing the angular movement of an arm supporting the stylus. A stylus may be pressure-sensitive, producing a darker or more intensely coloured line if pressed firmly. The position of the stylus on the tablet is input to the computer and used to position a cursor on the screen. Subsequent movement causes a drawing on the screen that matches the movements on the tablet. These devices are generally preferred to a mouse for computer drafting packages.

The stylus is being used on the tablet as a pen or a paintbrush.

Figure A4.2   Graphics tablet and stylus

Source: Volito by WACOM Europe. With permission from WACOM Europe.

PART A

Bitmapped graphics

is a method of creating images where a picture is held as a *bitmap* (see page 353) – that is, the state of each individual *pixel* (see page 197) is stored. Text in such a picture would also be stored in the same bitmap. Such drawings use a lot of storage space, because even 'blank' portions of the picture contribute to the size. They can also appear jagged when scaled up or down in size. However, for freehand drawings and graduated areas of tone, bitmapped graphics are better than vector graphics (see page 30).

Figure A4.3 Typical bitmapped graphics

Photo editing

including: layers, image enhancement
is the process of altering a digital photographic image, either for effect or to correct errors in the original. Typically, photo-editing software will allow the cropping and resizing of images, *colour correction* (see page 29), a variety of distortions (for example, to create buttons for Web sites), and the ability to add text or freehand drawing elements to the image (for example, to produce a labelled diagram). In addition, such packages usually convert images from one still image format or resolution to another (see Table A4.1, above).

Such packages usually allow an image to be seen as a number of separate *layers*, each of which can be moved separately and edited without affecting other layers. In this way, a part of one image can be superimposed on another and edited to blend in seamlessly.

Specialist *image-enhancement* software can take low-quality images (perhaps taken under poor lighting) and improve the picture by removing *noise* (see below) and strengthening outlines. Such techniques are now commonly used with images sent back from space probes.

PART A

In the original picture (1) the boats are too far away. The picture is cropped (2) to make a more pleasing composition. This has then been scaled up to make it a more appropriate size (3). This image in turn can be flipped (4), rotated (5) or (rather pointlessly) skewed (6). As well as changes to the size and shape of the image, the image itself could be modified in a number of ways.

Figure A4.4   Manipulation within a photo-editing package

Source: Adobe product screenshot reprinted with permission from Adobe Systems Incorporated.

Integrated graphics package

including: painting package, drawing package
is a package that incorporates both *vector* and *bitmapped graphics* (see above). At one time, it was common to use separate software to create and manipulate different types of graphics, stored on separate layers. *Painting packages* worked exclusively with bitmapped graphics, while *drawing packages* worked with vector graphics. It is now more usual to find both methods available in a single software package, particularly in photo-editing packages (see page 32).

Integrated packages will handle text separately from graphics, in separate layers, using the font definitions installed on the computer, and allowing the text to remain completely editable (as in a word processor) until the user wishes to export the combined image in a graphics format.

Clip art

While computer graphics software allows the user to draw their own illustrations, many publishers offer computer disks full of professionally drawn pictures that can be edited to suit an individual user's needs. These are popularly known as 'clip art' because of the way in which they are 'clipped' out of the file and 'pasted' into your own drawing.

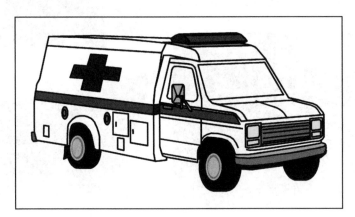

Figure A4.5 Typical clipart

Digital Still Imaging

Digital camera

is a stills camera that produces a digital image file of the scene photographed. This colour image may be printed directly from the camera or downloaded to a computer for storage or further manipulation (see *Photo editing*, page 32). It may also be possible to record short sequences of low-quality video.

Noise

is unwanted data in a digital picture. It often appears as random dots or patterning across the image. It is seen most often in images gathered by cameras operating in very low light, such as surveillance cameras.

Photo printer

is a printer of sufficiently high quality and resolution to print acceptable photographs. While photographs may be printed on plain paper using a colour inkjet or laser printer, the increasing popularity of digital stills photography has resulted in the introduction of affordable specialised printers that produce better-quality results through the use of glossy photographic-quality paper and through software designed to optimise the printing of photographs. Such printers often accept images directly from a camera or removable storage device (see below) without the need for connection to a computer. Sometimes, the printer will finish the process by cropping the print to a standard size. See also *printers* in B4 *Output*.

Photo-CD

is a proprietary format, introduced by Kodak, for storing photographic images on a standard data CD. Photographs that have been processed in the 'traditional' way may optionally be returned to the customer as a photo-CD, so that consumers without access to a digital camera can enjoy the benefits of *photo editing* (see above) on their computer. See also *CD*, page 187.

Digital camera storage

including: memory stick, compact flash card, XD card, smartmedia
generally consists of a small removable solid-state device that can be plugged into a special reader for input to a computer, or directly into a printer to produce a paper copy without the use of a computer. Most digital cameras (and also some video cameras that have a still photograph capability) use removable storage, but the cheapest cameras have storage built into the camera. In this case, photographs can be downloaded only by connecting the camera directly to a computer. These devices are not yet cheap enough for long-term storage of images, which are usually kept permanently on CD. There are several proprietary makes, incompatible with each other, including the *memory stick*, the *compact flash card, XD card* and *smartmedia*. See also B3 *Memory*.

PART A

Digital Video

Digital video camera

also known as: camcorder
is a movie camera that records digital images on to video tape or a small DVD. In the near future, we can expect digital video cameras that record directly to solid-state memory devices. Many video cameras can also record still photographs, either on to tape or disk or on to a removable still-picture storage device (see *Digital camera storage*, above). As the resolution needed for an acceptable moving image (72 dots per inch, dpi) is much less than for an acceptable still photograph (at least 300 dpi), this facility is unlikely to replace the dedicated digital stills camera.

Computer animation

is the creation of apparent movement through the presentation of a sequence of slightly different still pictures. The screen display of a computer is redrawn at least every 1/25 of a second, regardless of whether it has changed, because of the television technology used in many display devices. With a fast computer, it is possible to generate a new picture in this time, so that an impression of movement can be created, in the same way as a cinema film creates the illusion of movement from still pictures. Computer animation packages are now used routinely in the television and film industry, particularly where they can mix 'live action' with computer-generated images.

Video capture card

also known as: video digitiser
is a specialised analogue-to-digital converter that reads video signals from a video tape or video camera, digitises them, and stores them in a computer. The most recent video cameras record their data digitally, and strictly speaking a capture card is unnecessary. However, many users continue to use a capture card because other functions (such as *colour correction*, see above, or *real-time* effects, see in *video editing system*, page 37) are packaged on the card.

Codec

is short for 'coder/decoder'. It is the component that processes a video signal for storage and subsequent processing in a computer, and it may be implemented as software or hardware. While all codecs perform the same function, they are not equivalent; in order to recreate the video signal for playback to a TV set or video recorder, the coded data must be decoded by the same codec that was used originally. It is an important component of a *video capture card*, see above.

Digital video (DV) format

including: DV-in, DV-out, mini-DV, DVCam, widget

is the most widely accepted standard for digital video tape recording. Because the images are held and transmitted digitally, there is no deterioration of the picture when sequences are loaded into a computer, edited and re-recorded to tape. For this reason, the standard has become popular with both amateurs and professionals. The representation of the digital data is standard on all equipment, but there are two sizes of tape cassette; that most commonly encountered is the *mini-DV*, which is slightly smaller than an audiocassette. Professionally, most recording is done using *DVCam*, which uses identical cassettes and data format but spaces the data more widely on the tape to provide greater security from interference between adjacent tracks. Although a digital format, the DV system uses hardware *image compression* (see page 26) in the camera to produce data that are only 20% of the size captured originally.

All DV cameras will allow the tape to be replayed for downloading to a computer (*DV-out*); however, because of tax implications (video recorders are taxed more highly than players), not all manufacturers allow their cameras to *record* a DV signal (*DV-in*). This barrier may sometimes be overcome by modifying the camera using an electronic device known as a *widget*.

Video editing system

including: off-line editing, on-line editing, real-time editing

is a software package that allows the user (in this case, a video editor) to capture video material through a *video capture card* (see above) and organise it on the hard disk of a computer. Individual sequences may be trimmed to length and placed next to one another to assemble a final video programme. Transitions between sequences (dissolving from one to the other, or an animated 'page turn', for example) can be added, as can effects such as increasing the contrast of the picture or adding reverberation to the sound track. Titles may be created and added to the sequence, possibly by superimposing them over live action. Still images can be imported in a variety of formats and moved around the screen. Sequences may be speeded up or slowed down. Music and commentary may be added, either replacing the original sound or mixed with it through the use of sound-editing facilities in the package. When this creative work is complete, the finished sequence may be played back and recorded to video tape or DVD.

The video data remain in their original position on the hard disk, and the instructions for compiling the data into a finished sequence are stored as a series of references to the original files. Among other advantages, this allows a sequence to be

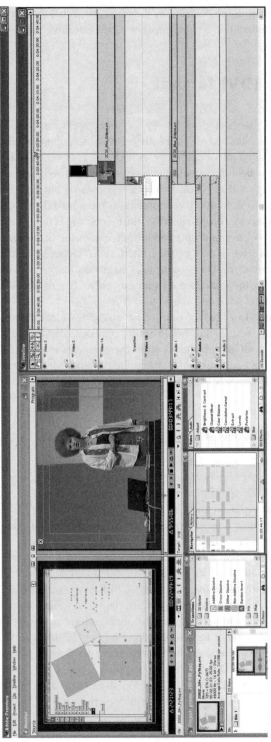

To the right, the various video clips being edited are arranged along the 'timeline'; the corresponding audio is displayed as a waveform below. To the left are two windows for replaying individual clips or the finished programme, and below are a variety of tool palettes and a master listing of available video. Many video-editing systems use two monitors, as here, in order to manage all this information.

Figure A4.6 Typical semi-professional video-editing system

reused without the need to create an additional (space-consuming) copy. Usually, these instructions can be saved independently of the video data, allowing the editor to delete the data but to retain a copy of the instructions, which can be used to re-create the sequence in the future by reloading the data.

Some terms have a very different meaning when applied to video editing by computer than when used in a more general computing context. Most edited video is only a small selection from the larger amount originally recorded. Where storage is an important consideration, it may be impossible to hold all the original material at the required quality.

Off-line editing is a method of working in which all the material is loaded, but at a very high degree of *compression* (see above); it is unacceptable for the finished sequence, but adequate for the editor to make decisions. When the sequence is complete, careful note is taken of the material actually used. The low-grade working data are then deleted, freeing up the space in the computer.

On-line editing, where only the material actually needed is loaded, at the best possible quality, follows this. Most video-editing systems allow this process to be automated.

Real-time editing has a similar meaning to that in *real-time system* (see page 17). Editing systems that are powerful enough to create effects and transitions without the need to *render* them (see page 27) are said to do so in real time.

PART A

# Sound

Other related terms, especially those concerned with modulation, may be found in D5 Communications Technology.

Electronic recording and reproduction of natural sound have been available for many decades through the use of tape recorders and gramophones. Similarly, the ability to generate natural sounds electronically – sound synthesis – was developed long before computers. What is relatively recent is the ability to process sound on computer equipment that is affordable by the consumer.

Sound is produced by the continuous vibration of air. This means that it has analogue properties. The electrical output from a microphone consists of a continuously fluctuating voltage and has to be converted into a digital form if it is to be stored on any digital device (for example, compact disc or digital audio tape) or if it is to be manipulated in a computer. The conversion of analogue signals to a digital form is achieved by **sound sampling**, a process in which special hardware measures the level of sound many times a second (typical up to 50 000) and records this as numerical data. The reverse process of turning digital sound data into audible sound is accomplished by using the data to determine the level of, for example, voltage applied to a loudspeaker or headphone.

Specialised sound equipment, such as mixing desks in a recording studio, use digital data in the same way as a computer, and hence contain microprocessors and storage devices such as hard disks.

Most personal computers are now supplied with a simple microphone for recording sound and a CD player for playing sound files. There is also at least a simple loudspeaker and possibly a more sophisticated stereo sound system for replaying sound.

While the most common applications of sound in computers are simple recording and playback, it is also possible to edit sounds using a suitable software package. This can involve simply removing unwanted portions of a recording, but it may also be used to alter the characteristics of the sound – adding echo or reverberation, for example, or removing hiss or crackle from older recordings. It is also possible to generate sounds purely by creating the digital data; the noises made by a computer when a key is pressed or an error message appears are examples of such 'artificial' sounds.

Any electronic music device that is controlled by a keyboard similar to a piano is called a (music) **keyboard**. The keys, which are arranged like the black and white keys on a piano, are frequently supplemented by switches, sliders and other ways of setting and changing the electronic signals produced by the device.

In order to understand fully what computers can do with sound, it is necessary to be aware of the nature and characteristics of sound entirely separately from computing. The medium that carries sound (most usually air, although sound can also travel through, for example, water) vibrates, and there are technical terms used to measure this vibration.

Characteristics of Sound

Waveform

is a representation of the vibrations that cause sound. A simple waveform is shown in Figure A5.1. This is the waveform corresponding to a real sound, and it is hard to see any regularity in it. Figure A5.2, later in this section, shows a simpler waveform (a single note) and how the terms explained below may be interpreted.

Figure A5.1 Waveform (the opening of a Strauss waltz)
Source: Reproduced by permission of Creative Labs.

Frequency

also known as: pitch
including: cps, hertz, Hz, kilohertz, kHz, wavelength
is the number of complete cycles made in one second. It is measured in cycles per second (cps, also known as *hertz*, *Hz*, after a German scientist). To avoid the use of large numbers, audible frequencies are also quoted in *kilohertz* (*kHz*); 1 kHz = 1000 Hz. The higher the frequency, the higher the sound heard by the listener. For example, the lowest note on a piano has a sound of 27.5 Hz, while the highest is 4186 Hz.

An alternative measure of the same characteristic is the *wavelength*. This is the distance between places where the vibration is in the same place. Higher frequencies correspond to lower wavelengths (see Figure A5.2).

Amplitude

including: volume
is the maximum amount that the vibrating particles move. It is basically the *volume* of the sound: the higher the amplitude, the louder the sound heard (see Figure A5.2).

Phase

is the amount of a complete cycle that has elapsed. It is measured in degrees – 360° is one complete cycle. We do not *hear* the phase of a sound, but it is important when sounds become out of phase. See *stereophonic sound*, below.

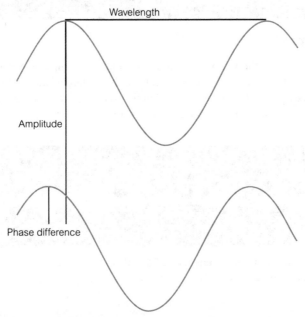

Two pure waveforms showing the same note. Wavelength and amplitude are marked and are the same in each case. However, the lower note starts earlier in time, and hence there is a phase difference between the waveforms.

Figure A5.2 Characteristics of a (sound) wave

Harmonics

including: timbre
It is possible to generate a 'pure' note electronically, or with a tuning fork, but the situation is considerably more complicated with a real musical instrument. Here, whenever a note is sounded, there will be other, higher notes present, called harmonics. Exactly which harmonics are present, and how loud they are, will depend on the instrument, and it is the particular blend of harmonics that gives an instrument its characteristic sound or *timbre*. Figures A5.3 and A5.4 explain this process.

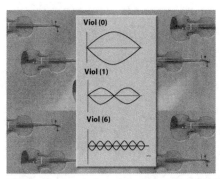
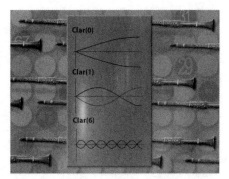

The basic note being played on a violin (left) and a clarinet (right) is shown at the top of each picture. Because violin strings are fixed at each end, the waveform is a closed loop. With the clarinet, which has an open mouth, the waveform is different. As well as these basic notes, a number of higher-frequency notes sound at the same time. These are added together to give the timbre of each instrument, as shown in Figure A5.4.

Figure A5.3 Harmonics and timbre (1)

Source: From a presentation of The Music of the Primes. Images designed by Shani Ram. With kind permission of Professor Marcus du Sautoy.

PART A

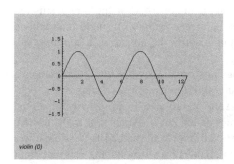
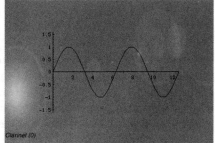
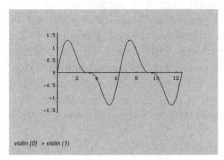
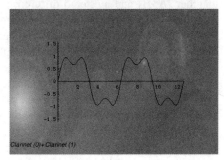

Three stages in the addition of the harmonics from Figure A5.3. The pure note at the top is modified in strikingly different ways. Although both instruments are sounding the same note, the resulting waveform, seen overleaf, is very different.

Figure A5.4 Harmonics and timbre (2)

Source: From a presentation of the Music of the Primes. Images designed by Shani Ram. With kind permission of Professor Marcus du Sautoy.

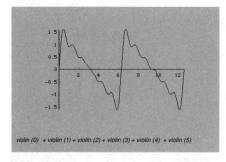

violin (0) + violin (1) + violin (2) + violin (3) + violin (4) + violin (5)

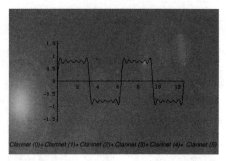

Clarinet (0)+ Clarinet (1)+ Clarinet (2)+ Clarinet (3)+ Clarinet (4)+ Clarinet (5)

Figure A5.4 (cont'd)

Stereophonic sound

also known as: stereo

including: stereo image, monophonic, mono, A&B, M&S

We hear sounds through our ears. Because these are on opposite sides of the head, sound takes different amounts of time to reach each ear. The human brain uses this time difference to create a three-dimensional picture of where sounds are positioned in relation to each other (sometimes called a *stereo image*). A single microphone cannot sense this three-dimensionality and records the sound as a *monophonic* (*mono*) signal.

In pursuit of realism, modern recordings and broadcasts use two microphones a small distance apart and play back the sound through a pair of speakers.

For simplicity of recording and processing, stereo signals are usually separated as left channel and right channel, sometimes called *A&B* signals. For transmission, particularly radio and television broadcasts, an improved method is possible. Two signals are sent, but these are a combined signal formed by adding left and right together (A+B) and a 'stereo difference' signal formed by subtracting one signal from the other (A−B). The difference signal would make poor listening by itself, as the B signal largely cancels out the A signal. However, the combined signal is just a (louder) version of what a mono microphone would have heard; a receiver such as a portable radio without stereo facilities can simply play this signal without further processing. A stereo hi-fi system can use the difference signal to re-create the left and right channels before they are sent to separate loudspeakers or headphones. This system, transmitting a mono signal, and a stereo difference signal, is known as *M&S* stereo.

The *phase* (see above) of a signal is important in stereo. While we cannot hear the phase in a sound, if the left and right channels of a stereo system are not perfectly in phase, one will tend to cancel out the other.

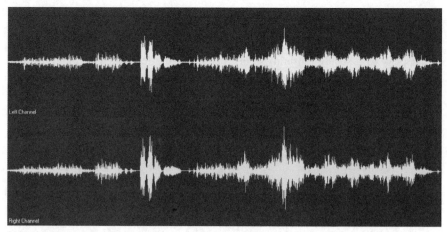

This is the same music as in Figure A5.1, but recorded as a left (top) and a right (bottom) channel. Although the waveforms are very similar, because the microphones are hearing the same sound, there are differences. For example, the peak of sound in the centre of this fragment is louder (has greater amplitude) in the right channel than the left. The instrument that produced this sound was positioned to the listener's right.

Figure A5.5 Stereophonic sound

Source: Reproduced by permission of Creative Labs.

Sound Processing

Envelope

including: ADSR (attack, decay, sustain, release)
is a shape used to describe the changes in volume (amplitude) or pitch (frequency) of a note as it changes with time. The form of a sound envelope is normally used in *sound synthesis* (see page 48). One commonly used way of describing a volume envelope is known as *ADSR*, short for attack, decay, sustain and release. See Figures A5.6 and A5.7.

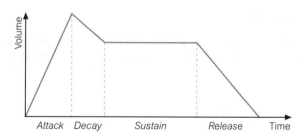

Figure A5.6 Volume envelope

Attack is the rate at which an envelope rises to its initial peak before starting to decay. For example, percussive sounds (piano, drums) have a high attack rate for their volume (amplitude). *Decay* is the rate at which an envelope falls from its initial peak to a steady (sustain) level. *Sustain* is the level at which an envelope remains whilst a key is still pressed after the initial attack and decay stages. *Release* is the rate at which an envelope fades away from its sustain level when the key is released.

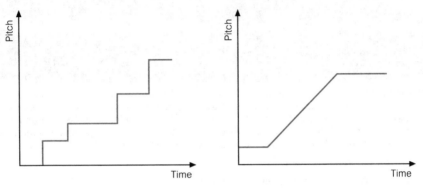

Figure A5.7 Two pitch envelopes

Frequency modification

also known as: frequency shifting

If a sound recording is played back faster than the speed it was recorded at, the frequency increases – voices sound like high-pitched squeaks. Using a computer to digitally process the sound by manipulating the sampled data allows the frequency to be adjusted so that a speeded-up recording sounds natural, but faster. It is even possible, within limits, to make me sing in tune!

SMPTE codes

are an agreed set of standards that make it possible to synchronise sound and video signals. SMPTE is an abbreviation for the (US) Society of Motion Picture and TV Engineers.

Sound sampling

including: sampling rate, sampling resolution

is the process of receiving analogue sound signals from a microphone (or other sound source) and analysing them in order to store them as digital data. By performing this analysis very quickly and very frequently, a faithful digital representation of the sound can be stored.

The quality of sound produced using sound sampling depends upon the sampling rate and the sampling resolution; the higher each of these is, the more faithful the sample, but the larger the amount of data storage required. It is not always necessary to strive for the highest quality; for example, a telephone uses the equivalent of a very low sampling rate because it is the message that is important, not the quality of the speaker's voice. It is simply perverse to attempt to listen to music on your telephone handset, however hard the manufacturers try to persuade us that this is a good thing!

Sampling rate is the frequency with which samples are taken. For theoretical reasons, to do with capturing not just the basic sound but also its higher frequency harmonics (see above), the sampling frequency is usually twice the highest audible frequency in the sound being sampled. For music, this indicates values around 40–50 kHz (40 000–50 000 samples per second).

Sampling resolution is the number of bits used for storage of each sample value. CD-quality sound uses 16 bits, but acceptable sound for use on the Internet or through a computer speaker may be achieved from only 8 bits.

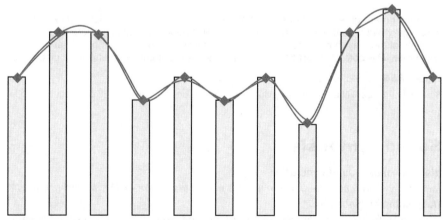

The dark green curve is part of a sound waveform. At regular intervals (the sampling rate), the amplitude of the waveform is recorded. When these samples are played back, it is the grey waveform that the listener hears. The effect of this is shown in Figure A5.9.

Figure A5.8 Sampling

Source: Key Stage 3 National Strategy-Communication: sound and video. DfES 0011/2003. HMSO.

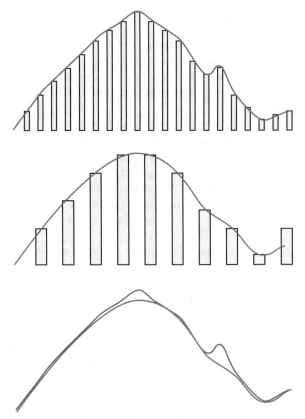

The upper (dark green) waveform has been sampled at twice the sampling rate of the lower (grey) waveform. As a result, the small high-frequency variation about three-quarters of the way through has been captured, while it is missed completely at the lower rate. The bottom illustration superimposes the two samples to show the difference.

Figure A5.9 Effect of sampling rates

Source: Key Stage 3 National Strategy-Communication: sound and video. DfES 0011/2003. HMSO.

Sound synthesis

also known as: sound generation
including: frequency modulation (FM), phase distortion (PD), linear arithmetic (LA), additive synthesis
is the use of electronic devices for creating sound, sometimes called sound genera-tion. The final audible sounds will be generated using analogue techniques, but digital methods may be used to transmit the sound before this final stage. With care, electronically generated sound can create notes that are like those produced by a variety of musical instruments.

In creating sound from scratch (that is, not using sound that has already been sampled), it is common to start from pure waveforms and modify these to mimic the characteristics of 'ordinary' sound. The most commonly used methods are:

Frequency modulation (FM), in which the frequency of a waveform is altered continuously to carry sound information.

Phase distortion (PD), in which the phase of a waveform is modified continuously.

Linear arithmetic (LA), in which sampled sounds are used as well as pure tones as the start of the process. Arithmetic operations are then carried out on the values of the bit patterns representing the sounds (see *Sound sampling*, above).

Additive synthesis, a software method in which the user selects a mixture of harmonics and the computer calculates the values for the waveform at very small successive time intervals. In all cases, the digital values for the sound are turned into sound signals by a digital-to-analogue converter. Different methods of creating sounds produce different qualities of sound.

Sound formats

including: lossless, lossy

A number of standard formats have been adopted for the storage and interchange of digital sound data; some of the more common of these are listed in Table A5.1. Generally, different formats are incompatible with one another. Some formats are *lossless*, in that they preserve all the information in the original sample; others are *lossy* and involve some degradation of the signal.

Table A5.1   Audio storage and compression schemes

Type	File extension	Comment
Windows waveform	.wav	A sampled lossless format, with selectable sampling rate
Audio Interchange File Format	.aif, .aiff	Sampled lossless format, with selectable sampling rate
Real Media	.rm	Sampled format, used for streaming audio (see below)
Motion Picture Experts Group	.mp3	A compressed, lossy format that is efficient. Usually used for downloading audio files over the Internet. Selectable compression rate
Windows media	.wma	A compressed, lossy format with selectable compression rate
Musical Instrument Digital Interface (MIDI)	.midi	A format for interchange only, not for storage. The sound itself is generated from samples already stored in the sound hardware; the MIDI file consists simply of instructions on how to play these samples

Note that the video file formats in Table A4.1 on page 28 generally have their own associated audio formats, which are not shown in Table A5.1

Table A5.2 The effect of sampling and format on file sizes

Method	File size		
wav sampled at 44.1 kHz	3.10 M b	= 3 100 000	bytes
wav at 22.05 kHz	1.54 Mb	= 1 540 000	bytes
wav at 12.025 kHz	854 kb	= 854 000	bytes
wav at 6 kHz	432 kb	= 432 000	bytes
mp3	303 kb	= 303 000	bytes
MIDI	2 kb	= 2000	bytes

One piece of music, encoded by different methods, results in the different file sizes shown in Table A5.2

Source: Adapted from Key Stage 3 National Strategy-Communication: sound and video. DfES 0011/2003. HMSO.

Streaming audio

is a technique used to allow audio to be played on a Web site without an excessive delay while a large data file is downloaded. The opening seconds of the sound must be downloaded before playback can begin, to provide a buffer. The player software starts to play this sound to the user and keeps the buffer filled by downloading the next sound while the first is playing. If transmission delays over the Internet cause the buffer to become dangerously low, the quality of the new sound is reduced to allow more of it to be transmitted, in order to catch up. One characteristic of this method of delivery is that once playback is completed, the user has no permanent copy of the audio on their computer. This can be an advantage, for example where a record company wishes to promote music from a popular record but not allow these extracts to remain in other hands.

Similar *streaming video* techniques can be used for moving image files.

Devices

MIDI (Musical Instrument Digital Interface)

including: MIDI channel, MIDI standard, MIDI code
A musical instrument digital interface, MIDI (frequently, but incorrectly, referred to as a MIDI interface), is a particular form of serial interface (see *interface*, page 356, and *interface card*, page 363) built into or added to the parts of an electronic music system. The interface allows electronic music data to be passed in both directions between parts of the system. The links between parts of the system are called *MIDI channels*. The form of the interface and the structure of the data are defined by the *MIDI standard*, which was agreed between the major manufacturers of electronic musical instruments in 1983. The standard defines the codes (*MIDI codes*) to be used for musical data, for example the pitch and volume of a note. These codes allow music data to be passed between devices from different manufacturers in the same

way that ASCII codes (see *character set*, page 307) allow alphanumeric data to be passed between different computers.

Music synthesiser

including: synthesiser, analog synthesiser, digital synthesiser, multi-timbral synthesiser, polyphony
is an electronic device for creating sounds. It is often simply called a *synthesiser*. The sounds may be generated electronically using either analogue or digital techniques (see *sound generator*, below). Most synthesisers have a piano-style keyboard and need to be connected to an amplifier with loudspeakers for the sounds they produce to be heard.

Analog synthesisers are usually intended to be used as musical instruments to be played, and most do not generally have the ability to store the sounds they create.

Digital synthesisers generally incorporate some form of digital storage and frequently have a built-in store of ready-made sounds. Digital synthesisers generally offer a much greater variety of sounds and a wider range of manipulation options than analogue synthesisers. For example, a *multi-timbral synthesiser* can play two or more different sounds at the same time or produce a number of different notes at the same time (*polyphony*), or a combination of both of these capabilities may be found in the same synthesiser.

Sound controller

including: musical instrument controller, audio controller
is a hardware device that controls sounds generated by a sound source. Controllers usually do not produce sounds themselves, though they may be made to look like (and be used like) musical instruments, for example a piano keyboard or a guitar. These are called *musical instrument controllers*. Some controllers use joysticks, sliders or wheels. These may be built into other controllers or attached to a musical instrument. Control of sounds is usually achieved by using MIDI codes (see *MIDI*, above). There are also *audio controllers*, which can generate (MIDI) control signals from audio sounds. With an audio controller looking like a microphone, a user can sing into it while 'playing' a synthesised sound from a connected sound generator, and thus control the sound produced.

Sound generator

also known as: sound source
is a digital device capable of producing sounds as part of an electronic music system; it is sometimes called a *sound source*. A range of such devices exists, which create sounds similar to those produced by particular musical instruments, such as drum machines, electric guitars and electronic organs. A *music synthesiser* (see above) is an example of a sound generator; it has a piano-type keyboard that is used to play it, but most sound generators have no direct means of being played as if they were musical instruments. Some have a collection of predefined sounds and some have

PART A

synthesising capabilities. The sounds may be accessed via *MIDI* (see above), to be used as input to a sequencer or a music controller, or the device may be attached to a computer as a dedicated peripheral.

Sound processor

is the general term for electronic sound equipment that can take a sound as an input, modify the signal and output the new sound. The processing may use either analogue or digital techniques, but the use of digital methods is now more common. Most sound processors have a particular function, for example echo units, reverberation units, graphic equalisers and noise-reduction units. All of these work in *real time* (see *sequencer*, below). Sound-processing software on a suitable computer can do the same things that individual sound-processing items achieve. Thus, a computer may be used as a general-purpose sound processor.

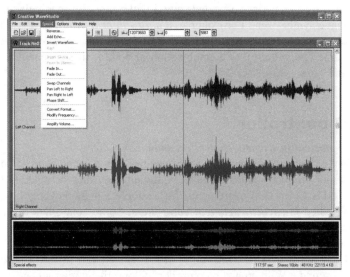

A stereo waveform is shown being edited in the larger window. The menu choices show that reverberation or echo may be added, a fade in or out can be applied, and the stereo image can be adjusted. Note the option to shift the phase of the recording (see Stereophonic sound, above) and to modify the frequency (see above).

Figure A5.10 Typical computer sound-processing package

Source: Reproduced by permission of Creative Labs.

Sound mixer

also known as: mixing desk
including: channel, music channel
is an electronic device for combining sound signals. It is commonly found in recording studios, where it is used to balance the loudness of sounds from a number of

sources and to add effects through use of built-in *sound processors* (see above). An operator (also often known as a sound mixer, in which case the hardware may be known as a *mixing desk*) selects how input signals are to be combined to form one or more output signals and adjusts the levels of individual sources and combinations. The independent input and output signals are known as *channels* or *music channels*.

Sequencer

including: real-time entry, step-time entry

is a digital device that can store a set of representations of notes, rhythms and other musical data for replaying at a later time. It may also include facilities for editing or for producing repeating patterns. Sequencers may range from the very simple, capable of storing only a small number of notes or a single chord, to the complex, capable of simultaneously handling many independent musical parts. Sequencers are often built into synthesisers (see *music synthesiser* above) and drum machines or other electronic music devices. One example of the use of a sequencer is to play a piece of stored music at different speeds without the distortion of pitch, which happens if the speed of a tape recorder is varied. Another is to change the sound of a series of notes entered previously, rather like changing the colours of parts of a computer-generated picture with an art program.

Music parts can be entered into a sequencer in one of two ways:

Real-time entry has the musical information provided by playing the notes with the correct relative time intervals. They need not be the actual intervals since the sequencer can modify the speed (tempo).

Step-time entry has the time interval between each note defined by the person entering the musical information.

Computer-based music system

including: digital sound system

is an arrangement of electronic music devices and a computer linked together so that music and other sounds, such as speech and singing, can be captured, stored, manipulated, generated or reproduced. These systems will probably contain both digital and analogue components. Where only digital processing components are used, they are referred to as *digital sound systems*.

Music workstation

is a collection of connected music-generating and sound-manipulating equipment. A typical arrangement will include a keyboard, a synthesiser and a sequencer. They are increasingly likely to include a computer with appropriate software. See *computer-based music system*, above.

PART A

A6 Multimedia and Virtual Reality

Multimedia systems are interactive computer systems that are concerned principally with the storage of data (and their associated information retrieval) for reference purposes. They are usually organised so that the user can obtain information in a number of ways. Often called **hypertext** systems, they store text in such a way that users are able to construct their own links between different parts of the text. The multi-level approach to text acquisition, storage, analysis, comparison, retrieval and editing includes a comprehensive command structure that allows users to move through a document. This may be achieved by the use of pre-programmed links, through techniques such as **browsing**, or by searching for specific words. The system will remember the path taken.

Multimedia is also known as **hypermedia** and is an extension of hypertext. It also includes related graphics (still, animated and moving video) and sound.

The data are held in a non-linear structure using nodes and, for each node, a small number of links (typically two, three or four) are available to related nodes. Using on-screen menus, often presented on a menu bar, it is possible to move through the system in a variety of search patterns. Starting with a main index, the user can choose a path that introduces the context of a particular subject and then, having noticed some point of special interest, can change the search pattern to follow the context of that new subject. The system might also allow the user to search for associated themes by using key words in the particular screen being displayed at that time.

The change in the type of information generated by calls into such a system can be dramatic. For example, in a system that apparently was associated with an art gallery, the user might choose to look at information about one particular artist, which could include a screen display of that artist's pictures. Then, seeing a subject of interest depicted in one of the paintings, they could choose to look at paintings by other artists on the same subject. If the subject happened to be people playing musical instruments, the next step might be to choose to hear some music associated with those instruments. This might then lead to a topic dealing with the production of sound, and then to information about the physics of wave motion.

The usefulness of such a system is dependent on the type of data structure that it employs, the size of the database and the access time. The ease of use might be related to the physical process of using the menus, where a touchscreen might have considerable advantages over a mouse or the arrow keys.

Multimedia Concepts

Multimedia

including: tutor

is the presentation of information by a computer system using graphics, animation, sound and text. The data may be stored in a variety of ways using conventional computer storage devices, together with a picture database on CD-ROM. Output might be through VDUs, sound generators and laser projectors.

Integrating a *tutor* program could allow the system to be used as a training resource. The performance of the user could then be monitored by recording the choices made in response to questions and evaluating this response using an expert system (see page 134). This performance output might then be sent to a remote trainer, who could assess the trainee's progress.

Interactive video

involves the use of a computer linked to a large-capacity data store such as a CD to provide random-access retrieval of images (including stills and continuous video) and sound. Data, once recorded, are not easily changed or added to, and access times can sometimes appear long. However, any disadvantage arising is generally outweighed by the amount, variety and quality of data that can be retrieved from one active device.

HyperCard

including: card, stack

is an application-building tool provided with Apple Macintosh computers that allows for interactive storing and retrieving on-screen '*cards*'. These can contain text, graphics, sound and video clips, and are grouped together in one or more related *stacks*.

Browse

is a feature of hypertext systems that allows users to build their own route through an application rather than following a predetermined one. The route so chosen may be remembered by the system so that it can be retraced back to the starting point of that route. This kind of browsing is particularly useful in applications such as computerised manuals, computer-aided learning packages and large databases.

Video clip

is a short section of film or video stored in digital form (both sound and pictures). It is easily incorporated in computer displays and hypermedia systems. The video clip would normally be stored in compressed form, otherwise the storage cost would be prohibitive. See also *image compression*, page 26.

Virtual Reality

Virtual reality

including: immersive virtual reality, non-immersive virtual reality
is a computer-generated environment that provides the user with the illusion of being present in that situation. Virtual reality is produced by providing feedback to our various senses: vision, hearing, movement and sometimes smell. As the user moves or acts, the image seen will change along with appropriate sound and movement. It usually requires high-powered computers.

Immersive virtual reality systems provide feedback to as many senses as possible by using specialised equipment. They attempt to provide the user with a very realistic situation and are used for training in critical and stressful situations. Examples include the training of aircraft crew (a cockpit simulator using a cabin mounted on hydraulic jacks to provide movement) and training maintenance engineers to work in nuclear reactors (using specialised peripherals such as *data gloves* and *headsets*, see below).

Non-immersive virtual reality systems use limited feedback to provide the user with the perception of a particular situation without attempting to convince the user that it is real. This can be done relatively cheaply using common equipment. The environment is displayed on a standard monitor using 3D graphics and can be controlled using a simple pointing device such as a special scalpel that a sculptor may use to carve a sculpture. Other examples include vehicle driver training and the ergonomic evaluation of a shop layout.

Data glove

is an input device worn on the hand by a user of a virtual reality system. Typically, it enables the position of the fingers and the orientation of the hand to be sensed by the system. In most systems, when the user 'touches' a simulated object, there is no physical sensation returned to the hand. Greater realism is possible in systems that do provide this kind of feedback. See also *haptic feedback*, below.

Haptic feedback

provides the user with a sense of feel and touch. When the user touches a virtual object, the input device stops moving freely and provides resistance to the user. An example is a sculptor using a special scalpel that moves freely until it starts cutting the virtual object.

Headset

is an input and output device worn on the head by a user of a virtual reality system. It gives the wearer the impression of being within the computer-generated scene, with sound provided through headphones and vision through small video screens in goggles worn over the eyes. The headset senses changes of position of the head and inputs this to the computer so that the simulation can be changed appropriately. Since the user is isolated from external sounds and vision, there is a very strong sense of being within the simulated environment.

Virtual reality cave

is a small room where the walls consist of back-projected displays, giving the user a more immersive experience without the need for a headset. For example, a driving simulator may consist of a car body at the centre of a virtual reality cave.

User Interface and Documentation

Other terms related to setting up interfaces and documentation will be found in C2 Describing Systems and C7 Describing Programs.

Cooks usually try to make their meals tasty and attractive as well as nutritious. In the same way, software writers try to make their products attractive to the user as well as effective and easy to use. Much time and effort are spent on designing ways in which the user interacts with the computer and the software. Most software users are more concerned with what a package can do than with how it works. They expect to be able to see and understand what the software can do and they want to be able to communicate their instructions easily and have quick and understandable responses from the computer.

As the scope of computer applications has increased and the number of computer users has also increased, a variety of ways have evolved for communication between the user and the computer; this is called the **user interface** or **user environment**. There are fashions in user interface design, just as there are in car and clothes design, but what is important is that the interface should achieve its objectives as efficiently as possible.

All user interface designs are limited by the capabilities of machines and people. Each design seeks to make the most of the strengths and avoid the weaknesses of computer equipment and its users. Aspects of computer hardware, for example processing speed, memory capacity, and input and output devices, restrict what software can achieve. Speech is the most common form of communication between people, and speech-recognition systems for communication from people to computers are now available for personal computers. Communication through text is limited by the speed at which people can read text presented on a screen and the time taken to type responses accurately on a keyboard. Recent improvements in hardware have greatly enhanced the graphics capability of small computers. Most software designers have chosen graphical ways of presenting the activities or concepts available for selection at any time: **icons** (small pictures with an easily understood meaning) are used widely, since graphical information should be independent of the user's language and can be used wherever the meaning of the icon is understood and not offensive. All user interface designs are compromises between what it is desirable to provide and what it is possible to achieve. All of this applies to the Internet and World Wide Web sites as well.

It is the combination of those parts of the hardware and software of a system with which the user interacts that make up the user interface. User interfaces are described in a variety of ways, whose names highlight their main features; for example, **graphical user interface (GUI)**, **menu selection interface**, **windows environment**, **forms dialogue**. There is no single kind of user environment that suits all applications or all users; the choice of an appropriate user interface depends on the amount of information to be presented or elicited, the experience of the user and the user's familiarity with the particular software.

Since taste and personal preference largely determine people's reactions to different user environments, there will always be scope for variety in their design. For those people who spend a long time working at a computer, it is very important that the user interface they experience makes a positive contribution to their efficiency. It is increasingly common for the user to be able to adapt (**customise**) the facilities provided by the system to fit the situation in which the system is used.

Additional arrangements can be made where there is a special user environment, such as where provision has to be made for people with disabilities. These may include the provision of customised input and/or output devices, such as touch-sensitive keyboards, and the appropriate additional software.

When a software package or piece of hardware is purchased, instructions on how to set up and use the software or the device will be needed. The instructions, known as **user documentation**, may be printed but are frequently seen on the screen when the software or driver has been installed.

Graphical Interfaces

Human–computer interaction (HCI)

also known as: human–computer interface
including: man–machine interface (MMI), user interface, user environment, graphical user interface (GUI)
is one of a number of terms used to describe the communication between people and computer systems. Other terms for this are *man–machine interface (MMI)*, *user interface* and *user environment*. Any of these terms is likely to be used in discussions of how people and computer systems interact and the ease of use of a system.

One way of classifying interfaces is by the style of communication they provide. Some are purely textual whilst others, known as *graphical user interfaces (GUIs)*, replace some or all of the words by *icons* (see below and also the introduction to this section).

PART A

WIMP environment

also known as: Windows Icons Menus Pointers environment
including: desktop
is a method of accessing the computer making minimum use of the keyboard by using a mouse (or similar device) to move a pointer over *icons* or text *menus* displayed on the screen. For example, selecting an icon may open a window and start a task. For definitions of the terms *window*, *pointer* and *icon*, see below; for *menu*, see page 62, and for *mouse*, see page 171. A combination of windows and icons is sometimes referred to as the *desktop*.

Window

including: active window, pane
is a temporary area opened on the screen displaying the activity of a program. There can be several windows on the screen at any one time, which can be moved if required or removed completely (restoring the original information on the screen). At any one time, only one window will be the *active window*, i.e. accessible for input by the user. Things may be happening in other windows, for example a clock may be showing the time, but this does not mean that the window is active. If several activities are being run at the same time, then each will be in a separate window but only one can be worked on at a time. It is possible to have more than one window visible and shift from one task to another by moving the cursor from one window to another. A window may be divided into parts, called *panes*, which can be used separately, for example headers and footers in a document.

Icons

also spelt: ikons
are small pictures or symbols, with an easily understood meaning, displayed on the screen as a method of offering a choice of activity. A pointer is moved to a selected icon using, for example, a *mouse*, *cursor* control keys or a *trackerball*, and the activity is started by *clicking* a mouse button or pressing an appropriate key. This method has advantages over text-based input for inexperienced users. Icons can be independent of the user's language, provided the symbols are generally recognised.

Menu-selection interface

is a form of user interface in which the computer displays a list of options from which the user must make a choice, either by typing the code displayed against the option or by moving a highlight to the option (using cursor keys, a mouse or a trackerball) and then pressing a particular key or clicking the mouse button. The response may be to carry out the choice, to request further information (using any of the communication styles) or to report an error. See also *WIMP environment*, above.

Highlighting

including: inverse video

is changing the appearance of a part of a screen display by altering it in some way so that it stands out, for example by changing colour arrangements or by putting shading around an area of the screen. One commonly used method involves the use of *inverse video*, in which black becomes white and colours change to the colour represented by the inverse bit pattern, for example the inverse of 00011011 is 11100100. See also *Word Processing*, page 22.

Highlighting changes **HIGHLIGHT** into **HIGHLIGHT**

PART A

Pointer

also known as: mouse pointer
including: cursor, cursor movement key, arrow key, caret

is an icon (sometimes in the form of an arrow) on the screen. It moves around the screen in response to the movements of a mouse (or other similar device) or the use of keys. The pointer often changes its shape depending on its position on the screen or the situation in an application. When the pointer indicates a position in text, it is usually called the *cursor*.

The *cursor* is the screen symbol that indicates where on the screen the next action will begin. To make it easier to find and follow in text-handling situations, the cursor may be made to flash on and off, or the present position might be emphasised by using *highlighting* (see above). When entering text, the cursor automatically advances to the next typing position after a key is pressed. Actions other than entering text require the movement of the cursor about the screen. These movements are controlled by a mouse (or other similar device) or by the *cursor movement keys*.

Cursor movement keys (up, down, left, right), which are sometimes referred to as the *arrow keys* ($\uparrow$, $\downarrow$, $\leftarrow$, $\rightarrow$), are one way of directing the movement of the cursor about the screen.

Caret is the name for a symbol used by printers to show that text needs inserting; for this reason, the name is used for the screen cursor for inserting text that is often in the form of a 'I'. Unfortunately, *caret* is also the correct name for the character $\wedge$, which is one of the symbols available on many keyboards.

Menu

including: submenu, action bar, menu bar, pull-down menu, pop-up menu, status bar
is a range of options offered to a computer user so that a choice can be made. A
menu may simply be a screen display that lists a number of choices. The user is
expected to press an appropriate key to select one of them; one of the choices offered
is likely to be another menu, known as a *submenu*. Sometimes a special panel
appears when a choice has to be made. This hides part of the screen, but the screen
is restored to its original state after the choice has been made.

Menu bar or *action bar* is a line of titles for menus across the screen (usually at
the top, but sometimes at the bottom). These are the menus that the user can choose
at that point. Clicking when the *mouse pointer* (see above) is on the appropriate
word, or else pressing an appropriate key, selects a menu. The choice is usually
displayed as a *pull-down menu*.

Pull-down menu is a menu that appears on request after its title has been selected
from the menu bar. It gets its name because it usually appears immediately below
the menu title.

Pop-up menu is a menu that appears on the screen wherever the user happens to
have positioned the cursor. It may be called up as the result of pressing a *hot key* (see
page 65) or because the program needs to offer the user a choice as a result of what
is being done at that instant.

Status bar is a line of information displayed on the screen, usually either at the
top or at the bottom, which shows some of the conditions in the task at the moment,
such as the page and line number in a word-processing application.

Clicking

including: double-clicking
Pressing a mouse button is called clicking, because this usually produces a 'click'
sound. If the user clicks when the pointer controlled by the mouse is on an *icon* (see
page 60) or a *screen button* (see page 64), then the operation represented by that icon
(or button) is selected. For example, clicking on the picture of the flag of a country
may cause its national anthem to be played.

Some software expects the mouse button to be pressed twice in quick succession,
which is called *double-clicking*; a single click may have one effect, while double-
clicking may have another.

Dialogue box

including: text box, list box, check box
is a window that appears when information about a choice is needed, or when
options have to be selected. For example, choosing Print from a File menu may
cause a dialogue box to appear, requiring answers to questions such as which pages
to print, number of copies, etc. (see Figure A7.1). Normally, a dialogue box will

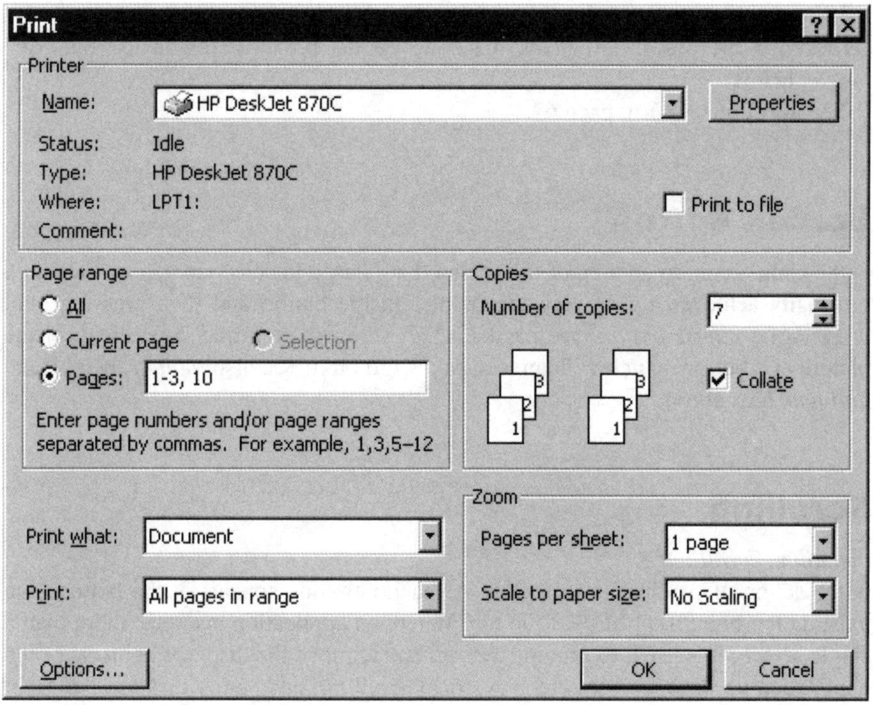

Figure A7.1   Dialogue box

offer the chance to cancel the request as well as the option to proceed. Dialogue boxes are intended to make it easy to obtain the necessary information quickly.

Where the user has to select from a limited number of options, this may be done by typing into a *text box* or by selection from a *list box* (see Figure A7.2), in which a list of options is shown and from which the user selects with the pointer. List boxes usually drop down to show several options.

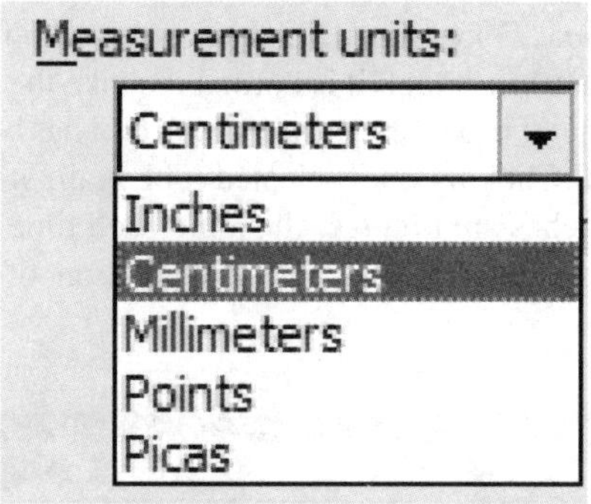

Figure A7.2   List box

PART A

In a *check box*, the feature is either activated if the box is marked or is not activated if the box is left blank. Clicking on the box will toggle its state. See *toggle*, below.

See also Figure A7.6, page 67.

Screen button

is the name given to an area of the screen that is used to select an action. Selection is usually achieved by moving the pointer to the button and then pressing (and releasing) a *mouse button* (see page 171). A screen button may be an icon or the picture of a button switch with an icon or a word on it. See also *toolbar*, below, and *dialogue box*, above.

Scrolling

including: scroll bar

is the action of 'rolling up' a screen. As each new line appears at the bottom, the existing top line disappears off the top. Where an application occupies more than a single screen, it is usual to provide a *scroll bar* to move the displayed portion of the application up or down the screen (vertical scrolling) and sometimes left and right across the screen (horizontal scrolling) (see Figure A7.3).

Figure A7.3   Horizontal scroll bar

Toolbar

including: tool, toolbox, toggle

is a line of *screen buttons* (see above) that represent the actions, *tools*, that are currently available to be carried out within an applications package or a system. This line of buttons is called a *toolbox*. For example, clicking on an icon for a brush in a drawing program will select a paintbrush tool. It is normal to make the icons behave like press switches (buttons), so that it is possible to see which tool has been selected or whether the tool is still selected. Clicking on a selected tool again will cancel the selection; this means that the switches are *toggles*, changing each time they are 'clicked'.

Toolbox is sometimes used to describe a collection of *utility programs* (see page 338).

Figure A7.4   Toolbar

Macro recording

including: script
is the action of recording a sequence of keystrokes that achieve a particular purpose and saving the recording, known as the *script*, for future use. By assigning a *hot key* (see below) to stand for this recorded sequence (see *macro*, page 265), it is possible to make frequently required actions easier to perform. For example, a single key combination could be used to type the whole of a frequently used phrase.

Drag

including: drag-and-drop editing
is the use of a mouse (or other similar device) to move an area of a screen display, which may be text or some part of a graphic display, bodily from one location to another. Before such movement can take place, the area concerned has to be defined in some way, such as by *highlighting* text (see page 61) or by marking the boundaries of a graphics item. Moving things around in this way is sometimes referred to as *drag-and-drop editing*, which may also be used to copy, as well as move, part of a screen display. One example of dragging is moving the icon for a file from one subdirectory to another as a way of repositioning the file within the directory; another would be moving a graphic item from an application running in one window on the screen to a different application running in another window. Drag is sometimes used to mean moving the mouse while holding down a button.

Hot key

also known as: quick key, shortcut key, keyboard shortcut
is a function key or a key combination (frequently combining *Control* or *Alt* with other keys) that causes an action (such as calling up a menu or running another program) whatever the user is doing. The name suggests the urgency of beginning a new action without fully breaking off from the existing task, or without the need to progress through a sequence of menus. The uses of *function keys* (see page 171) are sometimes defined as a menu on the screen or may be defined on a *keystrip* (see page 72) for the application.

Directory

also known as: folder
including: subdirectory, directory file, root directory
is a group of files or a group of files and *subdirectories*. A subdirectory is a directory within a directory; its contents may be files or other subdirectories, or both. A directory is held, in the form of a list of file and subdirectory names (the *directory file*), on the backing store to which it refers; stored with it will be information needed for files to be retrieved from the backing store. Directories are usually represented in

PART A

a tree structure, where the *root directory* is the entry point to the tree, as shown in Figure A7.5. See also *tree*, page 308, and *file*, page 10.

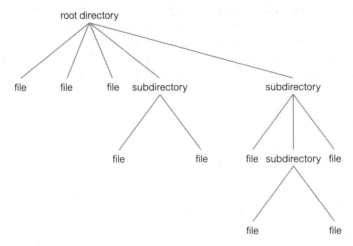

Figure A7.5 Directory tree

Screen saver

is software that removes the image from the display, either as a security measure or to reduce the risk of damage to the interior surface of the display screen. If the screen display is not changed for a long period of time, then the coating of the screen can become damaged.

Wildcard

is a symbol used in some commands or search instructions to stand for a range of characters. For example, ? is often used to stand for any single character, hence the command `type d????.doc` would cause all files of type **.doc** whose names have five characters and begin with **d** to be typed. The character * is usually used to stand for any group of characters (or perhaps none), hence `delete *.*` may be an unwise command, since it could cause all files to be deleted.

Other Interface Styles

Command line interface

including: command sequence
is a form of user interface in which the user types commands for the computer to carry out. As the term suggests, the command is usually restricted to a single line of

text, which may consist of any sequence of acceptable commands. The user has to know the conventions of the *command line interpreter* (see page 340). The commands may be combined to make up a *command sequence*, which can make this a convenient way of getting the computer to perform a sequence of actions (see *macro*, page 265). This form of interface can be efficient in the hands of experienced users, but it can be very frustrating for those who do not know the right commands to use.

Conversational interface

is a form of user interface in which the computer and the user appear to be holding a conversation or dialogue, using the screen for output and the keyboard for input. The user may be seeking information from the computer, but the computer may need to ask its own questions before it is able to provide the answer to the question originally asked. The example below, which could be a dialogue about a request to print a file, gives an indication of the kind of communication that might be experienced.

PROMPT (computer)	RESPONSE (user)
- - -	- - -
- - -	- - -
name of file to print?	MYTEXT.TXT
print all 10 pages?	no
which pages?	1 to 3 and 10
print pages 1–3, 10: correct?	yes
how many copies:	3:
- - -	- - -
- - -	- - -

Each line will appear one after another.

Figure A7.6   Conversational dialogue screen

Interactive computing

including: conversational mode

is a mode of operation in which the user and a computer system are in two-way communication throughout the period of use. In practice, most personal computer applications are interactive, whereas some applications on terminals attached to large central computer systems, for example in supermarket branches, are still run in batch mode, with data and command instructions supplied through the terminal. See also *batch processing*, page 17.

When a terminal user on a network appears to be in continuous communication with the central computer, getting replies almost immediately, it is described as *conversational mode*.

PART A

Forms dialogue interface

including: response field

is a user interface in which the computer outputs separate *prompts* (see page 68) and response fields for a number of inputs.

Response field is the place in a dialogue screen (Figure A7.7) where users may type their responses, in any order. There may be automatic movement of the cursor, depicting the entry point, from response field to response field. The process is similar to filling in a form on paper and allows the entries to be changed at any stage until the 'execution' key or button is pressed.

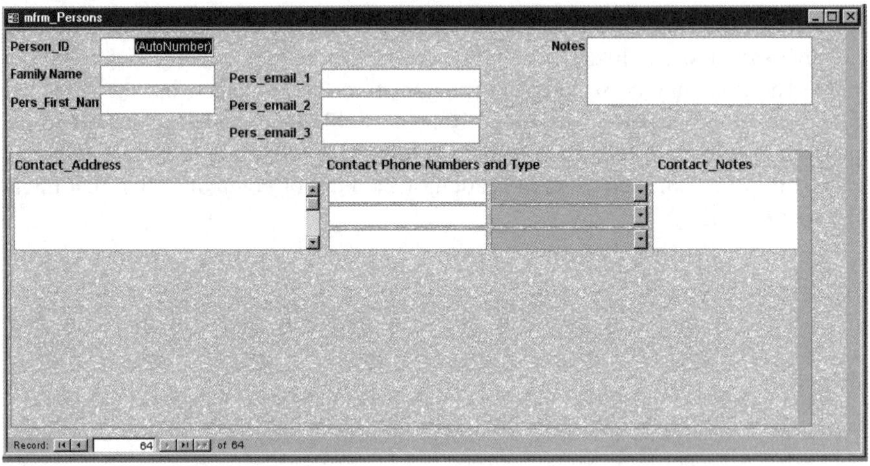

Figure A7.7 Forms dialogue screen

Prompt

is a character or message displayed on a screen to indicate that the user is expected to do something, usually to input data into the system. Sometimes a visual prompt is emphasised by a sound.

Screen editing

is the process of changing (editing) stored data or programs using a computer screen. The characters that are the data or programs are altered on the screen by adding, removing or changing individual characters or groups of characters.

Error message

is a message to the user indicating that something has gone wrong; it may include instructions on what action is needed. Well-designed applications packages will include comprehensive error-detection routines and helpful error messages. These routines will detect errors resulting from user mistakes, such as letting the printer run out of paper or failing to put the right CD into a CD drive, as well as errors occurring in the system itself.

Profile

is a file that holds data on how the system is to be presented for an individual user each time they log on. These customised interfaces are often available on network operating systems and on-line services.

User-friendly

is a term that describes a system, either hardware or software, that is 'kind' to its users. Since the user interface largely determines what a user experiences, generally it is the software system that is being described. However, some aspects of hardware, such as the feel of a keyboard, can improve or spoil user-friendliness.

User-transparent

sometimes: transparency
describes actions by a computer system, hardware or software, that are not apparent to the user. Nearly all hardware actions, other than those affecting the screen, are transparent, and most operating system actions take place without the user being aware of them. Well-designed user interfaces achieve high levels of *transparency*.

Wizard

also known as: assistant
is a feature of some applications packages that helps users to perform a task. By asking the user some questions, a wizard provides help in making best use of the available facilities. For example, a table wizard might help to create tables by offering a number of possible types, or a letter wizard might show how you could set out a letter for a particular situation.

Set-up Interface

User documentation

gives the user any information necessary for the successful running of a piece of software or hardware. This generally does not include many technical details, which will usually be found in *maintenance documentation* (see page 222).

Software documentation

is documentation received when a computer software package is bought, whether it is a computer game, a spreadsheet or a programming language. This may be anything from an instruction leaflet to a series of manuals. This user documentation is designed to introduce the package and to tell the user how to use the software to its best advantage. This documentation may be totally in printed form or, more likely, it may be seen on the screen when running the package. There may also be files on the accompanying disks called *Readme* or *Help* (see below).

There must be an overview of the package describing what it is capable of doing in fairly broad terms but also including some specific uses and features that are important with the package. This may include some sample screen displays and print-outs to show the users what to expect.

An early section should be on how to install the software (to make the software available on the user's system). These instructions might well include

■ how to make extra copies of disks (in case the working disk is damaged);

■ how to copy on to a hard disk and configure the software (where the user has a choice of options as to how the software is to work and what hardware will be used, such as the type of printer);

■ how to make hardware adjustments that may be needed. These may be described for the user to do or may require the help of a dealer.

Some of these operations may refer to hardware documentation. For example, reference may be needed to printer documentation.

It may be that the software has already been installed, so installation and configuration may not seem to be of interest. However, if the printer is changed, then the configuration process will probably need repeating, either by the user or by the supplier.

It is important that the novice user has access to tutorial material consisting of written instructions or similar sequences given as an on-screen tutorial. This is designed to speed the user through the simple aspects on to the more advanced usage that may have been in mind when the purchase was made. Equally, for the more experienced user, there should be some summary sheet or quick reference guide. It is useful to have a reference to the use of specific keys (such as the function keys), perhaps in the form of a *keystrip* (see page 72).

One of the first actions of the user should be to register the purchase with the publishing software company so that any upgrade or fault information can be passed on. With more sophisticated packages, there might be a telephone help line.

An index to the documentation should help the user to find how to do specific tasks and to find more detailed explanations of error messages.

Hardware documentation

contains the instructions on how to use the hardware. Usually a physical connection will need to be made between items of equipment, for example between a monitor and computer. This will specify details of the connecting leads and where they are to be connected.

Most computers can have add-on peripherals, such as scanners or hard drives, to attach to existing systems. Some hardware needs minor physical adjustment before connecting it to a computing system. Some hardware devices are attached via a *SCSI* (*Small Computer Systems Interface*, see page 363), and these devices need a unique device number. These could be set by the use of *jumpers* (see below). Printers commonly have switches that are controlled by either software or hardware. *DIP switches* (see Figure A7.8 for an example) are commonly used to specify the details of paper to be used, the characters to be printed and the type and speed of communication between computer and printer. These details may, alternatively, be specified by a special sequence of key presses on the device. Printers also may need to have paper-feed mechanisms fitted.

With a new computer system, the user documentation will also give the options that are controlled by software. These might include the type of monitor to be used, the type of printer to be used, and the speed of response of the mouse. Instructions on using the mouse, general care of the computer and use of disk drives are usually included. These will include how to *format* (see page 181) and copy disks and precautions that should be taken to prevent accidental damage and loss of data. Documentation may contain details on how your hardware may be *customised* (see page 14) for improving performance in a variety of circumstances. There is often a section on troubleshooting faults should your system not respond as it should, for example what to do if the printer produces gibberish or the screen remains blank.

More technical detail is usually available (at extra cost) from the manufacturer or a third party. The quality of such literature varies in its accuracy and clarity.

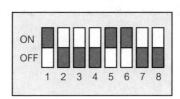

Figure A7.8   Bank of eight DIP switches

HELP system

including: context-sensitive help
is a means of providing helpful messages to guide a user when using a software package. It will give indications of how to answer prompts from the software and how to perform relevant operations. If the message responds to what the user appears to be doing currently, then it is called *context-sensitive help*.

README file

is a file that is provided on the medium with the software. It contains the latest details of using or loading the software.

Tutorial

provides the user with a guided tour through the software. It is a sequence of tasks to be carried out. This will help the user to find out how to use the software by experimenting with it and seeing the results.

Control panel

is a small display/keyboard on a device that enables the user to set options. On a printer, this may be used to set the print style or change the paper source.

DIP switch

is one of a set of small slide-operated switches mounted together in a bank (Figure A7.8, page 71). These are used to set options on hardware, such as printers. For example, they may control what alphabet to use or the size of font. (DIP stands for dual in-line package.)

Jumper

is a detachable flexible-wire connection between suitable socket points on a circuit board. Sometimes a rigid version may be found on printers and other peripherals, possibly arranged in banks like *DIP switches* (see above), for which they are an alternative.

Keystrip

is a piece of card or plastic used with a keyboard. It labels the operations performed by function keys within specific programs. For example, in a word processor the function key F4 might have Search/Replace above it (see Figure A7.9).

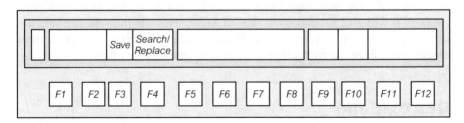

Figure A7.9 Keystrip

Install

is to transfer software on to the medium from which it is to be run. Installation is normally on to a hard drive, but it could be on to a CD-ROM or a network.

Uninstall

is to remove software from a medium – the process is the reverse of *install*, see above. This should remove all traces of the software and release the space from the storage medium. If there is a licence to install a limited number of copies, then deinstallation re-credits the disk (normally called the *key disk*, see page 155).

PART A

A8 Commercial Data Processing

Other concepts related to the design and implementation of systems to carry out commercial data processing are found in several later sections, especially C1 Systems Design and Life Cycle, C2 Describing Systems and C12 Managing Data.

Data processing in its broadest – and technically correct – sense covers every task that a computer carries out. Traditionally its meaning has been restricted to those particular computing applications and activities concerned with business and commerce.

The computing needs of business and commerce are very different from scientific computing, where complex mathematical calculations are performed, or indeed the personal computing needs of an individual, where the computer is a tool for use by a single person.

In many business applications, quite simple tasks are carried out but repeated for a very large number of individual transactions. For example, working out one person's pay is not difficult, but it has to be done for all employees, every week or every month. Typical of such application areas are accounting, payroll, record keeping, route planning and stock control.

A data-processing department has to provide a cost-effective and efficient service without expensive errors. The main elements in data processing involve automated data collection, prevention of errors, security of data, and procedures to collect, process and use large amounts of information. The terms discussed in this section reflect this focus.

The user organisations typically associated with these traditional data-processing applications are banks, government departments and a wide range of businesses. For any particular application type (for example, payroll), there is often a standard package, although many variations of it may be available. Although all users will need to use a particular type of package to do the same job, they may require a specific version because they have different hardware or operating systems or because they need to use the package in association with another application area.

In addition to its meaning as an operation, 'data processing' is also used as the title for the section of an organisation that carries out this area of work. Most data-processing departments will have a data-processing manager and a small team of support staff. These will have responsibility for seeing that the system provides a satisfactory service for the users, who may be either individuals or other departments. However, the individual departmental users are responsible for defining those data-processing tasks that the system is required to carry out for them. The maintenance of the whole system, both hardware and software, may be done by specialist employees of the organisation or by external contractors.

Data preparation

is the input of large quantities of data into a computer system for further processing. Input may be automatic, for example by scanning optical mark sense forms, or manual, when the data are typed and verified ready for processing. Data preparation is often performed by a smaller computer system to input the data. It is normal for all data to be entered before any are processed.

Direct data entry (DDE)

is the input of data directly into a computer system for immediate processing. Unlike a *data-preparation system* (see above), where the data are stored for later processing, direct data entry is used when data need to be available quickly to other users. As each set of data is entered, it will be processed.

Data capture

is the collection of data for entering into a computer. This may be done automatically, as in the scanning of bar codes in a shop, or manually, as in typing in a gas-meter reading. See also *data capture*, page 130.

Article number

including: ISBN, UPC, EAN
is the number given to a particular product (e.g. the *international standard book number* (*ISBN*) found on a book). This is often printed together with its *bar-code* representation (see page 76), so that it can be read both by people and automatically by a *bar-code reader* (see page 175) or some other *point-of-sale terminal* device (see page 127). The numbers are usually structured, and there are international agreements on how the numbers should be constructed for various types of goods. Two common forms of numbering systems are the *universal product code* (*UPC*) and the *European article number* (*EAN*).

PART A

Bar code

is a pattern of parallel lines of different thickness used to represent a code number, which can then be read automatically. It is a very cost-effective way of inputting data into a computer. For example, the article number printed on the back cover of this book is given with its bar-code version above it.

It is often used by shops to identify a product at the *point-of-sale terminal* (see page 75) so that its price can be found automatically from a computer. This is an alternative to a manual system, where prices are marked on goods and the prices are entered through a keypad. See also *article number*, page 75.

Electronic money

including: Mondex
is the use of a *smart card* (see page 174) to replace traditional money such as coins and banknotes. The card would have money transferred to it electronically by a special *automatic teller machine* (ATM; see page 78). Money would then be transferred from the card to a shopkeeper's point-of-sale terminal by a special card reader when money is spent. Although credit and debit cards allow a person to buy goods without having to handle large amounts of cash, they really only provide a cheap method of transferring money from one bank account to another, which is otherwise expensive. Electronic money, however, is stored on the smart card and can be used as easily and cheaply as traditional money. *Mondex* is currently one of the principal systems of electronic money.

Document reader

including: mark sense reader
is a kind of *scanner* (see page 175) used in business to input documents quickly and accurately into the computer system. It often incorporates a sheet feeder to enable the documents to be processed automatically. The documents can then be processed, for example using *optical character recognition* (see below). Document readers are also used to input *optical mark recognition* documents (see below).

A *mark sense reader* is a special document scanner that will detect the graphite in a pencil mark on the document. This is a reliable technology but has now been replaced by *optical mark recognition* (see below), which can be used with standard optical scanners.

Optical mark recognition (OMR)

is machine recognition of data recorded as simple marks on a document. The special forms (or cards) are printed to match a template in the computer. The hardware detects marks made in the predetermined positions, and software interprets this as data. The marks may be printed or put on the form by hand, for example with a pencil. The OMR software only detects marks, not characters such as letters or numbers. It is very reliable and suited to small quantities of multiple-choice data. The numbers recorded on some lottery entry forms are an example.

Timing information

including: index mark, clock mark, clock track
is required because mechanical devices cannot operate with the precision needed by computers. So, for example, an *index mark* in the form of an *index hole* is found on some floppy disks to provide a fixed reference point for reading and writing data. Another example is the *clock marks* making up the *clock track* that synchronise the reading of the items on a mark-sense document.

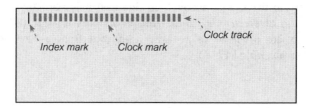

Figure A8.1   Clock track on a machine-readable document

Magnetic ink character recognition (MICR)

is machine recognition of stylised characters printed in magnetic ink. It is very reliable, so it is suitable for purposes needing accuracy, such as banking. The commonest application is the data printed on a bank cheque: the cheque number, the branch number and the account number. These characters are both machine- and human-readable. It is unlikely to be used for newly designed systems because it is expensive and bar codes provide a more efficient alternative.

Optical character recognition (OCR)

including: editable text
is machine recognition of printed characters: for example, the machine-readable section of a passport or the reading of typed postcodes when mail is automatically sorted.

Editable text results from using optical character-recognition software, which can convert a page of text from a scanned image into a text datafile. This text file can then be edited using a word processor. The software is not fool-proof, but it does include error messages to highlight characters that were not recognised. For most people, scanning an existing document and editing errors is much quicker than retyping the text. *Handwriting-recognition software*, see page 173, can also produce editable text datafiles.

Electronic funds transfer (EFT)

including: debit card, EFTPOS, cash dispenser, automatic teller machine (ATM)
is the use of computer networks to transfer money. This may be done between banks as an alternative to sending a cheque or a bankers' draft, especially where international transfers are involved. Most large companies now pay their employees by electronic transfer of funds into their personal bank accounts.

Increasingly, it is being used in retail stores as an alternative to payment by credit card or cheque. The purchaser offers a *debit card*, which is processed in the same way as a credit card but which initiates the transfer of money from the purchaser's account directly to the shop's account. In this use, it is normally known by the cumbersome title of *electronic funds transfer at point-of-sale* (*EFTPOS*). The same principles are involved in a cash withdrawal from a *cash dispenser* or *automatic teller machine* (*ATM*).

Turn-around document

is printed by a computer and then used to record additional data to be input into a computer later. This has several advantages:

■ the data identify the information accurately (the data came from the computer system);

■ the printed data need altering only if wrong;

■ errors, for example due to poor handwriting, are reduced;

■ the additional data may be simple enough to read automatically, for example using mark-sense reading.

Validation

including: range check, presence check, length check, format check, type check, look-up check, file look-up check, integrity check
is the automatic checking of data entered into a computer system.

Validation involves using the properties of the data to identify any inputs that are obviously wrong. Validation only proves that the data entered is a reasonable value for the computer to accept. It cannot prove that the data entered is the actual value the user intended. However, it does allow the computer to filter out obvious mistakes. The data are not processed until the validation succeeds.

The checking is done by software that can be either part of the input system or a separate program that checks the data at the following stage. For examples, see the descriptions of individual validation checks below. As the data pass through the system, they will also be verified; see *verification*, below.

Validation checks may include:

range checks to reject any data items outside an expected range; for example, an employee's age that was less than 16 or over 75;

presence checks to reject a group of data where required fields have been left blank; for example, information about a student would be of little use without including an identifier such as the student's name;

length checks to ensure that the data entered are of a reasonable length; for example, it might require that a name is between 3 and 15 characters long;

type checks to ensure that a data item is of a particular data type; for example, a number of pupils will be entered as an integer (whole number);

format checks to ensure that a data item matches a previously determined pattern and that particular characters have particular values, such as being letters or digits; an example is whether the data are valid as a UK postcode (which usually consists of two letters, two or three numbers and two letters);

look-up checks to ensure that the data match one of a limited number of valid entries; for example, subjects studied in a school should be selected from a list of Mathematics, English, etc. A *file look-up check* is used to compare the data against a larger list of items that are held in a datafile; for example, the product code of an item in a supermarket will be looked up in the stock file to confirm that such an item exists;

integrity checks to confirm the value of a piece of data by comparing it with other data; for example, an individual's date of birth can be compared with their current age, if known.

Check digits added to data items that allow the items to be *verified* (see below) may also validate the data implicitly.

Verification

including: double-entry verification, screen verification, check digit, batch total, control total, hash total, parity check, checksum, cyclic redundancy check (CRC)
is the use of checks to make sure data are consistent and have not been corrupted. Verification confirms the integrity of data as they are copied between different parts of a computer system. Copying should not change the data. Differences detected would mean an error in the transfer.

Verification can take place both when data are entered at the human–machine interface and when they are copied between other components within a computerised system (including from remote sensors or other computers). The data will also have been validated on input; see *validation*, above.

PART A

The verification checks at the human–machine interface may include:

double-entry verification to ensure that data typed into a computer system are entered accurately. The data are entered twice, by different operators, and compared by the system. Any differences can be identified and corrected manually;

screen verification to ensure that data being entered into a computer system are accurate. After being entered, the data are displayed on the screen, the user reads the data and confirms that they are correct;

check digits are extra digits added as part of a numerical data item (like a bar code or a stock number). They are worked out from the other digits in a way that can be repeated, enabling the data to be checked at a later stage by working out the check digit again and comparing the results;

batch totals are the total value of one or more fields in a batch of data. They are calculated in advance (manually) and then compared with the total as calculated by the computer;

control totals are batch totals that have a meaningful value, for example the total value of a batch of orders or simply a count of the number of transactions;

hash totals are batch totals which have no other meaning, for example the total formed by adding all the dates of the orders or the total of all the numerical fields for a particular record.

The verification checks within the hardware of the system are of particular importance when sending data between computers. These verification checks may include:

parity checks to ensure that a single byte or word of data has been transferred within the system correctly. A bit in each byte or word is reserved to be the parity bit. This parity bit is set to 1 or 0, depending on the data. If the data are corrupted, then the parity check is likely to fail.

checksums to ensure that a block of data has been transferred within the system correctly. Extra words of data are added to a block that are worked out from the value of the data in the block. At later stages, the checksum is worked out again, and compared with the original, to ensure that the data have not been corrupted at some stage in the system. This check is more complex than the *parity check* (see above) but is more suited to verifying quantities of data larger than single bytes or words.

cyclic redundancy checks (*CRC*), which are a particular type of *checksum* (see above). They are commonly used to verify blocks of data stored on disks or transmitted across networks.

Transaction

comprises the data and processes needed to update a computer system to reflect a single change in the information held. A single change in the information can involve several changes, or additions, to the data physically stored in the computer system. There may be other changes, such as to indexes used by the computer system. A transaction usually refers to a single piece of financial data or changes to a single *entity* (see page 89) in a database system.

Post a record

is the action to confirm that the *transaction* (see above) being entered is to be stored in the computer system. This usually occurs in finance systems to ensure accuracy and prevent fraud.

Before a record is posted, the data can be checked and altered. When it has been posted, a record is added to the datafile and it can no longer be altered. Any change must be made by posting a new record containing the change.

Back up

including: full back-up, differential back-up, incremental back-up
is to make copies of data or programs in case the originals are corrupted or lost. If the system fails, it can be rebuilt with accurate data. Back-ups should be made regularly and provision made for any changes made after the last back-up. These back-ups may be:

■ a *full back-up*, which copies all files to provide a complete snapshot of the data at a particular point in time;

■ a *differential back-up*, which copies only datafiles that have changed since the previous full back-up;

■ an *incremental back-up*, which copies only those datafiles that have changed since the last back-up, which could be a full back-up or a previous incremental back-up;

■ a *journal file* (see page 82), which provides a record of transactions since the previous back-up;

■ files using the *grandfather–father–son* method (see page 326);

■ (as a last resort) stored on paper.

A back-up of the total software of the system will be stored separately from the computer as a safeguard against physical dangers such as fire or hardware failure. However, a back-up of an individual file may simply be an additional copy stored on the computer system, for example a previous version of a word-processor file. See also *restore*, below.

Restore

is replacing corrupt or lost data using copies from a *back-up* system (see above). This generally involves copying the last full back-up back on to the system, followed by the differential back-up or any incremental back-ups. To return the system to the

PART A

state when it failed usually involves restoring the latest *journal file* or any *transaction files* (see pages 81 and 80).

Archive

is the storage of information for long periods of time. The data are likely to be compressed to take less space and stored on a cheaper storage medium such as *magnetic tape* (see page 182) or optical disks (see *optical disk storage*, page 178), freeing space on the main computer system. It can be accessed if needed but is not so easily available as the original information. There are legal requirements on most businesses to keep data for several years, and so old data will be archived.

Audit trail

including: journal file
is an automatic record made (in a *journal file*) of any transactions carried out by a computer system, such as updates to files. This may be required:

■ for legal reasons (so that the auditors can confirm the accuracy of the company accounts);

■ for security reasons (so that data deteted maliciously or accidentally can be recovered);

■ simply to monitor the performance of the system.

Spreadsheets

Spreadsheets are an important and powerful use of the computer. A spreadsheet is based on the idea of the computer looking like a large sheet of squared paper with the added advantage of being able to do arithmetic.

	A	B	C	D	E	F	G
1							
2							
3							
4							
5						hello	
6							
7							
8							
9							
10							
11							
12							
13							
14							
15							

Figure A9.1 Spreadsheet

The squares are usually called cells (sometimes slots), and each is identified by its column label (often a letter or letters) and its row label (often a number). In the example above, the cell with 'hello' in it has address F5, where F is the column label and 5 is the row label. The contents of a cell may be one of several types:

■ a **heading** or **message**: this is just plain text, i.e. a collection of characters.

■ a **number**: it is important to realise that there is a difference between a number as text and a number that is required for calculation – most spreadsheets allow for the conversion between a number as text and a number in a form suitable for calculation.

■ a **formula** that represents a calculation: in this case, what is seen in the cell is the result of the calculation rather than the formula itself. An example of a formula may be one that adds the contents of two cells together and multiplies the result by three: `=3*(A21 + B21)`

(If A21 contains the number 5 and B21 contains the number 6, then the cell containing the formula above will display the number 33. It still contains the formula after the calculation has been done, so that if the contents of A21 or B21 change, then a new calculated value will be displayed.)

■ an **instruction**: an example would be an instruction that takes the contents of a cell (a number) and uses it as a product code. The instruction then causes a table of product codes, prices and descriptions elsewhere in the table (or even a different spreadsheet) to be searched; when the correct product code is found, the description is inserted in the current cell that contains the instruction. In another cell would be an instruction to do the same but to insert the price.

Figure A9.2 is an example of a spreadsheet showing how many euros one would get for different amounts of sterling.

	A	B	C	D
1	Exchange Rate			
2	1.47	Pounds	Euros	
3		0	0.00	
4		5	7.35	
5		10	14.70	
6				

Figure A9.2 Spreadsheet for currency conversion

In this spreadsheet, you can see numbers (for example, in cell B4), labels and headings (for example, in cell C2), and the result of applying a formula (as in cell C4). However, a spreadsheet need not be used for just doing the original calculation; it will also respond to changes in the data. It is this ability to respond to 'what if?' questions that makes a spreadsheet such a powerful business tool.

What if the rate of exchange altered? You can cope with this simply by retyping the exchange rate in cell A2 and the freshly converted amounts of euros would appear in column C.

What if the amount of pounds that you wanted to exchange was not in the table? Type the amount in place of the zero amount in cell B3 and the converted amount will appear in cell C3.

In the above example, the formulas used in column C are all very similar but not quite identical; they all use A2, but this is multiplied by the appropriate entry in column B. On most spreadsheets, there is no need to type in each formula individually: by replication, you can repeat them automatically and make the system keep the reference to A2 every time but alter the reference to column B. Many spreadsheets also have a facility to take a set of figures and convert them into some type of graph (such as a pie chart, a line graph or a bar chart).

The printing out of a spreadsheet can pose problems. Some software will just print out everything that is being used. However, most allow the user to indicate the cells that are to be printed out; many allow the cells to be printed out in a different order from their 'natural' state, so that parts of the sheet that are separated by a lot of rows/ columns can be printed close together. Some spreadsheets even allow the sheet to be printed sideways to allow for a wide sheet to be printed. A further complication in printing is what should be printed out for some of the cells – should it be a formula or the result of the formula? Again, many spreadsheets allow the user to choose.

The use of spreadsheets has been extended beyond just numbers. Imagine a list of names and addresses; each one might consist of (say) four entries: (a) the name, (b) the house number, (c) the road and (d) the town. Each entry could be put into a different column and each row hold a different name and address, as in Figure A9.3.

	A	B	C	D	E
1	Name	No.	Road	Town	
2	Mr Smith	1	Acacia Avenue	Birmingham	
3	Mrs Jones	2	High Street	Luton	
4	Ms Black	77	Sunset Road	Liverpool	
5	Miss Green	12	Hillside	Leicester	
6					
7					

Figure A9.3   Spreadsheet used as a database

So you can use a spreadsheet as a simple database. Further to this, some spreadsheets can be used as word processors (in fact, the draft of this text was prepared on such a spreadsheet). Usually this means that the text is set out in one column of the spreadsheet, but the other columns can be used as well. This becomes even more powerful when you wish to include some calculations in your text: there are no calculations for the user to do since the spreadsheet will do them all!

Spreadsheet

is an applications package usually used to display financial or statistical information. It takes its name from the way data are arranged on the screen in rows and columns, as in the traditional layout of figures in account books. The user can specify that numbers displayed in particular positions are to be dependent on entries in other positions and are to be recalculated automatically when these entries are changed. Hence the effects of changes to one data item on, for example, totals, subtotals, profits and VAT can be explored.

Cell

also known as: slot
including: address, column, row, block
is the square on a spreadsheet in which only a single entry can be placed, sometimes called a *slot*. The single entry can be a number, a group of words or a formula. It can be referred to by its *address* in the spreadsheet using the *column* and *row* labels. The column label refers to a vertical group of cells and the row label refers to a horizontal group of cells (see Figure A9.3, page 85). A rectangular grouping of cells is termed a *block*. Usually the block is identified by giving the addresses of the upper left cell and the lower right cell of the rectangle, for example A3F12 would have six columns (A to F) of ten rows (3 to 12).

Formula

is the way a calculation is represented in a spreadsheet. As well as numbers, a formula uses the address of cells to identify other values to be used – the result is then displayed in the cell in which the formula was placed. If any of the cells referenced in the formula changes in value, then the result of the formula is changed to reflect the altered values.

For example, if the first side of a rectangle is in B3 and you wished to find the second side of the rectangle in C3, whose sides always add up to 12, the formula in C3 might be $=(12 - 2*B3)/2$

Function

is a special type of formula used in a spreadsheet. It has usually been set up to represent a formula that may be too complex or too long to expect an ordinary user to enter, or it may be just very useful. Examples of this are:

=SUM( ) a function to calculate the sum (i.e. the total) of a row or a column or a block of cells.

=MEAN( ) a function to calculate the average (mean) of a row or a column or a block of cells.

=FIND( ) a function to find where, in an area of the spreadsheet, a particular value is to be found.

Recalculation

is the term used to describe the process whereby the spreadsheet recalculates the values that may have altered because of the last input of data. The process of recalculation can be automatic – done after each and every entry in the spreadsheet – or it can be manual, whereby the user decides when it should be done and presses a particular set of keys to have the recalculation done. The advantage of having it set to manual is that the entry of data is quicker as the user does not have to wait for the updating (which can take an appreciable amount of time if the spreadsheet is large); the disadvantage is that the user has always to indicate when the recalculation should be done. It is sometimes important to know the order of the recalculation – whether it is by row (i.e. the first row, then the second, and so on) or by column (i.e. the first column, then the second, and so on). With many spreadsheets, it is possible to alter the order of calculation.

Replication

including: absolute reference, relative reference

is the process of copying a formula from one cell to another. As a formula usually involves references to cells, this means you should be aware of whether you want to keep the exact same reference to the cell (this is termed an *absolute reference*) or whether you want the reference to adjust itself according to either the row or column movement (this is termed a *relative reference*). An example of this is when you have a formula in cell A12 that calculates the sum of a column of figures – something like =SUM(A1...A10) – and this is then replicated into cell B12. Generally, you will want the result to represent the sum for column B; if you tell it that A1 and A10 are relative, then this will happen.

PART A

A10   Data Handling and Information Retrieval

Although a computer can store enormous amounts of data, these data are useless without appropriate links between individual data items. Imagine, for example, what a printed telephone directory would be like if it was simply two separate listings of telephone subscribers and their numbers, without the connection that is made by the printed layout between a particular subscriber and their telephone number. The data are also useless if they cannot be retrieved easily when required – imagine the telephone directory in random rather than alphabetical order.

The same applies to computerised collections of data. These are generally referred to as databases and can vary between a simple name-and-address listing and a massive collection of structured data that provides information for a large business. It is easy to be deceived when one is experimenting with techniques for accessing databases. If a demonstration database can be constructed with tens (rather than millions) of entries, then many of the techniques can seem unnecessarily long-winded. If you were certain that your data would never extend to more than 100 entries, then it would be sensible to store the data in a simple table. When the data grew, despite your plans, to millions of entries, no table would be capable of holding it, and your program would need to use sophisticated methods of data management.

Large databases usually have many potential users. Allowing simultaneous use of the same datafiles may lead to operating-system problems – the solution to these problems is usually embedded in a complex piece of software, known as the **database management system (DBMS)**.

Not all users will be experienced with computers, and simple user interfaces are often provided to access the data. The concepts used in designing and setting up a large database are complex and require specialist staff, but the data can be accessed easily without the less experienced user understanding the underlying structure.

Database

is a (large) collection of data items and links between them, structured in a way that allows it to be accessed by a number of different applications programs. The term is also used loosely to describe any collection of data.

Data model

including: entity, attribute, relation

is a diagram of a database. Designers of a large database will normally construct a diagram of the planned database. This will show the things represented in the database (the *entities*) and the information held about them (the *attributes*). The *relations* between entities are shown, and from this model the most efficient arrangement of the data will be worked out. See also *entity-relationship diagram*, page 230.

Database management system (DBMS)

is software that can find data in a database, add new data and change existing data. The database management system works automatically without users necessarily knowing how. It deals with finding the requested data, updates the data and performs other tasks, including maintaining indexes (see Figure A10.1).

The database management system may provide its own simple user interface or it may just communicate with other programs that request and use the data available to the database.

Large computer systems will have programs written for particular tasks. These programs use the database management system to handle the complexities of managing the database because it is easier than accessing the datafiles directly. Communication between programs and a database management system usually uses commands in *SQL* (see page 298).

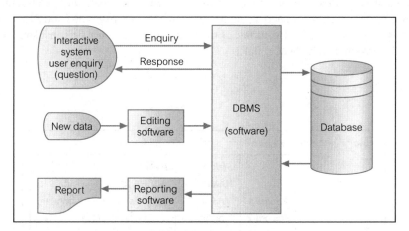

Figure A10.1   How a database management system works

Information retrieval

also known as: data retrieval

is extracting useful information from large amounts of stored data, such as a database. This usually involves specifying some form of *query* (see page 93) and also stating display and sorting instructions. This enables large amounts of data to be searched and the results to be output efficiently.

Data dictionary

also known as: data directory
is a file containing descriptions of, and other information about, the structure of the data held in a database. The data dictionary is not typically accessible to users. It is a tool for the managers of the database, for example when they need to alter the way data are stored.

Distributed database

is one where several computers on a network each hold part of the data and cooperate in making the data available to the user. If the particular data required are not available at a particular computer, the computer will communicate with the others in the network to obtain the data. Often each computer will keep a separate copy of frequently used data. Special methods are needed to ensure that the latest data are used.

Flat file

is a database held as a table and stored in a single file. The data will be structured with a row for each *record* and a column for each *field* (see pages 312 and 313). This allows only very simple structuring of the data, which can only be considered as a two-dimensional table (hence 'flat').

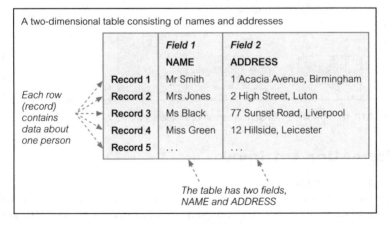

A two-dimensional table consisting of names and addresses

		Field 1	Field 2
		NAME	ADDRESS
	Record 1	Mr Smith	1 Acacia Avenue, Birmingham
Each row (record) contains data about one person	Record 2	Mrs Jones	2 High Street, Luton
	Record 3	Ms Black	77 Sunset Road, Liverpool
	Record 4	Miss Green	12 Hillside, Leicester
	Record 5	...	...

The table has two fields,
NAME and ADDRESS

Figure A10.2   Flat file or two-dimensional table

Hierarchical database

is a database where the data are held in a *tree* structure (see page 308). Each data item can be thought of by users as existing on one of a number of levels. There are links to related data items at the higher level and sometimes at a lower level. The data items at a lower level hold more detail about the item that they are linked to above.

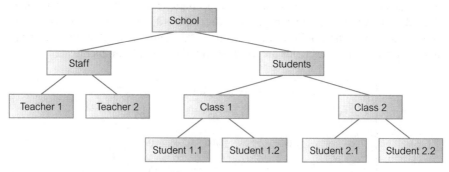

Figure A10.3 Hierarchical database

Relational database

including: table, view
is a complex database structure to hold a variety of different data. Where data items are related to each other, they are linked together by pointers stored in the database.

   Table is the name for each group of similar data with rows for each member of the *entity* and columns for each *attribute* (see page 89).

   The (relational) database management system provides tools for linking together tables and selecting items from within tables. In this way, each user can be given a different *view* of the data. An example of a view may be a table set up for a particular type of user, such as a receptionist, who would be able to access only data relevant to their job.

   Relational databases are especially powerful, because the method of storing data in tables makes no assumptions about how the applications programs will access the data and hence does not restrict the *queries* (see page 93) in any way.

Report

including: report definition, report layout, report format, display order, sort list, presentation order
is the presentation of selected data from a database. A report is usually printed in the form of a table. Reports may be defined in advance so that the user does not have to set up the report definition each time it is needed.

Report definitions require a query, a report layout and a display order to be defined. Normally the user will set a *query* (see below) so that the database will be searched, finding each record that satisfies the query.

Report layout or *report format* specifies which parts of the data are to be output and in what position. Often this is a list of *fields* (see page 313) to be printed as the columns of the report.

Display order, *sort list* or *presentation order* specifies the order in which records will be output. This is generally done by specifying the fields whose data will be used to determine the order of display. One specified field determines the main order in the display. Other fields may be used to affect the order when the records have the same value for the first field. In Figure A10.4, 'Surname' is used to determine the main order, and the other fields are used when the first fields are identical.

Report: Students taking Art			
Forename	Surname	DOB	Class
Fred	Able	10/02/83	10A
Jill	Baker	10/10/82	10Y
Martin	Baker	17/12/82	10C
Andrew	Cable	05/08/82	10C
Total Number: 4			

Header
Data in tabular form
Footer

Figure A10.4 Typical report

Schema

including: data description language, subschema
is the precise description of the data items to be stored, and the relationships between them, in a database system.

Managing the large amounts of data of different types stored in a modern database requires that descriptions of the data items are held, as well as the data items themselves. The description, the schema, will be written in a *data description language*. The *database management system* (see page 89) may reformat the data before presenting them to the user and will make use of individual *subschemas* that describe the data that a particular user can access (see *view*, page 91).

Normal form

is a way of structuring the data in a *relational database* (see page 91) according to theoretical rules in order to avoid problems of inefficiency in accessing and maintaining the data.

The *schema* (see page 92) is altered using certain mathematical processes to convert it into normal form. If the schema for a database is in normal form, errors and inconsistencies will be reduced; for example, data items should not be repeated, since there is a risk of error. See also *data protection*, page 142.

Query

including: interrogating, selecting, searching
is a question asked of the data in a database. The query is structured so that the answer is either true or false. To answer a query the computer must check each *record* (see page 312) of the data to see whether the answer is true. The result of the query is a list of all the data that satisfy the query. Querying a database is also referred to as *interrogating* the database, *selecting* data or *searching* for data. See also *search*, page 328.

An example of a general request might be: 'Which students in Year 11 take French?' This query is made precise by using words from the *query language* (see page 298) to link the names of the fields, 'year' and 'subject', in the database.

```
SELECT student WHERE year = 11 AND subject = "French"
```

Data filter

selects the set of records to be displayed. A data filter is often used in an interactive system to implement a query. Setting a filter, which is easily done but temporary, will involve entering a query. See also *query*, above.

Data warehouse

including: data mining
refers to large amounts of data that are stored together, usually in a single location, for further processing.

Many of the data collected by large businesses with many sites are used immediately for a specific purpose and are stored where they are collected and used. These data, particularly when analysed with other data, can provide useful information for future planning. The data warehouse is where these large quantities of data are collected together from a variety of locations for efficient analysis; it also provides a form of archive of the data. Since the data are being used only for further analysis, they do not have to be complete or up to date.

Data mining is the analysis of a large amount of data in a data warehouse to provide new information. For example, by using loyalty cards that connect purchases to a particular customer, supermarkets can gather information about the buying habits of individual customers. Combining all the information about customers helps them to establish long-term trends.

Modelling and Simulation

Imagine having to design and build a new bypass to divert traffic round a town. Before starting on such a venture, it would be wise to check on the cost and compare that with the advantages to be gained. Although it is quite possible to produce accurate costings, it is harder to work out how wide the bypass should be (should it be dual or single carriageway, for example) or what route it should take to reduce the traffic flow through the town. By the time the road is built, the money will have been spent and the bypass may not be effective. When data on current traffic flow have been collected and likely future traffic requirements have been assessed, then a model can be produced.

Modelling attempts to show what is happening now and the results of the intended alterations. The model produced is a mathematical description of the rate of traffic flow at all points of interest. The details of this model can be changed; for example, by increasing the expected amount of traffic in the bypass model we can determine whether this causes any problems. Once the model has been tested with these conditions, we can then judge how good the proposed changes would be. The bypass could then be built, with the likelihood that it would be worthwhile, or it could be abandoned as being not useful enough, having only had the cost of the exploration.

It is when you want to test and use a mathematical model that a computer would be used. The computer can quickly carry out the necessary calculations (many of which are repeated but quite simple) and show the results using tables of numbers or diagrams.

Simulation software uses the model that has been developed to show the effects of different conditions. To be of any use, the model used must be tested thoroughly. It is now possible to buy simulation programs that allow people to solve a range of similar problems. The simulation contains a model that has been developed and tested by the authors. The user may have little control over the model but relies on the work the authors have done to develop and test it. However, advanced simulation software may allow the user to build new models.

Weather forecasting uses computer simulation. Data are gathered from many sources at different times; from these data, the computer predicts what weather we are likely to expect soon or in the future. From experience, we know that weather-forecasting accuracy can vary from being very good to being dramatically wrong. Economic forecasting is performed in a similar way but often lacks the accuracy of even a weather forecast. Prediction can be only as good as the model. Any model is limited by human understanding and the need for it to be sufficiently simple to allow results to be calculated in a reasonable time.

Computer simulations are also used in training. A flight simulator is used to prepare pilots for anything from standard flying and landing to dealing with emergencies without putting anyone's life at risk. A flight simulator can range from a simple screen display to a full-size mock-up of the flight cabin with movement effects.

In education, computer simulation can be used to show a process that would normally be impossible to demonstrate because it would be too dangerous, be too expensive or would take too long. In a simulation dealing with a nuclear reactor station, alterations could be made that would not be allowed at a visit to such a station. Similarly, in the field of genetics, alterations could be simulated on a reasonable timescale rather than waiting months or years for even simple processes to be checked.

In silicon-chip design, a simulation is used to show how the circuitry would behave. The design is adjusted until the required response is achieved. This saves the expense and time of producing, testing and having to change a series of prototypes. In these circumstances, **emulation** software could be used to check computer behaviour for various programs before the new chip becomes available.

Model

is a sequence of ideas that attempt to represent a process realistically. At some stage, these ideas are expressed mathematically as a set (or collection) of equations. The accuracy of this model is limited by the knowledge of the process being modelled, the time available to produce the model, the availability of input data and how quickly results are required.

Modelling

is the construction of a *model* (see above) by a mathematical analysis of a situation. The model is refined by testing it in various known situations.

Simulation

is the use of a computer program to predict the likely behaviour of a real-life system. A mathematical *model* (see above) of the system is constructed and tested. The model is usually incorporated into a program that can be used to investigate other situations.

A simple model could be tested mathematically using a program such as a spread-sheet, but the final simulation may produce a graphical display and may react to real-time inputs. A more complex situation will require simulation software. By altering the input data for a simulation, the possible results of different actions can be investigated.

PART A

Forecasting

is the use of simulations to predict future events, such as forecasting the weather. To be of any value, the results of the simulation must be reasonably accurate. The models must be tested thoroughly by comparing predictions with actual events. If the model is accurate, it can then be used regularly to aid planning.

Emulation

is a very precise form of *simulation* (see page 95) that should mimic exactly the behaviour of the circumstances that it is simulating. See *emulator*, below.

Emulation may be used by printers to enable them to behave like a different printer. They may then be used with a wide variety of computer software.

Emulator

is a program that allows a computer to behave as if it were a different type of computer. An emulator enables:

■ software to be developed that will run on computers not yet built;

■ software to be used on a type of computer other than the type it was designed for;

■ software to be tested when it would otherwise use expensive resources;

■ a computer to be used as a peripheral, appearing to the host computer to have the characteristics expected. This enables microcomputers to act as terminals to larger computer systems.

An emulator is often much slower than the host computer because of the extra processing involved.

Monte Carlo method

A whimsical name that comes from the use of chance, usually random numbers rather than roulette wheels, in simulation. In exploring the behaviour of a complex system (which might be chemical, physical, biological, human, etc.), the overall behaviour of the system may be too complicated to specify confidently in mathematical terms. If the many small decisions in the system can be specified easily, then the behaviour of the system can be simulated, using random numbers to model a large number of small decisions. For example, migration of people between towns in the UK might be too complicated to specify mathematically, but information is available on how many people move from London to Edinburgh, say, each year. The overall behaviour of the population can be explored by selecting one resident of London, generating a random number to see whether that individual will stay or move, and, if so, to where. By repeating this for the whole population of the UK, predictions about future population trends will be possible, even if the mathematics are not understood fully. See also *random-number generation*, below.

Random-number generation

including: pseudo-random-number generator

Many *simulations* (see page 95) on a computer need to make use of random numbers in a similar way to 'tossing a coin' in order to make a decision. Most programming languages include a random-number function that gives the user a suitable number as if it had been chosen at random – numbers between one and six, for example, to simulate the throw of dice in a game. Because computer programs cannot be truly random, a *pseudo-random-number generator* is used, which gives numbers the appearance of being random. See *Monte Carlo method*, above.

PART A

Internet

This section is concerned with terms likely to be met when using the Internet. Many Internet terms are concerned with the transmission of data between computers within networks. Some of these terms and other related terms may be found in A13 Communications, A14 Networking, B5 Communications Components and D5 Communications Technology.

The Internet, increasingly referred to as the Net, interconnects a very large number of individual and diverse computer networks. Its name is a diminution of 'interconnected networks'. It uses a wide range of telecommunications media to provide a means of global information interchange that appears to be independent of the power of the user's computer or where in the world other systems or databases are.

Apart from saying that the Internet is very large, it is difficult to give realistic numbers. It is estimated that over 250 000 networks and 100 million computers around the world have some means of Internet access. Growing awareness of the potential of the Internet means that the figures are increasing rapidly.

Each connected network may be of any size, use any hardware or be situated anywhere in the world. These networks include very large and well-organised networks (like those of governments, universities and multinational corporations), small company networks and individuals using Internet service providers (ISPs).

For an individual user to access the Internet, their computer must be connected to a local network that has a connection to the Internet. If the user is using a terminal or personal computer on a company or educational organisation network, there may be a permanent connection to the Internet. If the individual has only a standalone computer, then a connection to an Internet service provider's network will be needed.

The principal requirement of any network that is connected to the Internet is the ability to communicate intelligently with it. To do this, the network must use the protocols – a set of rules in a sort of 'language' – required of all Internet users and have access to telephone, radio or other telecommunications links. Depending upon the types of data that users wish to receive or send, there are also requirements for the capacity of links to the Internet. The Internet has its own protocols, the definition of which is the responsibility of an Internet Committee. The usual protocol is TCP/IP (Transmission Control Protocol/Internet Protocol), although there are others.

There is also a Joint Board, which coordinates Internet naming procedures and the operation of major communication routes. Making sure that information from any one computer reaches its correct destination is the job of dedicated pieces of equipment, known as routers, located at strategic points around the world. Routers check the destination address for the message and either send it to the appropriate computer if it is on a network connected to the router or send it on to another router along the path. This process is repeated until the message reaches its destination. Figure A12.1 shows how communication from a computer passes through a number of nodes to reach its destination.

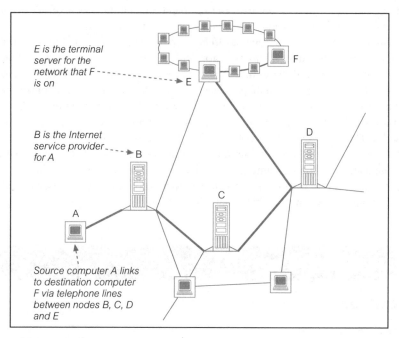

E is the terminal server for the network that F is on

B is the Internet service provider for A

Source computer A links to destination computer F via telephone lines between nodes B, C, D and E

Figure A12.1   Internet connection

Each machine connected to the Internet has its own unique address, which is a number. There is no central register of machines connected to the Internet; nor is there any formal index of either individual users or database addresses.

Essentially, the Internet provides three types of service:

- the *World Wide Web*, which gives access to remote databases, through browsing or searching;
- *electronic mail*, which provides one-to-one communication and exchange of information;
- *file transfer*, which makes it possible to transfer large amounts of information.

Additional services provide bulletin boards (broadcast mail), discussion groups and teleconferencing.

Most Internet resources are accessed using the World Wide Web ('the Web'), which is a multimedia information system. Each information provider makes their information available as a Web site, which becomes a part of the Web. In addition to information on the Web page, other facilities may be accessed by a user from a Web page, such as requesting information using file transfer, completing and returning a questionnaire or making requests for a search engine to locate information about a topic.

A variety of Internet applications have come into use, including *e-commerce*, *e-government*, *e-marketing* and *e-zines* (e-magazines), which allow governments and businesses to provide their services via the Internet. The principal savings to the provider organisation have been distribution (saving mail or delivery charges), printing costs (by passing these to the recipient), updating (latest offers instantly available) and direct marketing (to anyone with Internet access).

When using e-mail, a message has to be prepared and then posted into the e-mail system. Actual transmission may be automatic, or the message may be stored on the sender's computer until the e-mail system is next contacted. When the message is received by the e-mail system provider, it is prepared for onward transmission. Having passed through the communications system, often provided by the Internet, the message is delivered to and stored on the computer at the addressee's service provider. This message is later collected by the addressee from a mailbox.

All e-mail users must have a unique identifier or address. This ensures that any communication through the Internet finds its target. The identifier contains information to enable return communications to get back to the user. These user identifiers may be numerical or may use personal names.

User Perception

Internet

also known as: the Net
including: ARPAnet (Advanced Research Projects Agency Network), NSFNET (National Science Foundation Network), BITNET, JANET, SuperJANET
provides the facility to link computers worldwide, usually using telecommunications systems such as telephone lines. It allows fast communication between people, the transfer of data between computers and the distribution of information. Messages and data are passed from the source computer, through other computers, until the destination computer is reached. See *e-mail*, page 103, *file transfer*, page 102, and *World Wide Web*, page 000.

Any computer can be linked to any other computer attached to the Internet, communicating through intermediate computer systems. This is achieved by having common technical standards, a common identification system for computers and a common naming system for datafiles. See *TCP/IP*, page 110, *domain name*, page 107, and *URL*, page 106. In practice, most users either are part of a local area network, linked to the Internet by a *terminal server* (see page 111), or are linked by telephone line to a *host computer* (see page 127), which performs the Internet access.

Much of the initial success of the Internet has been due to the vast amounts of data made available by linking several very large networks to the Internet for academic and research purposes. These networks include the following:

ARPAnet (*Advanced Research Projects Agency Network*) is the US Defense Department Network that linked US university research centres to the Defense Agency from the late 1960s.

NSFNET (*National Science Foundation Network*) is the academic network used by US research facilities. It used the concepts from ARPAnet and it was extended to become the basis of the Internet.

BITNET is the academic network used by US universities. It is based on large IBM computers.

JANET is the UK Joint Academic Network that links British universities and research centres.

SuperJANET is a development of JANET providing much greater capacity for the twenty-first century.

Browser

including: kiosk-mode browser, line-mode browser
is a program that allows Internet users to retrieve information interactively on the Internet. A browser may be used to access the *World Wide Web* (see below) or to provide other facilities such as *file transfer* (see page 102) and *e-mail* (see page 103).

When browsing the World Wide Web, a browser retrieves Web pages from another computer on the Internet and displays them in the multimedia format used by the World Wide Web. Related pages can be retrieved easily by clicking on special links, which are usually shown in a different colour. The browser has facilities to save pages, print pages and move backwards and forwards through pages that have been accessed already.

Most browsers are very flexible and have many facilities, but two specialised browsers are:

Kiosk-mode browsers, which are designed for easy use by the public, allowing limited access to a range of information. They can be operated using robust interfaces such as touchscreens.

Line-mode browsers, which generally are character-based and unable to display graphics. Some may display a message in a box showing where a graphics image should have been. See also *Lynx*, page 114.

See also *HyperText Transfer Protocol* (*HTTP*), page 110.

World Wide Web (WWW)

including: Web site, Web page, home page, welcome page, personal page, surf
is a collection of information held in multimedia form on the Internet. This information is stored at locations called *Web sites* in the form of *Web pages*. A Web page is a single document. It may be too large to be displayed as a screen without scrolling.

Web pages are permanently available to any user of the Internet. Each organisation (and many individuals) providing information organises their information as a

Web site, often consisting of many pages. Web sites are an effective way of distributing information such as advertisements, technical information, comments and ideas.

Any Web page can be accessed directly if its full address is known, but to make locating information easier each Web site has a *home page* (*welcome page* or *personal page*) that provides a starting point for a user to search the site. Any Web site can provide links to other related Web sites.

Since *browsers* (see page 101) and *search engines* (see page 109) can quickly find pages of interest, users are provided with the tools to *surf* the Internet. Surfing means to search for useful information, following whatever routes may seem interesting.

Web pages are usually prepared using *HyperText Mark-up Language* (*HTML*), see page 303.

Internet portal

also known as: portal
is a Web site designed to be a first port of call for a user logging on to the Internet. It will be designed to carry links to pages the user is likely to want to access; it may even be *customisable* (see page 14), so that the user can specify which links he or she wants to see.

There is considerable commercial importance attached to providing a portal, as a page that will invariably be visited as the start of any browsing on the Internet is an attractive proposition, not least to advertisers.

File transfer

including: file transfer protocol (FTP), archive, anonymous FTP (anonymous file transfer protocol)
is a major use of the Internet involving the movement of information through the Internet as copies of files. Information providers store files containing data on computers that can be accessed from the Internet.

A user identifies which file contains the data needed and initiates a file transfer. If a file is copied from one location to another via the Internet, the transfer process has to conform to Internet protocols.

File transfer protocol (*FTP*) allows a user to send a message causing a copy of a file to be transferred between computers. The file can be saved by the user and the data can be read. The file transfer protocol controls the messages between computers and the sending of the file copy in sections (also called *blocks*, see page 188) and checks the data received for errors. To make the transfer faster, the files provided for file transfer are usually compressed and are referred to as an *archive*.

Anonymous FTP (*anonymous file transfer protocol*) is a service that offers users the facility to locate and copy files without having to identity themselves as the searcher. See also *Archie*, page 109.

Intranet

including: extranet

is a communication system providing similar services to the Internet solely within a particular company or organisation.

An intranet provides an organisation with services that are accessible only by authorised users and has good security for confidential information. It allows secure e-mail communication and the distribution of information using technology similar to the World Wide Web. It may use the Internet to allow access by its authorised users anywhere in the world. Part of the intranet may allow public access, which gives the organisation an opportunity to advertise itself using the Internet. This Internet access to an intranet is sometimes called an *extranet*.

Multi-purpose Internet Mail Extender (MIME)

is a protocol used to send e-mail messages containing forms of computer data other than text. Some e-mail systems are designed only for textual messages, and sending other computer data results in them being corrupted. MIME is a way of coding the data to avoid corruption. On receipt, the data will need to be decoded before use.

PART A

Electronic mail

also known as: e-mail
including: snail mail, mailbox, bounce, cross-post, spam

is sending messages from user to user through computer communication. These messages are the equivalent of traditional letters or memos; there is no provision for two-way conversation. Messages are delivered automatically and very quickly through telecommunications networks. In comparison, postal delivery is slow and derisively called *snail mail*.

Most e-mail services are provided by organisations linked to the Internet. This allows e-mails to be sent to anywhere in the world provided the recipient has an e-mail address, a *mailbox*. Many organisations have internal e-mail systems running on their own private, confidential networks.

Since e-mail is relatively cheap, and because the sending and receiving users do not have to be using their computers at the same time, it is a popular way for schools and colleges to communicate with colleagues in other countries.

E-mail system providers' computers will normally be able to receive mail at any time. If the recipient's mailbox cannot be located, the e-mail will *bounce*. This means that it will be returned to the sender, usually with a suitable message.

There are many kinds of electronic mail package, and the mail delivery information they present is not always the same. With the message, many packages provide information about it, the send time, the message arrival time, the name of the mail package used and the computer gateways that the message passed through. Some packages put this information after the message, others put it before the message, as in Figure A12.2 (see page 104).

```
line 1    From:        MX%"fred@rz.uni-jena.de"        26-MAR-1998 17:25:55.00
line 2    To: MX%"ngc@austin.ibm.com"
line 3    CC: MX%"thomas_ng@greenwood.notts.sch.uk"
line 4    Subj: Scotland
line 5    Received: from cnve.rz.uni-jena.de by greenwood.notts.sch.uk with SMTP; Mar, 26 Thur
          1998 17:25:53 GMT

line 6    Received: (from fred@localhost) by fsuj03.rz.uni-jena.de (8.7.1/8.6.10) id SAA16317;
          Mar, 26 Thur 1998 18:25:48 +0100 (MEZ)

line 7    From: Freda Smith <fred@rz.uni-jena.de>
line 8    Subject: Scotland
line 9    To: ngc@austin.ibm.com (ngc)
line 10   Date: Mar, 26 Thur 1998 18:25:46 +0100(MEZ)
line 11   CC: thomas_ng@vax.nott.ac.uk
line 12   In-Reply-To: <9703182135.AA20796@ng.austin.ibm.com> from "ngc" at Mar 18, 97
          03:35:51 pm

line 13   X-Mailer: ELM [version 2.4 PL23]
line 14   Content-Type: text

line 15   Hello......
```

Figure A12.2   An e-mail

The convention for an e-mail address is: *user@computer.organisation.country*

MX% (for Message Exchange) (**line 1**) is a piece of software that controls the store-and-forward routing and the delivery of electronic mail messages.

In this example:

User *'fred' from Jena University in Germany* (**lines 1 & 7**), **sent** a message to **user** *'ngc' at IBM, Austin, USA* (**lines 2 & 9**), and **carbon copied** the message to **user** *'thomas_ng' at Greenwood School, Nottingham, UK* (**lines 3 & 11**). The *Subject* of the message is *'Scotland'* (**lines 4 & 8**). The message was sent on *Thursday 26 March 1998 at 18:25:48 local time* (MEZ = Middle European Time Zone, one hour ahead of Greenwich Mean Time) (**lines 6 & 10**). The message was sent from a *localhost through fsuj03.rz.uni-jena.de* (**line 6**), then onwards to *cnve.rz.uni-jena.de*, and it arrived at *greenwood.notts.sch.uk at 17:25:53 GMT* (**line 5**). The message took five seconds to travel from *Jena University* to *Nottingham*. The name of user *'fred'* is Freda Smith. The mail package she used was *ELM* (**line 13**). This message is a reply to an earlier message sent by user *ngc on 18 March* (**line 12**). The message is made up of text (**line 14**). **Line 15** is the start of the message. See also E4 Geographical Domain Extensions, page 413.

It is possible to send copies of a message to more than one intended recipient at the same time; this is called *cross-posting* a message. It provides opportunities to send many, often unwanted e-mails, such as advertisements. This unwanted material is known as *spam*. See also *Multi-purpose Internet Mail Extender*, page 103.

Usenet

including: emotes, emoticons, three-letter acronym (TLA)

is the use of the Internet for interactive communication between individuals. Originally this formed a subset of the Internet, but now it refers to a range of personal communication facilities, including *chat* programs, *newsgroups* and *list servers* (see page 106).

Emotes or *emoticons* are primitive icons – usually formed by joining together a number of normal characters – used to indicate feelings in e-mail messages. They are often best interpreted at right-angles to the print direction. These icons are often known as 'smilies'. For example,

   : -)   and   : - (

Three-letter acronyms (*TLAs*) replace frequently used terms to minimise typing and connection time, for example BTW (by the way). However, many of these abbreviations actually have more than three letters, for example IMHO (in my humble opinion).

Web log

also known as: blog
including: blogging, blogger

is a personal diary kept on the Web and accessible to any user. A sudden burst of popularity of *'blogging'* in the early 2000s was believed to be due largely to two causes:

- the appearance of a number of Web sites offering simple blogging tools that allowed an unskilled computer user easily to generate and update their Web logs;
- a significant contribution to the flow of information from scenes of conflict, such as in Iraq, by *bloggers* actually in the thick of the fighting.

The format was adopted enthusiastically by many public figures, such as Members of Parliament and pop stars.

Chat

including: Internet relay chat (IRC)

is a program that allows Internet users to communicate interactively with other users. *Internet relay chat* (*IRC*) is one method of allowing many users to chat over the Internet without unreasonable delays in the communication.

Newsgroup

including: flame, frequently asked question (FAQ), lurk, moderated newsgroups, thread

PART A

is a message-storage area that is dedicated to a particular special-interest subject. Messages are sent by e-mail to the newsgroup, where they are stored. An interested user can read these messages and perhaps contribute to the group. Newsgroups enable contact and debate between people who do not know each other but have a common interest. See also *bulletin board*, page 115.

The interactive nature of newsgroups has allowed a very specialised vocabulary to develop, including the following:

Flame is an e-mailed message, often posted to a newsgroup, attacking another member of the group.

Frequently asked question (*FAQ*) is a list of questions and answers, usually in a mailing list or newsgroup. The purpose is to save time by avoiding the questioner having to send the questions and wait for the replies.

Lurk is to read messages in a newsgroup but never to post any.

Moderated newsgroups have a person (see *sysop*, page 115) checking all messages before they are made available. This prevents the misuse of the newsgroup by irrelevant, obscene or insulting messages being posted.

Thread is the initial posting and all associated comments linked to it that are being sent to a particular message area.

List server

is an automated electronic mail distribution system. This is a program that runs on a computer connected to the Internet. The list server can receive requests from people to join (or leave) the mailing list. The requests are processed automatically. A user on a mailing list can send an e-mail to the list server, which will copy it to all users currently on the mailing list. This is a useful way of distributing information to a group of users who have a common interest. See *Internet Service Provider* in *dial-up*, page 107.

Connection

Uniform resource locator (URL)

is the address for data on the Internet. Each resource, which is usually a file, has a name, its URL, which specifies the file or data and the location where it is stored. The URL includes the transfer protocol to be used, for example *http* (see page 110), the *domain name* (see page 107) where it is stored, and other information such as its individual filename.

For example, `http://www.bcs.org.uk/` will load the home page for the British Computer Society's Web site.

Dial-up

also known as: dial in

including: service provider, dial-up service, Internet Service Provider (ISP)

is to use an ordinary telephone line (and a modem or terminal adapter) to connect a local computer, or terminal, to a remote computer service such as the Internet.

In most cases, the facility to dial into the computer system is provided by a *service provider*, which runs the *dial-up service*. This may be provided by the IT department of a company with dial-up facilities for its employees or by a separate company that provides the service.

Many people access the Internet using a dial-up service provided by an *Internet Service Provider* (*ISP*). These companies provide a *host computer* (see page 127), which the user can connect to by dialling in. The host computer manages the communications and also stores data such as electronic mail, Web pages and files for its subscribers. This host computer is connected to the Internet, and subscribers can communicate with other computers on the Internet. The Internet service provider charges for these services and may provide other value-added services. See also *UNIX Internet host*, page 109.

Connect time

including: blink, flash session, off-line reader (OLR)

is the length of time that a user is connected to the Internet. This is related to the cost of using the Internet. If there is a telephone connection, it may be charged by the time used. Some *Internet service providers* (see under *dial-up* above) also charge users according to the time they are connected to the host computer. For a single session, these times ought to be the same.

To *blink* is to use an automated process to access the Internet very quickly, to collect electronic mail and perform file transfers, before processing the data off-line (see *off-line processing*, page 000). It is also called a *flash session*. One way of doing this is to use an *off-line reader* (*OLR*), which is a software package allowing a user to connect to an on-line system, such as that provided by an Internet service provider, and automatically download e-mails and any other addressed messages. After disconnection from the service provider, the software allows the user to read the messages and write replies while off-line. The software then transmits all replies and any other outgoing messages at a later time, which the user determines. This makes use of the Internet much cheaper than other methods of access.

Domain name

including: domain name system, domain name server, IP address

is the name for the apparent location, or site, of a resource on the Internet. Each location has a unique domain name, and this is part of the filename of each resource.

PART A

The *domain name system* defines how domain names are structured. Domain names are allocated and registered in this format by companies contracted to do this. Domain names, once registered, are stored on a large database, and a program called a *domain name server* accesses this database to provide the (physical) location of the data. See also E4 *Geographical Domain Extensions* page 413.

Each computer linked to the Internet has a physical address, a number called its Internet protocol (IP) address. The *IP address* uniquely identifies the physical computer linked to the Internet. The domain name server converts the domain name into its corresponding IP address.

Usually the domain name refers to the computer where the data are stored, but it is possible for the data to be stored elsewhere and, in this case, the domain name is a pseudonym for the real location of the data.

General

ITU (International Telecommunications Union)

formerly: CCITT (Committée Consultatif International Téléphonique et Télégraphique)
including: Internet Society, Internet Architecture Board (IAB)
is the international organisation that coordinates worldwide telecommunications. It is part of the United Nations. Originally it was based in France and known as the CCITT, a name by which it is still widely known. It seeks to obtain agreement on the setting and adherence to international standards for data telecommunications.

Various other organisations work with the ITU:

The *Internet Society* is an organisation representing the major Internet network owners.

The *Internet Architecture Board* (*IAB*) is a committee of the Internet Society and considers the use of appropriate Internet standards and protocols.

MUG (multi-user game)

including: modem play, network play, null-modem
is a networked game where several players take part at the same time. The players may play against each other or act as a group playing against the computer. Traditionally, the program controlling the game is run on a central computer with players dialling in directly or connecting through the Internet. Often the game runs continuously, with players leaving and new players joining all the time.

It is possible to link two computers running the same game, so that players can compete with each other rather than competing with the computer. This is called *modem play* or *network play*; it can be played by dialling in to the other computer or using an Internet link. An alternative to a network connection is a *null-modem* connection, where two computers are connected directly together to exchange data, usually using the *serial ports* (see page 363). A special null-modem cable is used because the output from one computer must be linked to the input of the other.

Cyberspace

is the complete set of information that can be accessed using the Internet. It can be thought of as an imaginary or virtual world, made up of all the sites and all the files available. This virtual world can be explored electronically in the same way as we may explore a real area of the world by moving around and looking for interesting things.

UNIX Internet host

including: Gopher, Veronica, Archie, WAIS (wide-area information server)
is a computer running the UNIX operating system that provides facilities for Internet users. UNIX is a powerful operating system particularly suited to network operation, and many Internet service providers use computers running it. The user operates a simple command-line interface or accesses one of the available menu systems. Few users now work with UNIX, preferring a *browser* (see page 101). See also *Internet Service Provider*, page 107, *UNIX*, page 127, and *host computer*, page 127.

Many programs were developed for UNIX systems, including:

Gopher: a menu system that helps the user find resources by searching its comprehensive indexes. There are many different gopher systems, and each has slightly different data in its indexes.

Veronica: a *search engine* (see below) that searches all the Gopher indexes to produce a list of resources in response to a user's request. See *Gopher*, above.

Archie: a *search engine* (see below) that holds indexes of all the files available for *file transfer* (see page 102) on the Internet.

WAIS (*wide-area information server*): a *search engine* (see below) that searches some of the databases attached to the Internet. There are several hundred databases, including news services, reviews and specialist document archives.

Information superhighway

is a name given to the Internet now that communication speeds are much higher. This name reflects the fact that large amounts of information can be communicated rapidly between users.

Search engine

including: Google, Yahoo, Lycos, Ask Jeeves, Alta Vista
is a computer program that searches a very large database to find data items matching a requested *query* (see page 93).

Search engines are useful for locating resources on the Internet. Search engines collect details of Internet resources and their locations, often automatically, and hold these data in a very large database for the search engine to use. A search engine uses a variety of methods to find the required data, such as finding alternative keywords using a thesaurus.

There are several proprietary Internet search engines, including *Google*, *Yahoo!*, *Lycos*, *Ask Jeeves* and *AltaVista*.

Virtual Reality Mark-up Language (VRML)

is a computer language used to define three-dimensional objects for a special type of Web page. A special *browser* (see page 101) may be needed to display VRML images.

Internet protocol

including: transmission control protocol/Internet protocol (TCP/IP), hypertext transfer protocol (HTTP), address resolution protocol (ARP), Internet control message protocol (ICMP), point-to-point protocol (PPP), serial line Internet protocol (SLIP), simple mail transfer protocol (SMTP), post office protocol 3 (POP3), UNIX to UNIX copy protocol (UUCP), user datagram protocol (UDP/IP)
is a standard set of rules used to ensure the proper transfer of information between computers on the Internet. Internet protocols define how data are to be structured, what control signals are to be used, and their meaning.

Some protocols deal primarily with how particular types of data are structured, such as *file transfer protocol* (FTP) and *hypertext transfer protocol* (HTTP), see page 102 and below. Other protocols are essentially technical, governing how the individual data elements are communicated over the Internet. Protocols include the following:

Transmission control protocol/Internet protocol (*TCP/IP*) is the set of working practices that allow all Internet users and providers to communicate with each other, whatever their equipment is. TCP/IP specifies how individual signals are sent over the Internet.

Hypertext transfer protocol (*HTTP*) is a protocol that defines the process of identifying, requesting and transferring multimedia Web pages over the Internet. These Web pages are usually constructed using *HTML* (see page 303). A secure variant, HTTPS, also exists.

Address resolution protocol (*ARP*) defines how to identify the technical destination of a message.

Internet control message protocol (*ICMP*) defines the messages used to report status and errors when communicating with another computer.

Point-to-point protocol (*PPP*) defines communication between two computers connected directly. It is commonly used between individual users and their *Internet*

Service Provider, see page 107, when using a telephone line. The Internet Service Provider will access the Internet on the user's behalf using the TCP/IP protocol.

Serial line Internet protocol (*SLIP*) is an Internet protocol allowing personal computer users to dial in to a suitable Internet service, using only a telephone line, but using the full TCP/IP protocol. Such a user has full Internet access.

Simple mail transfer protocol (*SMTP*) is a TCP/IP protocol used in the transfer of e-mail between computer systems. The user's incoming mail is stored on the service provider's computer. SMTP does not automatically download mail as soon as the user connects to the server but requires a specific request to do so. See also *POP3*, next.

Post office protocol 3 (*POP3*) defines the transfer of e-mail between computer systems. It provides more facilities than *simple mail transfer protocol*, see above.

UNIX to UNIX copy protocol (*UUCP*) defines the copying of files between systems running the UNIX operating system.

User datagram protocol (*UDP/IP*) is used by some applications instead of the TCP/IP protocol.

Remote login

including: Telnet
is a service that allows a user at one computer to log in to another computer on any connected network as if the user's computer is a terminal of the remote computer. This is achieved by the use of a program such as *Telnet*, which is a terminal emulator program used for remote access to computers linked to the Internet. This enables a user to have the power of the larger computer available for their use.

Point of presence (PoP)

is an access point to an Internet service provider's network. This is usually the telephone exchange where the transmitted data leave the public telephone network and enter the Internet service provider's network. See also *Internet Service Provider* (*ISP*), page 107.

Terminal server

is a computer that is attached to a *local-area network* (see page 118) and that accesses the Internet on request from any of the terminals attached to the local-area network. The network may be connected permanently to the Internet or may use a modem connection to dial in to an *Internet Service Provider* (see page 107) when required.

Post

is to send a message by e-mail. Where the message is available on a bulletin board, the message is described as being posted on the *bulletin board*, see page 115. See also *cross-posting*, in *e-mail*, page 103.

Postmaster

is a system controller with responsibility for e-mail.

White Pages

is a database holding a directory of Internet users, their correct Internet site names and their e-mail addresses.

Finger

is a program that lists the users on a remote system, often giving information such as physical addresses, telephone numbers, etc. See also *WhoIs*, below.

WhoIs

is a program that can find e-mail addresses using only the name of a known Internet user.

Internet information systems

are large, and often dispersed, databases that can be accessed from the Internet. There are many such systems, but three commonly used ones are *Gopher* and *WAIS*, see page 109, and the *World Wide Web* (*WWW*), page 101.

Site

is any individual computer or network that is part of the Internet.

Packet Internet Groper (PING)

is a program that checks whether a computer with a particular address is attached to the Internet. See also *IP address*, page 108.

Off-line

refers to a computer that is normally attached to a network but is operating in stand-alone mode. See also *off-line processing*, page 17.

On-line

refers to a computer that is normally attached to a network and is available for external connections to be made at all times on demand from users. See also *on-line processing*, page 17.

Netiquette

is the set of social conventions that seek to define good behaviour when using the Internet. These conventions try to encourage behaviour that does not cause inconvenience or offence to other users.

Server (software)

is software that allows one computer to offer a service to another computer. The software running on this other computer may make requests for services from the server. Sometimes the computer with the server software is itself called the server. See also *server*, page 125.

Robot (software)

is a Web-server program that receives a message and then takes some action appropriate to the message. A typical robot action may be to search for HTML documents by reference to links between them, building up a map of the information held on the *WWW*, see page 101. See *server (software)*, above.

Winsock

is a program that allows personal computers to communicate with other computers over the Internet, using the standard *TCP/IP communications protocol* (see page 110). Winsock converts commands from the PC into a correctly formatted message for transmission to a linked computer. Many personal computer communication programs use Winsock to perform the actual communication, although this is transparent to the user.

Freenet

is a service provider that allows free Internet access to a defined group of individual users. A typical example is access provided at a terminal in a public library.

Lynx

is a text-only *browser*, see page 101. It is particularly useful for users whose computer does not have facilities to display pictures.

Mosaic

is a UNIX-supported graphics *browser*, see page 101, that can be used to find many types of information on the Internet's *WWW*, see page 101.

e-Commerce

including: e-government, e-business, e-profiling, e-marketing, e-sales, e-zines
is the use of the Internet for ordinary commercial tasks such as retail sales and publishing. This reduces the need to exchange physical contracts in face-to-face meetings or by post. The advantages include the ability to:

- reach worldwide markets at a fraction of the normal advertising costs;
- eliminate the need for an expensive range of shops;
- provide a service 24 hours a day;
- test the range of customers' needs without extensive market research;
- shorten the time from ordering to despatching goods;
- shorten the time between launching products and advertising update.

   In the case of 'soft' goods (such as text, graphical images, computer software and electronic games), the delivery can be made using the Internet.
   e-Government, *e-business*, *e-profiling*, *e-marketing*, *e-sales* and *e-zines* are terms derived from this electronic method of doing business and providing services. They reflect the growing use of the Internet to increase market effectiveness in many areas of day-to-day life.

Communications

Other related terms may be found in sections A12 Internet, A14 Networking, B5 Communications Components and D5 Communications Technology.

The internal architecture of a computer involves electronic signals being passed from component to component. It is a natural extension of this idea to send signals out of the computer, to another computer, perhaps thousands of kilometres away. The technology to achieve this is discussed in Section D5.

The extension of these concepts and practices has produced the range of opportunities provided by the Internet. It has such a wide range of terms that are specific to it that Section A12 is devoted exclusively to the Internet.

On an electronic scale, the distance of a few metres to your printer is so large that it raises a new set of problems (is the printer actually switched on? what does the computer do if it isn't?). These problems are, surprisingly, not made much more severe if the printer is on the other side of the Atlantic, so it seems quite natural for a number of computer applications to have been developed that involve communication and information provision over large distances.

Many of the applications have become so much a part of modern industrialised societies that it takes us aback to realise that they involve computing technology – taking cash from a cash dispenser in the middle of the night in a strange town, sending a fax, reading the sports results on Teletext, and so on.

Bulletin board

also known as: bulletin board system (BBS)
including: system operator (sysop)
is the electronic equivalent of a notice board carrying short items that may be of interest to a wide number of people. Bulletin boards are sited on a computer, and the users access the computer by a *network* (see page 118), *electronic mail* (see page 103) or the *Internet* (see page 100). They can leave messages for anyone to read, review messages left by other users and sometimes take copies of software that has been placed on the board. The organiser of such a board is traditionally known as the *system operator* or, more familiarly, the *sysop*. Larger bulletin boards are run by organisations such as newspapers, computer manufacturers and universities, offering comprehensive information services as well as an opportunity to read or post messages.

Computer conferencing

makes use of *electronic mail* (see page 103) to allow a group of people with a common interest, but separated geographically, to share advice, opinions, information, and so on. The users are organised in a 'conference' and are able to examine messages left by other users, add their own comments, and generally participate in the work of the group. This is very similar to the idea of a *bulletin board* (see page 115), but there is a suggestion in a computer conference that users are all on an equal footing and are all expected to contribute equally.

On-line service

is a service, such as a *bulletin board* (see page 115) or an *email* service (see page 103), that is normally available at all times. It may be provided as part of a network, or it may be accessed via external communications systems.

Tele-conferencing

including: video-conferencing
is the use of communication links to conduct meetings between people who are separated geographically. The links might be voice-only, or they might include pictures, when it is usually referred to as *video-conferencing*.

Tele-working

is the use of information technology to allow people to work in their own homes, while still being in easy contact with the office. Typically, this involves use of *electronic mail* and *fax* (see page 6), as well as allowing remote users access to a central computer or network.

Header

is data at the start of a set of data, such as an email or document, that are used to identify the data. In communications, a header will contain data about the destination and route for the subsequent data.

Trailer

is data at the end of a set of data, such as an email or document, that indicate the end of the data in a *frame*, see page 197. Another kind of trailer is an *end-of-file marker*, see page 313, for a file.

Networking

Other terms and concepts related to networks and communications are to be found in A12 Internet, A13 Communications, B5 Communications Components and D5 Communications Technology.

Connecting pieces of communications and information equipment together in a network is not a new concept. The early telegraph systems, especially in America, where distances are so great, provided the stimulus for telegram services and the later development of telex communications, in which text information could be sent between any telex machines on the worldwide telex network using telephone lines. Passing messages internationally has been possible since the development of international cable links, which began in the nineteenth century. For over 70 years, the world's newspapers depended upon organisations that gathered news around the world and delivered it to their client newspapers through the telex network. These services are still provided by some of the same organisations, but in addition there are now e-mail and other services linking computers around the world.

In a computer network, a number of computers are connected together in order to exchange information. For example, an organisation having offices spread over a wide geographical area might install a network to enable employees to examine information held on computers in other offices many miles away.

The connections between computers may be wires, fibre-optic cables, microwave links, communication via satellite, or any combination of these. The interconnected collection of computers form the network. The computers may be large powerful machines, small personal computers or terminals. They may be capable of running on their own but will have the added advantage of being able to communicate with each other.

In a traditional network, users must explicitly log on (that is, identify themselves to the network) and explicitly move information around on the network by issuing the appropriate instructions. A **distributed system** is normally thought of as a network in which the existence of the other machines is not obvious to the user. Programs and data held on other machines can be used as though they were held locally on the user's computer.

A distinction is usually made between networks of computers that are all situated relatively close to each other – for example, in the same building or cluster of buildings – known as a **local-area network** (LAN) – and those in which the computers are geographically remote – known as a **wide-area network** (WAN).

A network offers the possibility of sharing work between the different resources available. For example, if one computer has a heavy load of processing, then some of the work can be moved to another machine on the network. A network makes all the resources of the network (programs, data and equipment, such as printers and disk drives) available to the whole network without regard to the physical location of either the resource or the user. Reliability is another advantage of networking. The effect of hardware failures can be reduced by switching work from a failed device to one that is still functioning. This can be particularly valuable in systems such as banking, where it is important that the system can continue operating even if there are some hardware failures.

Networks of small computers can be a cheaper way of providing computer power than using a single large machine. If a network of small machines has access to outside facilities, whose use may need to be purchased, such as a large specialist database, then the potential of the network is enhanced greatly. Linking a network to other networks, which are themselves linked to yet further networks, makes it theoretically possible to have the whole of world knowledge available to any computer on such a network.

The **Internet** now provides this kind of linking of networks. It works because there are thousands of networks each connected to other networks in such a way that it is possible for messages (data) to be sent from a computer on one of the networks to any computer on any other network, provided that both networks have access to the Internet. How such data travel through this 'network of networks' is illustrated in Figure A12.1, page 99.

Network

including: distributed network
is a linked set of computer systems capable of sharing computer power and resources such as printers, large disk drives, CD-ROMs and other databases. Sometimes the term 'network' is used to mean the arrangement of links between the equipment that form the network. See *network topology*, page 119.

In a *distributed network*, the sharing of resources is arranged by the (network) operating system without any action being required by the user.

Local-area network (LAN)

is a network in which the computer systems are all situated relatively close to each other, for example in the same building or cluster of buildings, such as a school. Since the distances involved are small, direct physical connection is possible. The network connections are normally wire cables, such as coaxial cable, but fibre-optic cable is increasingly being used.

Wide-area network (WAN)

is a network in which the computers are geographically remote. Wide-area networks make use of a range of connection methods typically using public telephone links, including microwave links, undersea cables and communication satellites.

Network topology

including: bus network, ring network, loop network, star network, central node, hub, nexus, backbone, FDDI (fibre distributed data interface), backbone
is the theoretical arrangement of components of a network. The actual arrangement will almost certainly be determined by the buildings or other locations for the parts of the network. The network descriptions indicate how the devices on the network, the computers, printers, servers, etc., are connected to each other. Since networks communicate serially, the actual connections will be capable of *serial data transmission* (see page 370).

A *bus network* has each of the devices connected directly to a main communications line, called a bus, along which signals are sent. The bus will frequently be a twin cable of some kind, for example coaxial cable.

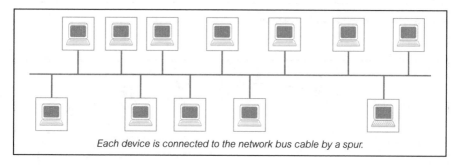

Each device is connected to the network bus cable by a spur.

Figure A14.1 Bus network with spurs

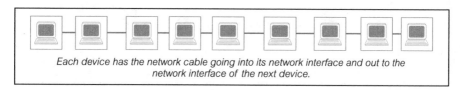

Each device has the network cable going into its network interface and out to the network interface of the next device.

Figure A14.2 Bus network

A *ring network* (sometimes called a *loop network*) has each of the devices on the network connected to a ring (or loop) communications line around which signals are sent. The devices may be connected to the ring by spurs, as in Figure A14.3, or the connections may pass through the *network interface* (see *interface*, page 356, and *interface card*, page 363) in each device, as in Figure A14.4; in this case, provision has to be made for the system to continue to work if one of the devices is switched off or fails to function properly.

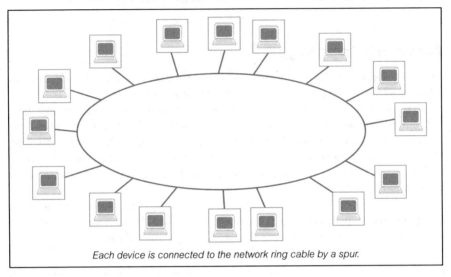

Each device is connected to the network ring cable by a spur.

Figure A14.3 Ring network with spurs

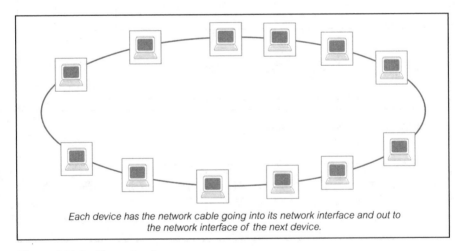

Each device has the network cable going into its network interface and out to the network interface of the next device.

Figure A14.4 Ring network

A *star network* has all the network devices connected to one central computer, which is often used as the *file server* (see page 125). The *central node* of the network, sometimes called the *hub* or *nexus*, is a computer that has separate connections to each computer or terminal.

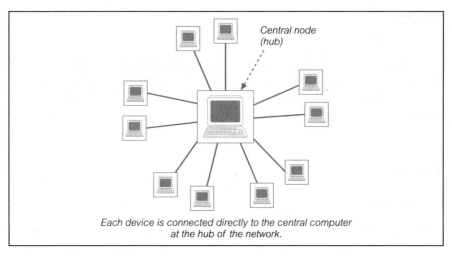

Figure A14.5 Star network

A *backbone* is a high-speed communication link used to provide the main links between the smaller subnetworks in a large network. The connections are fibre-optic cable. **FDDI** (*fibre distributed data interface*) is an ANSI-defined standard for high-speed fibre-optic cable communications with transmission speeds of 100 Mbps to 10 Gbps.

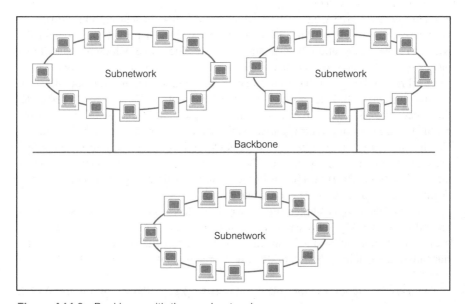

Figure A14.6 Backbone with three subnetworks

Cluster

including: cluster controller
is a group of computers in the same physical area, possibly on a network. A cluster sharing resources will usually be organised less formally than most networks. A *cluster controller* is the computer acting as controller for the cluster. See also *network controller*, page 127.

Gateway

including: bridge
is a computer system that links two dissimilar computer networks. Gateways usually provide a single point of entry to a secure computer network. The gateway converts data passing through it into the appropriate form for the second network. The gateway can monitor usage and also limit access between the networks to authorised users. In an Internet protocol-based network, a *firewall* (see page 147) provides most of the functions of a gateway.

A *bridge* provides a link between two local area networks. It may also convert the data into the appropriate form for the other system. It is simply a link, and there is no concept of it providing an entrance to a computer network.

Token ring network

including: token, Cambridge ring
is a *ring network* (see page 119) in which information is sent around the ring as variable-sized packets of data. In addition to the data, a packet will contain the address of the sender and the destination address. The *token*, which is a signal that passes round the network, can be thought of as a carrier for the packet. For a packet to travel round the ring, it has to be attached to a token. This is a method of avoiding data packets colliding on the ring and creating unreadable signals. In principle, the packet travels round the ring, attached to the token, until it is taken off at the destination address or it returns unread to the sender, where it is taken off as unread. The token then becomes free and continues round the ring ready to have another package attached to it by one of the network devices. The token continually circulates around the ring, picking up, carrying and dropping off packets at their destinations. Generally, there is only one token.

A *Cambridge ring* is a token ring network that has a number of tokens travelling around the network passing each device at equal time intervals. A network device wishing to send a packet simply attaches it to the first available free token. The data-transmission capacity of a Cambridge ring is much greater than a simple token ring network.

The network topology for token ring networks is shown in Figure A14.4, page 120.

Virtual network

including: virtual private networking (VPN)
is a network in which a specified group of computers can communicate with each other without detecting the presence of other stations on the physical network. Several virtual networks could share the same physical connections, without the user realising that any of the other virtual networks exist. Similarly, a virtual network could exist across several local area networks, or even across the Internet, but other stations could not get access to it. See also *Intranet*, page 103, and *station*, page 126.

The stations on a virtual network have specific individual network addresses. The security software that manages the virtual network ensures that communication is permitted only with other stations on the same virtual network.

Virtual private networking (VPN) is one way of implementing a virtual network by ensuring two-way secure communications between the stations. The virtual private networking system allows a client station to communicate with the server, using the Internet, to verify authenticity. The data are *encrypted* (see page 150) during transmission over the Internet. It provides extra security compared with ordinary communications.

Network number

including: station number
is the unique number assigned to a network when it is set up. All computers on the network have their own *station number* within the network, which is assigned through software. In addition, the *network interface* (see *interface*, page 356, and *interface card*, page 363) fitted in the computer has a unique number permanently stored in it. Communication between networks requires these unique numbers to ensure that messages get to the correct station in the correct network, since it is now possible for any network to communicate with any other network.

Ethernet

including: Ethernet hub, switched hub, router, repeater, wireless access point, media converter
is a popular general-purpose *local-area network* (see page 118). Different types of computer system can use the network, even at the same time. Network interfaces are available from many manufacturers. It uses wire connections, wireless links or fibre-optic cable. The software that makes up the *network operating system* (see page 127) has to be bought separately. Ethernet networks are used frequently in offices and schools. The transmission rate is usually 100 Mbp, although faster systems are available.

Ethernet networks consist of groups of computers usually linked to hubs in a *star configuration* (see page 120). These hubs are then linked together to form the local area network. See also Figure A14.6 for an example of a modern network.

The local-area networks can be linked to telecommunications systems using *gateways* (see page 122). The Internet is the ultimate example of a wide-area network formed in this way.

Ethernet networks are constructed from different types of networking components, including the following:

Ethernet hubs allow any two computers connected to the hub, or though other hubs, to send data to each other. A simple hub can deal with only one link at a time and can be slow if many computers are using the same hub.

Switched hubs act as hubs but have extra 'switching circuitry', which allows them to deal with many connections simultaneously. They are much more efficient than simple hubs.

Routers are sophisticated switched hubs. They hold information about the addresses of computers attached to the network and can forward data efficiently to the correct location via an appropriate route. They are generally used as *gateways* (see page 122), where a local-area network is connected to a larger network such as the Internet.

Repeaters are used to link two cable segments. Because of the loss of signal strength in network cables, a repeater amplifies the signals it receives before passing them on.

Wireless access points are hubs on the local area network. Any computer with a wireless network interface, which is within range, can communicate with the local-area network by radio to the wireless access point.

Media converters change the physical signals where different types of network link meet, for example between fibre-optic cable and twisted-pair cable.

Peer-to-peer network

is a simple network that provides shared resources, such as printers and storage, but may offer little else in the way of additional facilities, such as file security. The name comes from the fact that all the computers on these networks have equal status and can send data to and from each other. For example, one station may send data to another station, which can then print out the data, acting as a printer server. Similarly, one station can send data to another for storage on that station's disk drive. See also *server*, below, and *terminal*, page 126.

Client–server network

is a network organised around one or more *servers*. The server maintains a database of authorised users, passwords and access rights. Usually, but not always, a server also acts as a *file server*, but its prime function is to provide the security for the network. See also *server*, below, and *terminal*, page 126.

Network relationship

including: peer-to-peer relationship, client–server relationship
describes the way in which two computer systems work together when attached to the same network. Most networks operate with a mixture of network relationships depending on the functions being performed. The relationships can be either *peer-to-peer* or *client–server*.

Peer-to-peer relationship is a method of network organisation in which *network stations* (or *clients*, see *terminal*, page 126) can share resources on other network stations, so one station can use a printer on another station or save data on another station's local storage. There is no concept of the resource being owned by one station and then being given to other stations. This is simple but has the disadvantage that the data are not centrally organised or controlled, leading to duplication and errors.

Client–server relationship is a method of network organisation in which *network stations* (or *clients*, see *terminal*, page 126) make use of resources available at one or more *servers* (see below). The resource can be hardware (such as a printer), data (such as a database) or a software application. Many network organisations can operate with a client–server relationship. For example, this kind of organisation is seen in a *star network* (see page 120), in which one computer has the role of managing a particular resource for the network. One advantage of a client–server relationship is that the server does the required processing, with only the results being sent to the client, thus reducing network traffic. Another advantage is that the resource is in one place, and there are no problems caused by its physical distribution.

PART A

Server

including: file server, printer server, CD-ROM server, database server, Internet server, Web server, application server, terminal services server, mail server
is a computer on a *network* (see page 118) that provides a resource that can be used by any authorised *client station* (see *terminal*, page 126). There are a number of types of server:

A *file server* provides central disk storage for any users of the network. The file server software identifies each user's files separately so that other users cannot use them. Users can access their own files from any client station on the network or, given suitable *access rights* (see page 149), they can access other users' data.

A *printer server* allows all the client stations to use a printer controlled by it, and usually provides the facilities of a *print spooler* (see page 342).

A *CD-ROM server* allows all the client stations to obtain data from a CD-ROM disk currently being used by the CD-ROM server computer. Often a CD-ROM server will have access to many CD-ROM disks, either from a collection of several CD-ROM players or from a *CD-ROM jukebox* (see page 180).

A *database server* manages a large database. Client stations can access data in the database and, if authorised, can maintain the database. The server usually carries out the database processing, with the query being sent by a client station to the server and the results being assembled by the server and returned to the client station. This form of *client–server relationship* (see page 125) can ensure the consistency of the database, even in the simpler environment of a *peer-to-peer network* (see page 124).

An *Internet server* manages access to the Internet for all the users of the network. However, it is often called a *proxy server* (see page 147), since it usually combines the additional security features of a proxy server. It often provides a cache of Internet pages, which are pages stored when first accessed so they can be supplied later without the delay of accessing the Internet.

A *Web server* provides Internet pages for other computers through the Internet.

An *application server* stores application software (such as a word-processor program). Each time a user wants to use the software, it is copied temporarily from the server, making it easy to update the software centrally and to monitor its usage.

A *terminal services server* is a powerful server that both stores and runs the application software over the network for client stations. The software is not copied to the client station. See also *thin client*, under *terminal*, below.

A *mail server* manages the electronic mail for the network. It provides the users with e-mail addresses, stores incoming e-mails until collected by users, and sends outgoing e-mails to their destinations.

Any expensive resource can be made available to a large number of users by a server. A specialised example is a weather-station server obtaining and distributing current local-instrument readings or satellite weather data.

Terminal

also called: network terminal
including: network station, station, client station, thin client, point-of-sale (POS) terminal
is a computer or computer-controlled device that provides a user with access to a network. A network may have a variety of different kinds of equipment connected to it. For example, a supermarket network will probably have standard computers for its offices as well as the point-of-sale terminals (the checkouts) all connected on the same network. This may be linked to a wider network for the whole supermarket chain.

Network stations are any desktop computer terminals on the network that are available for use by users of the network. They are sometimes simply called *stations*; on a *client–server network* (see page 124), they are called *client stations*.

Thin clients are *client stations* that rely on a server to do the processing required. They have just enough computer power to process the input (keyboard and mouse) and display and to communicate with the network. The thin client does not store any data, and it cannot function without the network link to the server. This means that thin clients are very cheap and easily replaced if faulty, but they do require a powerful server. See *client–server relationship* (page 125).

Point-of-sale (POS) terminals are the specialised terminals used at supermarket checkouts. A point-of-sale terminal will have a variety of functions, which may include *electronic funds transfer* (see page 78) and *bar-code scanning* (see page 175) combined with getting the costs from a database on the network to produce the customer's bill.

Distributed processing

is the sharing of data-processing tasks between physically separated processors on a network.

Network controller

including: controller
is a computer dedicated to organising a computer network. It handles the communications between users and the shared resources, such as disks and printers. Some network arrangements (topologies), such as a *star network* (see page 120), in which the central computer is the network controller, can operate only with a controller; other arrangements may not use a controller. See also *server*, page 125.

Controller is sometimes used to mean a network controller, but it normally means a computer used in control applications to monitor *sensors* and control *actuators*, see page 130.

Network operating system

including: Appletalk, Novell Netware, Windows NT, UNIX
is the software needed to enable a computer to communicate with other computers (stations) using a network. All computers on a network must have the same network operating system software to be able to communicate through the network. Additional software is required for any servers. In particular, a file server needs additional software to enable it to provide secure data storage for users. Widely used network operating systems include *Appletalk*, *Novell Netware*, *Windows NT* and *UNIX*.

Host computer

is a computer used to control a multiuser, multi-access or distributed computer system. In particular, the term is applied to computers that provide access to the Internet. A host computer manages the communications and storage needs of its users, who may be subscribers to an *Internet service provider* (see page 107).

Network accounting software

provides statistics about the use of a network by its users. This may be about the use made of terminals on a multiuser computer system or about the use of facilities on a *peer-to-peer network* (see page 124). The information can be used to charge users for their use of resources or to monitor improper use of the network.

The information recorded can include such things as the connection time and the processor time used, a list of times and dates when the computer has been used on a multiuser system, disk storage space used, printer use, and e-mail use on a peer-to-peer network.

The accounting software can present the overall activity on the network in a variety of ways (tables, graphs or a log) and thus assist the network manager in optimising the system and, possibly, devising charging structures.

Value-added network service (VANS)

is a wide-area network with additional facilities such as a centrally provided database or information system for which users pay charges, which are usually based on their use of the facilities.

Workstation

is either a *station* on a network (see *terminal*, page 126) or a location where a computer, with its associated equipment, is used, such as a designer's work area; this kind of workstation may or may not be on a network.

Control and Monitoring

Other terms related to the use of computers in controlling processes and devices will be found in D5 Communications Technology.

The use of computers to make machines do what we want them to – called **control** – grew out of the extensive use of mechanical devices and electromagnetic switches (relays). In telephone exchanges, traffic lights and lifts, control used to be achieved by the use of mechanically operated switching systems. Other methods were designed to control the operation of machines, made up of devices that reacted to conditions in the environment, such as temperature, pressure, speed and position. Large manufacturing plants that were controlled by these methods were built.

The development of microprocessors and microcomputers made it possible to improve the reliability of existing systems and to make them more flexible. In a modern airliner, the computer system is capable of controlling take-off and landing as well as automatically maintaining course, speed and altitude. The computers used in cars take over part of the control of the car engine from the driver. The operation of washing machines and video equipment is frequently managed by microprocessors.

Control may be exercised remotely, in which case control signals are sent from the controller to the device. These signals may be transmitted in any of the ways that are used to pass data, for example through wires or as radio or infrared signals.

Control systems may be either passive or reactive. In a **passive system**, the controlled device, once it has been set going, will perform a predetermined set of activities regardless of the circumstances. A **reactive system** will vary its behaviour in response to different situations. By using programmable chips, connected to suitable sensors, it is now common for systems to respond to the information provided by these sensors. Combining control and observation, through the use of sensors, has made it possible to extend the scope of automatic **process control**, for example in the manufacture and packaging of chemical products.

Automation

is the use of machines or systems to perform tasks as an alternative to using people.

Actuator

is any device that can be operated by signals from a computer or control system causing physical movement, for example devices for opening windows in a computer-controlled ventilation system.

Servo mechanism

also known as: servo
is a mechanical mechanism for remote control of machines. A simple form is the motors that operate the control surfaces of a radio-controlled model aircraft, where the person flying the model plays an active part, continuously adjusting the position of the control levers. Servos can be controlled electronically through computer circuits, which may incorporate feedback to achieve automatic control; in these situations, human participation may be very limited.

Data capture

including: sampling, data logging
is the *sampling* (collection at specified intervals) of output from external sensors (see also *polling*, page 359). These data may be used to control a process. *Data logging* is the capture and storage of data for later use; thus, data captured in a control process may be logged for later analysis of the process.

Feedback

including: closed-loop feedback, open-loop feedback
is the use of data from sensors as input to the controlling program. In this way, the result of previous actions becomes input, which contributes to selecting the next action. If the response to the feedback is automatic (there is no human operator involvement), then the process is called *closed loop*; if an operator is involved, then it is called *open loop*. In most situations where feedback is used to control position, for example stacking boxes on shelves, the correct position is achieved by an iterative process, in which a move is followed by a position check, each move bringing it closer to the required position, until the correct position is reached.

Fly by wire

is a method of controlling an aeroplane in flight. The flaps, rudder and other control surfaces of the aeroplane are operated by motors. These motors are controlled by (electrical) signals, which are created as a result of actions by the pilot. This kind of flight-control system involves the use of computers to analyse the pilot's intentions and thus work out the right amount of movement of the control surfaces; the computers can override the pilot in situations that would endanger the aeroplane.

G-code

is a form of *intermediate code* (see page 294) that can be used by the control systems of machine tools.

Numeric control

also called: computer numeric control (CNC)
generally refers to the automatic control of machines such as lathes and milling machines. Some numerically controlled machines simply obey a preset programme of instructions, while more advanced machines can react to *feedback* (see above) from *sensors* (see page 132).

Paper tape

including: paper tape punch, paper tape reader
is sometimes still used as the means of program and data input to machine tools. A pattern of holes punched in the tape is used to represent the data. In order to prepare the tape, a *paper tape punch* is attached to the computer on which the program and data are prepared, while a *tape reader* is used as an input device to the machine tool.

Process control

including: integrated manufacturing
is the automatic monitoring and control of an industrial activity by a computer that is programmed to respond to the *feedback* (see above) signals from *sensors* (see page 132). The operation controlled may be as small as a single machine packing boxes or as extensive as the control of an automated bakery, where the mixing, cooking and packaging are controlled within a single *integrated manufacturing* process.

Robot

including: robot arm
is a computer-controlled mechanical device that is sufficiently flexible to be able to do a variety of tasks. Robots are frequently used to do jobs where consistent performance is required (such as paint-spraying motor cars) or where there is some danger to humans performing the task (such as the handling of toxic materials). A *robot arm* is a relatively simple fixed robot capable of picking things up, positioning them, etc.

PART A

Sensor

including: analogue sensor, digital sensor, passive device, active device
is a *transducer* (see page 211) that responds to some physical property, such as pressure, rate of flow, humidity or the proximity of ferrous metal. The electrical output from the sensor may be either analogue (an *analog sensor*) or digital (a *digital sensor*). Some sensors, called *passive devices*, require no external electrical source. Those that require an external voltage are called *active devices*.

Stepper motor

sometimes: stepping motor
is an electric motor that moves in small rotational steps. Suitably controlled and geared, a stepper motor can provide very small discrete movements, for example the movement of the paper rollers and the print head in a printer. The control circuits may involve the use of *feedback* (see page 130).

Telemetry

is the use of communications (usually radio) and measuring sensors to achieve control of machines and instruments at a distance, for example the control of satellites and space probes, or the monitoring and control of the performance of Formula 1 racing cars, where the technicians can adjust the engine control system on the car from the pits while the race is in progress.

Artificial Intelligence and Expert Systems

Artificial intelligence (AI) is a recognised discipline within computer science. It attempts to design software (sometimes with associated hardware) that behaves in a way that, if it were human behaviour, would be described as 'intelligent'.

The earliest artificial intelligence systems, in the 1960s, concentrated on such activities as playing chess and proving (mathematical) theorems. However, the techniques are now being applied to aspects of behaviour not normally thought of as requiring great intelligence, such as recognising objects, understanding simple text, speech recognition and general visual interpretation.

These activities, although often relatively straightforward for people, are, in fact, not so straightforward for computers. It is a challenging problem to write programs for a computer to perform these activities – so much so that we are still far from writing the programs successfully, except in the most simple cases.

One recent development in artificial intelligence is neural networks. These draw from and emulate the structure of the brain in terms of neurons. The networks are made to 'learn' from training sessions and then repeat what has been learnt when given new data.

An **expert system**, sometimes known as an **Intelligent Knowledge-Based System (IKBS)**, is an example of an 'intelligent' system applied to a real-life application. The computer performs at or near the level of human experts.

Examples of expert systems include PROSPECTOR, which advises geologists when they are out in the field. The system asks for certain data about the environment where the geologist is considering drilling bore-holes and provides advice based on this data and on 'knowledge' already stored in its knowledge base.

Other well-known expert systems include XCON, which gives advice on how to configure a VAX computer system – that is, how to make sure the correct units are specified and how they should be connected together for a certain application. There are a number of systems in the medical area; one of the better known is MYCIN, which gives advice on which drugs to use for certain types of bacterial infection.

Artificial intelligence (AI)

is the study and development of computing applications for tasks that would be described as requiring intelligence if they were done by people. Many of these applications involve systems capable of learning, adaptation or self-correction.

Cognitive science

covers a wide range of subjects that are concerned with the thinking processes (cognition) and are, to a great extent, people-oriented. Some, such as *artificial intelligence* (see page 134), computer vision and *human–computer interaction* (see page 59), are concerned with computers. Others are concerned with how people function; for example, cognitive psychology, which includes the study of the mental processes of memory, language processing and vision. Some cognitive scientists find it helpful to describe how humans function in terms of a computer model of information processing.

Neural net

is artificial intelligence software that allows a system to learn to recognise features or characteristics of situations that are input to it. The technique is based on a model of the logical properties of interconnected sets of nerve cells.

A neural net is made up of a network of very many junctions, or nodes. Each of these nodes will 'learn' features according to its input. Once the learning phase is completed, the neural net can be used to recognise features of the same type that were presented to it originally.

Neural nets have been used for visual recognition and for financial prediction.

Pattern recognition

is the process of identifying objects in a digitised picture, or in some cases digitised sounds, through analysis of the digital representation of the objects and comparison with stored knowledge about similar objects.

Cybernetics

including: robotics
is the study of the control of processes by a computer, for example an industrial process or a robot. *Robotics* is the study and design of robots. See also A15 *Control*, page 129, and *robot*, page 131.

Expert system

also known as: (Intelligent) Knowledge-Based System (IKBS), (KBS)
including: knowledge base, heuristics, rulebase, knowledge engineer, knowledge acquisition, knowledge elicitation, explanation, inference engine, shell
is an application of artificial intelligence to a particular area of activity where traditional human expert knowledge and experience are made available through a computer package.

Knowledge base is that part of an expert system that holds knowledge about the application area (or domain), such as drug side effects. Much of the knowledge is held as `IF...THEN...` type rules. For example:

`IF` a patient has high blood pressure
`AND` is anaemic
`THEN` avoid the use of a certain kind of drug.

From time to time, the knowledge base is updated.

Heuristics are rules that are not derived purely from logic but are derived from the experience of a person. These are known as 'rules of thumb'. Many of the rules in an expert system are of this type.

Rulebase is the part of the knowledge base that is made up of all the rules known to the expert system.

Knowledge engineers are the people who collect the information in the knowledge base. This information is collected from a variety of sources in a variety of ways; one of the most important is collecting information through talking to experts. The knowledge obtained is then formulated as a set of rules and facts.

Knowledge acquisition or *knowledge elicitation* is the process of gathering information for inclusion in a knowledge base.

Once the knowledge base has been constructed, the expert system is ready to be interrogated or consulted. The system requests the user to provide information and then searches the knowledge base to find appropriate advice for the user.

Explanations can be requested by the user. The system will provide the user with the reasoning behind the advice given. This is often in the form of a list of the rules tested by the system.

Inference engine (or *inference processor*) is a piece of software in an expert system that does the searching of the knowledge base. Searching the knowledge base uses standard searching methods that are independent of the application, for example a top-down or a bottom-up search.

Shell is a piece of software that is an 'empty' expert system without the knowledge base for any particular application. The user enters the appropriate rules and facts.

Expert systems have a clearly identifiable internal structure, which is illustrated in Figure A16.1.

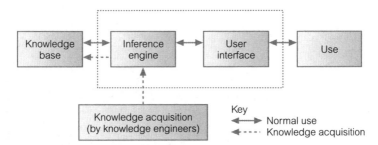

Figure A16.1 Expert system structure

The user communicates with the system through the user interface, which passes requests for advice to the inference engine. The inference engine processes the request, obtaining information – rules and facts – from the knowledge base as required and finally returns the answer to the user interface, and hence to the user.

In the knowledge-acquisition phase, the inference engine stores the information from the knowledge engineers in the knowledge base.

Computer Personnel

Further definitions related to the area of human–computer interaction are found in section A7 User Interface and Documentation.

The demand by people for information is the main reason why computers are needed. People who ask for systems and use them are normally not computer experts. The people who respond to users' requirements come from a wide range of computer personnel who specify systems, design and build systems, develop and enhance existing systems, implement systems, and manage them.

In many organisations, there has been an increase in both the number and the types of task that computers have been required to perform. This expansion of use has to be managed in a controlled and professional manner. Many computer-related job descriptions and responsibilities have changed, and many users' jobs have also been affected.

A **data controller** (previously designated as a data protection officer), to be responsible for ensuring that an organisation's notification complies with the requirements of the UK *Data Protection Act 1998*, should be appointed (see page 143).

Many large organisations have changed their operational methods; instead of employing a team or teams of information technology (IT) specialists, they have contracts with outside firms who agree to supply these specialist staff as and when required. This is known as **outsourcing**.

This section gives an indication of the types of computer-related work and offers a brief description of some of the jobs involved. A more detailed description of the wide range of IT roles, and the skill levels and competencies involved, can be obtained by examining the British Computer Society's **BCS Skills Manager**. The roles described in this section of the glossary fall roughly into three categories: systems development, including programming; information management; and support.

Systems development personnel

including: developer, programmer, systems programmer, applications programmer, information systems engineer, systems engineer, coder, systems analyst, systems designer, analyst/designer, software engineer, Web site developer, Web master

Developer, or *Programmer*, is the person responsible for writing and testing computer programs. Those involved in the writing of operating systems, general utilities (such as printer drivers) and specialist tools (such as a graphical user interface) are usually called *systems programmers*. Those writing programs for specific needs or user applications, such as database management systems, are known as *applications programmers*.

Those programmers working on the design and testing of computer systems, hardware as well as software, are often called *information systems engineers*, or *systems engineers*, whilst those who are involved mostly in translating statements into machine-readable form are called *coders*.

Systems analyst is the person responsible for the analysis of a system to assess its suitability both for computerisation and for any changes or upgrades to existing systems. Where change is decided upon, the *systems designer* will be responsible for building on the analyst's results to create the new computer-based system and will normally work up to the point where programmers can sensibly take over. People who are responsible for both the analysis and the new system design are referred to as *analyst/designer*.

Software engineer normally works as part of a team on a large installation and will have skills in a specialist area. However, they may be expected to undertake any of the roles from systems analysis, through design, implementation and testing, and including project management. They may be responsible for the design or enhancement of computer systems. They are also often employed in designing and implementing the software in *embedded systems* (see page 4).

Web site developers design and develop Web sites and Web pages. This involves designing not only the appearance and content but also the function to strict performance criteria. For example, a customer accessing a sales site should be able to explore information about products and place orders with ease, confident that credit-card or bank-account details are, and will remain, secure. A team designing Web sites will include people with artistic skills as well as systems designers with technical skills and experience. The *Web master* will be responsible for maintenance of and updating a Web site.

Information management personnel

including: data-processing manager, information manager, database administrator, database manager, information officer, decision-support specialist, data-entry staff

Data-processing manager is the person responsible for the overall running of a data-processing department. *Information manager* is the term for the person who manages the interface between the computer system and the organisation's user community.

Database administrator, also known as *database manager* or *information officer*, is the person in an organisation responsible for the structure and control of the data in the organisation's databases. See also *database management system*, page 89.

Decision-support specialist is responsible for organising database-interrogation procedures to allow business managers to access management information in appropriate formats.

Data-entry staff are those responsible for organising and entering data into the computer system. Data entry is increasingly undertaken as part of other jobs, such as administration, or by automated methods.

Data controller

is the named person in an organisation who is responsible for seeing that the organisation's registration is adhered to under the UK *Data Protection Act 1998* (see page 143).

User support personnel

including: technical support staff, software support staff, helpdesk, hotline
are those people involved in the day-to-day running of an organisation's computing installation and who respond to queries from computer users.

Technical support staff are computer specialists who are concerned with the integrity and functionality of the computer system. They may be hardware rather than software-oriented.

Software support staff are usually employed by software houses or specialist vendors in order to respond to questions relating to the use of particular pieces of software. Support staff are often referred to as a *helpdesk* and may be contacted quickly using the telephone *hotline* to give advice on problem solving.

Systems support personnel

including: network manager, computer operator, computer service engineer, computer engineers, maintenance engineers, service engineers
are those people who deliver, operate and monitor the computer systems in an organisation. These include the following:

Network manager is the person with overall responsibility for the smooth running of a network. This will generally include communications (software and hardware), access (user identifications and passwords) and shared resources, such as common data storage.

Computer operator is the person responsible for the operation and monitoring of larger computer systems, including back-up and archiving. Where appropriate, they respond to requests, which may be from the operating system or from remote users in a networked or time-sharing system.

Computer service engineer is the person responsible for the maintenance of the hardware and is often employed by a specialist servicing company under contract. They are also known as *computer engineers*, *maintenance engineers* and *service engineers*.

PART A

BCS Skills Manager

is a software package that sets out roles in IT work and details what is expected of a person performing computer-related tasks at each stage in a variety of career paths. An individual may have several roles within his or her job. The Skills Manager is designed and maintained by the British Computer Society. For more information, see the BCS Web site: www.bcs.org.uk

# Computer Security, Abuse and Related Law

This section includes terms from legal aspects of computing and terms relating to the security and control of data in computer systems.

Modern society is very dependent on computer systems and the data they contain. This dependence provides opportunities for antisocial behaviour, ranging from the annoying to the criminal. This section considers security measures and legislation that attempt to deal with computer abuse.

Computer abuse describes a wide range of behaviour, such as:

- unfair use of personal data, for example cross-referencing that reveals new, unrelated and perhaps embarrassing information;
- electronic vandalism, in which software or data are damaged deliberately, or where the operation of the computer system is affected;
- creation of viruses that cause random damage to software or data;
- theft of valuable information.

These problems are dealt with through the deterrent effect of legal punishment under the *Data Protection Act* and the *Computer Misuse Act* and through using a variety of security measures to make abuse difficult.

The *Data Protection Act* protects individuals from unreasonable use of their stored personal data. These data may be very embarrassing or perhaps could be used for blackmail – even if the individual has done nothing illegal. Computer data are potentially more dangerous than paper documents because:

- data can be retrieved electronically from a computer anywhere in the world;
- data can be searched very quickly to find patterns that are not obvious but that could be personally damaging or embarrassing;
- data from a range of computers can be combined, so apparently unrelated data can produce damaging information.

The *Computer Misuse Act* defines electronic vandalism, unauthorised access to computer systems and theft of information. It makes these activities criminal. There are penalties for individuals who attempt to interfere with another person's use of computers, such as:

- hackers, who try to beat security measures as a 'game';
- vandals who damage the software or data of a computer;
- virus writers, whose viruses can cause damage at random;
- thieves who break into computer systems to gain access to valuable information.

Security measures that can be taken may use either physical or software methods. **Physical** methods include:

- providing workstations with locks or keycards to prevent unauthorised use;
- locking offices containing workstations;
- positioning screens so that visitors are not able to see their contents;

Security measures using **software** include:

- using screen savers to hide the contents of the screen if the user leaves the workstation;
- using passwords to ensure that users are authorised;
- ensuring passwords are changed frequently;
- limiting the range of tasks that can be carried out at a particular workstation;
- setting access rights so that only some users can carry out some operations;
- having barriers (such as firewalls) to restrict access to a computer system by external users.

In addition to data protection and computer misuse legislation, there are also copyright laws that enable software producers to protect their investment in software development. These laws provide the means to penalise people who copy or use software without permission.

Computer systems in manufacturing, real-time processes and safety-critical applications need to meet particular design standards, and their implementation may have to conform to quality-assurance standards. Product liability and consumer protection legislation, particularly in the USA, imposes severe penalties on the producers of poor-quality computer products.

Data Security

Data protection

including: data consistency, inconsistent data, data integrity, data privacy, data security
is ensuring that data are correct and are kept confidential and safe. These concepts apply to all data, not just data that are confidential or about individual people.

Data can be corrupted, taken or lost in many different and unexpected ways, both by accident and by design. It is essential that these are prevented as far as possible and that the data can be recovered if required. Failing to protect data can be disruptive and often is very expensive.

Data protection involves the following issues:

Data consistency is the relationship between the input data, the processed data and the output data, as well as other related data items. If the system is working properly, the data will be correct at each stage (allowing for the processing done) and are said to be consistent.

Inconsistent data are found either when the result of a process is wrong or if two pieces of related data have the wrong relationship. For example, if a person's recorded age is not the same as their age when calculated using their date of birth, then this would be inconsistent. This inconsistency could be caused by the age or the date of birth being input wrongly, an error in the calculation program or a variety of technical faults.

Data integrity describes the correctness of data both during and after processing. Data may be changed by the processing but will still have integrity. Safeguards are needed to make sure that the data have integrity by detecting any accidental or malicious change to the data. See also *corruption*, page 329.

Data privacy is the requirement that data are to be accessed by, or disclosed to, only authorised persons. The *Data Protection Act* (see below) provides legal protection for individuals' data. Data privacy requires systems managers to build safeguards into their systems (both physical arrangements and software checks) to reduce the risk of unauthorised access.

Data security involves the use of various methods to make sure that data are correct and are kept confidential and safe (providing data protection). Data security includes ensuring the integrity and the privacy of data as well as preventing the loss or destruction of the data. An important part of data security is planning to ensure reliable backing up of the data and testing that the data can be restored effectively. See also *back up*, page 81.

Data Protection Act 1998

including: data controller, Information Commissioner, data-protection principles, data subject, sensitive personal data
is the UK Act of Parliament that sets out requirements for the control of stored data about living individuals, both on computer systems and in other forms (such as paper). The Act covers many aspects of data privacy (see *data protection*, above). The Act also defines *data controllers*, the individuals who are responsible for the uses made of the computerised data.

Data controllers are required to notify the *Information Commissioner*, providing details about the data they hold for the data-protection register. This register enables any individual to find out whether personal data relating to them are likely to be held, and they have the right to ask for a copy of the data from the data controller. If the data are incorrect, then the individual (as the *data subject*) is entitled to ask the data controller to have the data corrected.

The Act provides special protection for *sensitive personal data*, such as an individual's race, politics, religion, trade union membership, health, criminal record and sexual orientation. The few exemptions under the Act relate mainly to data held for certain limited purposes by government agencies, the police, the courts and the security services. There are also some exemptions for data intended for use by journalists or broadcasters.

The 1998 Act defines eight *data-protection principles*, which are given here in a simplified form:

1. Data should be processed fairly and lawfully (for example, there should be no deception in the collection of the information, and the subject should be told how the data will be used).

2. Data should be used or disclosed only for the specified notified purposes.

3. Data should be adequate, relevant and not excessive.

4. Data should be accurate and kept up to date.

5. Data should not be kept for any longer than necessary.

6. Access must be provided for individuals to check and correct their data, with a right of explanation when a computer takes automated decisions based on the data.

7. Security measures should prevent unauthorised access to, or alteration of, the data.

8. Data should not be transferred outside the European Community, except to countries with adequate data-protection legislation.

The Act applies only to data about living individuals, known as 'personal data'. The 1998 Act replaces a 1984 Act with new legislation, to comply with European Union requirements. There are many changes, and the Act was extended to cover non-computer data such as paper records.

Computer abuse

has no legal definition, but it is generally taken to be the wrongful use of computer systems and software for improper, antisocial or illegal purposes. Examples of computer abuse are the spreading of *viruses* (see page 152), data terrorism (actions against computer systems and data), computer-based fraud and computer pornography. Almost all examples of computer abuse involve breaches of laws such as the *Data Protection Act* (see page 143) and the *Computer Misuse Act* (see below).

Computer Misuse Act 1990

including: computer misuse
is the UK Act of Parliament aimed specifically at *hackers* (see *hacking*, below). It defines *computer misuse* as the unauthorised use of computer systems and relates

both to hardware (for example, using a computer without permission) and software (for example, accessing parts of a computer system without authorisation). The Act created new offences relating to unauthorised computer access and the unauthorised access to, the modification of, or the deletion of data.

Hacking

including: hacker
is attempting (with or without success) to gain unauthorised access to a computer system. This may be the unauthorised use of a computer or simply unauthorised access to particular programs or data stored on a computer (see *access rights*, page 149). A *hacker* is someone experienced in attempting to gain unauthorised access into computer systems.

Hacking often involves an unplanned approach to the attack on the computer system and the use of unusual and complicated techniques to solve problems as they arise. The term 'hacking' is also used to describe this approach when applied to the design and use of a computer system. The resulting software is prone to errors and is difficult to fix and maintain.

Digital signature

also known as: electronic signature
is part of a message that is specially encrypted and is used to indicate that the sender of the message is who they claim to be. If the recipient of the message can decipher the digital signature correctly, then forged data are unlikely to have been substituted. The digital signature confirms the identity of the sender; it does not encrypt the information. The message (including the electronic signature) will usually be encrypted again so the content is hidden as well. See also *digital certificate*, below, and *public key cryptography*, page 151.

Digital certificate

including: certificate, certification authority, trusted service provider, trusted third party
is an encrypted message provided by a certification authority that confirms that the individual is who they claim to be in an on-line communication. It includes a *digital signature* (see above), which can be confirmed by sending a secure message to the certification authority.

The *certification authority*, also known as a *trusted service provider* or a *trusted third party*, is a business that provides on-line certification facilities. These organisations are trusted to check the identity of the on-line users and provide them with

PART A

encrypted messages (the certificates) that can be confirmed by checking the certificate with the certification authority.

Key escrow

is a method of storing *cryptographic keys* (see page 151) to electronic communications so they are accessible to authorised agencies (usually governments). The keys to electronic communications are stored by an independent company, which will release them to appropriate government agencies in certain circumstances. This is primarily to allow the police access to criminal communications.

Secure socket layer (SSL)

including: secure electronic transaction (SET)
is a protocol that enables an encrypted link to be created between two computers using the Internet. It protects electronic communications from interception and allows a computer to identify the server it is communicating with. It is the standard security protocol used to provide security for commercial transactions (such as buying goods) taking place over the Internet.

Secure electronic transaction (SET) is a more sophisticated protocol developed by some major international banks. It is not used as widely as the *secure socket layer* protocol.

Firewall

including: personal firewall
is a computer application used in a network to prevent external users gaining unauthorised access to a computer system. A firewall may be software running in the main computer or a separate computer physically located between the system and the external access. It limits the data and instructions that can be received or sent to external users. For example, the firewall could block certain types of data, could allow access only from specific computers or could require additional user identification. It is usually used with a *proxy server*, see page 147. The firewall may restrict authorised users' external access to a small part of the system and may allow limited public access, for example to a Web server. The firewall can prevent a user (including users with limited authorisation) accessing data or executing any programs in the rest of the system.

A *personal firewall* provides the same protection for a personal computer where a single user may be linked to the Internet, a potentially hostile network.

Proxy server

is a computer application that accesses data on a different computer system or network. It controls the access of authorised users to data and allows the operation of the system to be isolated from control by external users. Proxy servers are often also *Internet servers* (see page 126).

This application receives requests from users, verifies them, accesses the required data and communicates the requested information back to the users. External users cannot run programs on the protected system but rely on the proxy server to access data for them. Instructions to the protected system itself are limited to specific types of requests, the effects of which can be controlled. Proxy servers can provide data for both external and internal users. External users cannot access the main system directly, whilst the internal users can be provided with controlled access to external systems, such as the Internet.

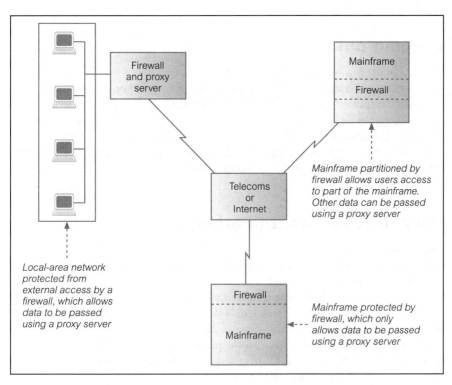

Figure A18.1 Firewalls and proxy servers

Intrusion-detection system (IDS)

monitors the operation of the network and the data transmitted to detect and warn when illegal access is attempted. The system may be server-based, detecting attacks on the operation of the file server, or it may be network based, watching the pattern of traffic across the network.

Logging in

also known as: log in, logging on, log on
is the procedure needed for a user to gain access to a computer system. It might provide access to a computer network, a multiaccess computer system, a specially set-up stand-alone workstation or just a specific application program. Logging in is a part of the security procedures to prevent unauthorised access.

Logging out

also known as: log out, logging off, log off
is the correct procedure to be followed when ending a session on a computer system. It cancels the authority to use the system obtained from the *logging in* procedure (see above). Logging out is a part of the security of the system preventing the work-station or application program being used until an authorised user logs in again. A user may be logged out automatically if the session has not been active for a pre-determined time or the network connection is lost.

User ID (user identification)

also known as: user name
including: password, personal identification device (PID), keycard, swipecard, personal identification number (PIN)
is a unique name or code used to identify a user to a computer system when gaining access (known as *logging on*, see page 148). The *network manager* (see page 139) or systems-management software allocates user IDs to new users.

Checks must be made to verify that the person logging on is the correct 'owner' of the user ID. Methods of establishing and checking include passwords, personal-identification devices and personal identification numbers.

Passwords are words or codes that should be known only to the user. A password is linked to a specific user ID. Although a user ID may generally be known to others, access can be gained only with the correct combination of user ID and password.

Personal identification device (PID) is a computer-readable object (such as a *magnetic stripe card*, see page 000) carrying data that identify the owner and act as an electronic key. This information can be read by a computer and used as a user ID. Unauthorised use is made difficult because a user must physically have the personal identification device. Additional protection can be provided by the use of a *personal identification number* (see below). *Keycard*, or *swipecard*, are other names for a personal identification device in the form of a plastic card. See also *smartcard*, page 174.

Personal identification number (PIN) is a number used as a password, particularly with bank cards and credit cards. For example, a bank card is the personal identification device, which provides the user ID, and is used with a personal identification number to obtain cash from an *automatic teller machine*, page 78.

Biometric

is a unique physical characteristic of an individual that can be checked automatically by a computer. The individual's biometric is measured by a special scanner and used with the *user ID* (see above) in a similar way to a password. Finding physical characteristics that cannot be copied has been difficult, but viable systems include fingerprints, iris scans and retina scans (the pattern of veins at the back of the eye). Face recognition and voiceprints have so far proved to be unreliable for use as biometrics.

Access rights

also known as: network privileges, privileges
including: ownership, password protection
control the extent to which a particular user can use or edit a program or datafile. Each user is assigned access rights that determine whether the user:

■ can access the file;

■ can copy, change or delete the data or file;

■ can read but not edit the data;

■ has no access at all.

Computer support staff may have more comprehensive rights than most users, including the right to alter other users' access rights. Access rights can also restrict the use of a file to a particular workstation or a particular user.

With the simpler operating systems used on stand-alone computers, the actual user may not be identified. The access rights can be changed easily but do provide a way of preventing some mistakes (for example, deleting important files).

The more complex network operating systems provide a way of identifying individuals (for example, by a user ID and password). The extent to which each individual user can access the resources is determined by the access rights (or privileges) set by the network manager. The user may have *ownership* of some files and can then set the access rights to restrict who else can use the files.

Some files have additional access restrictions provided by *password protection*. When a user attempts to gain access to one of these files, an additional *password* (see above) will be requested before access is allowed. This provides extra security since knowing a user's system password is not enough to gain access to the data. The password is often used as part of the *encryption key* (see below) to encrypt the data, making the data meaningless even if unauthorised access to the system is achieved.

Authorisation code

is a type of password needed to install or run a piece of software. By providing software that is protected in this way, the supplier can ensure that the software is used only by authorised users who have been provided with the authorisation code. In some cases, the user's identity is hidden in the code, allowing illegal copies of the software to be traced. This method usually involves some form of encryption.

Encryption

including: scrambled data, decryption, encryption key, decryption key, encryption, enciphering, coding, encoding, deciphering, decoding
makes data in a computer system unintelligible. The encrypted data appear to be meaningless and are sometimes described as *scrambled data*. Encryption provides security for the data (by preventing the data from being understood), both when stored electronically and when transmitted between computer systems. *Decryption* is converting the unreadable data back into an understandable form.

An *encryption key* is a word or code selected by the user to govern the encryption process. A *decryption key* is needed before the data can be understood.

In many systems, both encryption and decryption keys are the same, and therefore all users must have a copy of the key. If the number of users is small and the concern is for the security of stored data, then a single encryption key is usually sufficient. If transmission rather than storage requires extra protection, then different encryption and decryption keys may be used. See *public key cryptography* and *Data Encryption Standard*, below.

The terms *encryption*, *enciphering*, *coding* and *encoding* are often used loosely with the same meaning, as are *decryption*, *deciphering* and *decoding*.

Data Encryption Standard (DES)

including: Advanced Encryption Standard (AES)
is a standard method of encrypting data developed by the US government. The method specifies how a *key* (see *cryptography*, above) is used to encode the message in a standard way.

It was believed that the method was complex enough that the encrypted data could not be decrypted without knowledge of the key, even though the method was known. This meant that the method could be published, allowing computer manufacturers to develop software and hardware to encrypt and decrypt the data. Since it is a standard method, the Data Encryption Standard allows encrypted data to be sent between any computers whose manufacturers have implemented it.

The *Advanced Encryption Standard* (*AES*) algorithm is newer and much more complex. It may eventually replace the Data Encryption Standard.

Public key cryptography

including: public key, private key, one-way functions, trapdoor functions, RSA algorithm

is a very secure encryption method in which different keys are used to encrypt and decrypt the data. The key has two parts, a *public key* and a *private key*, which form a matched pair. The *public key* and *private key* are linked, and data encrypted with one key need to be decrypted with the other key. To send data, the sender uses the known *public key* to encrypt the data. The data can be decrypted only using the *private key*, which only the receiver has.

However, it would be easy to replace a message with a forgery (since the *public key* is well known). To prevent this, a *digital signature* (see page 145) is used. This often uses public key cryptography in reverse: the sender uses their *private key* to encrypt the data, which can be decrypted only using the known *public key*, showing that the sender must have used the *private key* and thus is genuine. To enable large numbers of users to use these digital signatures, they are often managed using *digital certificates*, see page 145.

The principles behind public key cryptography involve complex mathematical functions. Some mathematical operations are easy to do but, in practice, impossible to undo. As a simple example, it is easy to multiply together 11 and 13 to get 143, but it takes an amount of trial and error to work back from 143 to the (only) factors 11 and 13. If the numbers involved had hundreds or thousands of digits, rather than just two, the amount of trial and error involved would mean that even a fast computer might be unable to find the factors in an acceptably short time. Such operations – easy to do but impossible to undo in a realistic time – are known as *one-way functions*. If the operation is one like the multiplication above, where some secret knowledge (like the numbers 11 and 13) provides a shortcut, then they are known as *trapdoor functions*. These can be used as the basis for a simple but secure coding system, as shown in Figure A18.2, page 152. The best-known of these functions was developed by mathematicians Rivest, Shamir and Adleman and is called the *RSA algorithm*.

PART A

	A public directory is published – for everyone in the code system, it tells the whole world what **key** is used to send messages to that person. This is a (big) number that can be used to encode messages. The decoding part is secret: only one person knows it.
	I want to send a message to you. I write my message out, substituting A = 01, B = 02, etc., and get a (long) number that represents my message.
	Now I look up your key in the public directory and use it to turn my message into another long number – this is done in a way that no-one except you can decode – even I can't, unless I look back at my original message.
	You receive my message and, using your very secret decoding method, turn it back into the original message.
	How do you know that the message was really from me? Anyone could look up your key in the public directory and send a misleading message that claimed to be from me. I can prove it was from me, like this:
	With my message, I include my name and address, but before I code this, I use my own secret decoding key to turn the name and address part into a scrambled version.
	Now I code the whole message – the message itself and the previously scrambled name and address.
	You receive this two-part message and use your secret decoder to extract the plain message and the scrambled name and address. You read the message and need to check that it is from me.
	You take the scrambled part, look me up in the directory and see what my public coding key is. Using this will unscramble the name and address, and you are confident that it was from me, because I am the only person in the world who knows what my decoding key is.

Figure A18.2 How a public-key cryptosystem works

Viruses and Malicious Code

Virus

including: payload, infection, parasitic virus, macro virus, e-mail virus, worm
is a program designed to copy itself between and within computers to make a computer system unreliable. The virus includes instructions to do the copying automatically, via a disk or network. The virus may also include instructions to damage data (in the memory or on a disk) or to affect the computer's operation, such as displaying silly messages or filling up the computer's memory. These effects are often referred to as the virus's *payload*. They are often activated when some predetermined

conditions occur, such as on a particular date. Most viruses are specific to a particular operating system.

Infection occurs when a virus has copied itself on to a computer system, usually to its hard disk. Because of the potential damage a virus can cause, it has to be removed; see *anti-virus software*, below.

There is an increasing use of viruses with a malicious purpose. Viruses often exploit weaknesses in the security of either the operating system or the applications software.

Viruses include:

parasitic viruses, which hide themselves by attachment to a file that already exists until a specific event causes the virus to take action;

macro viruses, which attach themselves to the datafiles associated with the more complicated application programs that allow users to add *macro* programs (see page 265) to their documents;

e-mail viruses, which are attached to an e-mail and usually propagate themselves by sending e-mails automatically to contacts in the user's own address book;

worms, which are programs that spread themselves via network connections to other systems. Unlike a traditional virus, a worm does not require a host program or datafile but is a stand-alone executable program that exploits the facilities of the host computer to propagate.

Anti-virus software

also known as: vaccine utility
including: anti-virus monitor, virus checking, disinfection, quarantine, computer hygiene
is used to detect and remove viruses.

Anti-virus monitors are programs loaded permanently in memory and continually monitoring the system for the presence of tell-tale patterns indicating the presence of any of the thousands of viruses that have been identified. If any change is detected, the file is prevented from being run and a warning message is given. New data read into the computer are also screened for viruses and appropriate action taken.

Virus checking scans the files on a computer system to detect viruses.

Disinfection is the removal of viruses that have been detected.

Quarantine is the isolation of a file suspected of containing a virus. The file can then be investigated and the operation of the virus can be analysed.

Computer hygiene is the term used to describe the prevention and cure of problems caused by viruses.

PART A

Trojan horse

also known as: Trojan
including: logic bomb, backdoor Trojan, trapdoor Trojan
is a program that performs a normal process in the computer while also performing
another, possibly harmful process at the same time. Just as parasitic viruses attach
themselves to other files, Trojan programs are often hidden in other valid programs.
Trojans have been used by hackers (see *hacking*, page 145) to copy data from secure
files or to record information about security measures. Types of Trojan programs
include:

logic bombs, which are small programs included within a larger system and designed
to activate when a particular set of circumstances occur. For example, a programmer may include a logic bomb in the system they are developing to cause
damage if their name is deleted from the company payroll. They are used for
revenge attacks and blackmail;

backdoor Trojans, also known as *trapdoor Trojans*, are programs normally left
by a hacker that permit access to a computer system without the use of valid
authentication codes or passwords. They enable the hacker to avoid the computer's normal security systems. See also *trapdoor functions*, page 151.

Copyright

Software copyright

*including: software licence, licence agreement, end-user licence agreement (EULA),
single-user licence, multiuser licence, site licence, public-domain software, freeware,
shareware, concurrent user licence*
is the legal protection that authors and publishers have regarding the use of their
software. It is not always realised that computer software is covered by copyright
laws similar to those that apply to books and other publications. The *Copyright,
Designs and Patents Act* 1988 protects 'intellectual property' and establishes the
rights of the author.

When software is purchased, there will be a *software licence* (also known as the
licence agreement or *end-user licence agreement, EULA*), which sets conditions
for the use of the software. These conditions vary considerably between products.
Any use of the software not allowed by its licence is illegal. In practice, this means
that copying software bought by someone else is likely to be an offence. Special
licences are needed for some cases, for example multiple use on a network.

Various types of licence are used and the specific terms of each licence must be
adhered to. Examples of licence types include the following:

Single-user licence: the software can be used on only one computer. This is the
usual type of licence.

Multiuser licence: an organisation may install the software on an agreed number of
computers. A reduced fee is paid for each computer.

Site licence: any number of computers may use the software at a single location. One payment is made to allow the multiple installation. These are not common outside the UK educational sector.

Public-domain software has a licence waiving all rights and allowing free use of the software. This is a US legal concept that rarely applies in the UK. See *freeware*, below.

Freeware has a licence allowing free use (and usually distribution) of the software. The licence usually does not allow alteration or sale. The author usually provides little, if any, help and support. In the UK, freeware is often called *public-domain software*, see above.

Shareware has a licence allowing free use (and usually distribution) of the software for a trial period. If the user wishes to continue using the software, a fee must be paid, usually in return for improved versions, manuals and support.

Concurrent user licence agreements allow the user to operate the software on an agreed number of computers. The actual computers to be used do not need to be specified, providing that the total number in use at any one time does not exceed the number of licences.

Piracy

also known as: software piracy
including: protected software, unprotected software, dongle, copy protection, installation disk, key disk
is the illegal copying of software, whether for personal use or for resale. Software publishers lose considerable potential income due to illegal copying of their products and take a variety of measures to prevent it.

Protected software is supplied in a form designed to be difficult to copy. It may have copy protection or use a *key disk* (see below). *Unprotected software* has no special precautions against copying and relies on the legal authority of the *software licence* (see above).

Copy protection uses some physical changes to the data on the disk to prevent copies of the disk being made.

Dongle is a piece of hardware used to reduce the possibility of software piracy. It usually plugs into a standard interface on a computer. Without the correct dongle, the protected software will not run.

Installation disks contain the software in encrypted form. The software is copied on to the computer's hard disk before it can be used. The installation program may allow the software to be installed only a limited number of times. It may also make further copying difficult by embedding the owner's name or computer serial number within the installation disks.

Key disk is a floppy disk or CD-ROM disk used to install software that contains credits that are reduced by one on each installation. It may also be a disk that is required every time a program is run to ensure that it can be used by only one computer at a time. See also *software copyright*, above.

PART A

Specialised Computer Applications

Most information technology (IT) involves the use of the computer as a general-purpose tool capable of solving a variety of problems. However, some tasks are quite difficult to do with the standard IT tools of word processors, spreadsheets and databases. Some of these tasks could be done manually, but with the development of suitable computer software often they can be done much more easily using the processing power available in a computer system. The market for these specialised applications is obviously smaller than for general software, but the savings in time and money are sufficiently great, particularly in large organisations, to make it worthwhile for software producers to develop them.

Most specialised computer applications are expensive but are for complicated tasks that have to be repeated many times. To do this, they incorporate functions to load, edit and usually to save data for future use. This is common to most applications, whilst the actual processing will be different.

This section describes some of the more important specialised applications that have been developed.

Accounting package

also known as: finance package

records the use of money in a company or other organisation. A modern organisation is dependent on the accurate recording of financial information, which includes money received (from sales), money paid out (to buy goods or services), wages paid to employees, taxes paid and money transferred between departments within the organisation. Accounting packages can record this information accurately, allowing better use of resources and preventing misuse. Accurate accounting is also required by law to enable taxes to be collected fairly.

Any accounting package will maintain a database of financial transactions and provide spreadsheet-like facilities for financial planning.

Computer-aided design (CAD)

also known as: computer-aided draughting
is the use of a computer system to produce drawings as part of the design of some construction project; this might be the layout of components on a printed circuit board, the civil engineering design of a motorway, or the layout of furniture positions in an office or a home, for example. Most modern CAD packages also use the design data as the basis for calculations – for example, of costs, mechanical stresses, quantities of materials needed, etc. With the information available from the design stage, it is possible in many cases for the computer system to control the manufacturing process as well. See also *computer-assisted manufacturing*, below.

Computer-assisted manufacturing (CAM)

including: CAD/CAM
is the use of a computer system to control the production in a factory, including the supply of components, planning daily production and controlling the machinery involved.

Computer-assisted manufacturing is usually combined with a *computer-aided design* (*CAD*) (see above) system and is often known as *CAD/CAM*. In a CAD/CAM system, the designs are transferred electronically between the design system and the manufacturing system. This allows the machinery to be programmed automatically by the computer-assisted manufacturing system. The combined system becomes an integrated process in which the manufacturing is controlled automatically. This is important in the development of new products and allows minor improvements in the design to be implemented without stopping production.

Computer-aided learning (CAL)

including: computer-based training (CBT), computer-managed instruction (CMI), Computer-managed learning (CML), integrated learning system (ILS)
is the use of a computer to provide instructional information to a student, to pose questions and to react to the student's response.

Computer-based training (*CBT*) is the use of a computer as an instructional system in a training environment. The approach is the same as computer-aided learning, but the learning area is confined to a well-defined training objective.

Computer-managed instruction (*CMI*) is the use of a computer to manage a student's progress through a course of instruction. The student's performance is recorded by the computer, and new modules of instruction are defined or delivered as determined by the curriculum. A computer-managed instruction system may or may not contain computer-aided learning material.

Computer-managed learning (*CML*) is the use of a computer in a similar fashion to computer-managed instruction, but with additional emphasis on providing help, which depends upon the responses given by the student. Some computer-managed learning systems can build up a detailed learning profile for each student. This profile can be used for both reporting and directing the studies of an individual student.

Integrated learning system (*ILS*) is a computer system that combines providing the student with instructional material with monitoring the student's success and speed. This enables the computer to adjust the material presented to the student and provide analyses for the teacher.

Cryptography

including: secret message, cipher
is the science of creating and sending *secret messages*, or *ciphers*. When communicating by code, it is usual for everyone to use the same coding method but to have some personal and secret key that is used by the method in a way that makes the message remain hidden, even if the method is known. Modern cryptographical methods involve complex mathematical calculations to encrypt and decrypt the message. This is usually done by a computer. See also *encryption*, page 150.

Cryptanalysis

including: code breaking
is the analysis of encrypted messages to reveal the original information. This is often known as *code breaking*. Nowadays, this requires many mathematical calculations and is almost always done by computer. Captured cipher messages are analysed to see whether patterns emerge that will indicate the method of coding, after which further analysis may indicate the precise *cipher key* used in the enciphering. In some ways, the cipher key acts as a password to the information. See also *encryption*, page 150.

Geographical information system (GIS)

including: global positioning system (GPS), satellite navigation
stores complex geographical data and presents them as various types of maps. Since the data are stored separately from the map but linked to it, the GIS can easily produce scale maps to the user's requirements and plot the particular data that the user is interested in. This enables the maps to be clearer and relationships between particular types of data to be explored easily.

It is often used in conjunction with the *global positioning system* (*GPS*), which, by measuring the signals from satellites in space, can determine a position to within a few metres, anywhere in the world. These signals are used by *satellite navigation* systems guiding ships and aircraft as well as enabling maps to be constructed that are very accurate (essential for use in geographical information systems).

Management information system (MIS)

including: decision-support system (DSS)

provides understandable amounts of management-level information that individual users might require – such as summaries from larger collections of data. When data are collected, they usually consist of large quantities of simple information and need further processing before they are usable. This type of processed information may typically be used by managers as an aid to monitoring budgets, assessing sales targets or making business decisions.

Decision-support systems (*DSS*) are refined *management information systems* in which the emphasis is on providing senior management with key information for strategic decision making. Such systems use sophisticated analysis techniques and may include *expert systems* (see page 134).

Music-composition software

allows a composer to record their ideas using a computer. The music can be entered using either the normal keyboard or a music keyboard connected using a *MIDI interface* (see page 50). The composition can be played directly using the computer's sound system and changes made immediately. The output can be, for example, a print-out in a traditional musical notation or in electronic form, such as MIDI code, allowing it to be played on any MIDI musical system.

Presentation package

is used to produce multimedia presentations and displays. It allows the construction of a series of pages that can include sound and video clips as well as text and graphics. These pages can be linked together and displayed easily using a single key press or mouse click. The presentation can also be displayed automatically, with a new page being displayed after a given time. Presentations are usually displayed on a large monitor, which the whole audience can see, or projected on to a large screen by the computer.

TeX

including: Latex, Metafont

is a specialised text-processing system devised by an American mathematician and computer scientist, Donald Knuth. It allows much greater control over the display of mathematical and scientific formulas than conventional word processors and is often used by academic authors submitting technical manuscripts to journal or book publishers. The power of TeX makes it a difficult language for beginners, and a number of alternative user interfaces, such as *Latex*, have been designed – these offer facilities for the production of a number of common types of scientific document without the user needing to write pure TeX. As well as the text-processing features of these languages, there is an associated typeface definition system called *Metafont*.

Page make-up system

allows on-screen combination of graphics and text. The software allows easy manipulation of the layout to produce a professional-looking result that can be reproduced for leaflets, manuals, magazines, etc.

Desktop publishing (DTP)

is the use of a *page make-up system* (see above) and high-quality output devices to produce material that can be used directly as the first stage in the production process for printed leaflets, manuals, books, magazines, reports, etc. It does not include the marketing, sales or distribution carried out by many publishers.

Project-management software

allows the planning of complex tasks using a computer. The software allows the project to be split into small components, each of which can be planned separately. The various parts of the project can be linked together so that the computer can construct a plan or calendar of how the project will proceed. This should allow the computer to ensure that later components are not waiting for earlier related components to finish.

Scientific measurement and analysis

including: monitoring, telemetry
collects data from *sensors* (see page 132) and stores the data for later analysis. The sensors allow the computer to collect data that otherwise would have been collected by hand. The computer can collect a large number of readings reliably. The data can then be analysed without having to be re-entered into the computer. The analysis can involve statistical calculations or simply the production of graphs to illustrate how the experiment proceeded.

The process of collecting the data from sensors is generally known as *monitoring*. The data collected consist of a large number of readings from the sensors and are called the *telemetry*.

Mathematical applications

including: number crunching
allow the power of the computer to be used to solve mathematical problems. The computer can carry out the required arithmetic much faster and draw the results on the screen. This allows tedious problems to be solved much more quickly than by a human being. Examples include the solving of differential equations and geometrical construction. These applications that rely on the computer being able to do large amounts of simple arithmetic very fast are often referred to as *number crunchers*.

Statistical applications

allow the computer to process large amounts of data to find patterns and determine their accuracy. This requires a lot of simple and repetitive arithmetic, which used to be very time-consuming to do manually. The computer enables data to be processed quickly and accurately.

Accurate statistics are an important part of many tasks, allowing complex data to be analysed and forecasts made from them. An example would be the analysis of sales by a marketing department before and after a sales promotion.

Viewdata

including: Ceefax, Teletext, Minitel
is a standard for displaying textual information using fixed-size pages. It is very efficient and used where communications have limited capacity.

Each page can be displayed on a standard TV or monitor and requires a very small quantity of data to describe the information displayed. This means that each page of data can be sent using communication systems with low *bandwidth* (see page 373), for example as part of a TV signal or using a standard telephone line.

Ceefax and *Teletext* services are examples of viewdata and are provided by TV companies in the UK. They supply a variety of information, such as news stories, weather forecasts, train cancellations, and so on. The data are transmitted as part of the TV signal.

Viewdata is also used by businesses where communication must be fast and reliable, often over standard telecommunications media. Examples include travel agents communicating with tour companies to make bookings and public information systems to display travel information at railway stations and airports.

Minitel is another example, used by France Telecom to replace paper telephone directories with a small viewdata screen attached to the user's telephone. The low bandwidth of viewdata makes it ideal for use over the standard telephone system. This system provides other services similar to *Teletext* (see above) and also interactive systems such as on-line booking of trains.

PART A

Speech synthesis

including: speech synthesiser, voice synthesiser, phoneme

is the production of sounds resembling human speech by electronic methods. A *speech synthesiser* (or *voice synthesiser*) achieves this either by the use of software or by using standard sound-generating hardware. An example of a speech synthesiser is a talking word processor. The sound is produced either by selecting an appropriate sound from a collection of stored sounds or by breaking down the input data into its individual speech components which are output in sequence. These speech components are called *phonemes*. For example, the vowel sound in 'meet' and in 'meat' are the same phoneme.

Part B

What Computer Systems are Made of

Computer systems can be assembled out of a variety of different pieces of equipment in a whole variety of different arrangements. This part of the glossary defines terms that will be encountered when considering how computer systems are arranged, organised and connected to other computer systems. Terms related to the uses of computers are in Part A and terms concerned with the internal workings of computers are in Parts C and D.

PART B

Types of Computer

This section includes those terms that are descriptive of computers in general.

A digital computer is an automatic, programmable data processor. Every part of this definition is crucial to our understanding of what the modern computer is and how it works.

Automatic means simply that it operates without human intervention, except where this is expressly pre-planned and provided for. This feature alone distinguishes the computer from the simple pocket calculator, where each computation results from a manual key press.

Programmable means that the instructions to be followed automatically are held (as a 'program') within the store of the computer. If a repetitive calculation (a 'loop') is necessary, then the same instructions can be used and reused. The instructions are usually held in the same storage area as that used for data – computer programs and the data they operate on can coexist comfortably in the same sort of storage.

Digital means that the computer operates with quantities that take only distinct values from a known range; often these are binary quantities that take only two values, which represent the digits 0 and 1. The power of digital data is that sequences of 0s and 1s can represent a wide range of types of data, including pictures, music, text and others. Notice that because programs and data can occupy the same storage area in the computer, program instructions are also expressed digitally. Although digital processing is now almost universal, some computers do not work this way – see **analog computer**, below.

Finally, the term **data processor** simply expresses what a computer does – it uses digital data and it produces results.

Computer generations

including: first-generation computers, EDSAC, EDVAC, ENIAC, DEUCE, Pegasus, LEO (Lyons Electronic Office), Univac I, second-generation computers, Atlas, third-generation computers, ICL 1900, IBM 360, fourth-generation computers, fifth-generation computers
are a convenient way of distinguishing major advances in computer technology. The first three generations have well-accepted meanings, but the later generations tend to

be used by manufacturers to stress the more modern features of a particular machine; the generation terminology appears to be falling into disuse.

First-generation computers were the earliest designs. They used valves, mercury delay lines and electrostatic memories, and had very limited storage. Important first-generation computers include the experimental *EDSAC*, *EDVAC* and *ENIAC* (which lacked stored-program facilities and would now fail our definition of computer) and the production scientific computers *DEUCE* and *Pegasus*. Commercial machines were *LEO* (*Lyons Electronic Office*) and *Univac I*. These machines were all large, typically filling one or more rooms, and consumed large amounts of power.

Second-generation computers arrived when the transistor replaced the valve as the basic component. Consequently, they were much more reliable and consumed less power. They were cheaper but still out of reach for most businesses and certainly for individuals. One of the most significant machines was *Atlas*.

Third-generation computers saw the transistor replaced by the *integrated circuit* (the 'silicon chip', see page 366). Again, they were cheaper and consumed less power and became even more reliable. One consequence of new design methods was the ability to produce whole families of computers that were similar but of different computing power – the *ICL 1900* series and the *IBM 360* family, for example.

Fourth-generation computers are those commonly encountered today. There is no single technological advance that distinguishes fourth-generation computers from third-generation computers, except possibly the much greater use of *large-scale integration* (see page 368) of components on silicon chips, which resulted in increasing similarity of machine design. A dramatic fall in the cost of internal memory, and increases in the speed and capacity of external storage, led to new applications and new methods of programming. In addition, there was a growing realisation that standardisation of software, particularly operating systems, is necessary.

Fifth-generation computers are a vision of a totally different way of designing and using computer systems. It involves both novel computer architectures and new types of software, and the vision has been achieved in some respects. It focuses on virtual reality, expert systems and natural language interfaces that can interact with people.

Analog computer

including: hybrid computer

is a different design of computer from the digital computers we normally use. Instead of operating on digital data, these use continuously variable quantities. For example, the electrical current may represent the value of the data, which will vary continuously as a smooth change rather than in discrete jumps. In theory, every possible change can be represented, no matter how small. It is also possible to design mechanical analog computers.

This term is now mainly of historic interest. Inevitably, some computers, known as *hybrid computers*, used both analog and digital technology in combination.

Digital computers

including: computing power, Lisa, Macintosh, IMac, personal computer, PC, micro-computer, micro, IBM-compatible, desktop computer, tower, mini-tower, multi-media computer, portable computer, laptop computer, notebook computer, personal digital assistant (PDA), palmtop computer, mini computer, mainframe computer, super-computer

are computers that operate with digital data. These are quantities that take only two values, such as 'off' or 'on', which are represented by the digits 0 and 1. More complex data are represented by combining binary digits into binary numbers; see also C10 Data Representation and C11 Numeric Data Representation.

Originally, 'computer' meant something that filled a room, needed air-conditioning and required several operators to run it. Rapid technological advances allowed computers with the same power to become available in much smaller packages, leading to a range of computers of different sizes and capabilities. *Computing power* is a measure of the speed at which the computer works and the complexity of the operations performed. Newer computers tend to be smaller (and faster) than those they replace. Names are needed to distinguish each new type of computer.

The most significant development of the late 1970s was the introduction of a type of computer small enough and cheap enough to be bought by individuals. Apple Computers led the way commercially with their range of computers that evolved from the *Lisa*, offering the first convenient *graphical user interface* (see page 59), the *Macintosh* through to the *iMac*. IBM introduced the *personal computer* (or *PC*). A general name was needed for these types of small computer. The following names are all relative to one another and often are ill-defined. Most personal computers and Macintoshes now are more powerful than the earlier computers, whose descendants are now known as *mainframes*.

Microcomputer (or simply *micro*) became the general name, with 'PC' being the name for computers based on the original IBM design. These PCs were also known as *IBM-compatibles*. The various types of PC could run the same software without needing any changes to the software (but see also *software version*, page 226). The term used most often nowadays is PC.

Desktop computer is used at a desk as a tool for the individual user. It is a conventional micro with a full-sized screen and keyboard. It needs a mains power supply, so it cannot be described as easily portable. The box containing the central processor, disk drives and other storage usually provides the support for the monitor; however, the box may be in the shape of a *tower* designed to stand on the floor by a desk or be small enough to stand on the desk beside the monitor, when it is called a *mini-tower*.

Multimedia computer has facilities for handling sound and video as well as text and graphics. Most computers are now sold with a multimedia capacity.

As computers have become smaller, lighter and more powerful, *portable computers* have been developed. Most portable computers include facilities to transfer data to a larger machine or network (see also *docking station*, page 364); these include the following:

PART B

Laptop computer runs off battery power as well as mains electricity. It is normally between 2 and 3 kg in weight, and its *footprint* (see page 169) is about the size of an A4 sheet of paper, so it can be carried in a briefcase. It is suited for use whilst travelling and at meetings. Currently, users expect communications capability, significant storage and a CD-ROM drive. Many of them can be connected to a full-sized monitor. They are also called *notebook computers*.

Personal digital assistant (*PDA*) is very compact and is designed to be carried in a pocket.

Palmtop computer is a pocket-sized device, without a keyboard, that can be handheld. It is accessed through a pen-like stylus moving over the display; the software recognises handwriting.

Minicomputer is a larger, more powerful computer, usually accessed from several terminals. They are small and inexpensive enough to be bought by small and medium-sized organisations. Current applications include Internet communication and managing checkouts at supermarkets. Such machines may be used as *servers* on a network, see page 125. They are now often considered to be small mainframes.

Mainframe computer is the term for the large computer usually accessed from many (often several thousand) terminals, growing increasingly powerful. It is used mainly for large-scale data processing in businesses, such as managing central databases.

Super-computer is a very large computer that works very quickly. It is likely to have many processors working in parallel to achieve this. Data are processed simultaneously (in the parallel processors) as well as sequentially to complete tasks very quickly. Examples include computers used for weather forecasting and testing aircraft design.

Stand-alone computer

is a computer that is not connected to others by a network and cannot share devices such as data storage or printers.

Front-end processor

is a computer dedicated to managing communications devices or other computers linked to a more powerful computer system, generally a *mainframe* (see above). The front-end processor receives messages and commands from the communications devices and organises these before passing them on to the larger computer for processing.

Multiprocessor system

is a computer system with several *processors* (see page 348). These will work cooperatively, handling specific tasks (managing the screen display, doing arithmetic computation, handling peripherals) or simply sharing out the processing to enable parts of a task to proceed simultaneously (in parallel). See also *parallel processing*, page 353.

Quantum computers

are based on the properties of subatomic particles (quantum mechanics). These are at a theoretical stage of development. If their potential is achieved, they are likely to run billions of times faster than *super-computers* currently do (see above).

Word processor

is a computer dedicated to, or primarily for, word processing. Some have displays that are the proportions of conventional paper sizes. Some offer black text on a white or coloured background. Most provide an extended keyboard with function keys for the software provided with the computer. Nearly all these facilities are now available as standard on general-purpose computers.

Original Equipment Manufacturer (OEM)

including: badging, proprietary

is a firm that makes basic computer hardware for other manufacturers to build into their products. For example, a manufacturer assembles a washing machine using a microprocessor from an OEM as a control device, or a computer manufacturer fits another manufacturer's disk drive mechanisms into their computer. Many components of computer systems are made by only a small number of manufacturers and are then built into systems that are sold by other manufacturers under their own brand name; this practice is known as *badging*. Software or hardware may be marketed and sold under a name that is patented or is a registered trademark, which is known as a *proprietary* name.

Footprint

is the amount of space (area) taken up by a peripheral or computer on a desk.

PART B

B2 Input

Other related terms may be found in A5 Sound, A13 Communications, B5 Com-munications Components and D5 Communications Technology, A4 Graphics, Design and Digital Imaging, A15 Control and Monitoring and A8 Commercial Data Processing for automated input applications.

A computer operates on data (including instructions). The data, the **input**, must be entered into the computer. There are many devices that could be used for the pur-pose of entering data, called **input devices**.

Input devices are one type of the many peripherals that can be attached to a com-puter system to do particular jobs and that are frequently necessary for the effective use of a computer system. There is a range of devices, and any one computer system is unlikely to have all possible types provided. This section is not exhaustive, and some input peripherals have been covered in other sections. For example, **sound**, **communications**, **monitoring** and **control** each have their own input peripherals, and details will be found in sections listed above.

There are various means, requiring hardware devices and software techniques, to deal with the different ways in which the input is presented to the computer system. Input devices, which may be manual or automatic, deliver the data in a format that is suitable for processing by the computer system. The data may also be transferred into one computer system from another, for example over a network (including the Internet) or from CD-ROM, particularly for large volumes of data.

For **manual** devices, the data items are provided by the user's action, such as typing at a keyboard, moving a mouse or speaking into a microphone. The device converts the input to **machine-readable** form before it can be processed by the com-puter. Further conversion may be carried out by the software within the computer. The most familiar input devices are the **keyboard**, by which data are entered, together with the **mouse**, or its alternatives the **trackerball** and **trackpad**. **Personal Digital Assistants (PDAs)** have built-in input devices that allow direct input and recognition of handwriting.

Automated input devices read data items that are already encoded and machine readable, and transfer them directly to the computer for processing without further user action. This is used, for example, for data already stored magnetically on a credit card or a machine-readable passport. An important, but often overlooked, input is printed matter read into a computer using a **scanner**.

Manual Input

Keyboard

including: qwerty keyboard, numeric keypad, function key, embedded keyboard
is the typical typewriter-like input device used with all general-purpose computers. The number of keys on the keyboard will not be the same for all computer keyboards; nor is the arrangement necessarily the same, because it will vary according to the country where it is used and the application it is used for.

Part of the keyboard is likely to be arranged in the same way as a traditional typewriter; this is called a *qwerty keyboard*.

Sometimes the numerical keys are repeated as a separate block called a *numeric keypad*. This aids rapid one-handed data entry.

In addition to the keys for letters, numbers, punctuation marks and Enter (or Return), a typical keyboard will have special keys that, when pressed, change the effect of other keys on the keyboard. This includes ESC (escape), CTRL (control), SHIFT and ALT and some *function keys*. What these keys do will depend on the software, rather than the hardware, being used. For example, pressing F1 may call up a *help system* (see page 71).

It is sometimes possible for the user to assign part of the keyboard for special purposes. This part of the keyboard is called an *embedded keyboard*. For example, keyboards with a restricted number of keys, such as on laptop computers, allow a group of the keys to be assigned the role of a numerical keypad if the user wishes.

PART B

Mouse

including: mouse mat, scroll wheel, mouse button, mouse event
is an input device, similar in shape and size to a dormouse, communicating with the computer either by a thin-cable connection or by wireless. Moving the mouse (by hand) in contact with a special flat surface, called a *mouse mat*, causes a rolling ball on the underside of the mouse, or an optical sensor, to detect motion. This movement is echoed on the display screen by movements of a pointer or cursor.

A mouse has one or more finger-operated press switches, called (mouse) *buttons*. When a mouse button is pressed or released, it causes a 'click' and passes a signal to the computer. These are sometimes called *mouse events*. (See also *event*, page 247.) What effect such events have will depend upon where the pointer is on the screen and what software is being used. Mouse operations, such as *clicking* (see page 62), dragging (see *drag*, page 65) and combinations of these with the use of keys on the keyboard, provide a wide range of possible options at any moment. Some mouses have an additional control called a *scroll wheel*, which makes dragging and scrolling easier to control.

Alternatives to a mouse are a *trackerball* and a *trackpad* (see page 172).

Trackerball

also known as: trackball
including: trackpad, trackpoint
is an input device that is used to do the same actions as a *mouse* (see page 171). It is a ball, set into a cup, that can be made to roll in any direction by using a finger or the palm of a hand, depending on the size of the ball. The movements of the ball are echoed on the screen by a pointer, and finger-operated switches work in the same way as *mouse buttons* (see page 171). Trackerballs can be used on *laptop computers* (see page 168), being easier to use in a confined space than a mouse. An alternative to a trackerball is a *trackpad*, where movements of a finger over a sensitive plate are used to control the movements of the screen pointer. A *trackpoint* is a small extra 'button' on the keyboard that works like a joystick and responds to a finger movement to control the movement of the screen pointer.

Touch-sensitive device

including: touch-sensitive keyboard, concept keyboard, touchscreen, stylus, light-sensitive pen, light pen
is a device that responds to touch to enable the user to input data or instructions.

A *touch-sensitive keyboard* is a keyboard on which the 'keys' are areas on a sensitive surface. These keyboards are generally used in special situations, for example where there is a risk of dirt or liquids getting into a conventional keyboard. They are seen, for example, on checkout tills and in self-service restaurants. Overlays are put on the keyboard to indicate the areas and their meaning, and software interprets these for the computer.

A *concept keyboard* is a particular kind of touch-sensitive keyboard. This is divided into programmable areas to input information to the computer. It is often used with young users and people with disabilities.

Touchscreens are able to detect the position on the screen where a user's finger is touching or pointing. One way of doing this is by having a grid, consisting of two sets of fine wires embedded in the screen (one set across and the other down), which sense the finger position by induction. Another method is to use vertical and horizontal patterns of infra-red light beams, which are interrupted when a finger (or pointer) is close to the screen. With both of these methods, the software can calculate the position that has been touched.

A *stylus* is a device shaped like a pencil and used for drawing on a touchscreen or *graphics tablet* (see page 31). The movement of the stylus is detected by the screen or tablet and its software in one of a variety of ways, for example through the use of a wire matrix in the pad. In some specialist applications, the angular movement of a mechanical arm supporting the stylus is detected. A stylus may be pressure-sensitive, producing a darker or more intensely coloured line if pressed firmly.

An early type of stylus was a *light-sensitive pen* or *light pen*, which looks like a pen with a wire connecting it to the computer. The light pen is used to point at, and thus indicate, a position on the screen. Software calculates this position and performs an appropriate action.

Touchscreens are used by many *PDAs* (*personal digital assistants*) (see page 168). Data are created by moving a stylus over the screen as the screen is so small (see *handwriting recognition* below). See also *graphics tablet* page 31.

Pressure controls

including: pressure pad, pressure switch, touch pad, touch switch, single switch devices
in the form of sensor *pads* or *switches*, operated by pressure or touch, are used as input devices for some applications. They can be used in conjunction with special software to enable people with physical disabilities to select items displayed on a screen by touching (or pressing) the pad when the item needed is highlighted. They are often known as *single-switch devices*. See also *touch-sensitive keyboard*, above, and *graphics tablet*, page 31.

Handwriting recognition

is the analysis of handwritten input, comparing the result with samples already stored in the computer and turning it into characters that can be processed by the computer.

In simpler systems, the user has to write in discrete characters. Although some software can recognise cursive ('joined-up') writing, it needs greater processing power and the system has to be 'trained' to recognise an individual's handwriting.

Interactive whiteboard

is a large version of a computer display combined with the facilities of a *touchscreen* (see above). The image is displayed by either rear projection or front projection, although plasma screens are an expensive alternative. As the user writes on the board, it is scanned by sensors, either behind the screen or along its edge, and the image is fed to the computer.

Speech recognition

including: speech-recognition software
is analysing spoken words recorded through a microphone and comparing them with those known to the system. *Speech-recognition software* enables data or instructions to be spoken to the computer for use by software such as a word-processing package. Specialist vocabularies are available with additional words for particular types of

user, such as accountants and pathologists. However, the differences between the same words spoken by different people still make this an unreliable process, and the software has to be 'trained' to work with each individual user. For accurate recognition, words need to be spoken separately and consistently, although some software can accept continuous speech.

Automated Input

Machine readable

describes data or instructions that can be entered into a computer without the need for any preparation. These data may be stored magnetically, for instance on a credit card or travel ticket, or printed on paper that is also readable by humans.

See also *Magnetic Ink Character Recognition* (*MICR*), *document reader* (page 76), and *Optical Character Recognition* (*OCR*) (page 77).

Automated readers

also known as: card readers
including: magnetic stripe, (magnetic) card encoder, swipe cards, smart cards, radio-frequency identification device (RFID)
read or scan data already stored in electronic form on things such as credit cards, travel tickets and carpark passes. The data may be written on a *magnetic stripe* on the card by a *(magnetic) card encoder*. Such cards, which are swiped through a slot in the card reader, are known as *swipe cards*. The cards are easily read, but they contain only small amounts of data. See also *PIN* (page 149).

More complex readers will read data stored on, and send data to, a *smart card*, a plastic card with a microprocessor sealed inside it. A smart card is more versatile than a magnetic stripe card; in particular, it can:

∎ hold more information, which can be altered as required;

∎ encrypt the data, making it difficult for unauthorised users to understand (see *encryption*, page 150);

∎ ensure that a user is authorised to perform a particular action by the use of various security checks.

Readers can also be used to read *Personal Identification Devices* (*PID*; see page 148), giving secure entry to restricted areas.

Readers for *Radio-Frequency Identification Devices* (*RFID*) operate at a distance by sending a radio message, which is received, modified by the silicon chip on the card, returned and deciphered by the reader. One example is to read season tickets for toll roads.

Scanner

including: image scanner, flat-bed scanner, sheet-feed scanner, hand-held scanner, bar-code reader, bar-code scanner

is a device that systematically traverses a page or object with a beam of light in order to sense and retrieve an image, which may be stored in a computer. There are several techniques and devices to deal with the variety of types of input so that the computer can recognise, interpret and use the data.

An *image scanner* is an input device that scans a document (text and/or graphics) and sends to the computer an image of the input in a form that a graphics package can use, normally a *bitmap* (see page 353). Either a beam of light moves over the drawing or text, or the paper moves through the scanner past the stationary light. A detector senses the reflected light and separates out the colours and intensities. See also *Optical Character Recognition*, page 76.

In a *flat-bed scanner*, the object to be scanned is placed face-downwards on a flat surface (usually glass), and a light source and sensors move backwards and forwards across it.

In a *sheet-feed scanner*, the paper passes over the read head.

A user moves a *hand-held scanner* over the object to be scanned.

A *bar-code reader or bar-code scanner* is an input device used to read information in *bar-code* form (see page 76). Sometimes the reader is built into equipment such as a supermarket checkout terminal, where it is usually referred to as a scanner. This form of reader shines laser-light beams on to the object being scanned and interprets the reflected patterns of the bar code.

PART B

B3 Memory

Memory is the name given to that part of a computer system in which data are held. These data are made up of files, either program files or datafiles. Computer memory serves two purposes. The first is to hold programs or data that the processor needs immediately; for this reason, it is sometimes called **immediate-access memory**. The second is to hold data that may be needed at some time; it is often called *backing store*. Immediate-access memory must be able to be read (and be written to) very quickly, since most computer instructions require data to be moved around in the immediate-access memory. Back-up memory can have distinctly slower reading and writing times. Immediate-access memory is usually about 1000 times faster than backing store. The immediate-access memory is located very close to the processor, so that signals take the shortest possible time in coming from and going to the processor; the backing store can be in separate units connected to the processor by cables.

Memory and storage have meanings that overlap and are often used as inter-changeable words; however, memory suggests that data are immediately available, whereas storage suggests that data have to be retrieved. Sometimes memory is described as **primary** for the immediate-access memory, **secondary** for the principal backing store and **auxiliary** for other forms of backing store. A variety of other terms are used for immediate-access memory, such as 'IAS', 'main memory', 'the memory' and 'the store', and for backing store, such as 'back-up memory', 'peripheral memory' and 'off-line storage'.

Throughout the development of computers, there has been a continual search for ways of improving memory technology. The search has been for reliable, compact storage devices with low energy consumption. Whenever a suitable new device has been developed, ways of cheap mass production have been found.

Because of the different requirements for the two functions of memory, it is usual for completely different kinds of technology to be used in a particular computer system. For immediate-access memory, most present-day computers use some form of random-access memory integrated circuits, in which very large amounts of data can be stored in a single plastic encapsulated chip. For backing store, most computers use some form of magnetic storage, such as disks or tapes, or optical storage.

Immediate-access memory is sometimes in two parts. One part, called **cache** memory, is made up of a small-capacity but exceedingly fast memory and is located next to the processor. The other part is much larger, and a copy of some of its contents is put into the cache memory in readiness for instant use. The choice of size for the main memory of a computer is determined partly by the addressing methods used and the cost of memory components. It is usual for computers to be sold with the potential for later memory expansion.

Backing store consists of the medium (the material on which the data are stored) and any associated mechanisms. Most computers use magnetic backing store (tapes or disks); however, some use integrated circuit semiconductor memory and optical systems are also being used increasingly. As far as the user is concerned, the medium may be removable, for example tapes, floppy disks and optical disks, or fixed, for example hard disks. The advantage of using removable media is that an expensive mechanism can be used for a variety of purposes with cheap media. Fixed disks provide faster access and greater capacity than removable disks and are used to store programs and data that are needed frequently. Most computer systems now have both fixed and removable disks. A large computer system will have fixed disks, removable disks, tape storage and optical storage. A personal computer will have a hard fixed disk and an optical disk unit.

Memory may be **volatile** or **permanent**. Volatile memory loses its data when there is no power supply to it, whereas permanent memory does not require power. All magnetic and optical media provide permanent memory, as do some forms of integrated circuit memory. However, the most widely used form of integrated circuit memory for immediate access store is volatile; this means that when the computer is switched on, programs and data have to be loaded from backing store. If power is cut off for some reason, then all data in memory will be lost.

Memory is often described by the type of **access** that is possible. For example, all the storage locations in immediate access memory can be accessed directly and the access time for all locations is the same; this is described as **random-access memory**. In contrast, the data stored on a tape can be reached only by going through the tape, in sequence, until the right place is found; this is described as **serial-access memory**. Storage on a disk is in concentric rings and is a collection of small sequential lengths of storage. Since disk storage can be accessed so quickly, it is generally thought of as direct (random) access storage.

Some forms of memory can only be read (**read-only**) and normally cannot be written to except during manufacture. Some semiconductor memory chips are manufactured as a blank memory array that can have data 'programmed' into it at a later time. One advantage is that some of these programmable memory chips can have the data erased and rewritten if necessary. Uses for programmable chips include storing programs for controlling traffic lights and lifts, and computer games programs.

PART B

Storage

also known as: memory
is a general term covering all units of computer equipment used to store data (and programs).

Memory

also known as: store
including: store location, (store) address, main store, immediate-access store (IAS), primary store, (memory) cell

The memory, or store, is the part of a computer system where data and instructions are held for use by the central processor and where the central processor puts the results that it generates. The computer store is made up of a large number of identifiable units, called *(store) locations*. Each store location has a unique label, called a *(store) address*, which is recognisable and used by the central processor. Those store locations that can be addressed directly by the central processor are called the *main store, immediate-access store (IAS)* or *primary store*. A store location, sometimes called a *(memory) cell*, is capable of holding a single item of data, a *word* or *byte* (see page 14).

Backing store

also known as: secondary store, mass storage
including: magnetic disk storage, magnetic tape storage, optical disk storage, magneto-optical storage
is a means of storing large amounts of data outside the *immediate-access store* (see above). A computer system will have at least one form of backing store. Most backing store uses magnetic storage, but increasing use is being made of optical storage systems. Backing store is sometimes referred to as *secondary store* or *mass storage*.

Magnetic disk storage is backing store in which flat rotatable circular plates, coated with a magnetic material, are used for storing digital data. The data are written to and read from a set of concentric circular *tracks* (see *magnetic disk*, page 179).

Magnetic tape storage is backing store that uses plastic tape coated on one side with magnetic material. Digital information is stored on the tape as a set of parallel *tracks* (see *magnetic tape*, page 182), which are written to or read from simultaneously.

Optical disk storage is backing store that uses plastic disks on which the data are stored as patterns on the surface. One method uses hollows etched into the surface of the disk for pre-recorded data in the form of *CD-ROMs* (see page 187). Other methods, such as *phase-change optical disks* (see page 187), provide read/write optical storage.

Magneto-optical storage is backing store that uses plastic disks on which data are stored by a combination of optical and magnetic methods.

Disc Memory

Magnetic disk

also known as: computer disk, disk
including: hard disk, floppy disk, disk pack, exchangeable disk pack, diskette, track (disk), cylinder, platter
is a circular plate, usually made of plastic or thin rigid metal, coated with a layer of magnetic material on which data can be stored by magnetically setting the arrangement of the magnetic material. This is done by electromagnetic *read/write heads* (see page 186). Disks may have data stored on one side only (single-sided) or on both sides (double-sided). The disk may be rigid (a *hard disk*), when it is also known as a *platter*, or flexible (a *floppy disk*). Where a disk drive has multiple disks (a *disk pack*), these are generally rigid, hard disks on a common spindle with read/write heads for each disk. If the disk pack is removable so that it can be exchanged for another complete pack, it is called an *exchangeable disk pack*.

A floppy disk (sometimes called a *diskette*) has to be protected by an outer covering, which prevents the magnetic coating from being damaged and keeps out dirt. Floppy disks are made to agreed standard designs, which can be used on any drive for the same size of disk. The commonest size is 3.5 inches.

Floppy disks need to have some way of showing where the tracks start. In 3.5-inch disks, it is possible to fit the disk on to the drive in only one position. Floppy disks provide one of the most common ways of passing data and programs from one computer user to another.

The general layouts of recording surfaces on a disk and on a multi-surface disk pack are shown in Figure B3.1. Data are stored on disks in concentric rings, called *tracks*. In a disk pack, a set of tracks one above the other, for example the tenth track on each disk, is called a *cylinder*. It is normal to store data that need to be kept together on a cylinder rather than on one disk, because the read/write heads will not need to move to access the data.

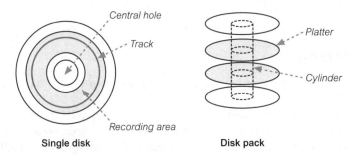

Figure B3.1 Tracks on a disk and a cylinder

Disk drive

also known as: magnetic disk drive
including: fixed-head disk unit, hard disk drive, Winchester drive, floppy disk drive,
CD-ROM drive, CD-ROM jukebox
is the unit made up of the mechanism that rotates the disks between the *read/write heads* (see page 186) and the mechanism that controls the heads. Most disk drives have one set of read/write heads for each surface and have to be moved to the required track. A disk unit with one set of heads for each disk track is called a *fixed-head disk unit*. This arrangement gives much faster access to data on the disk(s) but at increased cost.

Hard disk drives use rigid magnetic disk(s) enclosed in a sealed container. This has the advantage of allowing high recording density because the recording heads can be very close to the magnetic material on the disk. A small hard disk drive, sometimes known as a *Winchester disk (drive)*, is used widely in microcomputer systems as the principal back-up store in addition to one or more floppy disk drives.

Floppy disk drives use flexible disks that can be removed from their drives by the user, unlike hard disks, which are permanently mounted. See *magnetic disk*, page 179.

CD-ROM drives (sometimes called CD-ROM players) are very similar to audio compact disk players and read CD-ROM disks. A *CD-ROM jukebox* is a CD-ROM drive with a mechanism for automatically changing the current disk for another selected disk; it is similar to an old-fashioned jukebox used for playing gramophone records.

Disk array

including: RAID (Redundant Array of Inexpensive Disks)
is a set of hard disk units used as if they are a single mass-storage device. By using two disks to hold the same data, a disk-drive fault will be unlikely to have any effect on the operation of the whole system. By writing some of the data to each of a number of disks, storage and retrieval of data can be speeded up. This method of organising backing store for large computer systems is known as *RAID (Redundant Array of Inexpensive (or Independent) Disks)*. RAID systems provide a low-cost method of ensuring that losses of data are nearly impossible.

Disk format

including: track, sector, hard-sectored disk, soft-sectored disk, (disk) formatting,
disk verification
is the arrangement and organisation of the *tracks* (see Figure B3.2) on a disk. Each track is divided into a number of equal-length blocks, called *sectors* (see Figure B3.2). A sector is the smallest addressable portion of a track and is the smallest unit of data that is written to or read from a disk. Normally, each sector on each track

holds the same amount of data, even though outer tracks are longer than inner tracks, so the *packing density* (see page 184) depends upon the distance of the track from the centre of the disk. Some disk systems use variable-speed disks, which have different amounts of data on each track.

If the sectors are partially or wholly created when the disk is made, then the disk is called a *hard-sectored disk*. If the sectors are created by software on an unformatted disk, then the disk is called a *soft-sectored disk*. Floppy disks may be either hard- or soft-sectored.

The initial preparation of a blank disk for subsequent writing and reading by adding control information such as track and sector number is called *(disk) formatting*. When a disk is formatted, it is also *verified*; it is checked to ensure that all the tracks and sectors are fit for recording data. Reformatting a disk that contains data will erase all the data on it. Floppy disks for personal computers need to be formatted appropriately for the machine on which they are to be used, although some machines may be able to read disks in a variety of formats. Floppy discs are normally already formatted when bought.

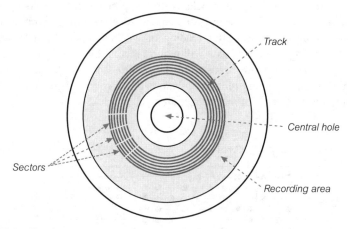

Figure B3.2 Tracks and sectors

Tape

Magnetic tape drive

also known as: tape drive
is the mechanism that winds the tape between the spools across the read/write heads. Tape drives are capable of sensing the presence of stored data on the tape. Tape drives for cassettes are similar to those in domestic audio- and video-tape recorders.

Magnetic tape

including: (tape) reel, (tape) spool, (tape) cartridge, (tape) cassette, serial-access storage, track (tape), frame, interblock gap

is a storage medium consisting of a flexible plastic tape covered with magnetic material on one side and kept on spools. The tape is similar to the tape used in domestic video systems, but it is of a higher quality, since computer tapes need to be accelerated and decelerated very rapidly. The tape may be held on *reels* (or *spools*), requiring an operator to change the reels and thread the tape, or in *cartridges* or *cassettes* (similar to the domestic video cassettes).

This form of storage medium provides *serial-access storage*.

There are a number of methods of data storage on tape, and a number of standard tape widths.

In older systems, many of which are still in use, the data are stored on the tape in parallel *tracks* using either a seven-track or a nine-track system on 0.5-inch tape. A single character is represented by a line of magnetised spots, a *frame*, across the tape; these represent the bits for that character in an appropriate code, such as *EBCDIC* (see page 307).

Data are written to the tape in blocks, with a gap between each block, called an *interblock gap*. The gap is needed for the tape to accelerate to the correct speed for reading or writing or to stop after reading or writing. Since the data are stored sequentially, finding an item of data will require that all the tape up to the data item is wound past the read/write heads until the required item is found. Figure B3.3 shows a diagrammatic representation of data on this form of magnetic tape; the data are stored as discrete areas of magnetism along each track.

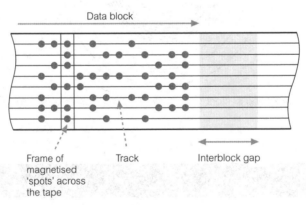

Figure B3.3 Data on 0.5-inch magnetic tape

More recent systems use the same technology as video recorders, where the data blocks are written on diagonal tracks (Figure B3.4) across the tape by a rotating head. This gives very high density and greater read/write speeds than the earlier tape systems.

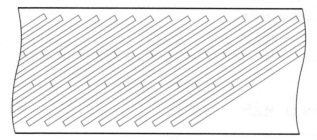

Figure B3.4   Blocks in diagonal tracks

Other tape formats include blocks arranged side by side on multiple tracks (Figure B3.5) and blocks arranged one after another in a 'serpentine' arrangement, with alternate tracks written in opposite directions (Figure B3.6).

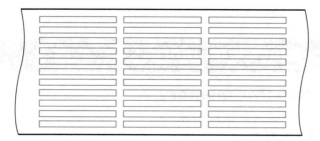

Figure B3.5   Blocks in parallel tracks

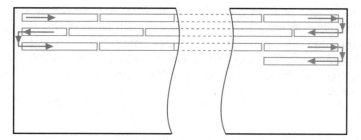

Figure B3.6   Blocks in serpentine tracks

Large amounts of data can be stored on a single tape. Tapes are used as back-up or archive storage and are very useful for storing data that are required only on planned occasions, or when the majority of records will be accessed in any processing, for example data that are updated monthly or quarterly. Applications that have very large storage requirements are increasingly using high-packing-density tapes for on-line purposes.

Tape streamer

is a small tape drive unit, usually using tape cassettes, with very large storage capacity. They are frequently used to make back up copies of data for security purposes.

Packing density

including: bits per inch (bpi), disk density
is a measure of the quantity of data that can be held per unit length of track on a storage medium. It is usually measured in *bits per inch* (*bpi*) and is the number of binary digits (or bits) stored in one inch (2.54 cm) along each track.

Terms such as single density and double density (DD), quad density (QD) and high density (HD) are used to describe the packing density of magnetic disks (*disk density*). The interpretation of these terms is not uniform, since the size of the disk, the age of the drive and the sophistication of the operating system cause differences in meaning.

Semiconductor Memory

Semiconductor memory

also known as: integrated circuit memory
including: MOS, CMOS
is a form of memory that uses integrated circuit semiconductor chips. The storage capacity of this form of memory is very high, the time taken to read a data item is very short, and the access is direct. There are a number of different forms of semiconductor storage; the more common ones use *MOS* (*metal-oxide-semiconductor*) or *CMOS* (*complementary MOS*) technology. The advantage of CMOS types is that they require little power to retain their contents; powered by small batteries they can be used as *non-volatile memory* while the computer is switched off. See *volatile memory*, page 189. Most current computer designs use semiconductor memory for immediate-access storage.

RAM (random-access memory)

including: static RAM, dynamic RAM (DRAM), memory refresh
is memory that has the same access time for all locations. Each location holds one *byte* (see page 14) and is addressable directly. RAM may be either *static*, which holds its memory so long as there is a power supply, or *dynamic*, which has to be *refreshed* by reading and rewriting the contents very frequently (about every two milliseconds). Dynamic RAM (*DRAM*) is used more widely than static RAM because it needs less power. Both dynamic and static RAM are *volatile* (see *volatile memory*, page 189). See also *semiconductor memory*, above.

RAM disk

also known as: silicon disk
is memory that is addressed as if it were a very fast random-access disk. It behaves as an extremely fast backing store for the user, but it is usually volatile and has to be loaded from backing store. It is normally an area of main memory reserved for this use.

ROM (read-only memory)

including: PROM (Programmable Read-Only Memory), EPROM (Erasable PROM), EAROM (Electrically Alterable Read-Only Memory), EEPROM (Electrically Erasable Programmable Read-Only Memory), flash PROM, cartridge
is memory for which the contents may be read but cannot be written to by the computer system. Read-only memory is used for both data and programs. There are optical ROM systems (see *CD-ROM*, page 187) and semiconductor (integrated circuit) ROM systems (see *semiconductor memory*, above).

The term *ROM* is frequently used to mean the (integrated circuit) read-only memory used to hold programs and associated data for building into computers. Software in ROM is fixed during manufacture, but there are other ways of putting programs and data into ROM:

PROM (*Programmable Read-Only Memory*) is a type of ROM that is manufactured as an empty storage array and is then programmed permanently by the user.

EPROM (*erasable PROM*) is a type of PROM whose data can be erased by a special process (e.g. by exposure to ultraviolet radiation) so that new data can be written as if it were a new PROM.

EAROM (*Electrically Alterable Read-Only Memory*) and *EEPROM* (*Electrically Erasable Programmable Read-Only Memory*), sometimes called *flash PROM*, are other similar types of read-only memory.

Some small computers and games computers use software on (integrated circuit) ROM that is packaged in plug-in modules called *cartridges*. This is a convenient way of preventing the software from being copied.

Cache memory

also known as: cache
including: disk cache
is a part of the main store between the central processor and the rest of the memory. It has extremely fast access, so sections of a program and its associated data are copied there to take advantage of its short fetch cycle (see *fetch–execute cycle*, page 349). The use of cache memory can greatly reduce processing time.

PART B

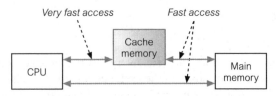

Figure B3.7 Cache memory

A way of speeding up the transfer of large amounts of data from disks is to use *disk caching*, that is using a section of memory for holding data that have been read from disk storage. See also *buffering*, page 354.

General

Read/write head

including: disk access time, seek time, latency, head crash, park
is the set of electromagnets and necessary circuitry used to magnetise the magnetic material used for storage. Tape units have fixed heads and the tape moves past them. Most disk units have the set of heads on an arm that moves them from track to track, but fixed-head disk units have a set of heads for each track, which greatly reduces the time taken to access data on the disk. Double-sided disks require a set of heads for each side. The time taken to get data from a disk, the *disk access time*, includes the time taken to move the heads to the correct track, called the *seek time*, and the time taken for the disk to rotate to the correct part of the track, sometimes called *latency*. However, some people use latency to mean the total waiting time.

Head crash is when the read/write heads hit the surface of a disk. This can cause serious damage to the mechanisms and loss of data. To avoid this happening with personal computers, for example when a machine is moved, the read/write heads are often automatically put in a safe position (*parked*), whenever they are not being used to access the disk. Following the proper procedures of closing all files before ending a session of work will ensure that the disk is parked properly. Some early personal computers required the user to give the command for parking the disk.

Optical storage

including: WORM (write-once, read-many), CD (compact disk), CD-ROM (compact disk read-only memory), CD-R (compact disk recordable), CD-RW (compact disk rewritable), multisession CD, laser disk, videodisk, DVD (digital video disk), digital versatile disk, photo-CD, magneto-optical disk, phase-change optical disk
uses laser technology to etch the surface of a storage medium to form minute patterns that represent the data. The scattering effect on a narrow laser beam is used to read the data which may be digital or analog. The storage medium can take any of several physical formats and various data formats. The data may include programs

as well as sound, graphics or text data. Optical storage with a computer capable of manipulating, storing and outputting high quality sound and graphics is a multi-media system. See *Multimedia*, page 55.

WORM (*write-once, read-many*) is an optical disk system that allows the user to write data on the next available portion of the disk. A portion of the disk can have data written on it only once, but all the data can be read as often as required. Some WORM disks allow the overwriting of data so as to spoil or erase them. See also *CD-R* below. (Not to be confused with *worm*, see page 153).

CDs (*compact discs*) are optical disks available in three formats, *CD-ROM, CD-R*, and *CD-RW*. They are nomally 125 cm in diameter.

CD-ROMs (*compact disk read-only memory*) are manufactured (pressed) with the data present and include data CD-ROMs and audio CD-ROMs. *CD-Rs* (*compact disk recordable*) use dye technology to enable data to be written to the disk. It may be read many times but it may not be subsequently changed. Once written they can be made to act as a CD-ROM.

CD-RW (*compact disk rewritable*) uses a different technology from CD-Rs which allows previously written data to be erased and fresh data written to the disk.

Multisession CD is a method of using CD-Rs to store materials created during separate work sessions. It allows an extra set of data to be added to an already used CD-R. A *photo CD* is a specialised way of storing digitised camera images, used by photographic processors.

Laser disk, sometimes called *videodisk*, is an early form of optical storage, usually 12 inches in diameter, now primarily used for the domestic market in the USA.

DVD (briefly *digital video disk*, but now *digital versatile disk*) is essentially a larger-capacity CD with a faster data transfer rate. This allows compressed moving video to be replayed, for example a movie. See also *image compression*, page 26. The DVD can also be used for data storage.

Magneto-optical disk is a rewritable or WORM optical disk that uses magnetic and optical techniques. Writing uses a laser beam to heat a small part of the surface of the disk and, at the same time, a magnetic field arranges the magnetic material in this heated area. Reading uses the effect that the magnetic field on the surface of the disk has on a weak laser beam.

Phase-change optical disk is a rewritable optical disk that uses a laser to read and write data. It uses three strengths of laser signal. The weakest signal is used to read data; the other two signals are used to write data, by making parts of the material of the disk surface reflective or non-reflective to the weakest signal.

PART B

Content-addressable storage

also known as: associative storage
is a physically separate module of storage designed to allow access to a location by its contents rather than by an address label. The normal address *decoder* logic (see page 392) is replaced by logic that compares the contents of part of each store with the address item. The remainder of each store contains indications of where the required data are stored.

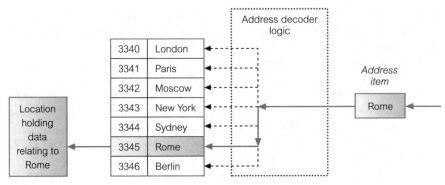

Figure B3.8 Using content-addressable storage

Block

including: bucket
is the name for the smallest unit of data that is transferred between backing-store and main store in one operation. In large computer systems, a *bucket* defines a unit of storage in random access memory. A *bucket* will contain a (variable) number of blocks. Access to the data is by reference to the bucket they are in.

Memory map

including: disk map, file-allocation table (FAT)
describes the way storage is organised in a computer. For example, sections of memory may be allocated to the screen display, program code or variables.

The memory map for disk storage is called a *disk map*. It describes how the information held on the disk is organised, and is kept on the disk. It may be held as a *bitmap* (see page 353). Details of where files are stored in backing store are kept in a *file-allocation table* (*FAT*), a file that is also kept on the backing store. See also *directory*, page 65.

Scratch pad

also called: work(ing) store
including: scratch file, scrap file, work(ing) file, scratch tape
is a section of immediate-access store reserved as a temporary working area for use by an application. It is also called a *work store* or *working store*. An area of file space on backing store assigned for this purpose is called a *scratch file*, *scrap file*, *work file* or *working file*. If tape is used, it is called a *scratch tape*. See also *clipboard*, page 19.

Virtual storage

is a means of apparently extending main storage by using backing storage as if it were main memory. See also *virtual memory*, page 351.

Volatile memory

including: non-volatile memory, permanent memory
is a form of storage that holds data only while power is supplied. This is in contrast to *non-volatile memory*, which keeps its contents even when the system is switched off. All currently used forms of magnetic storage and optical disk storage are non-volatile, but most other forms of storage are volatile. *Permanent memory* retains its contents regardless of power supply and cannot be erased or altered; many forms of read-only memory (ROM) are permanent.

Write protection

including: blocking ring, write-inhibit ring, write-permit ring, request verification
is the prevention of unintentionally overwriting data on backing store. This can be achieved either by hardware features or by provisions in software.

Hardware write protection is built into floppy disk drives and floppy disk cases; for 3.5-inch floppy disks, there is a sliding cover for a hole in the case. There are no similar standards for large disk units; each manufacturer provides their own system. There is no hardware write protection for small hard disks in personal computers. Tape units have removable *blocking rings* behind the tape spools, which act either as *write-inhibit* or as *write-permit rings*, depending on the system used; cassettes or cartridges have sliding tabs.

Software methods include double-checking a request (*request verification*) if it will overwrite or delete a file, checking the characteristics of file names to see whether they are protected and asking for passwords before overwriting or deleting any data.

PART B

B4 Output

Other terms and concepts relating to output may be found in A5 Sound, A13 Communications, B5 Communications components, D5 Communications technology and A15 Control and Monitoring.

We give instructions and data to computers. The computer uses the instructions that form computer programs to process the data to produce results, which are known as **output**. The results may be of various forms, for example sound, text and diagrams, data for external storage, messages to control equipment, and messages to send or receive e-mails or access the Internet. They may be dynamic images, visible on a computer screen, or static, such as that produced by a **printer**.

The **output devices** attached to the computer system make the output usable. The two output devices that are used most often, particularly by PC users, are display devices, i.e. **monitors** and **printers**. Specialised output devices are not necessarily provided as part of the computer system.

Human vision enables us to see objects in great detail and colour. Information and graphics in **colour** are more interesting, are remembered longer and can contain more detail than the same material in **monochrome** (shades of two colours – often black and white). For example, the software and user interface used to produce a word-processed document normally benefit from a colour display. The output from a printer may be in colour or monochrome. For business use, where **multipart stationery** is still prevalent and high volume and speed are required, monochrome printers are common.

Monitors give out light, so work according to the rules of transmitted light. White light transmitted from a light source may be split into coloured light of a spectrum of different wavelengths. The human eye has receptors for the three primary colours (primary additive), red (R), green (G) and blue (B), and perceives other colours as mixtures of varying amounts of light selected from these primary colours. The brain interprets the colours at both ends of the visible spectrum as a combination of red and blue, giving the effect of a colour wheel.

If a page printed in colour is illuminated by white light, some light is reflected and some is absorbed by the coloured pigments (inks); the eye then perceives the combination of primary colours that is reflected, not absorbed. Combining different proportions of the three secondary (primary subtractive) colours, cyan (C) (light blue), magenta (M) (deep red) and yellow (Y), gives the various shades. Mixing two secondary (primary subtractive) colours creates a pigment that absorbs two primary (primary additive) colours, leaving the eye to see the remaining primary (primary additive) colour.

Not all the light is reflected; some is absorbed by the pigment, so the printed image is less bright than that seen on the monitor. It is no simple matter to ensure that the colours displayed on your monitor will be matched by the output of your printer. Furthermore, human sensitivity to colour varies, so that no two people are likely to see a given colour or combination of colours in exactly the same way.

Images displayed by the most common types of monitors and printers are made up of patterns of dots. It is possible to produce any character or shape simply by arranging the dots in the right places. This method can be used for producing a piece of computer graphics (for example, a picture or a design) as well as for printing text. For example, the letter 'h' can be formed crudely by a simple pattern of dots, as shown in Figure B4.1. The quality of the output from both monitors and printers depends on the **resolution**, i.e. the numbers of dots per inch. By using a matrix with many more squares, it is possible to improve the shape of the letter. If the dots are very small and close together, the quality of display or printing can be very fine.

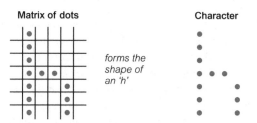

Figure B4.1   Character formed by a pattern of dots

The **pixel** is the smallest element of the display for programming purposes, made up of a number of dots forming a rectangular pattern. Coloured display screens are made up of dots that consist of three smaller dots of the three primary colours of white light.

Most monitors use the **cathode ray tube**. However, laptop computers require high-performance lightweight thin screens. This has been achieved by major enhancements to **liquid crystal** technology, which is used in pocket calculators.

The electronics that pass the information from the computer to the screen are generally specific to the type of screen device. These electronics have to be installed by fitting a specific interface board, called a **display adapter** (or **graphics card**), into the computer. For example, an SVGA display (a common display standard) consists of an SVGA screen device and a matching SVGA display adapter in the computer.

Printers are connected to a computer for the sole purpose of transferring the information from the computer to paper or other media, such as transparencies for overhead projectors. The version printed out is often referred to as **hard copy**. There are many types of printer varying in quality, cost and purpose.

Types of printers in common use are **inkjet printers** and **laser printers**. There are also specialist printers, such as **plotters**, **thermal wax printers** and **dye sublimation printers**. The quality of printing will depend on the type and quality of the paper as well as the resolution. In colour printing, one must also consider both the range of distinct colours that the printer can produce (**colour palette**) and the software that controls the printing process (**colour management**).

In summary, deciding upon an output device is not easy, as all monitors and printers today can display almost anything that your computer can produce. Often, the use of the output will determine the type of device. Cost, speed, quality of display and choice of output (colour or monochrome) are probably the main areas to focus upon.

Colour

Palette

also known as: colour palette
including: dithering

is the range of distinct colours that a computer system can produce. No computer system will be able to produce every possible shade of colour; the palette is the total set of shades available. Most computers have a palette of 16 million colours; this is a large number to work with, so the user can select their own palette of colours suitable for the task. The user may be allowed to change this selection.

In some situations, the user is unable to use the full range of colours and has only a smaller palette. Each of these colours can be chosen from the full range. Examples include artwork for display on the Internet, which has a standard palette, and desktop publishing work, which is restricted to the coloured inks to be used by the printer.

Dithering is reproducing a particular colour that is not in the palette by using a pattern of dots of a limited number of colours. This is used when the output device cannot reproduce a particular colour. For example, true orange may be produced by a pattern of dots of red and yellow (see Figure B4.2).

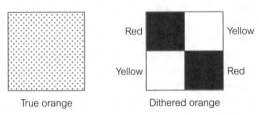

True orange   Dithered orange

Figure B4.2 Dithering

Colour mixing is often software-controlled. See *colour management*, page 193.

Colour model

including: spot colour, RGB colour model, CMYK model, hue saturation value, greyscale model
is the way in which separate colours are defined. Any colour can be defined using three values, but the different colour models do this differently. Each model is suitable for a particular application.

The range of colours that each model represents may be different, and when an image is converted from one model to another the colours will be changed to the nearest available colour. Sometimes, an additional colour, known as a *spot colour*, is needed to produce exact colour matching.

The usual models are as follows:

RGB model, or *RGB colour model*, defines the different amounts of red, green and blue, which are the primary (primary additive) colours and is ideal for use in display screens.

CMYK model, also known as *CYMK* and *YMCK*, defines the different amounts of cyan, magenta and yellow, which are the secondary (primary subtractive) colours. An extra value, the key (K) colour black, is added because imperfections in printing make it difficult to make black from CMY. The CMYK model is ideal for producing work to be printed.

Hue saturation value defines the hue (the different colours), the saturation (the luminosity or strength of colour) and value (the darkness). This is ideal for defining colours in, for example, photographic work.

Greyscale model defines the range of shades of grey from white to black, which is used for reproducing monochrome images. A colour model can be mapped on to a greyscale model. Two different colours of the same luminosity may look the same, as they have the same greyscale value.

Colour management

including: colour management system (CMS), Pantone
is the software process that controls the colours that are printed or displayed by a monitor, by managing the transfer of colour data between devices. The flow of data is shown in Figure B4.3, page 194.

The management of the transfer of colour data associated with different devices such as screens, scanners, CD-ROM readers and printers is handled by software known as a *colour management system* (*CMS*). The CMS may be included in the operating system or provided and installed separately. It works by comparing the colours for a device with independent colour standards and translating the colours for different devices so that they appear similar. When they cannot be matched exactly, for example the differences between a screen using the RGB system and a printer using the CMYK system, the CMS will select the nearest match.

Pantone is a *proprietary system* (see page 169) in which numbers are allocated to colours for exact colour matching. The Pantone numbers may be held in a *look-up table* (see page 248).

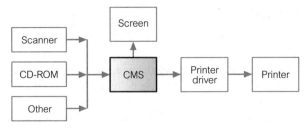

Figure B4.3 Dataflow in a colour management system

Colour separation

is the process needed for preparing colour data for (full-colour) commercial printing. For example, if a photograph is to be printed commercially, then the printer is supplied with four files, each containing the data for one colour, using the *CMYK model* (see above). Each file is a monochrome image, showing the intensity of the particular colour.

In order to print in colour, a coloured image has to be separated into its component colours. This is part of the process of preparing the data for a colour printer.

Quality

Resolution

including: low resolution, high resolution, screen resolution, dot pitch, low-resolution graphics, printer resolution, dots per inch, dpi
is the term for the clarity of text and graphics as they appear on a monitor screen or printed on paper. *Low-resolution* images have coarse dots and a 'grainy' appearance, with jagged diagonal lines and curves. *High-resolution* images have many small dots closer together and produce clearer images, with diagonal straight lines and curves both appearing smoother and less jagged. See also *raster graphics* (see page 197) and *vector graphics* (see page 198).

Screen resolution is usually quoted as the number of *pixels* (see page 197) in a row by the number of rows of pixels (horizontal × vertical), and the *dot pitch*, which is the distance between the centres of two dots on the screen. Values of between 0.28 and 0.38 mm for the dot pitch are considered acceptable; this is between 100 and 70 *dots per inch* (*dpi*).

Low-resolution graphics is generally applied to graphical display units where simple pictures can be built up by plotting large blocks of colour or by using special graphics characters. It is used for *teletext* images (see page 161).

Printer resolution is measured in *dots per inch* (*dpi*). The smaller the dots making up the printing, and the closer together they are, the clearer the image will be. Laser and inkjet printers normally have a resolution of at least 300 dpi for normal use, while high resolution of 2400 dpi is used by commercial printers.

Print quality

including: correspondence quality, letter quality, draft quality, condensed type
is a description of how well formed the characters are when printed. The descriptions are built into printers for use in business when only simple text printing is required. Desktop computers usually have the flexibility of printing the text as a graphical image, allowing for a wide variety of fonts, font sizes and effects.

The descriptions of characters are expressed in terms of the standards expected of printed output for different purposes:

Correspondence quality, also known as *letter quality*, is similar to the quality of a traditional typewriter, or of an ink jet or laser printer.

Draft quality is an option on some printers; the characters are not well shaped but can be printed quickly.

Condensed type is produced by some printers that can reduce the width of a character, so that more text can be fitted on a line.

See also *photo printer*, page 35.

Font

including: scalable, printer fonts, screen fonts, printer drivers, font cartridges, proportional spacing, monospace font, pitch, point size
is the set of printing or display characters in a particular type, style and size. Printer fonts may be produced by the same software as screen fonts and appear identical on the screen and in printed output. Such fonts are *scalable*; that is, they can be enlarged or reduced without changing their shape. See also *PostScript*, page 205.

Printer fonts are stored within the printer itself and therefore available for draft printing or faster printing in other circumstances.

Screen fonts are the way in which text of a particular style is displayed on the screen. Ideally, these will appear the same as the printer fonts, but for technical reasons they may be displayed differently. See also *WYSIWYG* page 20.

The font options, which can be selected by the user, may be stored in the computer and accessed through *printer drivers*, which are part of the system software that formats data for printing (see D1 Systems Software). Alternatively, fonts may be stored in read-only memory (ROM) *font cartridges* installed in the printer.

Proportional spacing is a way of printing text so that the spaces between letters and between words look the same. The letter 'i' is narrower than the letter 'm', and without proportional spacing there would be more white space around the letter 'i'. The software adjusts the space between letters. Not all fonts support proportional spacing. When using a *monospace font*, the *pitch* is the number of characters in an inch, which varies for different fonts, and is used mainly in commercial printing.

Point size is the maximum height of an individual character in a line of text. This is a traditional printer's measurement, each point being one-seventy-secondth of an inch.

Display

Monitor

also known as: visual display unit, VDU
including: monochrome monitor, colour monitor
is the term generally used for any device that displays information using a display screen, usually a *cathode ray tube* (*CRT*) (see below). All monitor displays are made up of illuminated dots on the screen. Monitors may be monochrome or colour.

Monochrome monitors give a display of varying intensity of a single colour, for example white, green or orange on a dark (black) background.

Colour monitors give a display with a range of colours determined by the colour circuitry in the monitor and the computer.

Cathode ray tube

also known as: CRT
including: interlace, non-interlace, multiscan monitors, multisync monitors, triad
is a glass tube used to form the screen in a monitor or television set. The cathode ray tube looks like a large electric light bulb with a flattened end; the viewer sees only the flatter end. The inside of the flat end is coated with phosphor. A beam of electrons is directed at the phosphor to make the end glow with patterns of dots. The electronics of the system controls the beam of electrons, and the number and nature of the excitation of these dots, and so determines the quality of the picture that the user sees.

The glowing substances on a cathode ray tube device have to be continually energised to keep the display visible. The screen is refreshed by the electron beam making a horizontal sweep over each line of dots. See *screen refresh*, page 197. In some systems, to avoid flicker on TV screens the screen refresh is done in two passes; every other line of dots is refreshed on a first pass, then the other lines are refreshed at the second pass; this is called *interlace* scanning and is the method normally used in domestic television. A system that refreshes all the lines of dots in sequence, called *non-interlaced* scanning, is used in a number of designs for computer display screens.

Monitors that can operate at variable refresh rates are called *multiscan monitors* or *multisync monitors*. The different scan rates are set by a *video adapter* (see page 198). Multiscan monitors are essential for high-definition display systems.

For a colour monitor or TV, the coating is arranged in horizontal lines of *triads*. A triad is a cluster of three dots: one will glow red, one green and one blue. The electronics of the system will excite different members of the triad to a greater or lesser amount, so as to produce a single glowing dot of the required colour and brightness. It is an arrangement of a large number of these dots that produces the final picture. Each pixel in the image may consist of several dots, depending on the *resolution* of the image and the *resolution* of the display device (see page 194).

Screen refresh

also known as: refresh
including: refresh rate
is to replace the image currently displayed on the screen by a new image, either because the image fades or because the data displayed have changed but are not reflected in the display.

The screen picture needs to be able to change quickly, to display anything from just simple text editing to a fast-moving graphics image. This ability to change is achieved because the picture is redrawn many times a second, even if it is not actually changing.

The *refresh rate* is the number of times the image is redisplayed per second. A low refresh rate tends to produce flicker. An SVGA monitor has a refresh rate of 72 scans per second. See also *video adapter* (page 198).

Frame

is used to describe a contained set of data treated as a single unit and which may change over time. Examples are a response frame for the input of data in a screen input data capture system, or a Web page.

In electronics, a frame is one complete screen picture. In a standard television set, this consists of 625 separate lines. A new frame is transmitted every one-twenty-fifth of a second as two *interlaced* fields. The first field is the odd-numbered lines and the second is the even-numbered lines. (See *screen refresh*, above.)

Raster graphics

is a method of producing an image on a display screen. The image is drawn as horizontal lines of dots, repeated for each line of the screen. The bitmap is encoded as a one-dimensional stream of bits, formed by each line of the display in order.

Each pixel in the image may consist of several dots, depending on the resolution of the image and the *resolution* of the *monitor*, see page 196. In general, any line that is neither vertical nor horizontal will have a jagged appearance. If very high-quality screen display of line drawings is required, then *vector graphics* (see page 198) is the appropriate system.

Pixel

including: pixel graphics
is a single dot of an image. It is usually rectangular or square, and it is the smallest element that can be displayed. Each pixel will be a single colour intensity and saturation. Pixel is a contraction of 'picture-element'.

PART B

Pixel graphics is a method of constructing a picture consisting of a rectangular array of dots. Each dot may be any of the colours available to the computer, but it is not possible for a dot to be split into smaller pieces. This means that it is impossible to have detail smaller than the size of the pixels.

Computer output on microfilm (COM)

is a technique for producing computer output directly on microfilm, for example the creation of computer-generated microfiches. This provides a very economical method of storing archive copies of documents and diagrams as well as making them generally available in microfiche form.

Video adapter

also known as: display adapter, graphics adapter, video card, video adapter card
is the circuitry that generates the signals needed for a video output device to display computer data. The data may be text only or text and graphics. The circuits are contained on a circuit board, which is installed in the computer with output via a cable to the display unit (the monitor).

A number of manufacturers have developed adapters with different screen proportions, such as a page-shaped screen for use in the newspaper industry. Computers that are not IBM-compatible PCs frequently use their own video adapters with different standards.

Video Ram (VRAM)

is a separate high-speed memory into which the processor writes the screen data, which are then read to the screen for display. This avoids the use of any main memory to hold screen data.

Graphical display unit (GDU)

is an output device incorporating a *cathode ray tube (CRT)*, (see page 196) on which both line drawings and text can be displayed. The term is used for display systems specifically for very high-quality graphics work. A graphical display unit is often used in conjunction with a light pen to input or reposition data. High-quality graphical display units normally use *vector graphics* (see below).

Vector graphics

is a screen display method using a *cathode ray tube (CRT)* (see page 196) in which each line of a drawing is produced on the screen individually. A line can be drawn in any direction (although there is a minimum width of a line), so the display is a more accurate presentation of the picture, with no jagged edges. The resolution of vector graphics screens is usually very high. Vector graphics is an expensive technique to implement, with the result that most displays use *raster graphics* (see above).

Liquid crystal display (LCD)

including: backlit screens
is a display technique that uses the phenomenon that certain liquids alter their ability to reflect or transmit light if a voltage is applied to them. Originally used for pocket calculators, it is now common for laptop computer screens.

In its basic form, liquid crystal display consists of a thin layer, a film, of fluid sandwiched between two sheets of glass or plastic. Complex wiring is used to apply voltages to different small areas of the film of liquid. The applied voltage alters the ability of the liquid to reflect or transmit light. Thus, a pixel display is built up of light and dark dots of varying intensity. One way of producing colour is to have three layers of different types of liquid, with different colour characteristics, where each layer has its own associated wiring. Some systems rely on reflected light and cannot be used in poor lighting conditions. *Backlit screens*, where the liquid films transmit light from a light source behind the screen, give a display that is viewed more easily than reflective systems.

Light-emitting diode (LED)

is a display that uses the property of some semiconductor diodes to emit light when a voltage is applied to them. Their power consumption is negligible, and they give off no heat. They are commonly used as indicator lights on devices such as disk drives. They are also useful for monitoring the logic state of lines in control applications.

Phase-alternating line (PAL)

is the UK standard method of encoding colour information in a television signal. The computer must contain a PAL encoder for colour if a domestic television set is used as a display device via the ordinary aerial socket.

Printing

Printer

including: monochrome printer, colour printer, print head, dot-matrix printer, inkjet printer, bubble-jet printer

is an output device producing characters or graphics on paper. *Monochrome printers* use a single ink colour, normally black on white paper. *Colour printers* use coloured inks, to produce the coloured image, as well as black ink. There are many methods of printing and of organising the operation of a printer; for example, some smaller printers use a moving *print head*, which travels backwards and forwards across the paper and carries the printing mechanism.

   Dot-matrix printers (see below) are relatively cheap, but the quality of printing may be poor. They include *inkjet printers* (also known as *bubble-jet printers*), which produce print quality rivalling that produced by a laser printer (but not as quickly). The advantages of *laser printers* are their speed and high quality of printing. They are used in offices as they are robust and the printed image is waterproof. Colour laser printers are available, but they are rather expensive. For a summary of information about printers see Table B4.1, page 203.

Impact printer

is a term applied to any printer that creates marks on the paper by striking an inked ribbon (or carbon paper) against the paper. The object that strikes the ribbon may be the shape of a complete character or may form a pattern of dots, which combine to reproduce a character or to produce a graphic image.

Character printer

including: daisy-wheel printer, golf-ball printer

is a printer that prints complete characters one at a time. A moving print head holds the mechanical part, a wheel (*daisy wheel*) or ball (*golf ball*), on which the set of characters are arranged, and can travel from side to side across the paper. The character is lined up with the striking position and then struck against a ribbon on to the paper. A change of font is achieved by replacing the mechanical part. These printers were based on the typewriter.

Matrix printer

is a printer that forms characters or graphics images out of ink dots in a rectangular matrix of printing positions (see Figure B4.1). The image is made up of dots in the same way that a screen image is generated using *pixel graphics* (see page 198).

Dot-matrix printer

also known as: pin printer
including: thermal printer
is a *matrix printer* (see above) that uses pins to print the dots. A print head moves in straight lines across the paper. Inside the print head is a vertical line of pins, each of which can print a dot on the paper. The dots are printed by pins striking a ribbon against the paper. By making a particular set of pins hit the paper at the right moment, it is possible to print a pattern of dots that looks like any character that is wanted. Some dot-matrix printers can print in colour by using a special ribbon containing the four *CMYK colours* (see page 193).

These printers are reliable, are cheap and can make multiple (carbon) copies at the same time because the impact can produce an image on several layers of *multipart stationery* (see page 205). They will work with almost any quality of paper, and generally they are able to print on either continuous paper or single sheets. They can be used in supermarket checkouts because the mechanisms are cheap and in industry, where several copies may be needed. The quality of print is not as good as that from other printers.

A *thermal printer* uses wires, arranged like the pins of a dot-matrix printer, which are heated to form dots on heat-sensitive paper. Thermal printers are very quiet, light and portable, but they do not produce good-quality printing. They are used in older facsimile (fax) machines.

Inkjet printer

also known as: bubble-jet printer
including: ink cartridge, print cartridge
is a printer that uses small bubbles of quick-drying ink to produce the printing. The ink is held in small containers, called *ink cartridges* or *print cartridges*. The printed image is created by forcing droplets of ink from the cartridge through fine holes on to the paper, forming the characters by patterns of dots. It can print text or graphics. A monochrome inkjet printer will print diagrams using shades of grey and characters in black. Colour inkjet printers usually have four separate cartridges for cyan, magenta, yellow and black (see *CMYK model*, page 193).

The print quality of most inkjet printers is much better than that of *dot-matrix printers* (see above); however, they tend to saturate the paper with ink, which can spread, giving a fuzzy outline and causing the paper to crinkle – special paper for inkjet printers removes this problem, but at a cost.

Models exist that can print on very large sizes of paper, but these tend to be large. Smaller portable models are also produced, which are carried more easily.

Photo-quality printer

is capable of producing print-out of a similar quality to traditional photographs. See *Photo printer*, page 35.

PART B

Laser printer

is a page printer that uses a laser beam to 'write' the image to be printed on to a light-sensitive drum. The drum then uses electrostatics (as in a photocopier) to attract toner (a fine plastic powder) to coat the image on the drum. Paper is pressed against the drum, transferring the toner to the paper. The paper is then heated to melt the toner on to the paper. This uses technology called xerography.

The computer software sends the image to the printer's memory, which requires that a laser printer has a fairly large amount of memory in order to print a page.

A monochrome laser printer will use black powder. In a colour laser printer, four passes of the paper are needed, one for each of the three colours cyan, magenta and yellow, and one for black (see *CMYK model*, page 193).

Thermal wax printer

including: dye sublimation printer
is a printer that works by melting coloured wax dyes on to special paper from a wax-coated roll. *Dye sublimation printers* work in a similar way, but with slight differences in the print head and formulation of the dye. They are used for high-quality realistic colour reproduction. Both types are expensive.

Line printer

including: barrel printer, print hammer, chain printer
is a printer that prints a complete line of characters at one time and, hence, is generally faster than other printers. The printers described below are large machines capable of printing at very high speeds and are generally used only with mainframe computers.

In a *barrel printer* the complete character set is provided at each printing position, embossed on the surface of a horizontal barrel or cylinder, and each printing position has a *print hammer*, which is used to press the paper against a ribbon to print a character. The barrel turns; as the correct character for a position occurs, its print hammer strikes the paper against a ribbon and on to the character, causing the character to be printed.

In a *chain printer*, the characters are carried on a continuous chain between a set of print hammers and the paper. The chain moves along the print line; as the required character appears at a print position, the print hammer strikes the paper against a ribbon and on to the character.

Unless these printers are well maintained, the quality can be poor, with the characters being badly aligned. Although they have mostly been replaced by other types of printer, some are still in use.

Table B4.1   Printers

	Character printers	Matrix printers	Page printers
Types of printer	Line printers (barrel, chain), golf-ball, daisy-wheel.	Pin dot-matrix printers, inkjet printers.	Laser printers.
Where in use	Obsolescent technology, but some line printers are still in use in large-scale data processing contexts.	Replacement for typewriter-style printers; generally compact machines; wide range of speeds and quality.	Have almost completely replaced the older line printers for large volume printing. Sizes range from desk-top to very large, floor-standing machines.
Application range	Obsolescent.	From personal printers to network printers on small networks, and specialised such as ATM printing devices.	Personal printers to large-scale data processing.
Printing method	Impact on a ribbon or carbon paper is used to form the characters. Characters are printed as complete characters in a single action.	Uses pins (impact or thermal) or inkjet to print the image. Text and images are made up of dots in a matrix pattern (similar to a screen image).	Uses photocopier principles. Prints a complete page at a time.
Mechanism	Line printers use a print hammer for each print position to strike the paper and ribbon/carbon paper against embossed type on barrels or chain loops when the right character is in position. Daisy-wheel and golf-ball printers print a character and then move to the next print position and have easily changeable fonts.	Print mechanisms move backwards and forwards over the paper, which advances after each pass by the print mechanism. Print quality is determined by the number of pins or ink bubble size and the minimum size of head and paper movements.	Image of the page is 'written' by lasers onto a special drum as an electrostatic charge. The drum attracts toner particles which are transferred to the page and heated to set the image.
Text / graphics	Text only.	Text and graphics.	Text and graphics.
Quality	Line printers – poor. Daisy-wheel, golf-ball – very good.	Print quality depends on the resolution (dots per inch).	Capable of very high resolution (dots per inch).
Fonts	Usually only a single (limited) font available at one time.	Wide range of fonts available through software.	Wide range of fonts available through software.
Line spacing	Restricted line spacing (often only full lines).	Flexible line spacing.	
Print area	Unlimited page length; fixed maximum width.	Unlimited page length, fixed maximum width.	Can print anywhere on the page print area (possibly excluding margins).
Stationery	Can print multipart stationery.	Pin printers – can print multi-part stationery. Inkjet printers – cannot print multi-part stationery.	Cannot print conventional multi-part stationery.
Colour	Usually only single colour, black, fixed intensity.	Can print in colour; inkjet can print a range of shades.	Can print colour; can print a range of shades.
Speed	Line printers can print at high speeds.	Slow to medium speed printing.	Can print at high speeds.
Current speed range	Daisy-wheel/golf-ball: 5–35 cps. Line printers: 200–2000 lines per minute.	Pin (impact): 25–250 cps. Inkjet or bubble jet: 4 mins per page to 8+ pages per min.	Laser 4–40+ ppm (up to 2500+ lines per minute).

PART B

Bidirectional printer

is a printer in which the return movement of the *print head* (see above) is also used to print, speeding up the printing often at the expense of quality.

Page printer

is a printer that forms and prints a whole page in one operation, for example a *laser printer* (see page 202).

Graph plotter

also known as: plotter
including: flat-bed plotter, digital plotter, X–Y plotter, incremental plotter
draws lines on paper by moving a pen in a holder relative to the paper on which the drawing is being made. In some designs, the paper is on a roller, and both the pen and the roller move. In others, known as *flat-bed plotters*, the paper is fixed on a flat surface, and all the movements are made by the pen. Colour is achieved by changing the pens. The software to control plotters is different from that used to control printers.

Digital plotters receive digital input specifying the coordinates of the points to be plotted, together with information about how the next point to be plotted is joined to the current point.

X–Y plotters create the drawing by plotting data at points defined by their x and y coordinates. They are used by architects and engineers for *computer-aided design* (see page 157) because they are very accurate.

An *incremental plotter* receives input data specifying increments to its current position, rather than data specifying coordinates.

Paper-feed mechanism

including: line feed, page feed, friction feed, tractor feed, pin feed, (cut) sheet feeder
is the means of making the paper move through the printing process. Many printers require *line feed*; that is, the paper is moved after a line (or sometimes half a line) has been printed. Laser printers eject one page at a time, i.e. *page feed*.

Friction feed is a mechanism for advancing paper by gripping it between rollers.

Tractor feed, also known as *pin feed*, is a mechanism for advancing paper by the use of perforations down the side of the paper and a toothed wheel (a sprocket).

Cut sheet feeder (also known as *sheet feeder*) allows ordinary separate sheets of paper to be fed in automatically for printing. Where a sheet feeder is not provided as part of the printer, it may be available as an accessory.

Print-out

also known as: hard copy
is computer output printed on paper.

Feed

is the process of making paper move through the printer. See *paper-feed mechanism*, page 204.

Continuous stationery

including: fan-fold paper, bursting, multipart stationery, decollate
is printer paper that is perforated to make pages and folded in alternate directions at each set of perforations to form a stack, *fan-fold paper*. *Bursting* is the separating of continuous stationery into individual sheets by tearing the paper along the perforations; it may be handled mechanically or by humans. Continuous stationery normally has a tear-off margin on both sides with holes for a tractor feed mechanism to use. It can be a series of pre-printed forms.

For some applications, it may consist of several sheets together, either with carbon paper in between or made of pressure-sensitive paper (termed *multipart stationery*) so that several copies are printed at the same time using an impact printer. To *decollate* is to separate the sheets of each page of multipart stationery. See also *pre-printed stationery*, below.

Pre-printed stationery

has certain fixed information already printed on each sheet so that the computer can fill in the gaps. This increases the speed of printing and improves the presentation. The paper may be cut sheets or continuous stationery. Common examples are customer accounts for gas and electricity and computer-printed cheques.

Printer buffer

is a store (usually in the printer but it can be in a separate box between the computer and printer) that receives the information for printing and stores it until it is printed. It is able to receive the information at a much higher speed than the printer can print, thereby freeing the computer from the printing task a little quicker.

Page-description language

including: PostScript
is a *high-level computer language* (see page 293) used to pass instructions to printers for setting up the data to be printed.

PostScript is a page-description language used by some laser printers for complex graphics and desktop publishing. The computer will code its print-out requirements, for example the size, direction and style of a piece of text or the format for a diagram. These will then be interpreted by the PostScript translator into the corresponding image of dots ready for printing. The PostScript translator is held as software in a processor in the printer.

B5 Communications Components

This section is concerned with terms used in describing the transmission of data between computers within a network. Other related terms may be found in A13 Communications, A14 Networking and D5 Communications Technology.

Communications and control require that information is passed rapidly and accurately between parts of a system. The origins of present-day communication systems are the electric telegraph, in which signals were sent as electric pulses, the telephone, in which sound is passed as a varying electric current, and radio, in which the signals are sent as electromagnetic radiation.

Modern communications systems are highly reliable, accurate and affordable. From the earliest days of computers until the late 1980s, it was necessary to install special-quality telephone lines between linked computers. Now it is possible to use standard voice-quality lines for connecting computers and remote devices. This is due partly to the use of digital signal systems and partly to the use of more reliable materials and devices for the transmission of signals in the public communications systems. The installation of digital telephone exchanges in many parts of the world, and the use of radio links where cables are not available, mean that it is impossible for a user to know whether a link between two telephones or two computers is by cables or via some terrestrial or satellite radio link. Where public communication links are not available, private links are installed.

The materials for connecting computers are wires of some form, fibre-optic cables, radio links or infrared radiation. Each has its advantages and disadvantages. If wires or optic cables are used, then the individual locations of equipment may be restricted to sites served by the cables; if infrared links are used, then receivers and transmitters have to be in sight of each other; if radio is used, then privacy may not be achieved easily. At present, nearly all local area networks are linked by some form of wire cable. Where these connect into the wider world, they require some device to make the connections to the outside world. These connecting devices arrange for the signals to be sent in an appropriate form, at the correct speed and with the necessary destination information attached. The computer user determines the content and destination of the messages, but the linking devices determine the way in which the messages are sent and often the route.

Modem (MOdulator–DEModulator)

is a data communications device for sending and receiving data between computers over telephone circuits. It converts the digital signals from the computer into audio tones for transmission over ordinary voice-quality telephone lines and converts incoming audio signals into digital signals for the computer. It is normally plugged directly into a standard telephone socket.

Terminal adapter

is an interface that is plugged into a microcomputer to link into an *ISDN* (*integrated services digital network*) (see page 374).

Private Branch Exchange (PBX)

including: Private Automatic Branch Exchange (PABX)
is a private telephone exchange. It provides the interface between a group of telephone extensions and the public network lines. There is usually a facility that allows any extension to dial any other extension directly and to dial into the public network using only a simple connect code and the outside number. Normally, external callers connect with the operator, unless they know the direct-dial number for an individual extension.

Digital *PABXs* can control and interconnect a mix of telephones, fax machines, teletext devices and computers all operating at different bit rates.

Multiplexor

sometimes spelt: multiplexer
including: Time-Division Multiplexor (TDM), time slice, statistical multiplexor, intelligent time-division multiplexor, Frequency-Division Multiplexor (FDM)
is a device that receives data from several independent sources for transmission along a single route to a single destination. A two-way communication multiplexor must be able to separate signals for each of the destinations. The demultiplexor could be a *front-end processor* (see page 168).

PART B

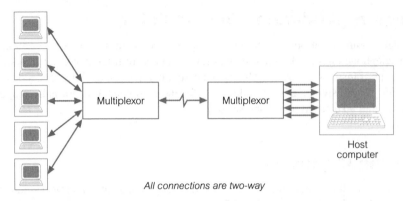

All connections are two-way

Figure B5.1 Multiplexors connecting remote workstations to a computer

A *Time-Division Multiplexor* (*TDM*) transmits the signals from two or more sources in successive short time intervals, called *time slices*. Each source gets the same duration of time interval. Where the multiplexor time allocation is proportional to the activity of each source, it is called a *statistical multiplexor,* or an *intelligent time-division multiplexor.*

A *Frequency-Division Multiplexor* (*FDM*) uses the available route link to transmit the data from the different sources at the same time. This is achieved by dividing the available channel *bandwidth* (see page 373) into a number of narrow bands, each of which is used for a separate transmission but at a slower speed.

Wireless communication

including: infra-red communication, microwave transmission, satellite
covers a whole range of possible methods of data transmission, which can be used for linking computers within networks or for links within computer systems.

Infrared communication uses the same systems as domestic remote control of a television. Examples of its use include the control of robotic devices and remote keyboards. It is necessary for there to be direct unobstructed line of sight between the transmitter and the receiver. Strong sunlight will interfere with infrared signals.

Microwave transmission is used as a method of communication within public telephone services. Many organisations use private installations to transmit data between key sites. Unlike cellular phone systems, which are broadcast systems, microwave transmissions use highly directional transmitters and receivers with dish aerials.

Satellite links are used for international communications by many providers of public telephone services. Unlike satellite broadcast systems, these links use highly directional narrow-beam two-way transmissions. A single channel is capable of carrying simultaneously a very large number of separate transmissions.

Wire connector

including: copper cable, coaxial cable, Twisted Pair (TP), Unshielded Twisted Pair (UTP)
is a standard form of wire cable used to provide the connections in a network.

   Copper cables are commonly used as connectors for local area networks, since they are readily available and have suitable electrical characteristics. Various types of copper cable are used, including the following:

Coaxial cable, which is made to a variety of specifications, is the same kind of cable that is used for connecting a television aerial to a television set. It has two conductors: one is a wire down the centre of the cable, which may be a single strand, insulated from the second conductor, which is made up of many strands braided around the insulation for the inner wire.

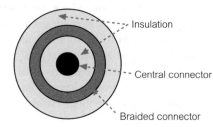

Insulation

Central connector

Braided connector

Figure B5.2   Section of coaxial cable

Twisted Pair (*TP*) cable is commonly used for data transmission. In its simplest form it is a pair of insulated copper wires twisted together and surrounded by a copper braid and external insulation. Some cables are made up of a number of twisted pairs surrounded by an overall (earthed) braid screen. In another form, stranded copper wires are twisted together in pairs with an earth wire. These pairs may be grouped to form a single multi-connector cable. These cables all have different specifications and, used in the correct situation, provide minimum interference data transmission.

Unshielded Twisted Pair (*UTP*) cable is similar to the *twisted pair cables* described above, but with no earthed shield. In suitable circumstances, they can be used for data transmission.

Fibre-optic cable

also known as: optical fibre
is a very fine glass strand that allows rapid transmission of data using modulated light beams. It is usual to put many strands together in a single cable, each one capable of carrying one or more data signals. Fibre-optic cable provides interference-free secure data transmission and, unlike metal wires, is not subject to corrosion.

PART B

Signal level

including: signal amplifier, signal booster
is the measure of the strength of a communications signal. In the same way that sound and light become weaker with distance, electrical signals passing down a wire become weaker as they travel along the wire. For this reason, *signal amplifiers* or *boosters* are built into communications networks at appropriate intervals. These increase the signal level before passing the signal on to the next part of the network.

Signal converter

including: digital signal, analog signal, analog-to-digital (A-to-D or A/D) converter, digitising, digital-to-analogue (D-to-A or D/A) converter
is a device that converts serial signals from one form to another. Signals may be *digital*, consisting of discrete bit patterns, or *analog*, consisting of a continuously variable voltage. Both analog and digital signals are used to represent data. Some devices generate analog signals or need to be supplied with data in analog form, while others generate or have to be supplied with data in digital form.

An *analog-to-digital (A-to-D) converter* converts analog signals into digital signals for subsequent processing. This conversion is sometimes called *digitising*. For example, the analog output from a microphone has to be digitised before it can be stored or processed by a computer.

A *digital-to-analog (D-to-A) converter* converts serial digital signals into analog signals. For example, the digital data for a computer display have to be converted into analog signals if they are to be used as input to a television.

Handshake

is the exchange of signals between devices to establish their readiness to send or receive data, for example the transmission of data from a computer to a printer. Handshaking is one of a number of methods used to ensure that both the sender and the receiver are ready before transmission begins.

Baud

including: baud rate, bits per second (bps), bytes per second (bps), bit rate, characters per second (cps)
is the unit used to measure the speed (the *baud rate*) of serial data transmission, for example the transmission of data along a telephone line or the speed of serial transmission to a printer. Generally, one baud is one bit per second, but it is important to note that there is no simple relationship between baud rate and the rate of data transfer between devices. Under any communications protocol, additional bits have to be transmitted to provide start and stop bits, error detection and other communications

controls. In addition, methods of communication, such as multiphase signalling and *data compression* (see page 329), can both increase the amount of data that are transmitted in a given time.

Other measures of speed of data transfer are:

bits per second (*bps*), sometimes called the *bit rate*, which is a measure of the speed at which data move between various parts of a computer. High bit rates are given in kbit/s (2^{10} = 1024 bps) or Mbits/s (2^{20} = 1 048 576 bps) (note: sometimes *bps* is taken to mean *bytes per second*, which is normally the same as characters per second);

characters per second (*cps*), which is a measure of the speed of character data transfer between devices. It is frequently also given as a measure of the speed of printers.

Transducer

is an electronic component that converts one form of energy to another. For example, a thermistor converts a temperature into electrical energy with a varying voltage, and a photo cell converts brightness of illumination into a voltage. The term is generally applied to devices that produce electricity rather than those that convert electricity into another form of energy.

Sampler

also known as: digital sampler

is an electronic circuit that takes samples of an electronic signal at intervals and stores them for future processing. In particular, they are used to take frequent measurements of analog signals for converting an analog signal into a digital signal, when it is known as a digital sampler.

PART B

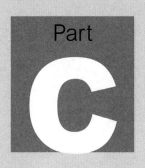

Part

C

How Computer Systems are Developed

This part is concerned with terms relating to computer systems development. These are frequently considered to be associated with computer science, unlike the terms in Part A, which are concerned with the needs of computer system users, and in Part B, which provides some technical information that may be helpful to both computer users and students following courses requiring some knowledge of computer systems and peripherals. Part D is concerned with the way computers work.

The range of terms covered in Part C, and the depth of treatment of individual terms, have been influenced by knowledge of the difficulties encountered by students who are studying courses that involve some computer science, whatever the name of the course.

PART C

Systems Design and Life Cycle

Related topics can be found in A7 User Interface and Documentation, C2 Describing Systems, C7 Describing Programs and C8 Implementing, Testing and Running Programs.

There is an enormous difference between the large-scale commercial production of software and an individual writing a computer program for their own use. The problems are much larger – too large for one person to manage – and usually have to be tackled by a team. A formal approach to the task is essential to plan and to enable members of the team to communicate both during and after development. In contrast, an individual writing a small program can do much of the visualisation and planning in their head.

For a purpose-built computer system, usually designed for a specific customer (for example, a large company), it is essential to establish exactly what the customer requires. The designers need to avoid the traditional complaints: 'Yes – but what I really meant was . . .' 'Yes – and while you're about it, can you just . . .' The aim is to produce a reliable system that prevents errors and is produced at the right time and for the expected cost.

When designing software that will be marketed in volume, such as word processors and spreadsheets, there is commercial pressure to ensure that it is useful to as many people as possible; for example, it should:

- have a range of attractive features absent from competing software;
- work within the limitations of the currently accepted level of hardware and, in particular, within the limits of any networking and communication systems;
- be able to be upgraded easily and cheaply from earlier versions (rather than users being tempted to buy a competitor's product);
- make it easy for users of competing products to use, for example by offering the ability to read (or import) files prepared in other software packages or by designing the user interface so that it has similarities with competing products.

The development team of a computer system or software application may also have to take into account the various rules that the designers of the operating system (such as Windows, MacOS or UNIX) have defined. This ensures that the software works reliably and will work in the future when the operating system is improved or upgraded.

There is the need to establish precisely what the customer requires; to organise the design and coding so that teams of people can work together; to keep track of the many changes that will inevitably be necessary; and to provide suitable documentation for the future maintenance of the software and suitable documentation for the user. This can be done using a defined development procedure, so that each member of the team knows exactly what is expected and can follow this procedure in a professional way.

This chapter defines terms and methods that are generally accepted for the development of computer systems. More detailed methodologies, such as structured systems analysis and design methodology (SSADM) and Jackson structured design (JSD), have been developed and are used commercially to provide a reliable method of computer systems development.

Typically, a **feasibility study** is done before any development starts. Estimates are made of costs, effort, effectiveness, reliability and the benefits to be expected from the new or improved system. A decision is then taken as to whether to proceed, based on the costs involved and the value of the benefits achieved. The development team then conducts an analysis of any existing system and of the requirements of the new system (**systems analysis**). The new system will be designed (**systems design**) and a **systems specification** produced of the desired system. This sets out the hardware and software requirements and the organisational and human implications. Only when all these stages are complete will work begin on the production of the system (**implementation of the design**). The final system will then be tested (**systems testing**) and installed (**installation**). When in use, the system will probably be adapted and modified (**maintenance**) by a different team.

It should be clear that designing computer systems (which may include hardware as well as software and manual procedures) is a task that requires considerable management and discipline. The development of large, complex systems (on which safety as well as profits may depend) is very similar to the design and construction of engineering projects such as bridges and buildings.

Concepts

System life cycle

including: system cycle

is the various stages that have to be completed in order to create a new or modified computer system, often known as the *system cycle*. These stages form a cycle because after a period of time, the system will need modifying or replacing and the process has to be repeated.

The system may include both hardware and software or just software. To ensure that a system is developed effectively, a planned approach is usually taken, which defines how the development takes place; see also *design methodology* (page 000).

There are various models for the different stages, but a typical system cycle is shown in Figure C1.1. The individual stages are described later in this chapter. See pages 219 to 222. See also Figure C1.4.

Stage	Description
Feasibility study	Of the users' requirements, including a preliminary analysis of the required system
Analysis	Of the system requirements, to provide a specification
Design	Of the new system, both the overall structure and details of the system components
Implementation (of the design)	Using the design from the previous stage, development of the software follows a similar set of stages generally known as the *software development cycle (see page 000)*
Testing	The implemented design: software, hardware and manual procedures
Installation (and commissioning)	Of the new system in its working environment
Maintenance	Of the new system to keep it working

- Formal documentation will be produced at each stage
- Each stage may be reviewed and repeated until the result is acceptable
- See pages 000–000

Figure C1.1   System life cycle

System development cycle

is the various stages in designing and implementing a new computer system. These stages, *analysis*, *design*, *implementation*, *testing* and *installation*, are part of the system life cycle performed by the main design team.

Figure C1.2 shows the stages of a typical system development cycle. Individual stages are described separately elsewhere in this chapter.

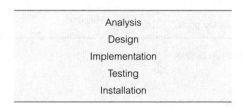

Analysis
Design
Implementation
Testing
Installation

Figure C1.2   System development cycle

Software development cycle

including: software life cycle

is the various stages required to produce the software component of a new computer system. The software development cycle is part of the *implementation* stage of the *system life cycle* (see above).

Software is often the most complicated part of a system. Hence, the software-development cycle is often considered separately, although the stages are very similar to those of the *system development cycle* (see above). A typical software development cycle is shown in Figure C1.3.

PART C

The *software life cycle* includes the additional stages of *feasibility*, *analysis*, *installation* and *maintenance*, which may be considered separately from the rest of the system. See pages 219–221. See also Figure C1.4.

Stage	Description
Overall design	Identifies what is required of the software and splits it into self-contained modules
Module design	Decides how each module will perform its task
Module production	Produces a computer program for each module (coding)
Module testing	Makes sure that each module works independently
Combining the modules	Produces the new software system
Integration testing	Makes sure that the modules work together

Figure C1.3 Software development cycle

The relationship between the system life cycle, the software life cycle and the system development cycle can be confusing. The system development cycle is, in fact, simply part of the system life cycle. Similarly, the software development cycle is simply part of the system development cycle. The software life cycle is the same as the system life cycle when the system being designed consists solely of software. Figure C1.4 shows the relationship between these various concepts.

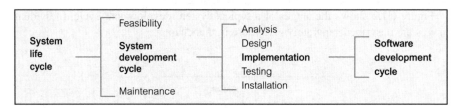

Figure C1.4 Relationship between the three cycles

Design methodology

including: Jackson structured programming (JSP), Jackson structured development (JSD), structured systems analysis and design method (SSADM)
is a set of rules to be followed when designing a computer program or a computer system. This ensures that all the steps of the system-development cycle are followed. Using the same methodologies means that different people can work together as a team. Design methodologies include the following:

Jackson structured programming (JSP) is a structured programming technique that uses diagrams as a step to developing programs. *Structured programming* (see page 227) emphasises an orderly approach to program development, breaking down large tasks into smaller subtasks. JSP is a particular form of this diagrammatic method that enables the design process to be managed efficiently.

Jackson structured development (JSD) is a method devised by Michael Jackson in 1983 for the analysis and design of computer software systems. JSD emphasises the need for orderly structure in the development and design of systems.

SSADM (Structured Systems Analysis and Design Method) is the standard method of analysis and design of large-scale software packages used within government departments in the UK and is widely used commercially. SSADM is very precise and divides the method into many small stages.

Stages

Feasibility study

including: problem identification
is the preliminary investigation of a problem used to decide whether a solution is possible and how it may be done. It may be carried out by the main design team or by a separate team, which will allow a suitable main design team to be chosen. It is similar to the *systems analysis* (see below), but at a much simpler level. It often:

- describes the context of the problem;
- contains an evaluation, or simple analysis, of the problem;
- identifies and justifies ways in which the problem may be solvable;
- involves a cost–benefit analysis to decide whether a solution is affordable.

Systems analysis

is an investigation into a problem and how a new system will solve it. The analyst will usually:

- research how the previous system and other similar systems work using interviews, observation, existing documentation, questionnaires and experience. In some cases, this may be documented formally to provide a basis for the new design;
- identify the main requirements for the system, i.e. the *requirements specification*, see page 227;
- identify what is input to and output from the system;
- describe the system using data-flow diagrams and a commentary;
- define the input, output and processing requirements for each process identified;
- develop a data model. This may include normalised entity descriptions and entity-relationship diagrams;
- identify the likely hardware and software constraints;
- specify the hardware and the software required to carry out the development.

Systems design

is the production of a detailed description showing how the new system will be constructed. One or more overall designs will be produced, and then detailed designs will be produced for the preferred solution. It will usually include:

- the overall design using a system diagram and commentary describing and justifying the solution;
- detailed design of user interface, and the validation and verification of the input data;
- detailed design of reports and other outputs;
- detailed design of the storage and organisation of the data;
- detailed specifications and structure diagrams of each process; see *functional specification*, page 227;
- a test plan for both the individual functions and the system as a whole. This will include the test data to be used.

Implementation (of the design)

is the process of constructing the working computer system. It will usually include:

- identifying and specifying the modules to be used;
- identifying the main data structures within the program;
- identifying the main algorithms to be used, describing them in *pseudo-code* (page 274) or as *structure diagrams* (page 237);
- producing the program and any other elements of the system.

Systems testing

is making sure that the system works as described in the specification. This is done by following the test plan as follows:

1. Test each individual system function.
2. Test that each individual function works with extreme or invalid data.
3. Test the whole system to ensure that the system produces the correct results for the data input.

Installation

also known as: systems implementation
including: parallel running, pilot running, direct changeover, big bang, phased implementation

is the process of starting to use an information system in a real situation after having designed and developed it. It may enable final testing in a real situation. Different approaches are used, depending on the size of the system and the properties of the data being processed.

Parallel running requires the new system to operate for a short period of time alongside the older system. The results can be compared to ensure that the new system is working correctly.

Pilot running requires the new system to operate alongside the old system but only processing part of the data. The results can be compared to check that the system works correctly, but pilot running cannot test how the system will operate with the larger quantities of data in a real situation.

Direct changeover or *big bang* requires that the new system replaces the old system without any overlap. In some cases, the nature of the system prevents parallel or pilot running, and a direct changeover is the only option, for example with an emergency-control system.

Phased implementation involves replacing part of a system with a new system while some tasks continue to use the old system. This enables training and installation to be spread over a period of time. For example, a supermarket chain might install a new system in a few of its branches to begin with and phase the introduction into its other branches as they are refurbished. This initial phase of the implementation will inevitably involve some parallel running.

Maintenance

is ensuring that the system continues to run smoothly and to meet changed requirements, for example:

■ addressing problems not identified previously;

■ modifying the software when circumstances change, for example the amount of data increases, the system is to be used in a new area or the data need to be processed slightly differently (for example, due to changes in legal requirements);

■ replacing the computer hardware;

■ adding new facilities to the software.

Documentation

including: technical documentation, maintenance documentation, systems documentation, program documentation
is the written information and diagrams that enable the development of the system to be planned professionally, help users use the system, and enable the maintenance and development of the system. The documentation usually consists of *technical documentation*, *user documentation* and, if appropriate, *installation instructions* (see below and *user documentation*, page 69).

Technical documentation describes how the system works. It is written for the computer professional rather than the user, and the reader will need to have expert knowledge. It will include both *systems documentation* and *program documentation* (see below). Some parts will be highly technical, for example the specifications of peripherals and their configuration. It is used mainly to develop and later adapt the system. It is sometimes known as *maintenance documentation*.

Systems documentation describes the results of the systems analysis, what is expected of the system, the overall design decisions, the *test plan* and the *test data* (see page 283) with the expected results.

Program documentation is the complete description of the software, intended for use when altering or adapting the software. It usually includes a statement of the purpose of the software, any restrictions on the use of the software, the format for input data, printed output produced, flowcharts, program listings and notes to assist in future modifications.

General

Benchmark

is a standard set of computer tasks designed to allow measurements to be made of computer performance. These tasks can be used to compare the performance of different software or hardware. Examples of tasks are how long it takes to copy a 1 Mb file across a network, how many pages can be printed in one minute, and how long it takes to save 1000 database records to disk. Users seeking to buy software or hardware may be able to obtain some information about the performance of possible purchases.

Benchmarks may also figure in *acceptance testing* (see *Figure C1.1*, page 217) of a computer system, by specifying performance that must be achieved before the system is considered finished. See also *software metric*, below, for a description of the theoretical equivalent of the more practical benchmark.

Software metric

is a value that can be associated with a piece of software to describe its efficiency, performance, ease of development, and other properties. *Benchmarks* (see above) measure how software actually behaves, while software metrics attempt to describe performance from a study of the program code alone. Simple and sometimes not very helpful metrics include the number of lines of code and the space occupied in memory.

Commissioning

including: decommissioning
is putting a new system into use. The suppliers make sure that the system is ready to be used, and the customer accepts that it meets their specifications. The customer will

have checked the operation of the system and can start using it to do the job it was designed for.

Decommissioning is taking an old system out of use. This involves more than simply switching it off. Data will have to be transferred to a new system or saved in a way in which they can be accessed later (such as on microfilm). Records will need to be made of outstanding problems that still need to be dealt with, and the hardware will need to be disposed of safely.

Compatibility

including: backward-compatibility, downward-compatibility, upward-compatibility describes how well different computer systems work together.

Backward-compatible (also known as *downward-compatible*) is used to describe a computer system designed to work with older systems. For example, programs can load files from older versions of the program, or computer hardware will run software designed for older types of computer. Backward-compatibility ensures that new software can be acquired without needing to buy new hardware and that the data from the old computer system can continue to be used.

Upward-compatible is used to describe a computer system designed to be extended and improved without the need to retrain staff or to alter any stored data.

Configuration management

is the automatic tracking and monitoring of changes to software during development, so that everyone involved is aware of the features of the latest version.

Bespoke system

is a system developed for a specific customer. It might include unusual hardware and will have to be specially programmed. This is expensive to do, but it may be the only solution to the customer's needs, particularly for a large organisation. It will take longer to develop and test, but the customer will get an efficient system that meets their requirements. In contrast, a *customised system* (see below) may not provide exactly the facilities wanted, although it is cheaper and quicker to develop and will need less testing.

Customised system

including: turnkey system
is a system consisting of standard hardware and software that is then adapted to suit a customer's requirements. Many users do not have the skill or resources to set up a new computer system. Such users will purchase a customised system from a supplier. See also *bespoke system*, above.

PART C

The supplier may simply alter the *defaults* (see page 15) and provide special templates to the customers requirements.

In a more complex system, several commercial programs may need to be combined to produce the required system. The cost of writing standard programs, such as word processors and databases, is very high, and it is much more cost-effective for, for example, a standard database to be purchased and a small program written to access it in the most efficient way for the user. See also *application program interface*, below.

The supplier could supply the system as a *turnkey system*. Such a system is installed quickly; when the user switches it on, it functions without further configuration.

Application program interface (API)

is the way in which a supplier of a software application enables a user to integrate this application with the user's own programs and with other software applications. This enables *customised systems* (see page 223) to be constructed easily and quickly using standard software packages. For example, a program may be written to take data from a payroll program and use the facilities of a spreadsheet program to present the data as charts.

The application program interface usually takes the form of standardised machine-code calls to subroutines in the software application. The supplier can alter the program code of the application and can adapt the application program interface to work with the new program. The user's programs will still work, because the way in which the application program interface is accessed has not changed. See also *customise*, page 14.

Developmental testing

including: alpha test, beta test, acceptance testing
is the repeated testing of a system so that the results can be used for further design and development. Commercial software is developed to an incomplete state, with some questions of design, command sequences and defaults left unresolved.

Alpha testing is the issue of the software to a restricted audience of testers within the developer's own company. This version may not be completely finished and may have faults.

Beta testing is when a version is released to a number of privileged customers in exchange for their constructive comments. This is after the results of the *alpha testing* have been studied and appropriate changes made. Beta-test versions are usually similar to the finally released product. They are made available to computer magazine reviewers, authors of independent 'how to' instructional manuals and developers of associated software or hardware products, who can work over a period of time with a near-complete package so that the final launch can be accompanied by valuable and informed publicity.

Acceptance testing is the testing carried out to prove to the customer that the system works correctly. This testing is done when system development is complete and the system is ready to be handed over to the customer. It will test all parts of the system and compare it with the requirements specified in the design. It is designed to ensure that the customer will get what they ordered. If the system fails any of the tests, then the supplier is obliged to correct the faults.

Formal methods

including: formal specification
is the name given to the mathematical techniques used to attempt to prove that software works, without having to test every possible route through the programs. With large complex computer systems, it is almost impossible to test that the system behaves properly under every possible combination of circumstances. Therefore, individual parts of the system will have a precise *formal specification* including inputs that they will recognise and outputs that they will produce that can be linked together with mathematics.

Process

also known as: subtask
is a task or operation that has to be carried out within a computer system, e.g. editing a record, sorting a file, inputting a set of data or printing a report.

Project management

is the organisation, planning and control of the various stages of the development cycle for a system. Project managers will set deadlines and ensure that all the tasks are completed for a particular stage before moving on to the next one. They will ensure that the necessary documentation is completed and reports are prepared detailing what has been achieved and what problems still have to be solved. Special software has been written to help manage large projects (see *project-management software*, page 160).

Prototyping

including: prototype, storyboard
is the construction of a simple version of the program, a *prototype*, that is used as part of the design process to demonstrate how the system will work. The prototype generally consists of the working *user interface*, but it will not actually process any data. The prototype can be reviewed by the user and changes made to the system at the design stage.

PART C

A *storyboard* is a diagram that shows the planned sequence of screen displays in a user interface. Unlike the storyboard in a film (which is linear), the storyboard may be a branching diagram showing the different paths available to the user.

Reverse engineering

is the analysis of existing software to produce an equivalent design. It is used if the original design documentation is lost to enable the maintenance of the system or the development of a replacement system. It may also be used illegally to reveal the techniques used in a competitor's product.

Shrink-wrapped software

is a computer application that is sold prepackaged for the user to install from the disks provided on to their own system. As the software is prepackaged, it can be sold through a variety of outlets such as computer retailers and even supermarkets. Help and support are likely to be limited to the manuals (or on-line documentation) provided, and possibly from a telephone support desk.

Software engineering

also known as: information systems engineering
is the science of designing and constructing new or modified computer systems based mainly on computer software (programs). The software engineer will develop a new system following the *system-development cycle* (see above). This will help to ensure that the new system has the required characteristics of *functionality*, *ease of use*, *robustness*, *flexibility*, *reliability*, *portability* and *ease of maintenance* (see page 251).

Software upgrade

including: version, migrate
is a new version of a program or computer application that is based on an older system but has been improved either to fix problems or to add new features. When purchased, the software upgrade often consists only of the files required to convert the older version to the newer version.

Version is a reference, generally a number, that indicates how old a particular program is. The version number is important because files produced by one version are not always usable by a different version, and having a newer version of the program may cure errors that were present.

Migrate is to move from using one version of a computer application to either a new version or to an application supplied by a competitor. This process may be quite complicated, as staff would have to be trained in the new program and files converted so they can be used by a new program.

It is also possible to upgrade a computer system from one set of hardware to a different hardware set-up. See also *porting*, page 251.

Specification

including: requirements specification, systems specification, functional specification
is a written document which defines precisely aspects of the system. Specifications may be written at different parts of the development cycle and serve different purposes.

Requirements specification is that part of the system documentation that sets out the customer's requirements for the system. It is produced as part of *systems analysis* (see page 219). It may be drafted as a formal contractual agreement between the customer and the software system developers. It will describe what is expected of the system and allow the final system to be assessed, making sure that it meets the customer's expectations.

Systems specification sets out the hardware and software requirements as well as the organisational and human implications. It is produced at the end of the *design phase* (see page 220) and is used by the programmers and others to produce a system that works as intended.

Functional specification describes exactly how the system will behave, showing what happens at each stage of the system as each process is performed. It is usually part of the *systems specification* (see above).

Structured programming

including: structured planning technique, top-down programming, stepwise refinement, bottom-up programming, modular design, module, functional decomposition, object-oriented design
is a methodical approach to the design of a program that emphasises breaking large and complex tasks into smaller subtasks. This is also referred to as *structured planning technique*.

Modular design is a method of organising a large computer program into self-contained parts (*modules*) that can be developed simultaneously by different programmers or teams of programmers. Modules have clearly defined relationships with the other parts of the system, which enables them to be independently designed, programmed and maintained. Some modules may be independently executable programs, while others may be designed to provide facilities for the suite of programs to which they belong.

Top-down programming, or *stepwise refinement*, is a particular type of structured programming, where the overall problem is defined in simple terms and then split into a number of smaller subtasks. Each of these subtasks is successively split and refined until it is small enough to be understood and programmed. It is an axiom of this approach that new ideas that were not in the original global design should not be added. This ensures that elements are not missed.

Functional decomposition is a method similar to top-down programming in which overall functions of the system are defined, which are then successively split down into smaller functions until they are small enough to be programmed.

Bottom-up programming involves designing a number of small modules before designing the larger structure. This is considered bad practice, since it is often difficult to ensure that an efficient system is developed by this method.

Object-oriented design involves identifying self-contained objects that contain both program routines and the data being processed. A program is split down into very small units, called objects, which can then be used by other objects to build a more complex system. Object-oriented design requires the use of an object-oriented programming language. See also *object-oriented programming*, page 242.

Undocumented feature

is a facility included as part of a computer system but that is not described in the official specification or documentation. The feature may not be tested fully or it may be provided to help engineers diagnose faults. The user cannot rely on the feature since it may be altered or removed at a later date.

Describing Systems

This section is concerned with the written comments and graphical illustrations that form the description of a system. The symbols and layout conventions referred to are those given in British Standards BS4058:1987 and BS7738:1994. Related topics can be found in A7 User Interface and Documentation, C1 Systems Design and Life Cycle, C7 Describing Programs and C8 Implementing, Testing and Running Programs.

Software systems will require some modification during their lifetime. If this is to be done satisfactorily, it is vital that good, complete and understandable documentation is available. Requests to modify software may arise for a number of reasons, which could include changes in company procedures, requests for improvements, errors in the software that were not found at the testing stage and changes in government regulations (for example, new taxation laws). The resources required at the maintenance stage of the **systems life cycle**, which is covered in C1 Systems Design and Life Cycle, frequently equal and indeed sometimes exceed the initial resources required to deliver the software in the first instance.

The original team that did the analysis and design, and the implementation, of the software may well not be available to carry out the maintenance stage. This makes it all the more important that good, up-to-date documentation is available throughout the life of the software.

A standard form of documentation may be followed, which may be specified by the company involved. There are a number of recognised system-development methodologies, for example **SSADM (structured systems analysis and design method)**. These specify, at various levels of detail, what documentation should be produced and in what form. Software tools also exist, such as CASE (computer-aided software engineering) tools, which can help to produce consistent documentation of changes.

Documentation produced at the design and analysis stage will include the **requirements specification**, which is sometimes signed off as a formal agreement between the customer and the software group. As the design develops, a range of diagrams will be produced; these will include:

■ diagrams showing the relationships between the data (**entity relationships** or **entity-relation diagrams**);

■ diagrams showing the relationships between the data and the processes or programs that manipulate and transform the data (**data-flow diagrams** or **system diagrams**).

The design task will be tackled in a hierarchical way, breaking it down gradually into smaller parts (subtasks), using methods such as **JSD** (**Jackson structured development**). Often, diagrams, such as those used by Jackson system development, use different shapes to indicate the use of a particular device or medium, in the same way that icons are often used in a graphical user interface.

As the programs are designed and developed, there will be other documentation for the programs. These have particular forms and are covered in C7 Describing Programs.

Flowcharts

Flowchart

including: flow line
is a graphical representation of the operations involved in a process or system. *System flowchart symbols* (see below) are used to represent particular operations or data, and *flow lines*, which connect the flowchart symbols, indicate the sequence of operations or the flow of data. Flow lines may use arrows to indicate sequence, or a top-down, left–right convention may apply if there are no arrows.

System flowchart

also known as: system diagram
is a diagram used to describe a complete data-processing system. The flow of data through the operations is described diagrammatically, down to the level of the individual programs needed to achieve the system requirements. The details of programs are not included, since these are covered in the *program documentation* (see page 222).

Entity-relationship diagram

including: entity relationship
is a diagram used to show how data (entities) are related to each other, for example how the different layers of data in a database are related and how access to one layer of data will automatically achieve access to related data items and related layers. An *entity relationship* is a formal statement of the way in which one data item is related to another, and of the way in which a class of data items is related to items in another class. See also *data model*, page 89.

Figure C2.1 illustrates two different classes of entity relationships, many-to-many and one-to-many.

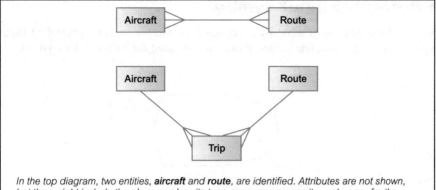

In the top diagram, two entities, **aircraft** and **route**, are identified. Attributes are not shown, but they might include the plane number, its type, passenger capacity, and so on, for the aircraft, and the starting point and destination for the route. There is a relationship between these entities: an aircraft can be used on many routes, and a route can be travelled by many aircraft. Such many-to-many relationships are not easy to implement in a database, so the designer breaks this relationship and invents a new entity called **trip**, which represents one specific journey over that route by one specific aircraft. One aircraft now makes many trips, but each trip is made by only one aircraft. Similarly, one route has many trips over it, but each trip is over just one route. Two such one-to-many relationships are more efficient to implement than one many-to-many relationship.

Figure C2.1   Entity-relationship diagram used in designing a database

System flowchart symbol

is a symbol used in a system flowchart diagram. Different shapes indicate the various kinds of activity described by the diagram. Sometimes, highly formalised shapes are used, each having a specific meaning; in other situations, very simple boxes with words are used. Provided the meaning is clear, either method is an equally acceptable way of representing a process or system. Examples of how these symbols might be used are given in Figure C2.9 (page 234), where rectangles are used for all processes, and Figures C2.10 and C2.11 (pages 235 and 236), which use more formal shapes.

Input/output symbol

also known as: data input/output symbol
is used for any input or output of data, however achieved.

or

Figure C2.2   Input/output symbol

PART C

Interactive input symbol

is used to indicate data input by a keyboard or another operator-controlled input system, such as a bar-code reader. It may also be used for on-line interrogation.

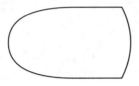

Figure C2.3   Interactive input symbol

Document output symbol

also known as: output document symbol
is used to indicate that data are to be printed.

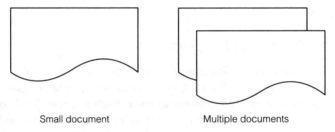

Small document   Multiple documents

Figure C2.4   Document output symbol

Process symbol

also known as: data-processing symbol
is used for the processing of data, for example by a computer program.

Figure C2.5   Process symbol

File symbol

also known as: data symbol
including: on-line datafile symbol, (magnetic) diskfile symbol, (magnetic) tape file symbol

A number of different symbols are used when processing datafiles. In most instances, the symbol shapes make it easier to recognise the process defined within the symbol.

The on-line data file symbol is used for data held on any on-line file, whatever the purpose.

Figure C2.6   On-line datafile symbol

The *(magnetic) disk file symbol* is used whenever the data are held on a disk.

Figure C2.7   (Magnetic) disk file symbol

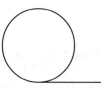

The *(magnetic) tape file symbol* is used whenever the data are held on a tape.

Figure C2.8   (Magnetic) tape file symbol

Flowcharts of a payroll system

The flowcharts in Figures C2.9–C2.11 describe the part of a payroll process where the wages information for each employee is processed. The transactions are validated, sorted and then used to update the wages master file.

The descriptions (printer, disk, etc.) may be altered, according to the particular medium being used; alternatively, the descriptions may be omitted completely if a less specific flowchart is required.

PART C

System flowchart (using simplified symbols)

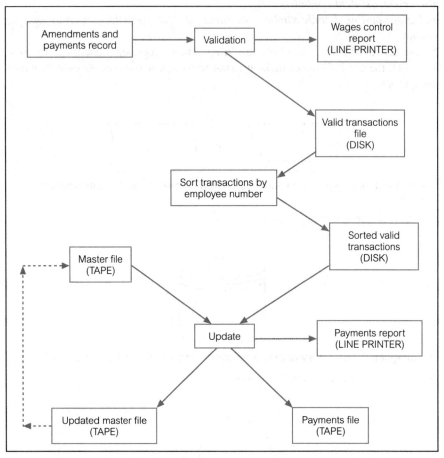

Note: the broken line between the updated master file and the master file indicates that the updated version replaces the original for the next run.

Figure C2.9 Example of system flowchart using simple symbols

System flowchart (using British Standard symbols)

Figure C2.10 uses British Standard symbols to show the process described in Figure C2.9. The annotations on the right of the flowcharts in Figures C2.10 and C2.11 have been used to describe the function of the symbols. A similar annotation method can be used to provide an explanatory commentary on the algorithm or process represented by the flowchart diagram.

An alternative set of symbols is used in Figure C2.11.

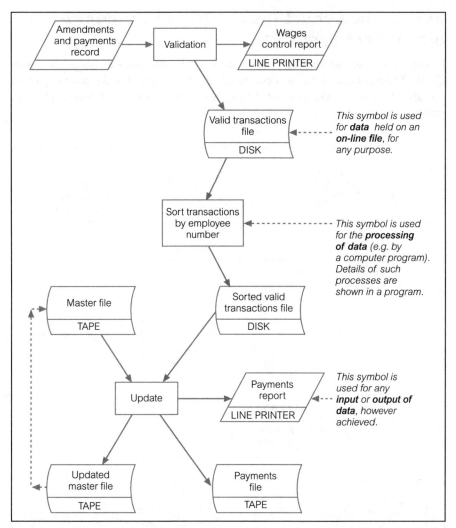

Note: the broken line between the updated master file and the master file indicates that the updated version replaces the original for the next run.

Figure C2.10 Example of system flowchart using British Standard symbols

System flowchart (using British Standard alternative symbols)

Figure C2.11 uses alternative symbols to describe the process shown in Figure C2.10. There are also other, less commonly used symbols. The document symbols can also be used for the input of data to a system by means of documents (e.g. written orders).

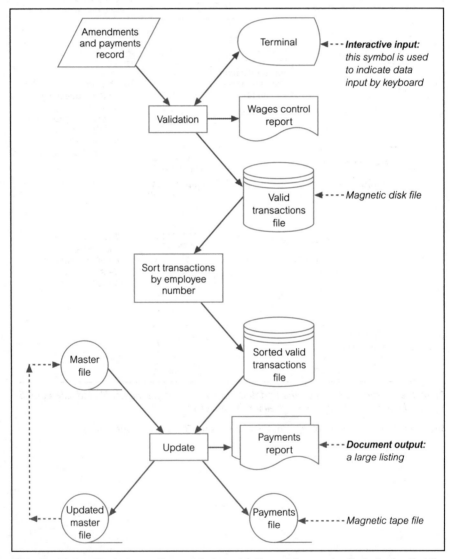

Note: the broken line between the updated master file and the master file indicates that the updated version replaces the original for the next run

Figure C2.11   Example of system flowchart using British Standard alternative symbols

Diagrams

Structure diagram

is a means of representing the design of a program or system. It consists of a number of levels, each of which describes the whole design, but at increasing levels of detail.

The structure diagram in Figure C2.12 shows another way of representing the payroll process shown in Figures C2.9–C2.11. This is based on the *JSD* (*Jackson structured development*) *notation* (see page 219). The hierarchical structure diagram is displayed in a top-down, left-to-right manner. At each successive level (labelled 1, 2, 3, . . .), the tasks are described in greater detail. The lower boxes expand the description of the task defined in the box in the level above to which they are connected. This process of expansion is continued to varying depths in different parts of the diagram until it is judged that sufficient detail is given.

The numbers are used to identify the boxes uniquely. The actual numbers are not significant, although they can be used to indicate levels; in this case, the first digit indicates the level, for example 3.59 would indicate a box at level 3.

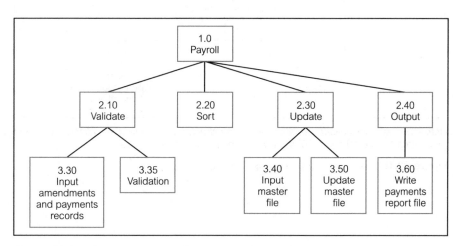

Figure C2.12   Structure diagram for the payroll process

At greater levels of detail, it can be helpful to draw the expanded version of a section in the structure diagram – in this case, the validation section – as a separate diagram (see Figure C2.13).

In this example, horizontal and vertical connecting lines are used. It is of no importance which type of connecting line is drawn, although it is normal to be consistent.

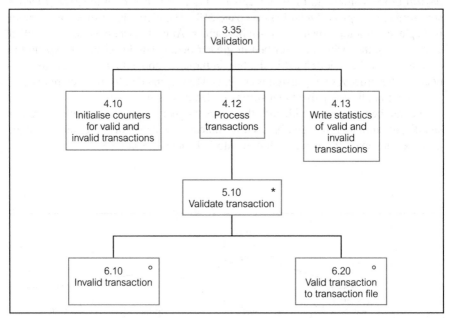

Note: The ∗ symbol indicates iteration (a looping structure). The ∘ symbol indicates selection (e.g. in modules 6.10 and 6.20, the transaction is either valid or invalid).

Figure C2.13   Expansion of process 3.35 in Figure C2.12

Block diagram

is a diagram made up of boxes labelled to represent different hardware or software components and lines showing their interconnections (see Figure C2.14).

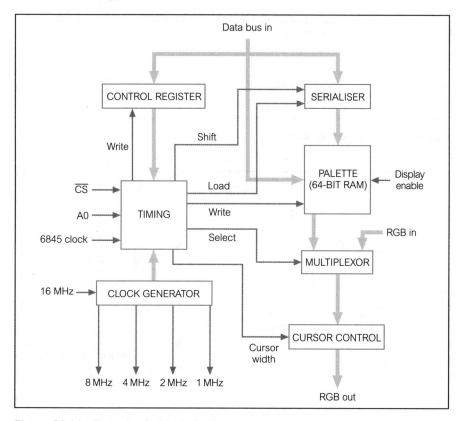

Figure C2.14 Example of a block diagram

Dataflow diagram

shows how data move through a system. It identifies where the data come from in the wider organisation, the processes the data pass through and where the data go to in the wider organisation.

Dataflow diagrams are used in *systems analysis* (see page 219) to show what happens to the data throughout the whole organisation, in both computerised and manual systems. Such a diagram is not usually linear and does not try to place the processes into order. This is done with a system diagram in the design stage.

Figure C2.15 shows a widely used set of symbols used for dataflow diagrams and Figure C2.16 shows a dataflow diagram for a traditional payroll system. Compare this with Figure C2.11 (page 236), which is the system diagram for the same problem.

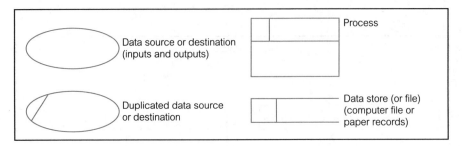

Figure C2.15 Dataflow symbols

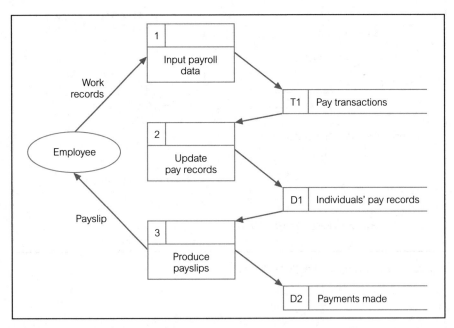

Figure C2.16 Dataflow diagram of the payroll process

Programming Concepts

The terms defined in this section cover a variety of techniques and concepts used to communicate ideas and algorithms. These terms are used both to communicate ideas before a program is written and to describe the program design so that other programmers can maintain the program at a later date. Related terms can be found in C4 Programming (Flow of Execution), C5 Programming (Subprograms), C6 Program Syntax and C8 Implementing, Testing and Running Programs.

The construction of any effective computer program is time-consuming and complex, requiring the application of a wide range of techniques, skills and processes. The programmer has to work at a very detailed level to make the computer do what is wanted, so that the resulting program works reliably and at a reasonable speed.

The actual computer program run on the computer has to be in the machine code used by the computer. There are ways of speeding up and simplifying the production of this program, such as using object-oriented programming styles, higher-level computer languages, program generators and specialised computer languages designed to produce particular types of programs, for example database managers. Many of the principles used by these various methods involve the same standard techniques that are used in traditional programming, and much of the technical language used is of value to anybody involved in developing computer software.

Regardless of the method used to develop computer software, the designer has to balance the properties of cost, speed, ease of use and reliability of the final product. A slow program can be used with a larger computer, but at a greater cost in computer time. Similarly, a complicated program will be more expensive to test. But if software is well designed, using a professional approach, then more efficient software can be developed at lower cost.

A computer programmer has to be prepared to choose between alternative programming strategies in order to get a usable program. The obvious method of solving a problem may be inefficient, as the user will not be prepared to wait while the computer carries out some apparently simple task. To avoid this, the programmer may use a variety of strategies (expressed as algorithms), some of which may be complex but without which it may not be possible to produce a usable program. One skill a programmer must have is the ability to understand and adapt a wide range of existing algorithms to new situations.

The user will expect a program to work reliably and produce no errors. The programmer may use standard algorithms developed and tested by other people as one way of reducing possible errors in a program. The program must be able to deal with any mistakes the user makes without introducing any errors, for example in the input data.

Object-oriented Techniques

Object-oriented programming (OOP)

uses the concept of self-contained objects, which contain both program routines and the data being processed. A program is split into smaller units, called *objects* (see below), which can then be used by other objects to build a more complex system.

Object-oriented programs are more reliable because the objects are self-contained and simple and thus easier to program. It may be possible to use the same types of object in different contexts within a program, and there is no hierarchical structure as in traditional top-down design.

Object

including: encapsulation

is a group of data and associated program routines used within an object-oriented programming system. An object is designed to be self-contained and contains both the programs that affect the object and the data that are being processed.

Each object may contain several program routines (called *methods*, see below) that act differently on the stored data (called *properties*, see below). When an object-oriented program is run, it may contain several copies of the object containing different data. Since the program routines are linked to and copied with the data, there is no possibility of a routine accessing the wrong data. It is also possible for the object to be defined differently in different situations. See *overloading*, *polymorphism*, page 244 and *inheritance* page 243.

Encapsulation is where the technical details of methods or properties are hidden within the object and can be changed only by using the appropriate methods, which will have been tested thoroughly. Ideally, all the methods and properties in an object will be encapsulated.

Method

also known as: member procedure, member function
including: constructor, destructor

is a program routine contained within an object designed to perform a particular task on the data within the object. For example, an object working out the total of a set of numbers would have a method to add a data item to the object, a method to return the results of the calculation or even a method to print the results directly to the installed printer. There are some methods that should always be provided when programming an object.

These include:

constructor, a method that correctly initialises and sets up a new copy of the object when it is created based on the object class;

destructor, a method that deletes the object, if necessary saving any data, warning other objects and freeing the computer's memory.

Property

also known as: data member

is data within the object that control how the object will operate. For example, the properties of an object displaying some text on the screen will include the text to be displayed and may have additional properties that control how the text is displayed, such as its colour and font size. Another example would be an object working out the total of a set of numbers, which would have a property storing the values of the numeric data.

Class

including: instance of a class, class library

defines the methods and properties for a group of similar objects. It is a template specifying program routines used for the methods and the data types of the properties.

Individual objects can be defined based on the object class but with specific properties. Each specific object is known as an *instance of the class*. The methods in the object class will be tested thoroughly, and a programmer can rely on this for the individual objects created, reducing programming errors and programming time. See also *inheritance*, below.

The *class library* is the set of class definitions that are built up over time and may be reused.

Inheritance

including: derived class

is the means by which the properties and methods from the object class are copied to the object being created so that that only the differences have to be reprogrammed.

A *derived class* is a class resulting from the inheritance process.

Overloading

including: polymorphism
is when a method is defined more than once in a class for use in different situations. The different situations involve different types, or quantities, of data being input into the *object* (see page 242) and the types of parameters supplied determine which method is used.

Polymorphism is a specialised form of overloading in which the method can adapt to process similar data in different formats, for example to allow for data that could be either a real number or an integer.

Traditional Programming Techniques

Address

including: memory location, absolute address, base address, offset, relative address
Each piece of data or program instruction is stored separately in the computer's memory and is located by its address. The address is the number for the position of a word of storage in the main memory. This number is used by a program as the identification of a particular *memory location*, which may contain a data item or the next instruction, when a machine-code program is branching.

If the address is the real address used by the internal electronics of the computer, then it is known as the *absolute address*. Many machine-code programs and operating systems use a method of addressing that allows a program to have its own (imaginary) addresses and convert these to the real addresses as the program is executed. The real addresses are worked out from a starting address number, called the *base address*, by adding another number, called the *offset* or *relative address*, to it.

One use of relative addressing is storing arrays. The location of any particular element of the array can be calculated from the element number and the base address of the (array) variable.

Array (machine-code programming)

The use of arrays is a fundamental technique in machine-code and low-level programming, since they make it possible to handle large amounts of related data efficiently. Each element in an array will be held sequentially in memory and so an index register or relative addressing can be used to access each element in turn. Since the array is stored as a single block of computer memory, the programmer has a variety of methods that can be used to manipulate the data easily, for example copying the entire block as one operation. See also *array*, page 310.

Algebraic notation

including: infix, prefix and postfix notation, Reverse Polish notation
is the way mathematical and logical processes are described when writing a computer program. Infix, prefix and postfix notations are different ways of writing the algebraic (and logical) expressions used by a program.

Mathematicians normally use *infix notation* (where the operators are placed between the operands, such as A+B). *Prefix notation* places the operator first (such as +AB) while *postfix notation* places the operator last (such as AB+). See Figure C3.1.

Prefix and postfix notations are easier for a computer to execute. Modern computers are sufficiently powerful that most users do not need to use either prefix or postfix notation.

Reverse Polish notation is a form of postfix notation in which brackets are not permitted and not needed. No rules about precedence are needed for different operations, which are carried out in the order met in the expression.

Reverse Polish notation has the advantage that any algebraic expression can be processed strictly from left to right. It is used widely by compilers that convert the infix notation that a programmer has used into reverse Polish notation. This reverse Polish notation is then easily converted into a machine-code program. It was devised by a Polish mathematician, Jan Lukasiewicz.

What has to be worked out:	Work out the perimeter of a rectangle, which is twice (**L**ength plus **B**readth)
*The formula in **infix** notation:*	2*(**L**+**B**)
*The formula in **prefix** notation:*	*2+**LB**
*The formula in **postfix** notation:* (also called **reverse Polish** notation)	2**LB**+*

Figure C3.1   Examples of different algebraic notations

Program algorithm

is a sequence of steps designed to perform a particular task. An algorithm may be constructed to describe the operation of a complete system or to describe a particular part of it. Standard algorithms have been developed to do specific common tasks, such as a particular method of sorting a set of data. Many have been published and are available for general use.

Algorithms include precise details about the operations to be performed and in which order. An algorithm is a sequence of instructions including information such as when sections are repeated or choices made.

Algorithms can be written in any suitable form, such as a programming language, *pseudo-code* (see page 274) or as diagrams. Often they are written in pseudo-code, which is communicated and translated easily into any suitable programming language (see Figure C3.2).

To count the number of words in a line of text:

```
begin  count words
  set  words = 1
  set  character = space                        for a space at the start
  while not end of line
  begin
    make  previous character = character        for unnecessary spaces
    get next character from line
    if  character = space
        and previous character not space        two spaces together
    then  add 1 to words
  end
  if character = space then subtract 1
     from words                                 space at end of line
end count words
```

Algorithms become complicated when covering all possibilities

Figure C3.2   Example of an algorithm in pseudo-code

Code

including: program code

refers to the actual set of instructions that form a program. This is either the source text of a program, which is later compiled, or the actual instruction codes of a machine-code program.

The term *program* (see page 266) is often applied to a complete software system (including items such as spellchecker dictionaries), but *program code* applies specifically to the instructions that make up a particular part of the overall system. See also *relocatable code* and *absolute code*, page 253.

Coding sheet

is a special form on which program instructions may be written. It has columns to ensure that instructions are presented in the correct format. These are now used very rarely, since most programmers now type their programs directly into the computer using a *text editor* (see page 346).

Assignment

is an instruction that gives (assigns) a value, which could be the result of a calculation, to a specified variable. The value is placed in the memory location corresponding to the given variable.

Working out an area in a program:

```
area:=height*width;
```

assigns the answer of 'height' *times* 'width' *to the variable* 'area'

Figure C3.3   Example of an assignment statement

Event

is an external change that is notified to the program by the operating system. This may be a key being pressed or a mouse button being clicked.

The term 'event' has a specific connotation related to multitasking operating systems used by personal computers. Events are occurrences that may apply to any of the programs running and are put into context by the operating system communicating with the programs. Events should not be confused with normal input, which is directed to a particular program, or with *interrupts* (see page 356), which are usually dealt with by the operating system. One effect of an interrupt may, however, be to generate an event.

Events are an important element in the design of multitasking programs where the operating system handles the input (from the keyboard) and output (to the screen). When a new input is received, a message is sent to the program informing it of the event and allowing it to take appropriate action.

Flag

including: set, unset, status word, status byte

is an indicator that has two states, often called *set* or *unset*. It enables the program to record whether a particular event has occurred, for example whether a list of numbers has been sorted or whether an interrupt has been sensed.

In a high-level language, a variable may be used as a flag. If a *Boolean* or *logical data type* (see *data type*, page 314) is used, then the two states true and false are equivalent to the flag states set and unset. To begin with, the flag may be unset (false) and when a particular case is detected it is set (true); when the action has been completed it is unset again (back to false).

Only one bit is needed to store a flag, so a machine-code programmer may use the bits in a single word to store several flags, which can be manipulated easily in machine code using a *mask* (see *mask*, page 249, and *masking*, page 359). Most central processors have a *status word* or *status byte*, which is the group of flags used in the control of the arithmetic/logic unit. When individual bits are used as flags, the two states are referred to as 0 or 1.

Carry flag

including: overflow flag

is a flag within the *status word* (see *flag*, above) of the central processor that is set to 1 (or true) when a carry condition occurs; otherwise, it is set to 0 (or false). This may be tested by the programmer if some special action may be appropriate, such as producing an error at that point.

Similarly, the *overflow flag* is set to 1 (or true) when overflow occurs during an arithmetic operation, because the result of a calculation is too big for the computer to store.

Heuristic program

is a program that attempts to improve its own performance as a result of learning from previous actions within the program. See also *heuristics*, page 135.

Initialise

including: initial value
is to set counters or variables to zero, or some other starting value, usually at the beginning of a program or subprogram. These values are known as *initial values*. A common programming error is to fail to initialise a variable. In this case, the program will execute correctly but will produce wrong results.

Default option

is the action to be taken automatically by the computer if no specific instruction is given. For example, in some versions of BASIC, arrays do not need to be declared, in which case they are given bounds 1–10. This is the default option. See also *default*, page 179.

Look-up table

is a table used to convert one set of values to another set. The table normally has two columns. The first column holds a list of data items and the second column holds a list of related values. For example, the first column might hold product codes and the second column their prices.

Another example is a tax table for VAT. Each product has a tax code, which is looked up in a look-up table to find the tax rate to be used. Look-up tables are particularly useful for non-linear values, and tax rates are often non-linear.

A further example is a sine table. Values of sine are calculated for a range of values and stored in the memory. Each time a sine is required, it is found in the look-up table rather than being worked out again. This speeds up the program because calculating sines is very slow.

Logical operation

including: AND, OR, NOT, XOR operations, mask, shift
is the use of *logic* (see *logical operator*, page 270) within a program. Logical operations are used frequently to determine the future progress of a program within selection statements, such as IF statements and REPEAT and WHILE loops.

Logical operations include *AND, OR, XOR* and *NOT*, which, when used with Boolean values, produce the results described in *logic gates* (see page 383). For example, when using a simple database of information about birds, a search might be written:

```
IF 'webbed feet' AND 'white feathers' THEN show picture ELSE
next item
```

The expressions 'webbed feet' and 'white feathers' can be either true or false; what happens next depends on the truth value derived from 'ANDing' them.

Logical operations can also be performed on *bytes* or *words* (see page 14) when a group of *bits* (see page 11) is processed together. Logical operations simply compare each bit, and the result is assigned to the equivalent bit of the result. An example of their use is the manipulation of a *status word* (see *flag*, page 247) by the operating system.

These operations can be performed using a *mask*, which is a user-defined binary pattern, to select which bits are to be changed while the other bits remain unchanged. See Figure C3.4. See also *masking*, page 359.

The bits in a byte, word or register can also be shifted. A *shift* moves the whole bit pattern one or more places to the left or right. Bits that move out are lost, and empty spaces are filled with a 0. See also *shift*, page 357.

The byte holds colour information:

The intensity of red is held in the colour byte below in the third and fourth bits from the right:

0 0 0 1 **1 0** 1 1	*The bold digits **1 0** are the red intensity.*
0 0 0 0 **1 1** 0 0	*A **mask** to select the bits we require.*
0 0 0 0 1 0 0 0	*The result of an **AND** operation on the mask and the colour byte: unwanted bits are set to 0.*
0 0 0 0 0 0 **1 0**	*The result of a **right shift** of two places.*
equals 2 (denary)	*The intensity of the colour red is 2.*

Figure C3.4   Logical operation on a bit pattern

Machine-code instruction

including: operation code field, address field, operand (field)

is a binary code that can be executed directly by the computer. Each type of computer has a set of binary codes that are recognised by its processor as instructions; see *instruction set*, page 349.

Each type of processor has a different instruction set. These are the only instructions that can be used to control the computer. Other instructions (such as those written in BASIC or Pascal) must be converted into appropriate machine-code instructions before they can be executed by the computer.

Each instruction is a binary pattern that can be decoded by the control unit. It consists of several fields, including the *operation code field* and usually an *address field* (see *single-address instruction*, page 250).

The *operation code field* is the part of the binary code for the instruction to be carried out (for example 'add' or 'jump').

PART C

An *address field* gives the *address* (see page 244) where the data to be used in the operation can be found. It is sometimes called the *operand field*, or simply the *operand*. See also *address calculation*, page 350.

Single-address instruction

also known as: one-address instruction
including: multiple-address instruction, two-address instruction
is the most common format of a *machine-code instruction* (see page 249). It consists of two fields, the operation code field and the address field.

A *multiple-address instruction* has more than two fields. There is always an operation code field and at least two address fields (giving several pieces of data that can be used by a single operation). In particular, a *two-address instruction* has three fields, the operation code field and exactly two address fields.

Other designs of processor may have different structures. For example, stack-based processors do not need address fields at all, just the operation code. Another example is microprocessors, which often use several bytes of storage instead of one word for each machine-code instruction. These are loaded separately but then treated as a single-address instruction.

For general-purpose computers, single-address instructions are more economical than other formats.

Mnemonic

including: symbolic addressing
is a code for an operation that is easily remembered. The meaning of the instruction is normally abbreviated into a related alphabetic code.

Mnemonics are used particularly in assembly languages, where each binary *operation code* (see *machine code*, page 294) is replaced with a mnemonic; for example, ADC could represent the binary instruction for ADD WITH CARRY. Mnemonics rather than binary numbers make the writing of programs faster and make errors easier to find. Assemblers are used to convert the instruction mnemonics into the binary machine-code instructions (see *assembler*, page 339).

The use of mnemonics or words to specify the address of a store location is called *symbolic addressing*. This is used in assembly language programming, where the address of a store location is specified by means of an *identifier* (see page 271), normally in the form of a word or mnemonic, rather than the numerical value of the memory address. See also *symbol table*, page 341.

Program maintenance

including: corrective maintenance, adaptive maintenance, perfective maintenance
is the modification of a program or system after its implementation has been completed. This may be needed to correct errors found in the system, i.e. *corrective*

maintenance. Maintenance may be necessary to adapt the system to changes within the organisation using it, to external changes such as new legislation or to allow the system to operate with new hardware, i.e. *adaptive maintenance*. Additionally, it may be advantageous to make changes that will enhance the performance of the system, i.e. *perfective maintenance*.

Maintenance normally cannot be carried out by the user, so specialist staff (often the team that designed and wrote the original system) are employed for this purpose.

Maintenance is much easier if the program is well-designed, well-structured and well-documented (see *structured programming*, page 227). *Ease of maintenance* (see below) is a desirable characteristic of a computer system.

Program characteristics

including: ease of use, robustness, flexibility, reliability, portability, port, (hardware) platform, ease of maintenance
are the general properties (which may be good or bad) of programs or systems that determine how successful the program may be in general use. The good properties that programmers will attempt to produce are as follows:

Ease of use means that users will be able to operate the program with limited training and support.

Robustness is the ability of a program or system to cope with errors and mishaps during program execution without producing wrong results or stopping. Events (such as a jammed printer) should not make the computer system fail. If failures do occur, errors can be introduced and customer dissatisfaction will result.

Flexibility is the ability of a program or system to be reconfigured easily by the user or adapted for use in a different situation. This may enable a program or system to be sold more widely or to be adapted to changing circumstances.

Reliability is how well a program or system operates without stopping due to design faults.

Portability is the ability of a program or system to be used on different computer hardware. Many large commercial systems remain in use for much longer than the original hardware and will be adapted or *ported* to new types of computer hardware, thus saving the expense of rewriting the system. Most software packages will work only on particular combinations of hardware and operating system, which are sometimes referred to as *(hardware) platforms*.

Ease of maintenance allows modifications that have to be made during the life of a system to be carried out easily and cheaply. *Program maintenance* (see above) is a major expense in the use of a computer system. *Structured programming* (see page 227) enables software to be designed in a way that enables ease of maintenance.

Overlay

including: overlays

is the process by which only parts (the *overlays*) of a large program are brought from backing store for processing, as needed. Only those overlays currently requiring processing are held in main store. The major part of the program (which also manages the overlays) is always held in the main store.

The use of overlays is a technique that enables programmers to reduce the amount of memory needed by a program. Similar techniques are *segmentation* (see page 345) and *paging* (see page 351), which is used by operating systems to make efficient use of available memory.

Pretty printer

including: printf, PRINT USING, format

is a subroutine that displays a line of text (on the screen or on paper) in a neat way. This may mean splitting the line between words, justifying it and displaying numerical variables to a defined number of decimal places.

Many operating systems provide pretty printers as machine-code subroutines for use by programmers, and some programming languages have predefined functions or procedures (such as the function *printf* in C and *PRINT USING* in some versions of BASIC). See Figure C3.5.

---

*Using the **writeln**, **PRINT USING** and **printf** functions*

If the variables a, b and c have the following values:

$$a: = 3.14159 \quad b: = 1.5 \quad c: = 1.5$$

In **Pascal**:

```
writeln('Answers  ',a:4:2,b:4:2,c:4:2);
```

will display: Answers   3.14   1.50   1.50

In **BASIC**:

```
PRINT USING "Answers  #.##  #.##  #.00",a,b,c
```

will display: Answers   3.14   1.5   1.50

In **C**:

```
printf("Answers  %0.2f  %0.2f  %0.2f",a,b,c)
```

will display: Answers   3.14   1.50   1.50

The examples display variables:

a rounded to two decimal places as 3.14
c padded to two decimal places as 1.50
b has the trailing 0 discarded by the PRINT USING statement, a facility not available as standard in the equivalent C and Pascal statements

---

Figure C3.5   Examples of display- and print-format statements

A pattern, known as a *format*, is used to determine features such as total width and the number of decimal places (Figure C3.6).

#.##	Numbers will be displayed rounded to two decimal places	2.52
#.00	Numbers will be displayed to two decimal places, with trailing zeros if needed	2.50
00000	Numbers will be displayed as a five-digit integer, with leading zeros if needed	00123
#.##e+00	Numbers will be displayed to three significant figures using scientific format	2.56e+02
(£#,##0)	Numbers will be displayed as a currency, with brackets for negatives	(£3,250)
dd/mm/yy	Date in European form, with obliques	02/05/95
mm.dd.yy	Date in American form	05.02.95
Mmmm d, yyyy	Date in American form, with month in words	May 2, 1998

The formats used vary between software; these are from a typical spreadsheet.

Figure C3.6   Examples of formatting numeric and date data

Relocation

including: relocatable code, absolute code, position-independent code

is the moving of a program from one area of memory to another by the operating system. This allows the operating system to make best use of memory, for example during compilation. Code that can be moved in this way is known as *relocatable code*, whereas *absolute code* must reside in a particular area of memory.

When a program is relocated, any memory addresses must be altered suitably, in particular any addresses in *jump* instructions (see page 258). This means that programs may need to be written in a special way to be relocatable. See also *relative address*, in *address*, page 244.

Ideally, when we relocate a program, we would not want to alter it, which will take time. It is possible, using special techniques, to write a program that will operate correctly wherever it is loaded into memory. Such a program has *position-independent code*.

Packing

is the compression of data in order to make the best use of storage space. If a computer has a large word length, then much space can be wasted when occupied by small pieces of data. For example, a character may need only 6 bits to store it, so a computer with a word length of 24 bits could pack four such characters into one word of storage that would otherwise store only one character. Packing is sometimes done automatically by the operating system.

PART C

Self-documented program

is where the program code describes the operations being carried out. This can be done by the use of comments, statements with meaningful variable names, formatting and clearly visible structures.

These features are in addition to the normal program documentation. They are valuable because they help to avoid mistakes being made when a programmer modifies the program. Modifications should always be based on the full program design documentation, otherwise the other effects of introducing changes cannot be predicted.

The use of a fourth-generation language helps this process, because these languages describe the underlying design of a system rather than the detail of its implementation. They rely on powerful compilers to convert the design into an executable system. See also *fourth-generation language*, page 166.

Terminator

also known as: rogue terminator, data terminator
including: rogue value
is a specified value that is not normally expected in the data and that is used to mark the end of a list of data items. The program can process the data in order until it reaches the terminator. The number of data items can vary, and the number of data items does not have to be known in advance.

The term *rogue value* often implies a *numerical* value (see *numerical data type*, page 322). It may also describe a special value, at some point in the data, used to indicate a particular situation, for example a deleted record.

Common values used as rogue terminators are 0, −1 and 9999. If the data are being entered from a keyboard, then simply pressing the Enter key can be the terminator (a blank input). When data are stored as a datafile, a special terminator, called the *end-of-file marker* (see page 313), is used to show where the data finish.

Programming (Flow of Execution)

Concepts and terms concerned with programs in general can be found in C3 Programming Concepts. Other related terms can be found in C5 Programming (Subprograms), C6 Program Syntax and C7 Describing Programs.

Computers derive much of their power from their ability to repeat groups of instructions within a computer program and to choose which instructions to execute. The effect is that the programmer can control the flow (or order) of execution depending on the data being processed.

The instructions that enable a programmer to do this are known as **control structures**. When using a high-level language, specific instructions are provided for control structures. However, when using assembly languages, the control structures have to be constructed from combinations of simpler instructions and, in particular, jump instructions.

The main control structures are **loops** and **conditional statements**. However, they are often referred to by the statements commonly used in programming languages such as **if . . . then, for loop, repeat . . . until loop, while loop** and **case statement**.

Control structure

is the general term for the different ways in which a group of instructions can be executed. Control structures allow the group of instructions to be repeated a variable or fixed number of times or to be executed selectively depending on the data currently being processed.

Loop

including: nested loop, iteration
is a group of instructions that is executed repeatedly. For example, to produce payslips for several workers, the instructions for one payslip are repeated many times with different data.

The instructions may be repeated a fixed number of times (as in a *for loop*, see page 256) or a variable number of times, with the instructions being repeated until some specified condition is satisfied (as in a *while . . . do* or *repeat . . . until* loop, see below).

A *nested loop* is a loop contained within another loop. The inside loop will be executed a number of times for each single execution of the outer loop.

Iteration is the process of repeating a sequence of steps. Iteration will involve a loop that is repeated (iterated) until the required answer is achieved. The first time the instructions in the loop are executed is the first iteration.

Count-controlled loop

including: for loop, do loop

is a type of *loop* (see page 255) that is executed a fixed number of times. This may be a constant (if the number of repetitions is known when the program is written) or may depend on the data being processed (but the number of repetitions is still fixed at the start of the loop).

With a high-level language, this is often called a *for loop* (*for . . . next loop*) or *do loop*; the names are derived from the program statements used to implement it. Traditionally the variables i, j and k are used as the control variables that record the number of repetitions executed. See Figure C4.1.

*In **Pascal**:*	`for i:=1 to 10 do`
	`begin`
	`...`
	`end;`
		i is a variable that holds the number of the current repetition

*In **BASIC**:*	`FOR i=1 TO 10`
	`...`
	`NEXT i`
		. . . indicates an instruction (or several instructions)

*In **C**:*	`for (i = 1; i <= 10; i++)`
	`{`
	`...`
	`}`	

Figure C4.1 Examples of count-controlled loops

Infinite loop

including: breaking, escaping

An infinite loop is a *loop* (see page 255) from which there is no exit; the instructions in the loop will continue to be repeated forever. This may be useful sometimes, for example in a program controlling a set of traffic lights, which continuously repeats the same instructions.

In most cases, an infinite loop prevents any other use of the computer. Interrupting an infinite loop may mean having to switch off the computer to reset it, but in a multiuser computer system the operator should be able to terminate the program without affecting other users. This is called *breaking* out of the program or *escaping* from the program. Control will return to the operating system and the user can issue further commands.

An infinite loop that cannot be interrupted results in a *hung* computer (see page 289).

Condition-controlled loop

including: repeat . . . until loop, while loop

is a type of *loop* (see page 25) that is executed continuously and finishes only when particular conditions are met. This enables loops to be written where the number of repetitions is unknown. The advantages of this approach include:

- the amount of data being processed need not be known in advance;
- mathematical algorithms can continue until an answer is found;
- more than one exit condition can be used, for example the loop could continue until the result is obtained or an error is found.

Two forms of condition-controlled loops are usually provided by high-level languages. These are often called *repeat . . . until loops* and *while loops*, names derived from the program statements used to implement them.

Both repeat . . . until loops and while loops act in a similar way. The repeat . . . until loop tests for its exit after executing the instructions; while loops test for exiting before any instructions are executed, thus allowing for situations where no action needs to be taken. See Figure C4.2.

PART C

	a *Repeat loop*	a *While loop*

In Pascal:	`i:=1;`
	`repeat`
	`    . . .`
	`    i:=i+1;`
	`until (i=10) or (flag=true);`
		`i:=1;`
		`while (i<10) and (flag=false) do`
		`begin`
		`    . . .`
		`    i:=i+1;`
		`end;`

In BASIC:	`i=1`
	`REPEAT`
	`    . . .`
	`    i=i+1`
	`UNTIL i=10 OR flag=TRUE`
		`i=1`
		`WHILE i<10 AND flag=FALSE`
		`    . . .`
		`    i=i+1`
		`ENDWHILE`

In C:	`i=1;`
	`do`
	`{`
	`    . . .`
	`    i++;`
	`} while (i<10 && flag==0);`
		`i=1;`
		`while (i<10 && flag==0)`
		`{`
		`    . . .`
		`    i++;`
		`}`

Figure C4.2 Examples of condition-controlled loops

If statement

including: else

is the name for a statement allowing selection within a program. A group of statements may be executed or ignored, depending on the data being processed at the time. The name is derived from the program statement used to implement this control structure (see Figure C4.3).

It is possible for the program to choose between two alternative groups of statements by using an additional keyword *else*.

	if ... then ... else *statement*	

In **Pascal**:	`if k=1 then`
	`begin`
	`. . .`
	`end`
	`else`
	`begin`
	`. . .`
	`end;`
		k *is a variable that holds the data
		on which the current selection depends*

In **BASIC**:	`IF k=1 THEN`
	`. . .`
	`ELSE`
	`. . .`
	`ENDIF`
		*. . . indicates an instruction
		(or several instructions)*

In **C**:	`if (k==1)`
	`{...}`
	`else`
	`{...}`	

Figure C4.3 Examples of selection statements

Jump

also known as: branch

including: conditional jump, unconditional jump

allows the order of execution of the statements in a computer program to be changed. Normally instructions are executed in the sequence they are stored, but this can be changed by a jump instruction that enables a program to choose which instruction to execute next.

Machine-code program instructions are stored consecutively in memory, and the control unit works through them sequentially using the *program counter* (see page 350). A jump alters the program counter and thus changes the next instruction to be executed.

Jumps are not normally used with high-level programming languages because they make the program harder to write without causing *logical errors* (see page 285). However, compilers change instructions such as for, while . . . and repeat . . . until loops into suitable combinations of jump instructions.

A jump may be either *conditional* or *unconditional*. An unconditional jump is always executed. A conditional jump is executed only if required by the result of a test, for example 'Is a certain variable zero?' or 'Has the loop been executed ten times?'

Case statement

is a statement allowing multiple selection within a program. One of several groups of statements may be executed depending on the data being processed at the time. The other groups of statements are not executed. This enables complex selections to be programmed easily and more reliably than using combinations of *if statements* (see above). The name is derived from the program statement used to implement this control structure (see Figure C4.4).

*In **Pascal**:*	`case k of`
	`    1:...;`
	`    4:...;`
	`    9:...;`
	`    otherwise ...;`
	`end;`
		k is a variable that holds the data
		on which the current selection depends

*In **BASIC**:*	`CASE k OF`
	`WHEN 1:...`
	`WHEN 4:...`
	`WHEN 9:...`
	`OTHERWISE ...`
	`ENDCASE`
		labels such as 1: and 4: are matched
		against the control variable data to
		determine which group of instructions
		is executed

*In **C**:*	`switch (k)`
	`{`
	`case 1:`
	`    ...`
	`    break;`
	`case 4:`
	`    ...`
	`    break;`
	`case 9:`
	`    ...`
	`    break;`
	`default:`
	`    ...`
	`}`
		...indicates an instruction (or several
		instructions)

Figure C4.4 Examples of multiple selection

PART C

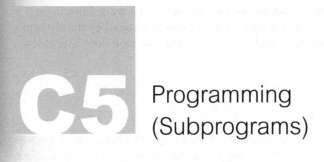

Programming
(Subprograms)

Concepts and terms concerned with programs in general can be found in C3 Programming Concepts. Other related terms can be found in C4 Programming (Flow of Execution), C6 Program Syntax, C7 Describing Programs and C8 Implementing, Testing and Running Programs.

One of the most powerful techniques available to a programmer is the use of subprograms. **Subprograms** enable a program to be split into a number of smaller and more manageable sections. Because they can be called in any order, any number of times, the use of subprograms is very flexible.

The design technique of splitting a program into subprograms, each designed and programmed separately, has certain advantages:

- each subprogram is understood more easily, so reducing errors;
- each subprogram may be small enough to be assigned to one programmer rather than a programming team;
- the subprograms can be tested separately and more thoroughly than a single large program;
- the subprogram can (and should) be written so that it cannot cause errors in other parts of the system.

Another benefit of subprograms is to avoid having to write the same routines many times. The same piece of program code can be used by different parts of the program, which means it has to be written and tested only once. Routines that perform general tasks, such as controlling the screen display, can be reused in different programs, thus saving programming time, testing effort and expense.

When using high-level languages, subprograms are usually implemented by defining **functions** and **procedures**. In machine-code or assembly language programming, subprograms are often called **subroutines**.

The supplier of the operating system will provide subroutines that allow access to the basic operation of the computer – such as displaying a character on the screen or reading data from a file. Operating systems often provide more sophisticated facilities, such as complex screen-drawing routines, loading and saving complete files to backing store and spooling print-out. These are all accessed as machine-code subroutines, which enables them to be shared between programs. They are effectively a library of subroutines always available to the user through the operating system.

Subprograms generally require data. With functions and procedures, the data are normally passed using **parameters**. Ideally, these parameters and any other variables will be **local** to the subprogram, so that the operation of the subprogram cannot affect variables in any other part of the program. If the results from a subprogram are required by the program, then the variables will be passed **by reference**. It is possible for a subprogram to act on **global variables**, but this is generally an unwise process, since it could produce adverse effects in other parts of a large program.

Function

is similar to a *procedure* (see below) but it returns a single value. The name of the function is used as a variable having that value. Every time the name is used in the program, the function will be executed and the result will appear like any other variable.

---

*In **Pascal**:*

*The function **square** is defined like this:*

```
function square(number:integer):integer;
begin
  square:=number*number;                    number is the parameter
end;
```

then it could be used as follows:

```
answer:=square(5);
```

or if `square(x)=25 then...`

Figure C5.1 Example of a function

Procedure

is a *subprogram* (see page 262) that is generally written using a precise formal definition. The procedure is defined and given an identifier (or name). This identifier can be used subsequently just like any other program instruction.

A procedure receives data from the program, manipulates the data in some way and makes the results available to the program.

Such procedures are usually associated with high-level languages, although sophisticated assembly languages also allow procedure definitions.

Standard function

is a function provided by a compiler or an interpreter that is so common that it is worth providing as part of the language. For example, almost all languages provide standard functions to work out mathematical results such as *log*, *sine* and *square root*.

PART C

Routine

is a part of a program used for a specific task. It may simply be a section of the main program, or it might be formalised as a procedure, function or subroutine.

Machine-code subroutine

is a subprogram stored in machine code. It may be called from another machine-code program, from an assembly-language program or from a high-level language program. The operating system often provides machine-code subroutines for common tasks, such as screen updating and printing, which can be called from any user program in any language.

Usually, when a subroutine is called, the current machine status is stored on the system *stack* (see page 311); when the subroutine is finished, the previous machine status is restored and the computer can continue running the program from where it left off.

When writing a machine-code subroutine, the programmer is manipulating the memory directly and there is no concept of local variables. If appropriate, the programmer could reserve a section of memory for use by the subroutine.

Common machine-code subroutines are often stored as a *subroutine library* (see below). These machine-code subroutines are often designed as *modules* (see page 227) and are frequently described as machine-code modules.

Subprogram

including: subroutine, call, return, exit, subroutine library, closed subroutine, open subroutine
is a set of program instructions performing a specific task but that is not a complete program. It must be incorporated into a program in order to be used. Different types of subprogram are known as *procedure, function, routine* or *machine-code subroutine* (see above).

The terms *subroutine* and *subprogram* are generally interchangeable, but some-times each of these terms could mean something more precise, such as implying a machine-code routine.

A program that uses a subprogram must have an instruction to transfer control to the subprogram. This instruction is known as a *call* to a subprogram. When a subroutine, procedure or function is called, the computer will start executing it.

When the subprogram has completed its task, it must transfer control back to the calling program, which can only continue from its calling position. This is generally done by a *return* (or *exit*) statement in the subprogram. A subprogram may have more than one return instruction.

Commonly used subprograms are stored in a *subroutine library*. This contains a number of prewritten and pretested subprograms, available to a programmer, which perform common tasks such as displaying a window, sorting a set of numbers or saving a file.

Subprograms can be used as either *open* or *closed* subroutines, depending on which is more efficient.

In a *closed subroutine*, separate calls to the subroutine use the same piece of program code. A closed subroutine should make the program shorter, although the program could be slower because of the extra instructions required to call the subprogram and return from it.

In an *open subroutine*, the instructions become part of the main program. The skeleton code of the subroutine is modified by the parameters passed to it and the resulting code is copied into the program where required. In some situations open subroutines may have advantages, for example avoiding the extra time taken to call closed subprograms.

Recursive subprogram

including: stopping condition

is one that includes, among the statements making up the subprogram, a call to the same subprogram. The subprogram will continue calling itself recursively, so it must have a means of finishing and continuing the calling program. This is done by a *stopping condition*, which causes the subprogram to exit rather than call itself again.

Some mathematical techniques involve repeating a process an indefinite number of times using the results of the previous calculations. See *iteration*, page 256. One method of managing this is the use of recursion where the same subprogram is called repeatedly (with the revised data). When the result is found, the automatic way in which the computer handles the return from the subprogram ensures that execution will continue from the calling point (see Figure C5.2).

PART C

The factorial of N is calculated as:

$$1\times2\times3\times4\times \ldots N \; \textit{(up to the number N)}.$$

So　　　　　　*factorial*(5) is　　5×4×3×2×1
which is also　　　　　　　　　　5×*factorial*(4)
and　　　　　　*factorial*(4) is　　4×*factorial*(3)　　and so on.

*In **pseudo-code**, the function **factorial** can be defined:*

```
function factorial(N)
    if N<=1 then factorial:=1; return      we stop and go back when we get to 1
    factorial:=N*factorial(N-1)            recursive call
    return                                 return to previous call of function
```

Figure C5.2　Examples of a recursive subprogram

Parameter

including: parameter passing, formal parameter, actual parameter, argument, by value, by reference

is information about a data item being supplied to a function or procedure when it is called.

With a high-level language, generally the parameters are enclosed in brackets after the procedure or function name. The data can be a constant or the contents of a variable (see Figure C5.3).

---

*In **Pascal**:*

when the function **length(side)** is called,

the **parameter** is the variable **side**

when the function **length('Fred')** is called,

the **parameter** has the value **'Fred'**

when the function **SIN(60)** is called,

the **parameter** has the value **60**

Figure C5.3   Examples of parameters

When a function or procedure is defined, a formal parameter, which is a *local variable* (see page 268), is declared; this can be used in the program code for the function or procedure.

When the function or procedure is used, the calling program must pass parameters to it (*parameter passing*). The *formal parameter* links the data in the calling program (which will change) to its use in the function or procedure. The data item supplied, known as an *actual parameter* or *argument*, is passed to the local variable (see Figure C5.4).

Function definition:

```
function increment(number:integer):integer;
```
*local variable is **number***
```
begin
    number:=number+1;
```
*adds 1 to **number***
```
    increment:=number;
```
function returns the value
```
end;
```
*assigned to **increment***

Main program:

```
begin
    fred:=2;
```
*variable **fred** starts at 2*
```
    bill:=increment(fred);
```
*fred is the **parameter**; its **argument** is 2*
```
    write(bill);
```
*variable **bill** is now 3*
```
end;
```

The value of *fred* after execution of the function will be different depending on whether the **parameter** *fred* is passed **by value** or **by reference**. The variable *fred* will still be 2 if passed **by value**, but it will be 3 if passed **by reference** (an example of the unplanned effects of using global variables).

Figure C5.4   Examples of parameter passing to a function

Actual parameters can be passed to functions and procedures either *by value* or *by reference*. If a data item is passed by value, a (local) copy of the data is used, which is discarded when the subprogram exits. If the data are passed by reference, the location (in memory) of the data is used. This means that any changes are retained after the procedure or function has been completed. Effectively, a single variable has two identifiers, with the subprogram using a pseudonym for the data item involved.

Re-entrant program

also known as: re-entrant subroutine, re-entrant subprogram
is a program in which the same physical copy of the program code can be used by several different tasks. The program must be written so that data about different tasks do not get mixed up. This is particularly important with systems software, where the computer can be executing the subroutine and an interrupt transfers control to a different program, which may then use the same subroutine. If this subroutine is not re-entrant, then data may be corrupted and errors may occur.

One example is an interrupt handling routine, which may still be handling one type of interrupt when a different type of interrupt is received.

Another example is the use of a high-level language interpreter on a time-shared system, where a single copy of the interpreter is used by the different users with different data depending on whose time slot is currently being executed. (See also *multi-threading*, page 343).

Macro

including: programmed by example, macro instruction
is a sequence of instructions that are defined as a single element. When a macro is *called* (see *call*, page 262), the sequence of instructions is used. A commonly used routine can be defined as a macro with an identifier, and the user can then simply call the macro, using the identifier, to save time and reduce errors.

Macros are used to provide a limited degree of programmability to applications software. They allow the user to customise the application and make it more efficient for their environment (see *human–computer interface*, page 59). For example, when using a word processor, a macro could be used to format and print a document quickly in house style. A macro will usually consist of a sequence of commands used by the software, although some software may provide additional commands to make the macros more useful. Sometimes a macro will be *programmed by example*, storing the user's operations as they occur. See also *macro recording*, page 65.

In a low-level language, a macro is also known as a *macro instruction*. Calling a macro (instruction) would insert the set of instructions into the program at that point, so that the program may include the same set of instructions several times. This is different from a subroutine, where the program jumps to the code to be used, although a macro is sometimes incorrectly called an *open subroutine* (see page 263).

PART C

Program Syntax

This section considers the various elements that make up a computer program rather than how they are used. Related material can be found in C3 Programming Concepts, C4 Programming (Flow of Execution), C5 Programming (Subprograms) and C9 Programming Languages.

A computer program, which must be written in a very precise way, is written in a programming language. Programming languages have a vocabulary of only a limited number of words, with precise rules describing how they may be combined.

Unless a program is written in machine code (which is very rare), it needs to be translated into some form of machine code before it can be executed. A program can be **assembled**, **interpreted** or **compiled**, which are all forms of **translation**.

Program

including: program suite

is a complete set of program statements that can be executed by the computer to perform some task. The program statements may be written in assembly language or a high-level language. In order to be executed, the program will need to be translated by a translator program into machine code.

If a program is not complete, then it will not work successfully. A correctly written program can be thought of as a specification of the algorithm that the design process has produced. Large software systems are normally *suites* of several programs used to do all the tasks required.

Syntax

is the precise way in which program statements must be written to be understood by the computer. It is the set of rules for combining the elements of a programming language (such as characters and reserved words) into forms that the compiler, interpreter or assembler can understand. The set of rules does not define meaning or the use of the final construction. However, it does allow programmers to know whether a statement they are making is structured correctly.

Semantics

is the meaning of the individual elements that make up a computer-language statement, such as the words, symbols and punctuation. The overall meaning of any statement, which is made by combining these individual elements, is determined uniquely by the semantics of the programming language.

Program statement

is any one of the instructions within a program. Program statement is usually taken to mean a statement in a source-language instruction that is human-readable, rather than a binary-code instruction. When a program statement is translated, it often generates several machine-code instructions.

Block

including: block-structured language
is a group of program statements that are treated as a single unit. Special *reserved words* (see page 271) or symbols are used to show which statements form a block. Blocks enable complex programs to be constructed from simple elements without any confusion about how statements will be executed (see Figure C6.1).

Programming languages that encourage the use of blocks are called *block-structured languages*.

*In **Pascal**:*	begin
	. . .
	end;
		. . . *indicates the statements*
		that form the block

*In **C**:*	{
	. . .
	}	

Figure C6.1 Examples of block structure

Declaration

is a statement in a program that gives the translator the information it needs. It is not an operation carried out as the program is executed, but it is needed for the correct translation of the program. For example, in Pascal the declaration

var area: integer

informs the translator that whenever the program uses the variable 'area', it must be treated as an integer (a whole number) rather than a real number, string or other data type. Declarations provide information about things such as array sizes, variable types, constants, functions, procedures, library routines and memory allocations. See also *directive*, page 272, and Figure C10.4, page 311.

Label

is an identifier (normally a name) that identifies a particular statement in a program. Labels are normally needed only to indicate the destination of a *jump* (see page 258), which is the next instruction to be used after the jump instruction.

Variable

including: global variable, local variable, strongly typed languages, dynamic variables, static variables

is the identifier (or name) associated with a particular memory location used to store data. By using a name, the programmer can store, retrieve and manipulate data without knowing what the data will be.

Global variables can be used anywhere in the program, but *local variables* are defined for use in only one part of the program (normally a function or procedure). They come into existence when that part of the program is entered and the data they contain are lost when execution of that part of the program is completed. Using local variables reduces the unplanned effects of a variable being used in another part of the program and accidentally being changed. In a large system, global variables should be used only for data that need to be shared between sections and should be documented clearly at the design stage.

The data item that is identified by a variable can be a number (such as integer or real number), a character, a string, a date, a set, a file, an array, a sound sample or any other kind of data. This is called the *variable type* or *data type* (see page 314). In a high-level language, the type may need to be declared when the variable is first used, so that adequate storage space is provided. In a machine-code program, the programmer has to manage the different types of data, although they still need to be identified and defined in the design process.

The special features of the data types provided in many high-level languages enable a programmer to write better programs (see *program characteristics*, page 251). These features include:

strongly typed languages, which *validate* (see *validation*, page 328) the data and prevent the wrong kind of data being assigned to a variable;

dynamic variables, which store the data in the most efficient way, often by using a pointer to locate the data that are held in a different location. The programmer has limited control over how or where the data are stored;

static variables, which are stored in a known format in a known location, allowing the programmer to use unorthodox methods to manipulate the data. Static variables can also be used to preserve local data between the calls to a subprogram.

Scope

is the range of statements for which a *variable* (see above) is valid. This will normally be the subprogram in which it is declared and any other subprograms embedded within that subprogram. A variable cannot be used outside its scope, as it appears not to exist.

This concept enables the same identifier to be used in different parts of the program for different purposes without conflict. This concept defines which variable will apply in any given situation during compilation. In a large software project, several programmers may be used; this characteristic of variables means that the programmers will not have to coordinate their use of identifiers.

Dummy variable

is a variable (or identifier) that appears within a program but that is not actually used. This may be because the syntax of the programming language requires a variable but the data contained are not needed.

One use of a dummy variable is illustrated in Figure C6.2. An assignment statement is used to produce an outcome that is desirable, and a dummy variable has to be present to accept the (unwanted) result of the assignment.

```
110  PRINT "Press any key to continue"
120  dum □ GET
130  CLS
```

In line **120**, *the statement* **GET** *provides the code of the key being pressed and this is stored in the variable* **dum**. *This value is not needed and is ignored.*

Figure C6.2   Example of the use of a dummy variable

The identifiers used in the definition of a *procedure* or a *function* (see page 261) are sometimes called dummy variables because they will be replaced by other identifiers when the program is executed. Better descriptions for these are *parameters* (see page 264) and *local variables* (see above).

Operator

including: binary operator, unary operator, arithmetic operator, string operator, relational operator, Boolean operator, logical operator
is a symbol used to indicate that a particular operation is to be performed and gives a shorthand method of indicating in a computer program how data are to be manipulated. An obvious example is the '+' sign to mean 'add', but most programming languages now provide a wide variety of operators for different contexts.

PART C

Two different uses of the '+' operator:

```
5 + 7 means 12
```
  in the context of the addition of numbers.

But `'Fred' + 'Smith'` *means* `'FredSmith'`

  in the context of the concatenation of strings.

Figure C6.3   Example of '+' operator

In **Pascal**:

 unary operators: **not** `end_of_file`
           `- 5`

 binary operators: `result` **and** `end_of_file`
           `length` **+** `width`

Operators are in **bold**.

Figure C6.4   Examples of unary and binary operators

The important distinction between an operator and a program instruction is that an operator manipulates one or more pieces of data. Most operators are *binary operators*, which combine two pieces of data, although *unary operators*, which act on a single piece of data, are also commonly used.

Arithmetic operators manipulate numbers by carrying out normal arithmetic tasks such as addition and subtraction.

String operators combine or manipulate strings by performing tasks such as concatenation (joining strings) and replication (replacing part or all of a string).

Relational operators compare data and produce an answer of *true* or *false* (see *truth value*, page 380). This answer can control the flow of a program using IF, WHILE and REPEAT UNTIL statements. Examples of relational operators include equals '=' and less than '<'.

Boolean (or *logical*) *operators* combine Boolean values using operators such as AND, OR and NOT to produce a Boolean result, *true* or *false*. This result can control the flow of a program using IF, WHILE and REPEAT UNTIL statements. See *logical operation*, page 270.

In these examples, the operators = and > are shown:

Are two numbers equal?
 maybe   `if number = 5 then ...`

Is a string alphabetically after another string?
 maybe   `repeat ...`
                    `until word > 'FRED'`

Figure C6.5   Examples of relational operators

Identifier

is a name or label chosen by the programmer to represent an object within a program. The object could be a variable, a function, a procedure, a data type or any other element defined within a program. It is wise to make identifiers as meaningful as possible by using longer, more descriptive words (such as 'sales' rather than 'S'). See also *variable*, page 268.

Constant

is a data item with a fixed value. In a high-level language, it is assigned to a variable that cannot be changed when the program is executed. For example, if the following declaration is used:

```
const pi = 3.14159265;
```

then the programmer can use the variable name **pi**, which will make writing the program easier.

Similarly, the declaration:

```
const tax_rate = 17.5;
```

allows the programmer to use the variable name **tax_rate**, the value of which is also easy to change at a later date if circumstances change. However, the program would need recompiling. Only one *declaration* (see page 267), rather than the many occurrences throughout the program, would need altering.

Machine-code programs also use constants in the form of either a directive assigning a value to a particular mnemonic or a data item stored when the program is assembled, which makes it part of the program rather than its data.

It is generally more efficient to use constants, because the data are inserted directly into the program code, rather than variables, which the computer will have to retrieve from memory every time they are required.

PART C

Reserved word

also known as: keyword
is any word in the vocabulary of a programming language that can have only the meaning which is defined in the language.

For example, many programming languages have an instruction FOR, which is a reserved word, so a variable or other identifier cannot be named FOR.

Directive

is a statement in a program that influences the translation process. Examples include controlling the use of memory, producing a program dump, producing debugging information and using declarations. While a declaration provides information for the program, a directive affects the environment of the translation process. See also *declaration*, page 267.

Describing Programs

This section is concerned with the written comments and graphical illustrations accompanying a program. The symbols and layout conventions referred to are those given in British Standards BS4058:1987 and BS7738:1994. Related topics can be found in A7 User Interface and Documentation, C1 Systems Design and Life Cycle, C2 Describing Systems and C8 Implementing, Testing and Running Programs.

Program documentation is the documentation that is produced for those stages of the **software life cycle** that are concerned with module development and integration. Program documentation is particularly important at the maintenance stage of the **system life cycle**.

Software will need to be modified during its lifetime, and the original programming team is unlikely to be fully available to assist with modifications, hence the team making the modifications will need to rely heavily on the original program and system documentation.

Each module will need to be documented individually at various levels of detail, depending upon its size and complexity. Some of this will be within the programs, using comment facilities to describe, for example, the data used and the processes carried out. This notion of a **self-documenting program** is an important element in program documentation. As well as the use of comment facilities, there are other functions that can improve the readability of code; these include the use of indentation (for example, for the body of a loop) and the choice of meaningful names for identifiers.

The history of a module is important, for example who wrote it, where and when it was written, when it was modified and by whom, details of modifications made, and testing history including some test data and the results obtained. As with other information about a module, some of this can be included in the module listing as comments. This is often included at the start of the listing, where a standard format to the header defines the information expected.

Diagrams, such as a set of **program flowcharts** or **JSP (Jackson structured programming)** structure diagrams, help to show the flow of a module. They can be particularly valuable for showing how modules are integrated into subsystems and then into the completed fully integrated software as it is to be delivered.

Another tool that is also helpful at the module design stage is **pseudo-code**, which is a formalised English-like way of describing the steps involved in a program routine.

Listing

also known as: program listing
is the printed sequence of program statements. This may also include lists of the data required for the program.

Program flowchart diagram

also known as: program flowchart
including: flow line
is a graphical representation of the operations involved in a computer program. Symbols are used to represent particular operations, and *flow lines* indicate the sequence of operations. Arrows on flow lines may be omitted if the flow is from top to bottom or from left to right.

A program flowchart forms part of the permanent record of a finished program; it is needed for maintenance purposes. Examples of *program flowcharts* are given in Figures C7.8, C7.9 and C7.11 (see pages 278–280).

ECMA (European Computer Manufacturers' Association) symbols

are standard symbols used in system and program flowcharts. Examples of the use of some ECMA symbols in *system flowcharts* are shown in Figures C2.9 and C2.10 (see pages 234 and 235). Their use in *program flowcharts* is shown in Figures C7.8 and C7.9 (see pages 278 and 279). In addition, there are British Standard symbols for flowcharts.

Pseudo-code

is a method of describing a program or system design. It uses control structures and keywords similar to those found in programming languages, but without the strict rules of programming languages. It may be presented in a form that looks like a combination of English and a programming language. (See the example of *pseudo-code*, Figure C7.10, page 279.)

Decision table

is a table that specifies the actions to be taken when certain conditions arise.

The example in Figure C7.1 illustrates possible decisions in the problem of how to go to work. Y and N indicate the values of the condition (Yes and No). X indicates that the action is possible. Blank entries indicate that the action is not possible or that no action decision is needed. For example, column four indicates that on a week day, after 8.00 a.m. (which is also after 7.00 a.m.), the decision has to be to go by bus without having breakfast.

Condition	Value of condition		
Action	Value of action		
Week day	N	Y	Y	Y
Before 7.00 a.m.		Y	N	N
After 7.00 a.m.		N	Y	Y
After 8.00 a.m.		N	N	Y
Breakfast		X	X	
Walk		X		
Go by bus			X	X

Figure C7.1   Decision table

Program flowchart symbol

is a formalised symbol used in a program flowchart diagram. Different shapes indicate the various kinds of activity described by the flowchart. Sometimes, highly formalised shapes are used, each having a specific meaning; in other situations, very simple boxes with words are used. Provided that the meaning is clear, either method is an equally acceptable way of representing a process or system.

Examples of program flowcharts showing how these symbols might be used are given on pages 278–280. In Figure C7.11 (page 280), rectangles are used for all processes; more formal shapes are used in Figures C7.8 (page 278) and C7.9 (page 279).

Connector symbol

also known as: continuation symbol
is used to indicate that the flowchart is continued elsewhere at an identically labelled connector point. To simplify layouts, connector symbols may be used to replace lengthy flow lines or to indicate that the flowchart continues on another page.

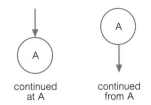

continued
at A

continued
from A

Figure C7.2   Connector or continuation symbol

Input/output symbol

also known as: input symbol, output symbol
is the program flowchart symbol used for any input or output operation. The description in the box may include the device or medium for the process.

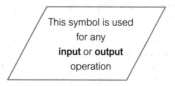

Figure C7.3 Input/output symbol

Decision box

also known as: decision symbol
is the flowchart symbol used to indicate points in a program where decisions are made. There are a number of different ways of representing decisions diagramatically. One set uses the diamond shape in a variety of ways. A decision box may have more than two exits. Four forms are shown in Figure C7.4.

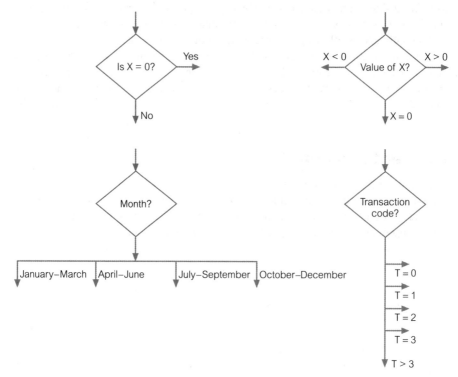

Figure C7.4 Alternative forms of decision box

Process box

also called: operation box, process symbol, operation symbol
is a box used as a flowchart symbol for any operation or sequence of instructions that
does not involve a decision. The box can be any suitable size.

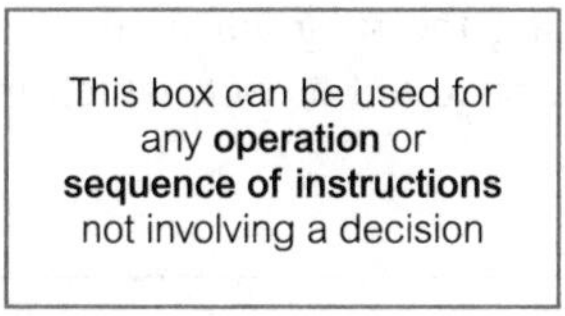

This box can be used for
any **operation** or
sequence of instructions
not involving a decision

Figure C7.5 Process box or symbol

Start/stop symbol

is the flowchart symbol used for both starting and stopping points in a flowchart. A
flowchart will have only one start point, but there may be more than one stop in a
flowchart.

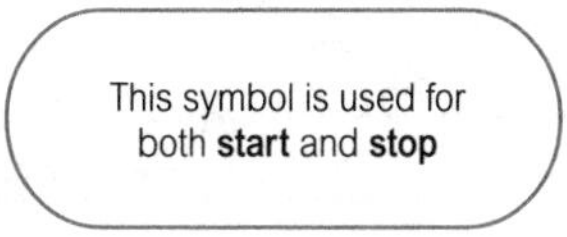

This symbol is used for
both **start** and **stop**

Figure C7.6 Start/stop box or symbol

Subroutine symbol

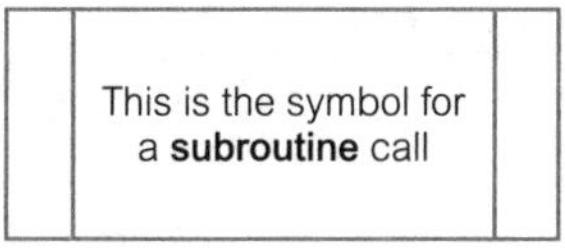

This is the symbol for
a **subroutine** call

Figure C7.7 Subroutine box or symbol

Example of a program module

This program module reads a series of records from a transaction file and uses the valid transactions to update a master file. Details of invalid transactions are output on a line printer, together with a summary of the numbers of valid and invalid transactions processed. Figures C7.8, C7.9 and C7.11 give flowcharts for this module. Figure C7.10 shows the module expressed in pseudo-code.

In this method of presenting the program module, an English-like approach is combined with the use of a structured layout, which is closely akin to some computer languages.

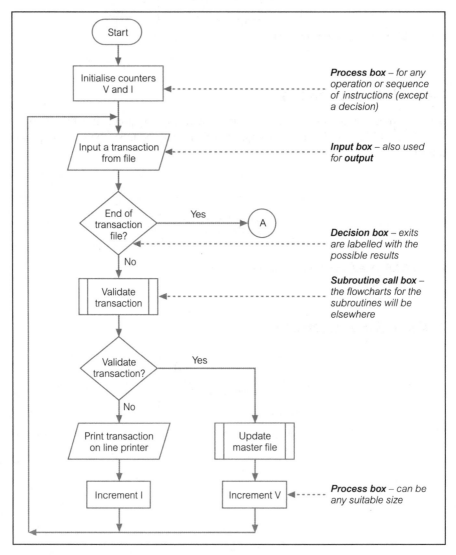

Figure C7.8 Example of program module flowchart (in traditional form)

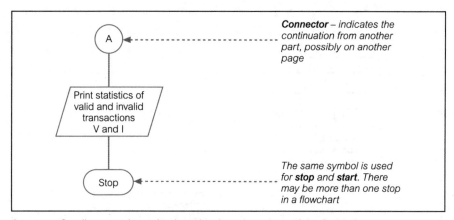

Arrows on flow lines may be omitted, as they have been here, if the flow is from **top to bottom** (or from **left to right**).

Figure C7.9   Example of program module flowchart (continuation)

```
BEGIN
Initialise counters V, I
WHILE more transactions
  BEGIN
  Input transaction
  Validate transaction
  IF valid transaction
    THEN BEGIN
       Update master file
       Increment V
       END
    ELSE BEGIN
       Print transactions
       Increment I
       END
  END
Print statistics of valid and invalid transactions
END
```

Figure C7.10   Program module in pseudo-code

PART C

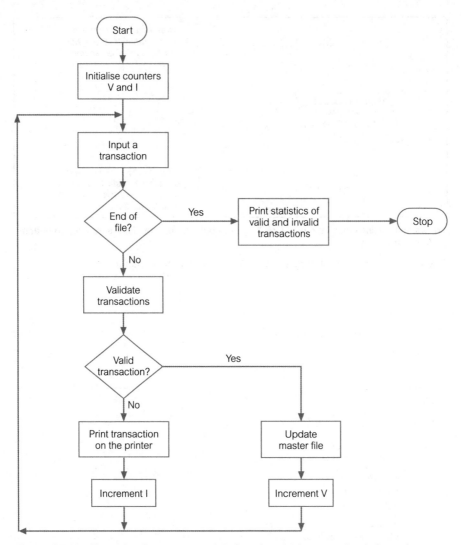

Figure C7.11 Example of program module flowchart (using very simple boxes)

Implementing, Testing and Running Programs

Other related material can be found in C1 Systems Design and Life Cycle, C3 Programming Concepts, C4 Programming (Flow of Execution), C5 Programming (Subprograms), C6 Program Syntax, C9 Programming Languages and D1 Systems Software.

Computer systems need to be reliable. Depending upon the task that they are designed to do, different levels of reliability are appropriate. Software on these systems ranges from that used for office activities, such as word processors and spreadsheets, through software used in financial institutions, all the way to safety-critical software, such as that used for controlling aircraft in flight.

The way software is developed and tested ultimately affects its reliability. A long process of development and testing is undertaken to ensure that it works well for the customer.

The complete software-development cycle is described in Section C1. This section describes the methods and tools used to produce software.

Software systems are normally designed as small interacting modules, possibly by different teams of people. These modules can be independently **coded**, **compiled** and **tested**. Errors found during the testing are investigated and corrections made to the module (**debugging**). This cycle is then repeated until the criteria are satisfied that specify the level of testing to be achieved. The modules are then combined, one at a time (**integration**), tested at each integration stage (**integration testing**) and debugged. Once all the modules are combined successfully, the whole system should be tested (**system testing**) and the remaining known errors corrected.

The testing process for each phase is carried out using a **test plan**, designed to test the widest possible range of situations. However, software can be highly complex. This means that, in most cases, without infinite time and resources it is impossible to test every logical path through a program. As a result, test cases must be designed carefully to execute the areas of software, or trigger conditions within the software, that are most likely to provoke errors. There are various techniques that are used to improve the effectiveness of testing, some of which are supported by software tools. All these techniques can be classified as either **black box** or **white box**.

Testing should not be delayed until an executable program is completed. Before the software is coded, requirements, specifications and design documents can all be inspected to eliminate errors early on in the software-development life cycle. An inspection is most likely to be performed by a team consisting of designers, developers and clients. Guided by a checklist, the team will review the documentation and look for errors. Code can also be inspected or may be subjected to a manual **walk-through** to determine whether there are any errors.

The later an **error** is detected in a piece of software, the more costly that error is to fix. It is therefore good practice to aim to catch errors as early as possible in the software-development life cycle or, better still, to prevent errors being made in the first place. Unfortunately, even after testing has been completed and software is released, errors may remain and will need to be corrected. Some errors may not be detected until the software has been in operation for a period of time. Some time after the initial software release, a new version or **patch** may be issued to fix many of the known errors. However, software that has been specified adequately, designed well and tested thoroughly will have a minimum number of errors remaining.

Source program

including: object program, source language
is the program as written by the programmer using a programming language. It is normally written using a *text editor* (see page 346) and is an understandable document rather than consisting of binary codes. It must be assembled, compiled or interpreted before it can be executed.

When a source program is compiled or assembled, a new program called the *object program* is generated. This is the program that is executed. The source program is kept in case any changes have to be made, in which case the modified source program would be recompiled. It is not generally possible to modify the object program if the source program is lost. It is the object code that is sold and this cannot be modified by the user.

The object program is normally in the machine code of the computer being used. There are some exceptions to this, where *intermediate code* (see page 294) is produced. When the program is executed, the intermediate code is translated easily into machine code.

The programming language in which the source program is written is known as the *source language*.

Execution

sometimes: program execution
is the operation of a computer program. Unless the program is being interpreted (see *interpreter*, page 340), it must be in machine code. If the machine code is produced by compiling a high-level language program, it is the *object program* (see above) that is executed. If the machine code is produced from an assembly language program, it is the assembled program (see *assembler*, page 339) that is executed.

Testing

including: test plan, test data, test case, black box, white box, inspection, walk-through

is the process of detecting errors in a piece of software. It can be carried out at all stages of the *software-development life cycle* (see page 217). For each stage, a *test plan* will exist. The plan will describe each item that needs to be tested. It will provide instructions or operations to be carried out and *test data*, which are the inputs to be used. It will also provide the expected outcomes. Each set of test data and the expected outcome forms a *test case*.

Unfortunately, there is an infinite number of test values that could be applied to a piece of software. However, various techniques can be applied that aid the selection of test cases, which will force out the largest number of errors. These can be split into black-box and white-box techniques.

Black-box techniques see the software as a 'black box' with inputs and outputs but no understanding of what is happening within the black box. When testing, suitable inputs are selected based upon the interfaces of the system, or module.

White-box techniques analyse the structure and logic of the program. This is then used both to help monitor the depth of testing and to guide selection of appropriate data that will cause areas of code to be run that have not yet been executed.

Test cases are usually applied to code that is executed. However, errors can also be found by examining the code manually, such as using inspections and walk-throughs.

Inspection is a technique in which a small team reads through the code during a group meeting, analysing it with a *checklist*. The checklist documents common problems, which the team will be looking for explicitly during the inspection.

Walk-through is a similar technique. In this case, the team will manually execute the code using inputs from defined test cases. This is a formalised team version of a *dry run* (see page 285).

Debugging

including: diagnostic aid, debugging tool, diagnostic program, debugger, cross-referencer, trace, variable check, step mode, single-stepping, post-mortem routine

is the detection, location and correction of faults (or bugs) causing errors in a program. The errors are detected by observing *error messages* (see page 284) or by finding unexpected results in the test output. The location of the faults may be obvious (identified by the error message) or may require extensive investigation. Tools are available to help in this process, particularly with assembly-language programs, where comprehensive error-reporting may not exist. These *diagnostic aids* and *debugging tools* include the following:

PART C

Diagnostic programs attempt to detect and locate faults in another program or system by supervising its operation and providing additional information about possible errors.

Debuggers are programs that provide a range of facilities enabling the programmer to investigate the conditions when errors occur.

Cross-referencers are programs that identify where variables are used in a program. This allows errors such as unplanned use of duplicate names to be identified.

Traces are print-outs that show the statements executed as the program is being run and may include the values of variables. The program flow can be compared with the *trace table* (see below) to identify where an error has occurred.

Variable checks list the contents of variables at specific points in the program. This allows their contents to be compared with the expected values, perhaps from a *dry run* (see below). *Breakpoints* (see page 287) provide a way of stopping the program to look at the contents of variables.

Step mode or (*single-stepping*) is the execution of a program, one statement at a time, under user control. It allows the user to observe the effects of each statement after it has been executed.

Post-mortem routines display or print the values of variables at the point when a program failed. In some systems, it is a list that indicates where the program failure occurred and gives the latest values of registers, stacks and other variables. See *register*, page 349 and *stack*, page 311.

Dry run

including: trace table

is working through a section of a program manually. This is useful for locating errors, particularly run-time errors. A dry run can be performed on a section of an assembler program or on a high-level language program. A dry run would usually be carried out on parts of a program rather than on a whole program.

Working from the listing of a section of a program, a *trace table* is constructed with a column to identify the instruction executed and columns for the contents of each variable. The programmer follows the instructions from the listing, adding a new line to the trace table each time an instruction is executed. The new line of the trace table should indicate the instruction, either by its machine address or by its line number, and show any changes to the variables (see Figure C8.1).

Example of a **trace table** for a very simple program in an assembler language:

Current address	Instruction	Accumulator	&98FF	&9800	&9801	Display
&8001	INP &98FF		5			
&8002	INP &9800		5	15		
&8003	LND &9800	15	5	15		
&8004	. . .					

Example of a **trace table** for a very simple program in a high-level language:

Program statement	H	W	A	Output	Comment
1: Input H	5				Get height
2: Input W	5	15			Get width
3: A = H * W	5	15	75		Calculate area
4: Print A	5	15	75	75	Print area
5: GoTo 2	5	15	75		Go back for new pair of values This is the error, this line should be GoTo 1
2: Input W	5	20	75		Get width – we haven't updated the height
3: A = H * W	5	20	100		

An alternative form of trace table for the simple program in a high-level language (showing the position after statement 4 of the program):

Many programmers simply use a box for each variable, making changes to the boxes as instructed by the program but without constructing a formal trace table:

Statement 1 2 3 4	H 5	W 15	A 75	Output 75

Figure C8.1   Examples of trace tables

Error

including: bug, error message, listing file, execution error, run-time error, compilation error, linking error, syntax error, statement syntax error, program syntax error, structure error, logical error

is a fault or mistake in a program or information system causing it to produce wrong results or not to work. A *bug* is a fault in a program that causes errors. Most computers attempt to indicate the likely source of an error by producing *error messages*. Usually these messages are produced either on the user's screen if the error is attributed to the user or on the operator's console for more serious errors.

When a program is being developed, many simple errors will be detected during the compilation process. A *listing file* can be generated during compilation; this will contain the source program with error messages and other diagnostic information.

The many types of error can be classified as follows:

Execution errors or *run-time errors* are errors detected during program execution. These errors, such as overflow and division by zero, can occur if a mistake is made in the processing algorithm or as a result of external effects not catered for by the program, such as lack of memory or unusual data.

Compilation errors are errors detected during compilation and are usually *syntax errors* (see below).

Linking errors occur when a compiled program is linked to library routines, for example if a particular subroutine is not present in the library or the number of parameters provided is wrong.

Syntax errors occur either when program statements cannot be understood because they do not follow the rules laid down by the programming language (*statement syntax errors*) or when program structures are nested incorrectly (*program syntax errors* or *structure errors*). Examples of statement syntax errors include wrong punctuation and misspelling of reserved words and variables. Examples of program syntax errors include control structures that are nested incorrectly or terminated incorrectly.

Logical errors are mistakes in the design of a program, such as a branch to a wrong statement or the use of an inappropriate mathematical formula. A logical error will be recognised because the program produces wrong results or an incorrect display. It is unlikely to generate an error message because the error is in the program design.

Run

including: run-time

is putting a program or information system into action so that it can perform the data processing it was designed to do.

Run-time is the time during which a program or information system is in operation. Often data have to be provided during run time and some effects, such as *run-time errors* (see page 284), can be detected only when the system is operating.

Breakpoint

is a position within the program where the program is halted as an aid to debugging. While the program is halted, the programmer can investigate the values of variables, memory locations and registers. This provides additional information to help locate errors, particularly run-time errors.

This facility is often used with assembly-language programs and may be incorporated into the operating system or provided by a *debugger* (see page 284). The machine-code addresses of breakpoints can be set, the progress of the program can be monitored and the program will halt when the instruction at a breakpoint address is reached. A debugger allows the contents of computer memory to be displayed. It may be possible to resume execution after stopping the program at a breakpoint.

A programmer may insert breakpoints in a program as part of a testing strategy. These will be deleted when the tests are successful.

Dump

including: screen dump, memory dump, core dump
is to copy the contents of a file, or the contents of part of immediate-access store, to backing store or an output device. The output is known as the dump and may be used to test the integrity of a datafile or to assist in program-error detection. A dump may also be made as part of a backup process. There are various types of dump, including:

screen dump, which is a representation of the screen stored as a datafile or produced as a print-out. A screen dump is an easy way of printing data collected together on the screen and produces a copy of the current screen display;

memory dump, which is the output of an area of memory to a file or the screen, usually showing the information in binary or hexadecimal numbers;

core dump, which is a memory dump of part of the main memory of the computer. It usually occurs when a program is terminated abnormally by an internal error.

Patch

including: service pack, update
is a small fragment of code provided by a software supplier to enable a user to modify or correct their copy of software without requiring a complete replacement. A *service pack* is a collection of programs and datafiles that correct problems in released software. It is installed to overwrite parts of the originally released software. An *update* is a minor release of software that incorporates corrections but that does not usually include any significant new features. It is now common for manufacturers to publish these updates on their Web sites, enabling users of the software to download them. See also *software upgrade* (page 226).

Run-time system

is the complete set of software, including any *library programs* or *library routines* (see page 338), that must be present in a computer before a particular program can be executed.

PART C

Process state

including: ready, running, blocked, suspended, stopped, completed, deadly embrace
is the status of a program submitted to a computer system for *running* (see *run*,
page 286). The concept is particularly useful with *multiprogramming systems* (see
page 342), in which several programs may be being processed at the same time. This
includes multiuser computer systems, which will be operating using some form of
multiprogramming.

Programs submitted to a computer, either for batch or for interactive processing,
are added to a job queue and are then in one of a number of process states (see
Figure C8.2).

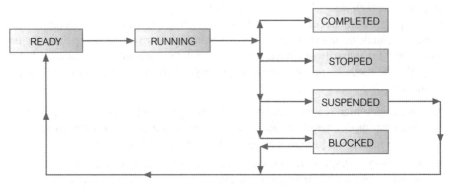

Figure C8.2   Program process states

Ready: a program waiting to continue execution by the central processor. Several
    programs may be ready at any one time, waiting for execution.

Running: a program being executed by the central processor. A central processor
    can execute only one program at a time, so only one program will be running
    (except in a computer with several processors). Execution may be interrupted,
    in which case the program will be either suspended or blocked.

Blocked: a program waiting for a peripheral. The peripheral may be in use by
    another program or already committed to a task for this program. When the
    peripheral becomes available, the status returns to *Ready*, allowing the central
    processor to continue executing the program when it can.

Suspended: the operating system decides that a program has to be interrupted, per-
    haps because it is taking up too much time. The program status will be returned
    to *Ready* to await a further time allocation.

Stopped: a program has been *aborted* (see *abort*, page 289).

Completed: a program has run to a proper conclusion. It will then be deleted from
    the job queue.

Deadly embrace: a condition in which no processing takes place at all and the
    system appears to be *hung* (see page 289); this could be the result of a number

of situations, for example process A is waiting for process B to complete, which it cannot do until process C is complete, which it cannot do until process A is complete . . . ; the chain could, of course, be even longer.

Down time

is the time when a computer system is not available (*down*) to the user. This may be because the computer is being maintained, it has broken down, there is a failure in the operating system or there is a communications failure.

Abort

is stopping the execution of a program or system before it has reached its normal conclusion. The run may be aborted by the program itself, the operating system or an operator.

A program may be aborted if an error is detected or if the operator requests it. An error such as a missing file will cause a program to be aborted. If the program appears to be working incorrectly, then the operator may request that it is aborted. Sometimes the operating system may not be able to abort a run; in this case, the computer will not respond and will have to be reset. See also *hung*, below.

Crash

also known as: bomb
including: system crash, hung
is a term used to describe the situation when a computer system unexpectedly stops working correctly. This could be caused by a hardware failure, an error causing the program to *abort* (see above) or an error causing the computer to be hung.

A *system crash* is a major failure of a computer leaving it inoperable and all users unable to continue.

A computer is *hung* if it does not produce any output and appears to have ceased to operate. This is often caused by an *infinite loop* (see page 256). The operator will then attempt *recovery* (see below); if that is not possible, the computer will need to be *reset* (see page 290).

If a crash occurs on a personal computer, it is possible that any recent unsaved alterations to work or data will be lost.

Recovery

including: warm start, cold start, reset
is the process of returning the system to normal operation after an error. The procedures may differ, depending on the type of program in use and the type of error

PART C

(whether due to hardware, software or data). Recovery will include identifying any data that have been corrupted and deciding on the restart process:

Warm start: execution is continued from the point at which the error occurred, using data that may already have been processed and stored in memory. Because the computer's memory is not initialised, there is a risk that corrupted data may cause further errors. A warm start enables a fast recovery of the system, if possible.

Cold start: the system is started again from the beginning. The computer's memory is initialised and the system should now work as expected. This can be a slow recovery, since the system may have to repeat processing already performed. See also *crash*, above.

Reset: the system is returned to its initial state, as if it had just been switched on or started. This is often used after a program has caused a computer to crash or behave erratically, when the computer may continue to work, but corruption of the contents of critical areas of memory may lead to erratic behaviour and loss of data.

Immediate mode

is the use of a command or program language statement outside the program that has been running. The instruction is executed and any results are produced before the user can enter the next instruction. Usually, immediate mode is available only with interpreted systems.

Programming Languages

Other related material can be found in C1 Systems Design and Life Cycle and D1 Systems Software.

Programming languages are the means of generating the software that makes the computer work. A computer operates by executing a **program**; that is, following a sequence of instructions. This is held in memory as electronic patterns, known as **machine code**. The programmer starts with a design of what the program is intended to do, or algorithm, then writes it in a programming language. The written program is known as the **source code** and is translated into **object code** (or machine code).

Programming languages are not the same as human languages – most obviously because (at present) they are only written and never spoken. However, the term 'language' is a very appropriate one. Languages have a **grammar** (or **syntax**), which states the rules of the language. This makes it possible to recognise 'wrong', ungrammatical uses of language to avoid spending time and effort trying to understand something that has no meaning. The syntax of a language is not simply a collection of 'correct' uses – it is a set of rules that allow programmers to combine elements of the language into a statement and know it is acceptable to the computer. Statements in languages also have meanings (or **semantics**). One important difference between human and computer languages is that computer languages are never ambiguous – a statement always has just one meaning (even if it isn't the meaning that the programmer intended).

Historically, the first languages were developed to simplify the process of programming the electronic patterns instead of entering them as 1s and 0s – binary digits, or bits. If the pattern 101010 was the code for ADD, then it was easier to allow the programmer to write 'ADD' and let the computer substitute the appropriate code. These languages are known as **assembly languages** because they assemble instructions that could be coded directly as bits. The instructions are translated into machine code by **assembler** programs. Assembly languages are very close to the actual machine code of a computer. A different assembly language is needed for each type of computer. Because of this close link, such languages are known as **machine-oriented** or **low-level languages**.

As programming became more sophisticated, languages were designed to allow programmers to write instructions that are closer to the way they think about the problem. If a running total is located in 1101101, then it is easier to give this location a name, e.g. TOT, and let the computer substitute the location. The programmer can work more efficiently and has less to remember, so mistakes are less likely. A translation program will turn, for example, a mathematical computation expressed in mathematical symbols into the (often quite lengthy) sequence of machine-code instructions to perform that computation. This also allows the programmer to use a single language for different computers, provided that the language is translated by a translation program appropriate for the computer in use. Such languages are at a different level from the details of how the machine works, and they express programming steps in a way that is more suited to the problem than the computer. These languages are known as **problem-oriented languages** or **high-level languages**, an example being Visual Basic.

With a completely developed program, the translation process is performed only once, so it need not be very fast, provided that the machine code that is produced is efficient. There are several ways of organising the translation. Some translators take in a written program and produce working machine code; others translate into assembly language and use an existing assembler for the last stage of translation. Yet another way is to produce **intermediate code**, which is easier to translate than the original program during execution; Java is of this type.

Translation programs that produce another program at a lower level (machine code, assembly language, intermediate code) are called **compilers**. After compilation, programs can be executed again and again without needing the original translation program.

Some programs are translated while they are being executed, a process known as **interpreting**. This allows the programmer to make changes easily without long delays whilst waiting for compilation. A disadvantage is that all of the translation program, known as an **interpreter**, needs to be present when the program is executed, so even a quite small program will need a lot of memory when it is running.

Interpreters normally translate and execute programs line by line, converting each program statement into a sequence of machine code instructions and executing these instructions without retaining the translated version. In a program with a loop, this means that the same statement will be translated every time it is encountered. For this and similar reasons, interpreted programs are usually slower in execution than compiled programs. Nevertheless, both the disadvantages – space and time – are outweighed by ease of use.

Interpreters begin execution of a program immediately and they can work on an unfinished program, hence they are commonly used interactively, where it is important to see the results as soon as possible. Compilers are best used for software that will be used many times without change, such as systems software and applications packages.

Over a period of time, a number of programming techniques have developed, and programming languages have been written with characteristics that support the various programming styles. However, machine code is **imperative**; that is, it specifies the operations, the order in which they must be carried out and the memory locations to be used. All other language types, such as **declarative**, **functional** and **logical** languages, have to be translated (compiled or interpreted) into an imperative form for execution. Programming techniques such as **structured**, **procedural** and **object-oriented** programming are designed to enable effective programs to be developed and maintained, particularly when several people are involved in the design.

New languages are designed when existing languages no longer provide adequate facilities – specialist graphics and statistics languages have emerged, for instance. At present, their translators are often written in a particular high-level language called **C** (or its successors, **C++** and **C#**), which has its own features to allow the easy design of such systems software. Specialised tools are available to simplify the process further.

Computer users are becoming increasingly aware of **mark-up languages**. These are not programming languages in the normal sense, but rather a way of defining the structure and format of a document – for example, a Web page.

Comparative information about some significant early programming languages that are no longer used for program design appears in Table C9.1; programming languages typically used today for program development are given in Table C9.2.

Types of Language

High-level language

including: problem-oriented language, third-generation language (3GL), fourth-generation language (4GL), application-generation language

is designed to help a programmer express a computer program in a way that reflects the problem that is being solved, rather than the details of how the computer will produce the solution. These languages are often described as *problem-oriented languages*. The programmer will certainly be allowed to use long descriptive names for the variables and to structure the program into subroutines or functions to help keep the logic of the solution clearly visible. Certain mathematical notation will be permitted, allowing calculations to be specified in the same way as in written mathematics. When the language is translated, the *compiler* or *interpreter* (see page 340) will take care of the details of the many machine-code instructions necessary to cause the computer to execute the program. Compare this with the definition of *low-level language*, page 294.

Languages that were developed at the time of *third-generation computers* are known as *third-generation languages* (*3GL*), and many are still in current use.

Fourth-generation language (*4GL*) is used to describe languages aiming at end users rather than specialist computer practitioners. A characteristic of these languages was the recognition that computing power was becoming available more freely and cheaply, and that popular software would be that which could reduce the time taken to *develop* users' programs. 4GLs are also known as *application-generation languages*.

Comparative information about some significant high-level languages appears in Tables C9.1 and C9.2 (see pages 300 and 301).

PART C

Intermediate code

Computer programs are generally translated into instructions for the computer to follow in one of two distinct ways, compilation or interpretation. There is also a possible 'mixed' approach, in which the program is first compiled into an *intermediate code* made up of simpler instructions, which are then interpreted when the program is executed. The intermediate code translator is an *interpreter*. If a program is compiled into intermediate code, it can be run on any computer for which an intermediate code translator is available. The same computer-specific intermediate code translator can be used as the final stage for any programming language that can be translated into that intermediate code. One advantage of this approach, which has not been exploited as fully as might be hoped, is to improve the portability of high-level languages. Java is currently the most common programming language using intermediate code. See also *compiler* and *interpreter*, page 340.

Low-level language

including: machine-oriented language
Some programming languages are necessarily related closely to the design of the machine; the available instructions reflect the way the machine is built. *Assembly language* and perhaps even *machine code* itself (see below) are good examples. Because *high-level languages* (see above) generally prevent the user specifying memory locations directly, low-level languages are necessary for programming tasks connected with the running of the computer, particularly where speed is important. For this reason, they are described as *machine-oriented languages*. They are not generally good for problem-solving, for which high-level languages are more suitable.

Assembly language

is related very closely to the computer's own machine code. Instead of writing actual machine-code instructions (which would typically need to be entered in binary or hexadecimal), the assembly-language programmer is generally able to make use of descriptive names for data stores and mnemonics for instructions. The program is then assembled (by software known as an assembler) into the appropriate machine-code instructions. See also *machine code*, below, and *assembler*, page 339.

Machine code

is the set of all possible instructions made available by the hardware design of a particular processor. These instructions operate on very basic items of data, such as bytes or even single bits. They may be given memorable names in the associated documentation, but they can be understood by the computer only when expressed in binary notation. Hence, machine code is very difficult to write without mistakes. In practice, machine-code programming is achieved by the programmer writing in *assembly language* (see above), which is related closely to machine code.

Microcode

is the specialised code that controls the logic operations of the processor when implementing machine-code instructions. It is part of the physical design of the processor and cannot be changed.

Language Characteristics

Imperative language

is a language in which the programmer specifies the steps needed to execute the program, such as program statements, declarations and control structures, and the order in which they should be carried out. Most early programming languages were imperative.

Current high-level imperative languages generally have features that would enable them to be used as *procedural languages* (see below).

Procedural language

is an imperative language in which the program statements can be grouped in self-contained blocks called *procedures* and *functions* (see page 261). These procedures have their own variables, not accessible outside the procedure. The logic of the program is expressed as a series of *procedure calls* (see page 262).

Although a well-written program expressed in a procedural language is generally more comprehensible to the reader, procedural languages are nonetheless imperative (see above), in that the responsibility for specifying what steps should be taken, and in what order, falls on the programmer. See also *functional language* (page 296).

Object-oriented programming language

is a procedural language that provides the necessary structures to produce object-oriented programs. It enables the programmer to design self-contained objects, which contain both program routines and the data being processed. A complex system can be built up from these small objects. See also *object-oriented programming*, page 242.

PART C

Declarative language

is a language in which the program consists of declarations, i.e. statements that specify the properties that the result should have. In contrast to an *imperative* language (see page 295), the outcomes are described, but how they are to be achieved is not described. The order of these declarations should not be important. Currently, most existing so-called declarative languages rarely achieve these characteristics, owing to the difficulty of implementing such a system. See *PROLOG*, page 299.

Functional language

is a *declarative language* (see above) in which each call producing a value is returned to the statement being executed at the time the function was called. The logic of the program is expressed as one single function call that calls other functions in order. These functions in turn may call others directly or call themselves recursively. Consequently, a well-written program in a functional language making good use of recursion has a structure that looks different from that of an *imperative* program (see page 295).

Logic programming language

is a type of *declarative language* (see above) that makes use of logic formulas. It is based on procedures, ideally these would be unordered, although this is often not the case, for example *PROLOG* (see page 299) or CPL. See Figure C9.1 for an example.

List-processing language

manipulates data strings (lists of data items, see page 315) and uses linked lists (see page 311) as its primary data structure. It has very few primitive operations, but these are very powerful and use recursion very efficiently. (See also recursive subprogram, page 263.) Such languages are used mainly in expert systems and generally have not been used commercially, as they are less comfortable for general-purpose programmers. Examples are *LISP* and *Logo* (see Table C9.2, page 301).

Declared facts, such as	Philip is male	
	William is male	
	Elizabeth is female	
	Philip is parent of Charles	
	Elizabeth is parent of Charles	
	Charles is parent of William	
Declared rules, such as	A is child of B **IF** B parent of A	*Note: all variables are local to the rule in which they occur*
	A is father of B **IF** A is male **AND** A is parent of B	
	A is son of B **IF** A is male **AND** A is child of B	
	A is daughter of B **IF** A is female **AND** A is child of B	
	A is grandparent of B **IF** A is parent of C **AND** C is parent of B	
	A is grandchild of B **IF** A is child of C **AND** C is child of B	
	A is granddaughter of B **IF** A is female **AND** A is grandchild of B	*etc, etc*
Now can ask	Is William granddaughter of Elizabeth?	
	which X **if** X is grandson of Elizabeth	*To speed up subsequent deductions, results of these could be added to the knowledge base as additional facts (if they are not there already) by an imperative statement*
	which X **if** X is father of Charles	
	which A **if** X is grandparent of William	

Figure C9.1   Example of use of a logical language

Extensible

languages allow additional operations, data structures or data types to be defined, as if they were part of the original definition, using the existing language facilities. These can then be incorporated into the language and used in the same way with the same syntax as existing ones. See *FORTH*, page 299. Collections of extensions may be made available to others (see also *library routine*, page 338).

PART C

Query language

including: Structured Query Language (SQL), Query By Example (QBE)
Large database management systems (DBMS) (see page 88) must allow the user –
who may not be a skilled programmer – to ask for information to be extracted; for
example, 'How many invoices more than three months old are recorded in the
database that have not yet been paid?' Query languages are simplified programming
languages, restricted to querying a database.

A few keywords are used to link the names of fields in the database and to specify values for comparison:

```
SELECT invoices WHERE date-sent < 16-04-1998
AND total-owing > 0
```

Popular query languages that you might come across include *Structured Query
Language* (*SQL*) and *Query By Example* (*QBE*). See also *database*, page 88.

Report generator

including: RPG II (Report Program Generator II)
is a piece of software that allows a business user – who may not be a skilled computer programmer – to specify a printed report that draws on values from a database
or the results of calculations performed by the computer. Such software is closer to
an applications package than most items considered 'languages', but it is generally
included in listings of available computer programming languages. The structure
of the software allows the user to design the report using statements that are very
similar in appearance to programming language statements. Table C9.1 (page 300)
includes *RPG II*, the *Report Program Generator II*, as the commonest example of
such a report generator.

Data-manipulation language (DML)

is a form of high-level language, usually part of a *database management system* (see
page 89), that is designed to allow the user to access (query), store (insert) and
change (update) data in a *database* (see page 88). SQL is an example (see above).

Authoring language

including: authoring tool
is a language designed to assist in the preparation of teaching or presentation
materials that are to be presented on a computer. These materials may be learning

material for computer-managed learning, Web pages or any other situation for which computer presentation is desirable or appropriate. These authoring languages are sometimes referred to as *authoring tools*.

An authoring language for computer-managed learning allows the author to specify which material will be displayed (this might include the use of sound or video) and which questions are to be asked of the student. Answers to these questions will be listed, together with the action to be taken in response to each one, and the section of the teaching that follows; in this way, remedial lessons can be offered to students who score badly, while students giving correct answers can be directed along a faster route through the material. See also *computer-aided learning*, page 157.

Other specific authoring languages include *Virtual Reality Mark-up Language* (see page 110) and *HyperText Mark-up Language* (see page 303).

PROLOG

including: knowledge base, logic engine
is a high-level programming language. It is a type of logic programming language, but procedures are not unordered fully as would be required of a true logic language. The name comes from 'PROgramming with LOGic'. It is used in *artificial intelligence and expert systems* (see page 134).

Programming in PROLOG involves building a *knowledge base* by declaring a large number of rules to the system, using mathematical logic notation, and facts, and then asking the PROLOG system to deduce conclusions from the knowledge base. PROLOG sometimes uses imperative statements to add deduced facts to the knowledge base.

The necessary processing is accomplished by a logical inference machine together with a *logic engine* program emphasising the extensive use of mathematical logic concepts.

FORTH

is an extensible low-level programming language, well suited to control applications. It is functional (see page 296). The language consists of a number of predefined 'words' at a level very close to machine code. The programmer then defines new words, which are added to the language, just as if they were part of the original definition. Because speed of execution is important, the language uses *Reverse Polish Notation* (see page 245), in which to add 1 to 2 you would write `1 2 ADD`.

It is stack-based, so there is little use of variables, threaded, so it is highly extensible, fast to compile and execute, and basically imperative.

Table C9.1 Early programming languages generally no longer used for program development, although some are still in use

Language	Date	Derivation of name	Translation	Characteristics	Notes
ALGOL	1958–68	*ALGOr*ithmic *L*anguage	Compiled	Imperative	Originally for (paper) description of algorithms – an influential language with several distinct versions (Algol-60, Algol-68)
ALGOL 68	1968	*ALGOr*ithmic *L*anguage	Compiled	Imperative	Developed from Algol, with more structure
APL	1957–68	*A P*rogramming *L*anguage	Interpreted	Functional	Easier to write than to read Uses symbols not always found on regular keyboards – requires large memory Operates on vectors
COBOL	1959–60	*CO*mmon *B*usiness-*O*riented *L*anguage	Compiled	Imperative	Easier to read than to write Large memory requirements, hence a mainframe language Highly structured data suited to business use
FORTH	Late 1960s	Pun on 'fourth'	Mixed	Unique, functional	Very different from other languages: used in control and graphics applications – see separate description in this section
Pascal	1968–71	After Blaise Pascal	Compiled	Imperative	Mainstream general-purpose structured language of the 1970s and 1980s
PL/1	1963–64	*P*rogramming *L*anguage 1	Compiled	Imperative	Union of COBOL and FORTRAN Introduced new simple concepts but never gained popularity Big, and defaults should be context-dependent
POP-11	Late 1960s	Author: Dr R. J. Popplestone	Interpreted	Functional	Artificial intelligence uses
RPG	1964	*R*eport *P*rogram *G*enerator	Compiled	Imperative	Almost an applications package for business reports
RPG II	1970	*R*eport *P*rogram *G*enerator II	Mixed	Imperative	Enhanced RPG
Simula	1965	From *simula*tion	Compiled	Object-oriented	Simulation First object-oriented language
SNOBOL	1962–68	*StriN*g-*O*riented *SymBO*lic *L*anguage	Compiled	Functional	String-manipulation language

The date is that of initial development; most languages have been improved continuously since invention.
Translation indicates the most usual method, not necessarily the only one.
Structure indicates:
■ whether the language is used by giving instructions on how to solve the problem (an algorithm or conventional program) – 'imperative';
■ whether the language is based on functions or procedures applied to sets of data – 'functional' – or whether its basic structure is that of an object-oriented programming language.
FORTH is a rather unusual language and is described on page 000.

Table C9.2 Programming languages typically used today for program development

Language	Date	Derivation of name	Translation	Characteristics	Notes
Ada	1975–83	After Ada, Countess Lovelace	Compiled	Imperative	Used mainly for large military systems; sponsored by US Department of Defense
Ada 95	1995	Updated version			Superseded Ada
BASIC	1964	*Beginners All-purpose Symbolic Instruction Code*	Interpreted	Imperative	Easy to learn and (in modernised versions) the world's most frequently encountered programming language, especially in schools
C	1972	See Notes	Compiled	Imperative	Systems-programming language, derived from 'B', which derived in turn from BCPL, which derived from CPL
C++	1979–83	C plus a bit more	Compiled	Object-oriented	Object-oriented features added to C
C#	2001	C++ and more	Compiled	Object-oriented	Client–server distributed applications Pronounced 'C sharp'
Delphi	1995	Object Pascal	Compiled	Object-oriented	Extension to Pascal by Borland
FORTRAN	1954–57	*FOR*mula *TRAN*slation	Compiled	Imperative	Mainstream scientific programming language Too early to be a structured programming language
FORTRAN 90	1990	Updated version			There have been different generations
Java	1991–95	Its 'exotic, exciting, adrenaline-pumping connotations'	Compiled to intermediate code, then interpreted	Object-oriented	Platform-independent related to C++ for the Internet Use of applets and bytecode for distributed applications across the Internet
Lisp	1959	*List Processing*	Interpreted	Functional	Artificial intelligence uses Influential language, in that many other languages have been derived from it
LOGO	1966–68	Greek for 'thought'	Interpreted	Procedural, list-processing	Based on list-processing features, but noted for its 'turtle graphics' subset Popular in education as it is considered to teach thinking as well as programming
PROLOG	1972	*PRO*gramming in *LOG*ic	Interpreted	Logical	Artificial intelligence uses A very different language
Smalltalk	1972–80	To emphasise nature of language interface	Compiled	Object-oriented	Forerunner of most graphics interfaces
Visual BASIC	Early 1990s	*Screen-based extension of BASIC*	Interpreted or compiled	Imperative	Provides quick and easy means of creating interface applications for MS Windows™
VBA	Mid 1990s	Visual Basic for Applications	Interpreted	Imperative	Later development of Visual Basic

The date is that of initial development; most languages have been improved continuously since invention.
Translation indicates the most usual method, not necessarily the only one.
Characteristics indicates:
∎ whether the language is used by giving instructions on how to solve the problem (an algorithm or conventional program) – 'imperative';
∎ whether it is based on functions or procedures applied to sets of data – 'functional' – or whether its basic structure is that of an object-oriented programming language.
PROLOG is rather an unusual language and is described on page 299.
Java, and some other languages, may be encoded into an intermediate code, which can then be interpreted on other systems.

LOGO

including Turtle Graphics, turtle
is a *functional* language based on list processing and is easily *extensible* (see page 297). It was developed as an educational language for use with young children and encourages children to think in a structured way. It contains graphical operations that are easy to use.

The subset of LOGO commands dealing with graphics is called **turtle graphics** because it is used to control the movements of a *turtle*. The turtle can be a small robot with wheels and a pen moving across the floor and drawing or simply a point moving and drawing on the screen.

Another subset of LOGO allows the production of music (see also *Sound*, page 40).

Backus–Naur form (BNF)

including: replacement rules
is a way of describing the syntax of a computer language. The name comes from its two inventors, although it is sometimes held to be 'Backus *normal* form'. A BNF description is expressed as a series of *replacement rules* that describe how some element of the language is built up from choices of simpler elements. See Figure C9.2 for an example.

Part of a possible definition of the LET assignment statement in the BASIC language:

```
<LET-statement>: :=[LET] <numeric-variable> = <numeric-expression>|
                 [LET] <string-variable> = <string-expression>
```

This says that the LET statement can take either of two forms, shown by the vertical bar, which represents alternatives.

The first form is:
 the word LET (which is optional, because it is shown in square brackets),
 followed by a numerical variable,
 followed by the equals sign '=',
 followed by a numerical expression.

Items shown in angle brackets '<' and '>' have definitions elsewhere in the full language specification.

 For example, it is likely that elsewhere you would find the line:

```
        <string-variable>: := <numeric-variable>$
```

 showing that a string variable obeys the same rules as a numeric variable but is followed by a dollar sign '$'.

Items shown in curly brackets '{' and '}' may occur any number of times, including none.

 For example, the definition of a numerical variable may be:

```
        <numeric-variable>: := <letter>{alphanumeric}
```

 showing that the variable name must start with a letter but that following characters, if any, may be either letters or numbers.

Figure C9.2 Example of Backus–Naur form

Mark-up languages

including: Standard Generalised Mark-up Language (SGML)
are document description languages used for multimedia documents; they are not truly programming languages. They were intended to describe the structure of a document, without specifying how it was to be laid out when printed or displayed on a screen (but see *HTML*, below). The document is made up of elements such as text, pictures, sound, etc., and the structure is defined by means of *tags* inserted in the document (see *HTML*, below). These tags are quite separate from the elements and might specify, for example, that a particular block of text is a heading, a complete paragraph or the author's name. The interpretation of these tags is not defined in the language, and different users elect to display these elements in their own ways. Because the tags are expressed as plain text, and without special codes specific to one particular user, documents defined in a mark-up language are completely portable.

Standard Generalised Mark-up Language (*SGML*) was the original language and had no specific reference to computers. Later versions, incorporating developments for computer use, are HTML, DHTML and XML.

HyperText Mark-up Language (HTML)

including: tag, DHTML, XML
is a mark-up language developed for multimedia documents, such as World Wide Web pages.

Tags in HTML are instructions for the browser, telling it how to display the text. The tags themselves are never displayed. Each tag consists of a name, sometimes followed by an optional list of attributes. Many tags generally occur in pairs, bracketing elements of the text. Such tags are an instruction about how the text between the tags should be treated. For example glossary indicates that the single word 'glossary' should be emphasised, and this generally results in the browser displaying it in *italic* text. Table C9.3 shows some of the important tags.

As with all mark-up languages, an HTML document is just text and can be transmitted rapidly. Portability is enhanced further by the required behaviour of a browser on encountering an unknown tag, which is simply to ignore it. It is thus possible for a Web page to capitalise on features present in later browsers, while still displaying satisfactorily in earlier versions.

In the original specification, the text to be displayed was marked with tags, and it was the responsibility of the user's Web browser to display the text in an appropriate way. This allowed the user to specify their own preferences. For example, a visually handicapped user might instruct their browser to use a larger or more readable font, and it was unnecessary to consider this in the design of the Web page. However, there was understandable pressure from Web page designers, asking for more control over the display of their pages. This resulted in the addition of extra tags: bold and italic text is now more commonly specified through explicit <b> and <i> tags, and the ability to specify a particular type face, colour and size of text

PART C

Table C9.3 Small selection of important HTML tags

Tag	Example	Result or description
strong: `<strong>` . . . `</strong>`	The `<strong>`glossary`</strong>` text	The **glossary** text
emphasis: `<em>` . . . `</em>`	The `<em>`glossary`</em>` text	The *glossary* text
combining style tags	The `<strong><em>`glossary`</em></strong>` text	The ***glossary*** text
image: `<img>`	`<img src="picture.gif">`	The image 'picture.gif' is displayed within the page
anchor: `<a>` . . . `</a>`	`<a href=page2.html>` Click here to see the next page `</a>`	Produces a link to another page
	`<a name=linkname>`Contact details`</a>`	A label within the current page. This label can be used to link directly to this location within the page
	`<a href=linkname>` Click here to see the contact details `</a>`	A link to a label within the current page
paragraph: `<p>` . . . `</p>`	`<p>`This is the text to be displayed in a paragraph`</p><p>`This is another paragraph`</p>`	This is the text to be displayed in a paragraph This is another paragraph

unordered list: `<ul>` . . . `</ul>`
list item: `<li>` . . . `</li>`
	`<p>`The following is a bulleted list:`</p>`
	`<ul>`
	`<li>`First item on the list`</li>`
	`<li>`Second item on the list`</li>`
	`<li>`Next item on the list`</li>`
	`<li>`Last item on the list`</li>`
	`</ul>`
		The following is a bulleted list:
		
		■ First item on the list
		■ Second item on the list
		■ Next item on the list
		■ Last item on the list

ordered list: `<ol>` . . . `</ol>`	`<p>`The following is a numbered list:`</p>`
	`<ol>`
	`<li>`First item on the list`</li>`
	`<li>`Second item on the list`</li>`
	`<li>`Next item on the list`</li>`
	`<li>`Last item on the list`</li>`
	`</ol>`
		The following is a numbered list:
		
		1. First item on the list
		2. Second item on the list
		3. Next item on the list
		4. Last item on the list

has been incorporated. This has taken HTML further from the concept of a 'pure' mark-up language, but it has provided much greater (but sometimes misused) functionality for Web pages.

It is possible to define a Web page by adding the tags to the text using a text editor, but most page design is done using special editors, which save the designed page as an HTML file with all tags inserted automatically.

Extended versions of HTML (which require extended versions of browsers to read them) include:

DHTML (dynamic HTML), which allows more user interaction within the browser. It also allows the user to read from and write to specific database files;

XML (from eXtensible), which has taken HTML back towards the original concept of a pure mark-up language. It can be used to define the structure of data with existing and user-defined tags. This basic structure can then be interpreted not only by Web browsers but by any software. For example, a medical database structured in XML can be used unchanged as the data source for a query program and for a tutorial application.

# Data Representation

Related material, particularly about numbers and their representation, can be found in C11 Numerical Data Representation.

The essence of any computer is its ability to store and manipulate data. The data are stored electronically, and this section looks at the principles used to interpret the stored data as understandable information.

Within the computer, all information is represented as some combination of physical properties. What these properties mean depends on how we interpret them. Indeed, a particular set of these properties could represent a number, a letter, a word, an instruction or a variety of other things. What a particular set of properties is taken to mean depends on the context it is in when interpreted by the computer's central processor.

In a digital computer, these properties are made up of individual elements that can have one of two values (often voltages). It is convenient for us to think of this element as a binary digit (a **bit**), which can be written as either 0 or 1. Binary digits can then be grouped to form patterns, which are used as **codes**. These codes provide a way of thinking about how the computer works internally, but the technology actually used can vary from computer to computer.

The codes allow us to describe how data are stored and manipulated in a way that is common between computer systems. We can also consider the codes as binary numbers, which allows us to use mathematical theory to manipulate the data.

Data representation is about the way in which binary digits are grouped to provide codes, how these are interpreted and how larger groupings, such as arrays, stacks and lists, are used for sets of data.

Concepts

Data

are information coded and structured for subsequent processing, generally by a computer system. The resulting codes are meaningless until they are placed in the correct context. The subtle difference between data and information is that *information* is in context, data are not.

Character set

including: character, character code, control character, non-printing character, internal character code, EBCDIC (Extended Binary Coded Decimal Interchange Code), ASCII (American Standard Code for Information Interchange), ISO 8859, code page, ANSI (American National Standards Institute) character set, teletext character set

is the set of symbols that may be represented by a computer at a particular time. These symbols are called *characters*. They can be letters, digits, spaces and punctuation marks. They include non-printing and control characters.

Individual characters are represented by a single code number (the *character code*) stored as a binary integer. Any textual data will be stored as a sequence of these codes. When the data are displayed or printed, the code is converted into the appropriate shape.

The shape assigned to a particular code number can be changed, and the resulting display will be different. In particular, this occurs when the screen display character set is different from the printer character set, in which case the print-out will be different from the screen display.

Many character sets also have codes for *control characters*. These *non-printing characters* are used for special purposes. Examples of control characters are end-of-record and end-of-file markers in a file, carriage return and line feed for a printer, and begin and end transmission with a modem, and cursor movement on a screen.

All the symbols available form a character set, which could be specific to a particular computer or application. A microcomputer system will usually use *internal character codes*, which are the code numbers produced by pressing the keys on the keyboard. These internal character codes will usually be converted into standard codes for use by applications software.

Many computer systems now have the flexibility to use several character sets as required, for example to provide foreign-language characters or for compatibility with earlier systems. In practice, most computers use internationally agreed character sets, such as the following:

EBCDIC is an older character set used by large computer systems for internal communication and data storage. It stands for *Extended Binary Coded Decimal Interchange Code*.

ASCII was devised for use with early telecommunication systems but proved to be ideal for computer systems and forms the basis for almost all other character sets. It stands for *American Standard Code for Information Interchange*.

ISO 8859 is the current international standard for computer character sets and has several variations for use in different cultures. The variations are known more usually by their names, such as *Latin1 alphabet*, *Latin2 alphabet* and *Greek alphabet*.

Code page is the name for optional character sets defined for use with IBM-compatible microcomputers.

PART C

ANSI character set provides various lines and shapes as additional characters. These simplify the production of screen displays involving lines and shapes. ANSI stands for *American National Standards Institute*.

Teletext character set enables screen displays involving simple graphics to be constructed. These are very compact and can be transmitted economically.

The ASCII code uses 7 bits, giving 32 control codes and 96 displayable characters (an eighth bit could be used for error checking). Most modern character sets are extensions of the ASCII code, using 8 bits, which provides the possibility for more characters, but letters, digits and common punctuation characters retain the same code numbers. The most noticeable effect of character-set variations is that some characters appear to change; for example, '£' may appear as '$' or '#'.

Collating sequence

is the order in which a computer will sort character data. This could be the order in which a particular application sorts data, but it is often the sequence of characters in the order of their character codes. Obviously, letters such as A–Z will be in the usual alphabetical order, but various computer systems may differ in whether 'A' comes before 'a' or whether '1' comes before 'A', depending on the codes used in the system. The use of a standard code such as ASCII avoids such differences between computer systems.

Structures

Data structure

is a group of related data items organised in the computer. A data structure allows a large number of pieces of data to be managed as a single set. Each type of data structure makes it easy for the programmer to find and process the data in a particular way. Each type of structure has its own strengths and weaknesses. Examples of data structures are *arrays*, *lists*, *tables* (see page 310), *trees* (see below), *strings* (see *string data*, page 315) and *files* (see page 324).

Tree

including: node, branch, leaf node, terminal node, parent node, child node, root node, binary tree
is a non-linear data structure in which the data items can be thought of as occurring at different levels. There are links between items at one level and their descendants at the next. Each data item has data that relate it to its unique parent node. See Figure C10.1.

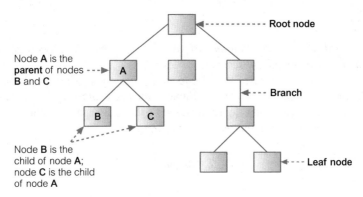

Figure C10.1   Typical tree structure

The data items are usually called *nodes*, with the links known as *branches*. A node may have any number of descendants, but it may be the descendant of only one other node. This data structure is often encountered in a directory of files, where directory nodes are linked to subdirectories. It is usual in computing to draw a tree diagram upside-down, with the 'root' at the top.

Data can be added to (by creating a new node) or removed from (by deleting a node) the tree. The tree can be traversed using a variety of algorithms, but only by following the links between nodes.

Some nodes in a tree have particular characteristics. Of particular importance are leaf nodes, parent nodes and root nodes.

Leaf nodes or *terminal nodes* are nodes in a tree without any branches further down the tree. In the conventional way of drawing trees (upside-down), the leaves occur at the bottom.

Parent node is the node immediately above a given node, at the next level up. There can be only one parent node for each node, but different nodes, known as *child nodes*, may share the same parent.

Root node is the entry node where we would start before moving around the tree. It is the only node in a tree without a parent node. In the conventional way of drawing trees (upside-down), the root occurs at the top. A tree has exactly one root node. If the data suggest that there should be two or more root nodes, then the data structure has to be viewed as several trees.

One particular form of tree is the *binary tree*, in which nodes have, at most, two branches down the tree. Binary trees are easier than other forms of tree to implement on a computer. Some of the advantages of a binary tree are:

- there is a way of representing all trees as binary trees;
- a fixed amount of space can be reserved for its branches;
- efficient algorithms exist for adding items to the tree and searching it.

PART C

Array

including: subscript, list, one-dimensional array, dimension, two-dimensional array, table, array bound, subscripted variable
is a set of data items of the same type grouped together using a single identifier. Each of the data items is addressed by the variable name and a *subscript*; for example, in Figure C10.2, NAME(4) is the fourth element of the array NAME. A column of data like this is called a *list* or a *one-dimensional array*.

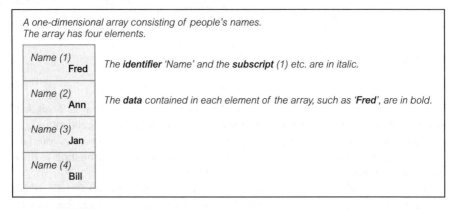

Figure C10.2 One-dimensional array

Arrays may have many *dimensions* and may have a *subscript* for each dimension. In Figure C10.3, STOCK(3,2) is an element in the *two-dimensional array* called STOCK. On paper, two-dimensional arrays are the same as tables (with rows and columns); they are sometimes called *tables* in the computing context.

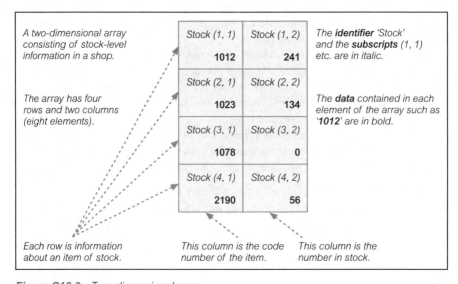

Figure C10.3 Two-dimensional array

Before an array can be used in a program, it must be *declared* (see *declaration*, page 267) and its size defined, so that the computer can allocate a part of memory for the array. Examples of array declarations are given in Figure C10.4. The limits of the array are known as the *array bounds* and it is usual to declare the array by stating its name and giving the maximum values of each dimension.

A *subscripted variable* refers to an individual element of an array, for example AGE(20) or STOCK(3,2).

Two-dimensional array of stock items	One-dimensional array of the results of throwing two dice
In **Pascal**:	
var **stock** : array [1..10,1..5] of real;	var **dice_score** : array [2..12] of integer;
In **BASIC**:	
DIM **STOCK**(10,5)	DIM **DICESCORE** (12)
In **C**:	
float **STOCK** [10][5]	int **dice_score** [12]
This example defines an array (of real numbers) that has two dimensions, with upper bounds of 10 'rows' (the first subscript) and 5 'columns' (the second subscript).	This example defines an array (of integers) for a problem using subscripts 2–12. Pascal allows the lower bound to be set at 2, rather than the more normal lower bound of 0 or 1.

Figure C10.4   Declaring array dimensions

Stack

including: last in, first out (LIFO), push, pull, pop
is a list in which items are added to or deleted from the same end. The operation of a stack is *last in, first out* (*LIFO*), i.e. the most recent item to arrive is dealt with first.

Push is the term used for adding an item to the stack. *Pull* and *pop* are terms used for taking an item from the stack. Taking an item from the stack makes the next item in the stack available. Items in other positions in the stack cannot be accessed.

Stacks are often represented by an array with a pointer to the top of the stack where the elements are added and removed.

Linked list

is a list in which each item contains the data together with a pointer to the next item. There may be an additional pointer to the previous item. This means that the items can be accessed in order, even if they are not stored in order; they do not have to be stored in adjacent memory locations.

Queue

including: first in, first out (FIFO), circular queue, circular buffer
is a list in which any new item is added to one end, and items are deleted from the other. The operation of a queue is *first in, first out* (*FIFO*), i.e. items are dealt with in the order they arrived.

Queues are often represented using an array with pointers to the first and last elements of the queue.

A *circular queue* is a queue in which the storage area is fixed and the first item is held in a location that is logically next to the storage location for the last item of the queue. Data items can be thought of as being arranged in a circle; for this reason, it is sometimes called a *circular buffer*.

Record

including: record format, logical record, physical record, blocking factor
is the basic unit of data stored in a datafile. It is a collection of items, which may be of different data types, all relating to the individual or object that the record describes, and it is treated as a unit for processing. Most datafiles contain records that have the same types of information but about different individuals or objects.

The contents of a record are described by the *record format*, which specifies the record in terms of its *fields* (see below).

Where it is necessary to distinguish between the content of a record and the computer-stored record, the terms *logical record* and *physical record* are used. Logical record is used to refer to the information held in a record, but a physical record is a *block* (see page 188) of memory in backing store, which can hold one or more logical records.

The number of logical records in each physical record, which will depend on the size of the logical record and the structure of records and blocks on the backing store, is called the *blocking factor*.

Variable-length record

is a record in which the number of bits (or characters) is not predetermined but is governed by the amount of data to be stored. This is useful when textual data are to be stored, which would leave a lot of wasted space in *fixed-length records* (see below). However, fixed-length records are processed more easily.

Fixed-length record

also known as: fixed-format record
is a record in which the number of bits in a record is decided in advance at the design stage. This length is constant and cannot be changed later. The length of a fixed-length record is often thought of in terms of bytes or characters.

Elements

EOF (end-of-file) marker

is a marker written to a file by the operating system immediately after the last record to signal the end of that file to the controlling program. A programmer can use this to process a variable amount of data in a file, processing records until the end-of-file marker is found. This is similar to using a *rogue terminator* (see page 254).

Field

including: field name
is part of a *record* (see above) designed to hold a single data item of a specified type. Most datafiles contain records that have the same fields of information but about different individuals or objects. Each field is referred to by a *field name*, which identifies the data in the field and makes it possible to generalise about the data being processed.

A **datafile** *holding details of club membership.*

Each **record** *would contain* **fields** *of a member's data:*

Name, initials, date of birth and membership number.

The **field names**:

Name, Initials, Date_of_Birth and Membership_Number

identify the data present, rather than being the actual data, which may be:

Smith, F, 12/3/78, 458923

Each **record** *would have the name, initials, date of birth and membership number of a different member.*

Figure C10.5 Fields and records in a datafile

Key

including: key field, sort key, primary key, key-field order, secondary key, composite key
is the field (the *key field*) within a record used to identify the record; for example, a bank-account number identifies a customer's account. The key can be used for finding the record within a file or as the *sort key* for sorting a file into order.

Most datafiles will have a *primary key*, which is unique and used to identify the record. If the records in a datafile can be accessed *sequentially* (see *sequential access*, page 327), then the records will be accessed in *key-field order*, which is the order in which they will be when they have been sorted using the key field.

PART C

Datafiles may also have *secondary keys*, which enable the file to be accessed in a different order. *Composite keys*, made up of more than one field, can be used to sort a file. The use of composite keys is shown in Figure C10.6.

In the example (Figure C10.5) of a datafile holding details of club membership containing **fields** *for:*

Name, Initials, Date_Of_Birth *and* **Membership_Number**

the **Membership_Number** *could be the primary key field because it is unique and identifies who the record is about.*

Name *could be a* **secondary key**.

Date_Of_Birth *or* **Initials** *could not be* **key** *fields because without the other fields they are out of context (and the data are unidentifiable and meaningless).*

Date_Of_Birth *could be a* **sort key** *because the resulting list would be in order of age, which is useful.*

Name *and* **Initials** *(i.e.* **SmithF**) *could be a* **composite key**.

If the file is sorted using this as a sort key, then all the **Smiths** *would be together, in alphabetical order according to* **initial**.

Figure C10.6   Key fields in a datafile

Data type

including: variable type, field type, user-defined data type, alphanumerical data, character data, string data, Boolean (or logical) data, sample data, sound data, video data, video clip, date data

is a formal description of the kind of data being stored or manipulated within a program or system, for example alphabetical data, numerical data or logical data.

Variable type in a high-level language describes the kind of data held by a *variable* (see page 268).

Field type describes the kind of data stored as a *field* (see above) within a datafile. The specification of data types is important because:

- it provides a limited validation of data;
- different operations can be performed on different data types;
- memory can be allocated efficiently to store data.

Different programming languages provide different data, variable and field types. Many allow programmers to specify their own data types; these are called *user-defined data types* and are often combinations of existing data types.

Some systems provide a wide range of data or field types, such as date, sample (sound recordings) and video (moving pictures). These are particularly useful in database systems.

Data, variable and field types can be specified for any data item that has an identifiable structure. Some of the more important ones are detailed below:

Alphanumeric data is a general term used for textual data, which may include letters, digits and punctuation. It includes both character data type and string data type.

Character data comprise a single character represented by the codes from the character set in use on the computer. See also *character*, in *character set* page 307.

String data are textual data in the form of a list of characters, for example words and punctuation. String data are made up of character data and will usually vary in length.

Boolean data or *logical data* can have only one of two values, *true* or *false* (see *truth value*, page 380). This makes it easy to use the values of Boolean variables to control the flow of a program. See also *D6 Truth Tables and Logic Gates*, page 380.

Sample data (digitally recorded *sound data*) and *video data* (a *video clip*) are large complex data structures containing all the information needed to enable a suitable subroutine to play a sound sample or display a video clip.

Date data are in a form recognised as representing a date, for example 1.2.04 or 1 February 2004. Date data must represent a valid date; for example, 11/12/89 is allowed, but 31 April 1995 is not allowed because April has only 30 days.

Numeric data can have a variety of types (see *numeric data type*, page 322).

PART C

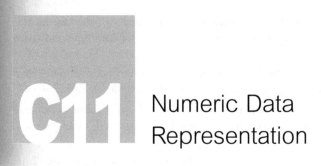

Numeric Data Representation

This section defines terms associated with some of the methods used to store numbers in ways that can be processed efficiently. Other related material can be found in C10 Data Representation.

Many of the data stored in a computer are numbers of some kind. Numbers create special problems for the computer scientist because they vary in type and size in an unpredictable way.

A number such as 123 could be treated as the three separate **characters**, '1', '2' and '3', but if it is necessary to store its **value**, 'one hundred and twenty-three', then there are several of ways of doing this. Storing numbers as values has the advantage that it is easier to perform arithmetic efficiently on numbers that are stored as values rather than as characters.

A number could be very large or very small, positive or negative, a whole number or a fraction. Whatever it is, it must be converted to a binary pattern for storage and manipulation in a computer. For a given number of bits, there is a finite number of patterns available to represent number values, and this places limits on the numbers that can be stored. Figure C11.1 shows the number of patterns available for different numbers of bits.

1 bit	Example: 1	2 patterns (0 and 1)
2 bits	Example: 11	4 patterns (00, 01, 10 and 11)
3 bits	Example: 101	8 patterns (000, 001, ... 111)
4 bits	Example: 1101	16 patterns (0000, 0001, ... 1111)
7 bits	Example: 1101100	128 patterns
8 bits	Example: 11011001	256 patterns
. . .	. . .	. . .
16 bits	. . .	65 536 patterns
. . .	. . .	. . .
32 bits	. . .	4 294 967 296 patterns
. . .	. . .	. . .

Figure C11.1   Number of patterns provided by different numbers of bits

The way in which numbers are stored involves a compromise between the **range** of values needed and the **accuracy** with which these values can be represented.

For a limited range of whole numbers, each number can be represented exactly using one of the available code combinations. As the required range of numbers increases, eventually there will not be enough codes for each code to represent a single value. A longer word length (more binary digits) could be used to extend the range of values, but there will always be a limit at some value, and using a very long word length all the time would mean that the computer would be slower and could run only smaller programs.

To store an even larger range of numbers with the same set of codes, two or more numbers close to each other will have to use the same code, which could introduce errors into the results of calculations. Similarly, if provision is made for negative numbers, then the largest value that can be stored will be halved, since one of the binary digits is used to indicate the sign.

Even larger numbers require different methods of representation, which may introduce errors into computed results because similar numbers will share the same codes. To represent very large numbers and fractions, **floating-point representation** is used. This enables a wide range of numbers to be represented to a known accuracy. Figure C11.2 illustrates the range of numbers that can be represented in different forms.

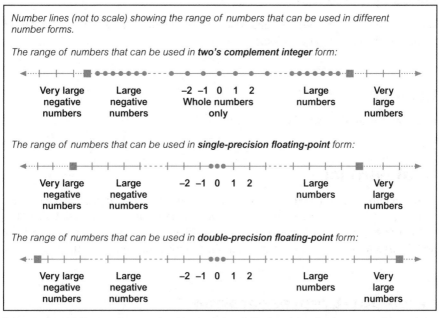

Number lines (not to scale) showing the range of numbers that can be used in different number forms.

*The range of numbers that can be used in **two's complement integer** form:*

| Very large negative numbers | Large negative numbers | –2 –1 0 1 2 Whole numbers only | Large numbers | Very large numbers |

*The range of numbers that can be used in **single-precision floating-point** form:*

| Very large negative numbers | Large negative numbers | –2 –1 0 1 2 | Large numbers | Very large numbers |

*The range of numbers that can be used in **double-precision floating-point** form:*

| Very large negative numbers | Large negative numbers | –2 –1 0 1 2 | Large numbers | Very large numbers |

In any representation, numbers can be stored only to a limited predetermined accuracy, the number of significant figures.

*In **floating-point form**, numbers **very close to zero** cannot be represented accurately, shown by the gaps between the dots, •.*
*Also there are limits to the range for **large numbers**, both positive and negative, shown by ------- ▋.*

Zero is a special case and has a unique representation (all noughts) in floating-point form.

Figure C11.2   Number ranges for different number forms

An additional constraint is that the computer has to perform arithmetic with the resultant codes; in particular, it has to be able to add and subtract them. The methods used to represent values have to be related to the way the computer does arithmetic, in particular the way it deals with negative numbers.

A programmer normally has control of the types of representation used. A program can be optimised to work as fast as possible, to handle numbers with great accuracy or to handle a wide range of numbers. Some compromise is normally essential, since these properties are often mutually exclusive.

Binary notation

is the number system using base two and the digits 0 and 1. It is a convenient way of representing numbers in an electronic computer. Most computers do arithmetic using binary numbers, and other representations need converting into binary form before the computer can do anything with them. For example, 123 (denary) is 1 111 011 (binary). See *denary notation*, below.

Denary notation

is the familiar number system using base ten and the digits 0–9. It is often referred to incorrectly as decimal notation.

Integer

is any whole number, whether positive or negative.

Real number

is any number represented with a fractional part. In most high-level languages, real indicates that *floating-point representation* (see below) is to be used when the number is stored or manipulated. This implies that the number may contain a fractional part and that it is processed to a limited number of significant figures.

Fixed-point representation

is the form of representation in which numbers are expressed by a set of digits with the decimal (or binary) point in its correct position. During operations in the computer, the position of the decimal (or binary) point is generally maintained by instructions in the program. The size of fixed-point numbers is limited by the construction of the computer, but operations are generally very fast and preferred for most commercial data-processing work.

Floating-point representation

including: mantissa, exponent
is a form of representation in which numbers are expressed as a binary or decimal fractional value, called the *mantissa*, which is non-zero, together with an integer *exponent*. The use of floating-point representation increases the range of numbers that can be represented, although the number of significant figures remains constant for any given system. Generally, the advantage of the extra range available when working in floating-point representation is gained at the expense of processing time and precision. Floating-point numbers are often called real numbers in a computing context, although this meaning is different from the strict mathematical use of the term real number.

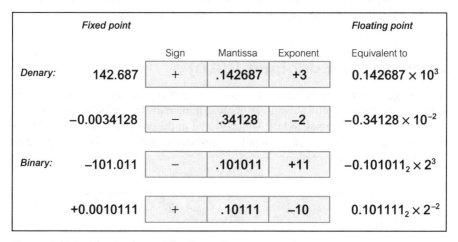

Fixed point		Sign	Mantissa	Exponent	Floating point Equivalent to
Denary:	142.687	+	.142687	+3	0.142687×10^3
	−0.0034128	−	.34128	−2	-0.34128×10^{-2}
Binary:	−101.011	−	.101011	+11	$-0.101011_2 \times 2^3$
	+0.0010111	+	.10111	−10	$0.101111_2 \times 2^{-2}$

Figure C11.3   Fixed-point and floating-point representation

Negative numbers

including: sign bit, sign and magnitude, sign and modulus, complementation, one's complement, two's complement
are represented within the computer by binary patterns that enable the computer to do arithmetic easily. Generally, one bit, called the *sign bit*, is used to indicate the sign of the number – usually **0** for positive and **1** for negative. Common methods of representing negative numbers are as follows:

Sign and magnitude (or *sign and modulus*) is a method of representing numbers by allocating one bit of a binary word, usually the most significant bit, to represent the sign of a number whose magnitude is held in the remaining bits of the word. For example, in the 16-bit number **1000101010101000**, the **1** at the left-hand end is the sign bit, and the remaining 15 bits are the magnitude (or modulus) of the number.

Complementation is a method of representing positive and negative numbers. This system requires numbers to be represented by a fixed number of bits. There are two forms of complementation, one's complement and two's complement, which are illustrated below. Two's complement is preferred because subtraction can be performed by adding the two's complement of the number to be subtracted. For example, 43 (denary) is represented as an 8-bit binary number by **00101011**.

One's complement is formed by changing each 1 bit to a 0 and changing each 0 bit to a 1. For example the one's complement of **00101011** (+43) is **11010100**, and this complement could be used to represent −43, but more often the two's complement is used.

Two's complement is one greater than the corresponding one's complement. For example, the two's complement of **00101011** (+43) is **11010101** (11010100 + 1), and this complement is normally used to represent −43.

Binary-coded decimal (BCD)

is a coding system in which each decimal digit is represented by a group of four binary digits. This is useful sometimes because it maintains the relationship between the place values in decimal and the values stored in the computer. It is not efficient for the computer to store and manipulate numbers in this form, but it may have advantages in some applications.

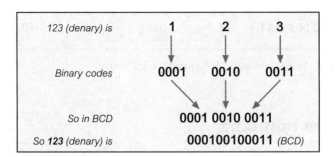

Figure C11.4 Denary to BCD conversion

Octal notation

is the number system using base eight and the digits 0–7. It has similar advantages to *hexadecimal* (see below), in that it is related to the binary pattern (each octal digit represents 3 bits). Most people use hexadecimal in preference to octal.

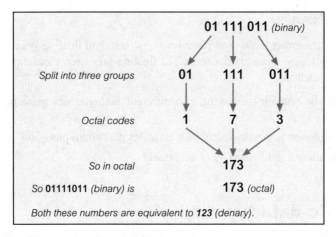

Figure C11.5   Binary to octal conversion

Hexadecimal notation

also known as: HEX

is the number system using base 16, the digits 0–9 and A–F. It is often used in computing because long binary patterns can be written as short hexadecimal numbers without losing the relationship between the value and the individual bits in the pattern, with each group of 4 bits being represented by one hexadecimal digit (see Figure C11.6).

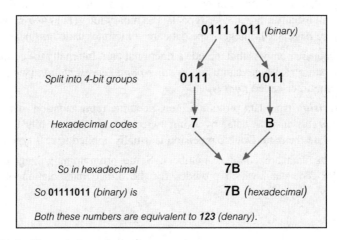

Figure C11.6   Binary to hexadecimal conversion

PART C

Normalise

is to change a number in floating-point form into standard floating-point representation format. Using a standard format for floating-point representation has some advantages, such as:

■ avoiding the problem of having two different binary codes meaning the same thing;

■ the form chosen is usually that which provides maximum precision;

■ multiplication is performed more accurately.

Numeric data type

including: numeric variable type, numeric field type, integer type, int type, real type, float type, double precision, single precision, complex type
is a formal description of the kind of numeric data being stored or manipulated within a program or system, for example *integers*, *real numbers* (see page 318) and complex numbers.

Numeric variable type and *numeric field type* specify the kind of numeric data held by a *variable* (see page 268) in a high-level language or as *fields* (see page 313) in a file.

In many cases, the same numeric value can be stored using any of the representations available; the one that is chosen by the programmer will be the most appropriate to the task being programmed. Some of the more important numeric data types are detailed below:

Integer-type data are whole numbers, either positive or negative. Internally the computer will usually store integer-type data as binary integers in *two's complement form* (see page 320). Integer-type data are sometimes called *int type*.

Real-type data are numbers that include a fractional part. Internally the computer will usually store real-type data using *floating-point representation* (see page 319). It is sometimes called *float type*.

Double-precision-type data provide a more accurate representation than the usual *single-precision-type* data, by using twice the number of bits to store and manipulate the data. Double precision is usually applied to real-type data.

Complex-type data are complex numbers. Some programming languages allow complex-type data, which provides for the direct manipulation of complex numbers.

Managing Data

Related topics can be found in A3 Word Processing and Text Manipulation, A8 Commercial Data Processing, A9 Spreadsheets, A10 Data Handling and Information Retrieval, B3 Memory, C10 Data Representation and C11 Numeric Data Representation.

Computer users tend to keep their programs separate from the data they operate on. The data are usually held as one or more **files** on backing storage, and the systems software encourages the user to believe that the file is held here (for example, on a disk) all the time. In fact, when a program wishes to use the data in a file, it is necessary for the portion of the file being worked on to be copied into primary storage in order to work on individual items of data. The systems software is responsible for copying between backing and primary storage, ensuring that the correct portion is readily available, without explicit action by the user. Because of this automatic management, it is necessary for users to access files in a formal way.

If the file is a new one, it must first be **created**; this might include specifying how large the file will become and how it will be organised. Before any use of an existing file, it is necessary to **open** the file, when a section will be copied to primary storage and other programs will be notified that the file is in use. Any changes will be made to the copy; when access is requested to a part of the file not currently in primary storage, the systems software is responsible for making the changes to the permanent version and loading a fresh copy of the required portion.

When access to the file is no longer needed, it must be **closed**, so that any remaining changes are written back to the permanent version and other programs can be notified that the file is no longer in use.

A file may be **deleted** from backing store, but it is usual for the systems software simply to mark the file in some way so that the space it occupies may be used for other files, rather than physically erasing the contents.

PART C

Files

File structure

including: serial file, sequential file, random file, address-generating algorithm, hashing algorithm, random access file

is the way in which data are physically stored in a file. The requirement for any file is that knowledge of the *key* (see page 313) for any record allows that data to be retrieved. The choice of physical storage method can help (or hinder) this process, depending on the *file-access method* (see page 327).

Common file structures include the following:

Serial file is a file in which the data are physically stored in the order in which they were acquired. To retrieve any particular record, it is necessary to read through every preceding record. If the record does not exist, this will not become apparent until you read to the end of the file. New records can be added only at the end of the file. Deleted records will leave a gap that cannot be reused unless the file is completely re-created. Serial files are associated mostly with linear storage devices, such as tape drives.

Sequential file is a serial file in which the data are physically stored in key order. If a record does not exist, this will become apparent as soon as the appropriate value of the key is reached.

Random file is a file in which the physical location of the record is derived from the record key. Unlike most file structures, there is no concept of storing data in a physical linear order; hence, the data may appear to be scattered randomly. Usually, the file uses a dedicated area of a storage device, such as a disk, and may not even appear as a file to the operating system. The algorithm for deriving the location from the key is known as an *address-generating* or *hashing algorithm* (see *hashing*, page 329). This structure allows particular records to be accessed directly, without reading other unrelated records.

Random-access file is a file in which the records are stored serially but that can be accessed directly like a random file. This may be done by using the position of the data in the file as its 'address'. See also *File access*, page 327.

Table C12.1 summarises the suitability for these structures for various access methods.

Record number

is a unique number that identifies the position of a record in a datafile. This means that record number one identifies the first physical position and the data in that position. The concept of a record number is not used in some file structures, such as *random files* (see above), and in some *relational database* systems (see page 91).

Table C12.1   Suitability of file-access methods

File structure	Access method		
	Serial	Sequential	Direct
Serial	Yes	No	No
Sequential	Yes	Yes	No
Sequential (indexed)	Yes	Yes	Yes
Random	No	No	Yes
Random access	Yes	No	Yes
Notes	Not suitable for large quantities of data	Particularly suited to searches with a high hit rate, as in batch processing	Particularly suited to real-time and interactive systems, and transaction processing

Many datafiles can be processed serially by working through the file one record at a time and, in this situation, the record number identifies the position of the record currently being processed. A record number may serve as a *pointer* (see page 327). See also *file access*, page 327.

Archive file

is a file containing data no longer in use but held for historical purposes, perhaps for auditors. It is often stored away from the computer system, in a secure location.

Back-up file

is a copy of a current file kept as a security measure in case the original is corrupted in any way. As with an *archive file* (see above), it is often kept in a secure location away from the computer system.

Reference file

is a special type of *master file* (see page 326) that is not updated during the job being processed. It contains fixed data that does not change. When changes are necessary, this will be achieved by a separate program.

Master file

including: transaction file
is the principal source of data for an application. It holds data that are mostly static but that can be added to or amended by updating as necessary during processing. In a traditional commercial batch-processing application, such as a payroll, the master file (of all employees) is updated by reference to a *transaction file* of hours worked in the current month, leave, sickness, promotions, etc.

Grandfather, father, son files

are the three most recent versions of a file that is updated periodically, for example the *master file* (see above) in a batch-processing application such as a payroll. The most recent, the *son* file, is used for the next run of the program; if an error occurs that corrupts this copy of the master file, the *father* version is still available and can be used with an archive copy of the *transaction file* (see above) from the previous run, to re-create the damaged son version. The *grandfather* version provides an additional level of security.

Index file

is a file used to access a large datafile quickly. It contains key field data from the file that the index is for. The key data are in a format that can be searched quickly, and the attached addresses are used to access the data.

Operations

File operations

including: read, write, update, insert, append, read-only
are those activities that can be performed on an existing datafile.
   Reading is the operation of taking a copy of a data item from a file.
   Writing is the operation of saving any changes to a file.
   Updating is altering an existing data item already written in the file.
   Inserting is adding a new data item to an existing file. This implies moving all later items to make space.
   Appending is adding a new item at the end of an existing file.
   In multiuser systems, problems can arise if more than one user is allowed to access a file at any one time. Only the first user who requests access to a file will be allowed to update it or append to it. Until the first user has released the file, subsequent requests for access may be denied or allowed *read-only access* to the file or individual records.

File access

including: serial access, sequential access, direct access, random access, index-sequential access method (ISAM)

The way in which a file is to be accessed by users influences how it is stored and the information that the systems software needs to hold in order to allow for efficient reading and writing.

Serial access is where the items are read one at a time from the physical start of the file in the order in which they are stored. Items may vary in length, provided there is some marker to signal the end of one item and the start of the next.

Sequential access is where the items are read one at a time from the logical start of the file, in key value order. Because the records in a file held on a *serial-access device* (see *magnetic tape*, page 182) need to be sorted into the order in which they are to be processed, serial access has sometimes been referred to as sequential access.

Direct access is where any item can be retrieved immediately, provided its position in the file is known. This often means that items must have a known length, so that software can calculate where in the file the required item is located. Direct-access files are commonly called *random-access* files because they are usually held in storage that permits random access. See also *magnetic disk*, page 179, and *random-access memory*, page 184.

Index-sequential access methods (*ISAM*) index the records of a sequential file. This allows both sequential and index approaches to be used, for example to search an index-sequential file of surnames. To locate 'Smith', an index is first consulted to discover the first item beginning with 'S', after which the file is searched sequentially. For this to work, both the file and the index must be in alphabetical order.

Pointer

is the address or reference of a data element that allows it to be retrieved without further searching.

For example, a database that stores information about students may use pointers to identify students in a particular class. It may use one pointer to locate the first student and further pointers between the students. In this way, to find the students in a class, the pointers allow the next student in the class to be accessed without searching other parts of the database.

Pointers allow fast access to data because little searching is required. When used on data stored in the computer's memory, the pointer is usually the address of the data in the memory. However, in a database system, the pointer may be the *primary key* (see page 313) or the reference number of the related record.

Merge

is to combine two or more ordered data structures, such as files, into a single ordered structure.

PART C

Sorting

is the process of arranging data items in a predetermined order (such as alphabetical or numerical). When the data items are themselves structured – a record in a file, for example – then one particular part of the structure must be specified as the item to be used in determining the ordering: this item is known as the *key* (see page 313). In a file of names and addresses, for example, the surname might be used as the key.

Search

including: hit, hit rate, serial (or linear) search, binary search
is the process of examining a file to see whether a given data item occurs in it. A successful location of an item is called a *hit*, and the success rate is the *hit rate*. Unless the file is in some useful order, searching may involve examining every entry in the file until the item is found or the end of the file is reached, a *serial* or *linear search*. Efficient *sorting* methods (see above) are important in searching. If the file is in alphabetical order, then a particularly efficient search method is the *binary search* (Figure C12.1).

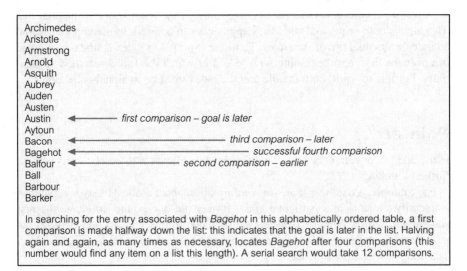

In searching for the entry associated with *Bagehot* in this alphabetically ordered table, a first comparison is made halfway down the list: this indicates that the goal is later in the list. Halving again and again, as many times as necessary, locates *Bagehot* after four comparisons (this number would find any item on a list this length). A serial search would take 12 comparisons.

Figure C12.1   Example of a binary search

Validation

including: data vetting, range check, check digit, batch total, control total, checksum
is computerised checking to detect any data that are unreasonable or incomplete. It is also known as *data vetting*. There are many methods, chosen to suit the data being processed. Some operate on single data items:

a *range check* would signal any data items outside a plausible range (e.g. a worker's age that was under 15 or over 75);

check digit is an extra digit added as part of a numerical data item (like a part number); it is derived from the other digits in a way that can be repeated.

Other methods operate on batches of data:

a *batch total* of the number of separate records in a batch might be calculated manually and added to the data as a check that none had been missed;

a *control total* formed by adding up some field from each record could accompany the batch as a double-check.

Where the data are computer software, a *checksum* formed by simply adding up all the instructions, treated as numbers, is often added to a file to make sure that it has been copied without error. See also *hashing*, below.

Hashing

including: hash total, hash table, collision

is the process of calculating a numerical value from one or more data items. While this value obviously depends on the value of the data item(s), it does not depend on the meaning attached to them. It can be used as a *control total* (see *validation*, above) to check for errors in copying the data, when it is known as a *hash total*.

It is also an important technique in storing values in a data structure known as a *hash table*. The calculated value can be used to mark the position in the table where the data item should be found, enabling it to be accessed directly rather than forcing a sequential search.

A *collision* occurs when two data items give the same value under hashing, and should therefore be stored in the same place in a hash table.

General

Corruption

is the introduction of errors into data or programs during storage or copying. It is usually due to physical causes, such as electrical *interference* (see page 378) or faulty equipment.

Data compression

is the technique of reducing the space occupied by a large file. There are many different methods, suited to different types of data.

The first paragraph of the introduction to Section C12 (page 323) contains 747 characters, including spaces. It can be reduced in size, without losing any of the information it contains, by replacing certain common pairs of letters by a single character (we have illustrated this by using numbers). For example, there are 18 occurrences of the pair 'th'. If these are replaced by '0', then 18 characters have been saved. Making the changes listed in Figure C12.2, the introduction is reduced to 635 characters, a saving of 112 characters, or about 15%. The file must be re-expanded before it can be used, of course, but space has been saved in storage.

Comput9 us92te6 to keep 0eir program2separ73from 03d7a 0ey op973on. 03d7a i2usually held82on3or mol *file2* o4backi5 storage,86 03system2softwal encourage203us9 to believ307 03fil3i2held hel (for example, o4a disk)8ll 03time. l4fact, whe4a program wishe2to us303d7a i4a file, it i2necessary for 03portio4of 03fil3bei5 worked o4to b3copied into primary storag3i4ord9 to work o4i6ividual item2of d7a. 03system2softwa1 i21sponsibl3for copyi5 betwee4backi586 primary storage, ensuri5 07 03cor1ct portio4i21adily8vailable, wi0out explicit8ctio4by 03us9. Becaus3of 0i2autom7ic management, it i2necessary for us92to8cces2file2i4a formal way.

Replacements:

0 = th	1 = re	2 = s'N'	3 = e'N'	4 = n'N'
5 = ng	6 = nd	7 = at	8 = 'N'a	9 = er

(a space is represented by 'N')

Figure C12.2 Simple example of data compression

Download

including: upload

is the term commonly used to refer to the transfer of a file from one computer to another. This may be from a larger computer to a smaller one, for example from a mainframe to a personal computer, or across a network such as the Internet. Generally, the term is used when the user who starts the process is operating the computer that will eventually receive the file. When the user is sending the file to another site, the term used to describe the operation is *upload*.

Overwriting

is the erasing of a data item by writing another in its place.

Raw data

are data as input to a computer, before any *validation* (see page 328) or processing.

Overflow

including: numerical overflow, stack overflow, underflow

is a general term describing what happens when something becomes too large to be processed satisfactorily. For example, the result of a numerical calculation may become too large to be stored in the space reserved for numbers (*numerical overflow*); or a data structure, such as a stack, may have space reserved for just 100 entries, so that attempting to add another one would cause *stack overflow*. *Underflow* is also possible, in the case of a number that is too small (close to zero) to be represented in the computer or an attempt to remove an item from an empty stack.

Rounding

including: rounding error

is the approximation of a numerical data item by its nearest equivalent to a given number of significant figures or decimal places. For example, 1.36 rounded to one decimal place is 1.4. *Rounding error* is the error introduced by rounding (+0.04 in this example). See also *truncation*, below.

Truncation

including: truncation error

is the approximation of a numerical data item by ignoring all information beyond a given number of significant figures or decimal places; for example, 1.36 truncated to one decimal place is 1.3. *Truncation error* is the error introduced by truncation (−0.06 in this example). This use of the term 'error' comes from mathematics and is important in situations where numbers are represented in a fixed-length format but should not be confused with other uses of the term. See also *error*, page 284, *floating-point representation*, page 319, and *rounding*, above.

PART C

Part

D

How Computers Work

This part is concerned with terms relating to how computers work. They are frequently considered to be associated with computer science, as opposed to the terms in Part A, which are concerned with the needs of computer system users. Part B provides some technical information and Part C is concerned with terms relating to computer systems development. This Part may be helpful to both computer users and to students following courses requiring some knowledge of computer systems and peripherals.

The range of terms covered and the depth of treatment of individual terms has been influenced by knowledge of the difficulties encountered by students who are studying courses that involve some computer science, whatever the name of the course.

PART D

Systems Software

Other related material can be found in C1 Systems Design and Life Cycle, C2 Describing Systems and C9 Programming Languages.

A computer system requires a layer of software that enables users to operate it without having to know about the underlying processes that are going on all the time inside. This includes the **operating system** and other forms of **systems software**.

A computer needs separate instructions for even the most elementary tasks. Computer users are interested in solving their problems without having to program every detail into the computer. The systems software is provided by the manufacturer and enables a user to give a few simple instructions, which the systems software translates into the millions of minor operations needed for the computer to function in an easy-to-use way.

Every computer is provided with an operating system that controls the vital parts of the computer's operation – using the keyboard, screen display, loading and saving files and printing are some examples.

Additional programs (such as disk formatters and device drivers to control peripherals) are provided, which are useful in the operation of the computer. They do not enable the user to get answers to problems (**application programs** do that), but they do make using the computer easier by allowing resources to be organised and controlled better. They improve efficiency by making the computer easier to use.

Systems software can be classified in a variety of ways, depending on whether it:

- is necessary to run the computer (**operating system software**);
- provides other useful functions for operating the computer (**utility programs**);
- provides for frequently required tasks (**library programs**);
- enables software to be produced and maintained (**compilers** and **assemblers**).

Software that is essential to the performance of the computer is usually sold with the computer. Other systems software may be purchased separately to enable the computer to be used for particular types of task.

In brief, systems software is the collection of programs available for the total control of the performance of a computer system.

PART D

Concepts

Systems program

is one of the programs that control the operation of a computer system, enabling the computer system to be developed and to be more efficient. Examples of systems programs are compilers, monitor programs, disk formatters, network software and print spoolers. Many systems programs are part of the *operating system* (see page 336).

Systems programs can be contrasted with *applications programs* (see page 5), which perform some end-user task. These tasks, such as producing a letter, are not part of the actual operation of the computer.

Operating system

including: disk operating system, DOS, MS-DOS, PC-DOS, OS/2, Presentation Manager, Risc-OS, UNIX, Linux, Windows, MacOS, MacX

is a program or suite of programs that controls the entire operation of the computer. It is normally provided by the manufacturer and deals with the basic functions of the computer, such as detecting what has been typed in, displaying data on the screen and loading and saving to backing store. Most modern operating systems include *utility programs* (see page 338), which make the operation of the computer easier, such as a program to format a disk. At a technical level, the operating system handles the basic and central functions such as *input* and *output* operations (see *BIOS*, page 338) and *interrupts* (see page 356).

The design of the operating system is often modular, allowing new features to be added and new hardware to be accommodated. One part, the portion of the operating system that deals with access to and management of files and programs stored on disk, is often provided separately. This is the *disk operating system* (commonly abbreviated to *DOS*). The *network operating system* (see page 127) provides similar facilities for use with local area networks.

Many modern operating systems also include a *graphical user interface* (*GUI*) (see page 59), either incorporated into the operating system or provided separately.

These are general terms, and most manufacturers have their own proprietary names for either the operating system or the disk operating system; among these are the following:

MS-DOS is an operating system written by Microsoft originally for the IBM-PC. It is now the most common operating system used with personal computers. It provides an operating system for the Intel 8086, 186, 286, 386 and 486 and Pentium microprocessors. A version called *PC-DOS* was supplied as the operating system on the original IBM-manufactured Personal Computers.

OS/2 is a development of the PC-DOS operating system for IBM PCs and compatible microcomputers using more powerful microprocessors than the original

Intel 8086. This operating system allows *multitasking* (see page 343), which makes it more suitable for use in a complex or network environment.

Presentation Manager is the graphical user interface developed by IBM and Microsoft for use with the OS/2 operating system.

Risc-OS is the operating system and graphical user interface developed by computer manufacturer Acorn for their computers. The operating system and graphical user interface are integrated, making the system easy to use with all the operations performed using the graphical user interface.

UNIX is an operating system originally written for large machines. Versions are now available for a variety of machines, ranging from mainframes to personal computers. It was designed to improve software portability. It has been highly successful as an operating system for minicomputers, because it is particularly suited for running multi-user and networked systems. It is also adapted easily for the specific requirements of each multi-user or networked system.

Linux is an operating system designed to be similar to UNIX. It was intended originally for personal computers, but now it is used more widely. It was developed collaboratively and so does not have any licensing costs associated with it, making it cheap to implement in large organisations. The source code is available free on the Internet, allowing developers to improve it and check it for flaws.

Windows is a combined graphical user interface and operating system. Many new personal computers are now supplied with Windows software. Users do not need to be aware of what operating system is used, as the Windows interface appears to do most of the required system operations.

Mac OS is the operating system used in Apple Macintosh personal computers. It incorporates a *graphical user interface* (see page 59). Later versions include *Mac X*.

Boot

including: booting, system prompt, boot file, config.sys, autoexec.bat, reboot
is a short sequence of machine-code instructions used for loading the program that starts up the computer. It is normally held in read-only memory and activated when the machine is switched on. This process is sometimes referred to as *booting*. It loads or initialises the operating system ready for use. A *system prompt*, indicating, for example, which drive or directory is current, will be displayed on the screen. See *prompt*, page 68.

The users of a personal computer are often given the opportunity to start it up automatically configured as they want. This is done by placing the required commands in a file, called a *boot file*. This file will be executed automatically by the computer after it has booted the *operating system* (see page 336).

MS-DOS and similar operating systems use two files as part of the start-up sequence. These files must be called *config.sys* and *autoexec.bat*. These files do not have to be present, but if they are, then they are used automatically. The file *config.sys* is a datafile containing values and settings to be used by the operating system; it may include the file names of files to be used by the operating system. The file *autoexec.bat* is a list of commands (see *batch file*, page 341) that the user wishes to be executed when the computer is started up.

To *reboot* the computer is to restart the system, usually after a hang-up (see *hung*, page 289). All parameters will be reset to their initial values and data that were not saved will be lost. See also *cold start* and *warm start*, page 290.

BIOS (Basic Input Output System)

is the part of the operating system that handles the input and output of the computer. It enables the operating system to use the particular features of the hardware being used. The name refers specifically to a single part of some operating systems, which can be altered easily to allow the same operating system to be used by a variety of hardware designs and manufacturers. If the BIOS is altered, then the other parts of these operating systems will not need any alteration.

Utility program

including: full backup, incremental backup
is a *systems program* (see page 336) designed to perform a commonplace task, for example the transfer of data from one storage device to another, sorting a set of data, or a disk editor for directly editing the contents of a disk.

A *full backup* utility creates a backup of all the files on a disk, as opposed to an *incremental backup*, which copies only files that have been altered since the last backup.

Software library

also known as: library, program library
is a collection of software held either permanently accessible on backing store or on removable media such as tape or disk. It will include complete software packages, package modules that will be required only occasionally, and machine-code routines for loading into user programs.

Library program

including: library routine
is a program that is available to all users of a multi-user computer system, typically to carry out common tasks (such as file maintenance) required by everyone. Some tasks may be carried out by *library routines*, which users can incorporate into their own programs. See also *software library*, above.

Development

Translator

is a computer program used to convert a program from one language to another (for example, from a low-level language to machine code). This is a general name for the three types of translation programs, *assemblers* (see below), *compilers* (see below) and *interpreters* (see page 340). See also C9 Programming Languages, page 291.

Assembler

also known as: assembler program
including: assembly language, assembly, macro assembler, cross-assembler
is a program that translates a program written in assembly language into machine code.

An *assembly language* is a special type of programming language in which the instructions are related closely to the computer being programmed (rather than a common language that is similar on any type of computer). In general, each assembly-language instruction is changed into one machine-code instruction, but programming can be simplified by the use of *macro instructions* (see page 265).

The program is written in the assembly language of the computer being used and then translated (assembled) into the machine code of that computer by software called an assembler. This process is called *assembly*.

The assembler program is specific to a type of computer and is often provided as part of the systems software, since the assembly process automates the task of producing machine-code software required to operate the computer.

A *macro assembler* is a more complex type of assembler that offers the facility of expanding *macro instructions* (see page 265).

A *cross-assembler* is an assembler that runs on one computer but that produces machine code for another. It enables software developers to produce programs for computers that are still being designed or to convert software between different types of computer.

PART D

Compiler

including: source code, compilation, lexical analysis, syntax analysis, code generation, cross-compiler
is a program that translates a high-level language program, *source code*, into a computer's machine code or some other low-level language. Generally, each high-level language instruction generates several machine-code instructions. It produces an independent program that can be run.

This translation process is known as *compilation*. Compilation involves analysing the language structure of the source program, determining whether it is valid, and producing suitable machine code. Compilation involves a number of steps:

Lexical analysis: the stage in the compilation of a program that puts each statement into the form best suited to the syntax analyser. The standard components of each statement, such as PRINT, IF, etc., are replaced by their tokens (a unique fixed-length code) and programmer-defined names are entered into a *symbol table* (see page 341). The lexical analyser also removes unnecessary characters such as spaces.

Syntax analysis: the stage in the compilation at which language statements are checked against the rules of the language, errors being reported if a statement is not valid.

Code generation: produces a machine-code program that is equivalent to the source program.

A *cross-compiler* is a compiler that runs on one computer but that produces code for another. It enables software producers to develop programs for computers that are still being designed or to convert software between different types of computer.

Interpreter

translates and executes a program one statement at a time. The program may be in a high-level language or an intermediate code.

The interpreter is actually a machine-code program. It is used as an easy, if slightly inefficient, way of executing programs not in the machine code of the computer. For example, when an interpreted program contains a loop, the speed of execution will be slow because the analysis of each statement has to be repeated for each time round the loop; however, there are advantages in using interpreted languages. See also C9 Programming Languages, page 291.

Command line interpreter

including: batch file, command file
is the portion of the operating system that analyses a system command typed by the user and performs the appropriate actions. Most operating systems work by asking the user for commands to be typed in, as a line of text after a *prompt* (see page 68), analysing the commands and taking appropriate action. Modern operating systems provide a *graphical user interface* (see page 59), which is often easier to use, but usually the command line interpreter is still available.

Some graphical user interfaces simply convert information from the mouse into an equivalent system command processed by the command line interpreter. Commands may be:

- read from a text file (called a *batch file* or *command file*);
- provided remotely from a peripheral or another computer through an interface;
- provided from within a program.

These commands are all processed automatically by the command line interpreter.

Disassembler

is a program that translates from machine code back to an assembly language. They are generally used to decipher existing machine code by generating equivalent symbolic codes. This is useful for programmers maintaining and modifying machine-code programs.

Loader

including: linking loader, linking, linker, link editor
is a program that copies an *object program* (see page 282) held on backing store into main store ready for execution.

Often, common routines are provided already compiled in a *library* (see page 338); when the program is loaded, these routines also have to be loaded and links made to these routines. This is performed by a *linking loader*.

Alternatively, the library routines can be added when the program is compiled or as an additional *linking* operation between compilation and loading. A *linker*, or *link editor*, is the software tool that allows already compiled object code files or modules to be combined with the compiled program and then converted directly into an executable file. This also involves completing address links to and from the program.

Symbol table

also known as: name table
is the table created and maintained by a compiler or assembler relating programmer-defined names to machine addresses. It may also hold information about properties of data, such as data types.

When translating a program, the compiler or assembler works through the program for the first time (the first pass), replacing some parts with tokens and building the symbol table that contains the actual address in memory of each variable, label or subroutine. The program is then processed a second time (the second pass), when each identifier can be replaced with its actual address in memory.

Parsing

is the breaking down of high-level programming language statements into their component parts during the translation process, for example identifying reserved words and variables.

Operations

Spooling

is the temporary storage of input or output data on magnetic disk or tape, as a means of compensating for the slow operating speeds of peripheral devices or when queuing output from different programs to one device, such as a printer (see *printer spooler*, below).

Printer spooler

also known as: print spooler
including: print job, print queue
is a program that stores data ready to be printed. Each set of data to be printed is known as a *print job*. When the print job has been received from a program and is complete, the printer spooler can send these data to the printer. Several programs or terminals can send data at the same time for printing, because the data are stored in files by the printer spooler and sent to the printer when appropriate. A printer spooler is normally part of the operating system.

If a printer spooler is used, programs do not have to wait whilst printing is being done (printers work more slowly than computers). This is particularly important with personal computers and interactive computing, as users do not want to waste time waiting for data to be printed out. See also *printer server*, page 125.

The *print queue* is a list of work waiting to be printed by a printer spooler. Normally, it is a list of the files holding data ready for printing. Each file will hold the data from a particular task, which will be sent to the printer by the printer spooler when the printer is free. A task could be a single letter or a large batch of commercial documents.

Multiprogramming

including: time slice
is a method of benefiting from the speed of a central processor compared with slower peripheral devices, allowing two or more programs to be processed apparently simultaneously but actually in bursts, controlled by an operating system. For example, while one program is waiting for an input or output operation to be performed or is

using a peripheral, another may have access to the central processor. To control this process, priorities may be assigned to jobs.

A *time slice* is the predetermined maximum length of time for the bursts during which each program is allowed to run in a multiprogramming system.

Executive program

also known as: monitor program, supervisor program
is a control program that schedules the use of the hardware required by the programs being run in a multitask or multiprogramming situation.

Multi-tasking

including: single-tasking
is a method of organising computer use that allows several different tasks or applications to be available at the same time. The users of a *multi-access system* (see page 17) will be working on different tasks apparently at the same time, although only one program is actually being executed at any one time. Similarly, modern personal computer operating systems allow users to have several tasks apparently running at the same time, with the user switching freely between applications or tasks.

Some operating systems will not support multi-tasking; these *single-tasking* systems allow only one program to be in use at any time.

Thread

including: multithreading, concurrent thread, single thread
is the processing performed on a single set of data in the system.

Multithreading is the use of a single copy of a program to process several sets of data that are at different stages of processing. This is most useful in a multitasking situation, where tasks may need to be launched at any time. Only one copy of the program needs to be loaded, which saves memory. The program design ensures that the data for each thread are kept separate and that the appropriate program instructions act on the thread that is being executed.

Concurrent threads are two or more threads being executed at the same time using *multitasking* (see above).

A *single thread* is one set of processing. This may be the traditional simple program (which is not designed to multithread) or one thread out of several being processed in a more complex system.

Processing mode

is the way in which the processing tasks carried out by a computer system are organised to make the most of the potential of the system. Sometimes the choice of mode

PART D

is given to the user. For example, the user may have a choice between *single-tasking* or *multi-tasking* (see page 343) when running a program, or a choice between *foreground* or *background processing* (see below).

Different processing modes can also be selected by the central processor for different types of tasks. For example, some types of instruction may be available only to the operating system, reducing the possibility of a user program affecting the rest of the computer's operation.

Job

including: job control language (JCL), job queue
is a data-processing term for a package of work regarded by the computer as a single unit. Typically, a data-processing department will run programs on behalf of its clients. These programs may be small (a single report) or large (a complete payroll). Once started, each program will proceed automatically to completion; from the data-processing department's point of view, each is a single task or job to be run.

A specialised language, the *job control language* (*JCL*), is used to control the execution of a job in a computer. It enables the operators to specify the requirements of a job (such as which printer to use) when the job is executed. The programmer does not need to deal with these decisions when writing programs. A job control language also enables a series of small jobs to be linked together and executed in one larger, more efficient operation.

In a *multiprogramming* system (see page 342) or a *batch-processing* system (see page 17), the jobs wait in a *job queue* until the computer system is ready to execute them. This will normally be in the order in which they are submitted, although in some systems priority levels can be assigned to jobs to ensure that some are executed earlier than other less urgent jobs.

Remote Job Entry (RJE)

is the use of a remote terminal to initiate a *job* (see above) on a computer within the network to which the terminal is attached. One example is the use of a terminal in a supermarket to transmit the record of the day's transactions to the central computer for the chain and initiate the appropriate funds transfer and ordering routines. Another very simple example is a request for a bank statement from a customer using a cash machine.

Foreground/background processing

including: foreground job, background job
is a method of organising a computer system so that certain important tasks (*foreground jobs*) may claim the sole use of the computer when required, while other less pressing tasks (*background jobs*) utilise the remaining time.

For example, a user can continue typing in a word processing program (the foreground job) whilst the computer sends data to a printer (the background job) using processing time that is idle whilst waiting for user input.

The same concept applies to a *multiprogramming system* (see page 342): the foreground job will have priority, but if the processor is idle (for example, waiting for disk access), then a background job will use that time.

Segmentation

including: segment, interleaving

is the splitting of a large program into a number of smaller programs or *segments*. Each segment is a complete program that is executed separately. The function of the large program is achieved by running segments consecutively. Segmentation allows a large program to be executed on a computer with insufficient memory to store the whole program.

The segments of several programs can be *interleaved*, which allows several large programs to be run concurrently, in parts, to make optimum use of resources. These techniques are not used widely nowadays due to the relatively large memory of modern computers. Similar techniques are *overlays* (see page 252) and *paging* (see page 351).

Scheduling

including: round-robin

is the method by which central processor time is allotted in a multi-access system. The scheduling algorithm may be as simple as the *round-robin* that deals with each user equally in turn, or as complex as a scheme of priorities distinguishing between users and between tasks.

Systems Application Architecture (SAA)

including: Common User Access (CUA), Systems Network Architecture (SNA)

is a set of standards for achieving both consistency and compatibility between software running on various types of IBM computer, including a consistent user interface. A number of standards are defined for the various parts of the systems application architecture, including:

Common User Access (*CUA*), which is the set of standards for the screen and keyboard layout, labelling and functions;

Systems Network Architecture (*SNA*), which is the standard for distributed processing, providing for communication between terminals and a host computer.

PART D

Garbage collection

including: fragmentation, defragmentation

is a 'housekeeping' task carried out by software. Many applications packages and systems software programs do not immediately rearrange their immediate-access storage when data are deleted, and the 'free space' becomes distributed throughout memory. In order to reuse this efficiently, software will need to collect the space together; this tidying up is called garbage collection.

A similar problem occurs with some *disk operating systems* (see page 336), where files may be split and stored on different parts of the disk. This *fragmentation* usually happens when a disk is almost full. The access speed of the disk and hence the performance of the system will be improved if the separate elements of these files are collected together, a process known as *defragmentation*.

Text editor

also known as: editor

including: screen editor, line editor

is a program that enables the user to input, inspect and alter text files, which may be programs or data. Text editors are particularly used by computer programmers who need to produce text files suitable for compilation or assembly. Most text editors have special features that make the programmer's task easier.

In a *screen editor*, the user interacts with a file by moving the cursor to the required position in the file, which is displayed on the screen, as in a word processor. In contrast, a *line editor* requires the user to specify a particular line of the file, for example a line number in a BASIC program.

Machine Architecture

Other related terms can be found in B3 Memory, D3 Interfaces and Buses and D4 Physical Components.

The structure of a computer, or more properly the **central processing unit (CPU)**, and how the particular components are related to each other is called machine architecture. The working of the computer can still be considered in terms of binary patterns and codes. The physical characteristics of the central processor affect the way the computer is used and also determine the speed, power, cost and suitability of the computer for a particular application.

The choice of integrated circuits and other components can determine how fast the computer will operate. This is important when selecting a computer for a particular application. For example, an important part of the specification of a personal computer is its **microprocessor** (such as a 386, 486, Pentium, 68010 or ARM600), since this tells the purchaser something about the complexity of the programs that it will run. Other parts of the central processor can affect a computer's performance for particular jobs; for example, a **floating-point unit** will make a computer much faster at solving scientific problems but may be of little value in an office context.

An important factor in the design of the central processor is the selection of the binary patterns used internally. For example, the number of bits used as an address affects the maximum size of the main memory, and the number of bits used to store a number affects very large and very small numbers.

There are ways of getting around these problems, but always at the expense of performance and at a price. Various techniques may be employed within the hardware of the central processor to enhance performance, but further development of a type or series of computers will be limited by these technical factors and the initial design decisions.

PART D

Processor

Central processing unit (CPU)

including: central processor, processor
is the main part of the computer, consisting of the registers, arithmetic logic unit and control unit. See *control unit* (page 349) and *register*, page 349, and *arithmetic logic*

unit, page 355. Usually, the central processing unit includes the main memory (see *immediate-access store*, page 178). It is sometimes called the *central processor* or *processor*. Many computers have more than one processor.

A special form of central processing unit is the *microprocessor* (see below), which is used in microcomputers and small computerised devices, for example the control circuits of washing machines.

Microprocessor

including: Complex Instruction Set Computer (CISC), Reduced Instruction Set Computer (RISC), Z80, 6502, 8086, n86, Pentium, ARM, 68000, Transputer
is an integrated circuit in which the components of the *central processing unit* (see above), excluding the main memory, are combined as a single unit. Microprocessors are manufactured in large numbers for use in microcomputers and small computerised devices. The general user has to obtain software suitable for that type of processor, since software cannot usually be used on different types of central processor.

Two of the main approaches to the design of microprocessors are the *Complex Instruction Set Computer* (*CISC*) and the *Reduced Instruction Set Computer* (*RISC*). A complex instruction set computer design produces a complicated and expensive integrated circuit capable of performing a large variety of complex operations. A reduced instruction set computer design produces a simple, cheap integrated circuit with a basic range of operations. It is, however, faster and relies on its speed to perform complex operations by using several machine instructions.

There are many types of microprocessor available, including:

Z80 microprocessor, which was used in many early microcomputers and computerised control systems. It is now obsolete;

6502 microprocessor, which was used in some early microcomputers, including the BBC microcomputer. It is now obsolete;

8086 microprocessor, which was used in the earliest IBM PC and similar computers. It is now obsolete;

186, *286*, *386*, *486* and *Pentium* microprocessors, which are further developments of the original 8086 microprocessor. Each succeeding newer design is much faster than its predecessor, but they share a similar *instruction set* (see below), so that most software written for earlier IBM PC-compatible computers can still be used without modification. These microprocessors were originally designated 80186, 80286, etc.;

ARM2, *ARM3*, *ARM250* and *ARM600* microprocessors, which are used in Archimedes and Acorn computers. They are based on *RISC* (see above) design principles and so they are fast-operating and inexpensive. Their design is modular and variants are produced to control devices such as laser printers and personal organisers;

68000 microprocessor and its variants, which are used in the Macintosh series of computers;

Transputer microprocessor, which includes the *main memory* (see page 178), hence its nickname 'computer on a chip'. Combining processor and store in the same chip makes it very easy to build parallel processing arrays containing many processors.

Instruction set

is the complete collection of instructions that are used by a particular type of central processor. These are the instructions available for use in machine-code or assembly-language programs for that computer. The instruction set is part of the design of a central processor or microprocessor, and so the machine codes of different types of computer are rarely compatible. See also *machine-code instruction*, page 249.

Control unit

including: fetch–execute cycle, instruction cycle, instruction decoder, fetch phase, execute phase
is the part of the central processor that manages the execution of instructions. A characteristic of all computers is the ability to follow a set of instructions automatically. The control unit fetches each instruction in sequence, and decodes and synchronises it before executing it by sending control signals to other parts of the computer. This is known as the *fetch–execute cycle*. See also *program counter*, page 350.

The fetch–execute cycle is the complete process of retrieving an instruction from store, decoding it and carrying it out. This is also called the *instruction cycle*. Part of the control unit is the *instruction decoder*, which decodes the machine-code instructions during the fetch–execute cycle and determines what actions to take next. The cycle consists of two phases, the *fetch phase*, in which the instruction is copied into the control unit and decoded, followed by the *execute phase*, in which the instruction is obeyed.

Register

including: program counter, instruction address register (IAR), next instruction register, sequence control register (SCR), address register, memory address register (MAR), memory buffer register (MBR), memory data register (MDR)
is a location, normally used for a specific purpose, where data or control information are stored temporarily. Some registers are used in the different parts of the *fetch–execute cycle* (see *control unit*, above), whilst others may be available for use by the program being executed. Registers usually are much faster to access than the immediate-access store, since they have to be accessed so often.

The various registers include the following:

Program counter in the control unit that contains the address of the next machine-code instruction to be executed. *Instruction address register* (*IAR*), *next instruction register* and *sequence control register* (*SCR*) are alternative names for the program counter.

Address register in the control unit that holds the address part (see *address field*, page 250) of the instruction being executed.

Memory address register (*MAR*) in the central processor that stores the address of the memory location currently in use. In the fetch phase, this would be the address of the instruction being loaded; in the execute phase, it would be the address of the data being used. The memory unit has access to the MAR and switches the address selection circuitry to access the appropriate location.

Memory buffer register (*MBR*) in the central processor that stores the data being transferred to and from the immediate-access store. It acts as a buffer, allowing the central processor and memory unit to act independently without being affected by minor differences in operation. A data item will be copied to the MBR ready for use at the next clock pulse, when it can either be used by the central processor or be stored in main memory. *Memory data register* (*MDR*) is another name for the memory buffer register.

Memory

Address calculation

including: direct addressing, indirect addressing, vector, immediate addressing, indexed addressing, index register, address modification
is working out which *memory location* (see *address*, page 244) is to be accessed by a machine-code instruction. Part of a machine-code instruction is called the *address field* (see page 250), which contains data about which memory location the instruction is to use. There are a number of alternative methods for determining the address of the memory location, including the following:

Direct addressing uses the data in the address field without alteration. This is the simplest method of addressing and also the most common.

Indirect addressing uses the address field to hold the address of a location that contains the required address. The action of a program can be changed easily by altering the data in the location pointed to by the instruction. The location holding the real address is known as a *vector*. One use of a vector is to provide access to library routines. Program control is passed to the address in the vector. The locations of the vectors are defined for other programmers to use. Routines can be changed without all the programs using them also being changed. This is because the address of the vector remains the same, but its contents can be altered to point to the new start address for the routine. See also *vectoring*, page 359.

Immediate addressing uses the data in the address field, not as an address, but as a constant that is needed by the program. An example is a routine counting up to 10, which may have the constant '10' supplied in the address field of an instruction. Although the address field cannot hold numbers as large as those that can be stored as data in a memory location, because space has to be left for the *operation code field* (see page 249), this is a particularly convenient method of loading constants into the accumulator.

Indexed addressing modifies the address (either direct or indirect) in the address field by the addition of a number held in a special-purpose register, called an *index register*, before the address is used. Index registers are altered quickly and easily, providing an efficient way of accessing a range of memory locations, such as in an array.

Address modification is changing the address field of a machine-code instruction as the program is running, so that each time the instruction is executed it can refer to a different memory location.

Memory management

including: memory management unit (MMU), bank switching, virtual memory, paging, pages, page turn, page fault, threshing, direct memory access (DMA)
is organising the flexible use of the computer's main memory, the *immediate-access store* (see page 178). This can be done by the *memory management unit* (*MMU*), often a single integrated circuit in a microcomputer, which allows the addresses used by the *central processing unit* (see page 347) to be stored at a different physical location. The memory management unit automatically converts the logical address provided by the central processor into the physical address in memory.

This allows programs in a multi-user or multi-tasking computer system apparently to use the same memory locations. The memory management unit places them in different physical parts of the immediate-access store. Four memory management techniques that can be used are bank switching, virtual memory, paging and direct memory access.

Bank switching is used for overcoming the limitations of computers that can address only a limited amount of immediate-access storage. Several 'banks' of storage are provided, each one occupying the same place in the computer's memory map. Only one bank may be active at any one time, and the required one is selected as needed by the software.

Virtual memory is used when sufficient immediate-access store is not available. Part of a disk drive is allocated to be used as if it were main memory. When accessing these memory locations, the software has to copy the contents of the relevant disk block into a reserved area of main memory, having first copied its existing contents back on to disk. This is very slow, and the software will attempt to use the immediate-access store if possible.

Paging is the organisation of memory into fixed-size units, called *pages* (for example, a page of 32 kb). The immediate-access store is organised as a number of physical pages. The logical pages used by the central processing unit can be assigned by the memory management unit to any page in physical memory. A form of *virtual memory* (see page 351) can be used with less frequently used pages being stored on disk, but when required they are reloaded into the immediate-access store as a complete page.

Page turn is the movement of a page to or from backing store. The movement of pages is counted in page turns, which are sometimes, confusingly, called *page faults*. Monitoring the rate of page turns can lead to improved efficiency by indicating where unnecessary movement is taking place. Rapid uploading and downloading of pages is known as *threshing* and can be recognised by a very high rate of disk access. In extreme cases, something close to a *deadly embrace* (see page 289) may occur, because tasks cannot continue for any effective time before being interrupted and while new pages are loaded.

Direct memory access (*DMA*) is the use of part of the immediate-access store independently from the operating system or the memory management unit. This is usually used in the design of games for use on microcomputers, where the screen display is accessed directly, allowing a faster and more complex display.

Array processor

is a central processor designed to allow any machine instruction to operate simultaneously on a number of data locations (data arrays). This design enables problems involving the same calculations on a range of data to be solved very quickly. Examples of suitable problems are weather forecasting and airflow simulation around a new aircraft. See also *floating-point unit*, below.

General

Floating-point unit

including: maths co-processor, floating-point accelerator (FPA)
is a component that can be added to the central processor to make arithmetical operations faster. It provides registers sufficiently large to handle floating-point representation of numbers as single units. It contains micro-code routines optimised to perform floating-point arithmetic operations very quickly.

Floating-point units may be included in a microprocessor or manufactured as a separate integrated circuit for use in suitable microcomputers where they are called *maths co-processors* or *floating-point accelerators* (*FPA*).

Floating-point units increase the performance of a computer when carrying out large numbers of calculations. They do not improve the performance of text processing or peripheral handling. They are used widely in graphics applications to perform the calculations needed to plot screen images, for example in a computer-aided-design system.

An alternative approach to complex mathematical problems is the *array processor* (see page 352).

Parallel processing

is the simultaneous use of several processors to perform a single job. A job may be split into a number of tasks, each of which may be processed by any available processor.

Bitmap

including: disk map, screen map

is a pattern of bits describing the organisation of data. For example, the arrangement of data on a disk might be represented to the operating system as a bitmap in which each bit represents one sector on disk: 1 for sectors in use and 0 for unused sectors.

A bitmap for a disk is called a *disk map*. A graphic screen prepared in a painting or drawing package may be held as a bitmap, often called a *screen map*, each bit relating to the setting of an individual pixel on the screen.

Bus

including: address bus, data bus

is a common physical pathway shared by signals to and from several components of a computer. For example, all input and output devices would be connected to the I/O (input/output) bus. In practice, each bus has two parts, an *address bus*, which carries identification about where the data are being sent, and a *data bus*, which carries the actual information. The principle of a bus is that the same wires go to each component in turn. The components watch the address bus until an address that they recognise, by using an address *decoder* (see page 392), is present. When this occurs, they take action, either retrieving the data from the data bus or placing new data on the bus for the central processor.

Local bus

including: video bus, VESA and PCI buses

is an additional bus in a microcomputer normally with a specific function. Some functions of modern microcomputers (such as maintaining the VDU and sending data to and from the disk drives) can require the computer to move vast amounts of data. This can use between 10 and 50% of the microcomputer's power. One way of increasing the power of a microcomputer cheaply is to provide a special bus for one or both of these functions, so relieving the load on the main bus. This special bus

PART D

doing a specific function is known as a local bus. If the local bus is simply maintaining the screen display, then it is sometimes called a *video bus*.

VESA (*Video Electronics Standards Association*) and *PCI* (*Peripheral Component Interconnect*) are standard designs of local buses used by various types of IBM-compatible microcomputers.

Buffer

including: buffering, single buffering, double buffering
is an area of computer memory allocated to transferring data between the computer and a peripheral, for example a printer buffer. Sometimes, a buffer is used between components within the computer (see *memory buffer register*, page 350). Using a buffer provides a barrier between devices with different working speeds or data organisation.

It is much more efficient to send or receive data as a *block* (see page 267) of many words or bytes. Magnetic disks and tapes require data to be read or written in such a way that a block of data is moved in a single operation. The computer and the peripheral have to be capable of sending or receiving a whole block of data at high speed when required.

The management of block data transfer is done by *buffering*. An area of memory is allocated as the buffer; when information is to be transferred, it is stored in the buffer until an entire block is compete. This block is then sent, leaving the area it occupied free for assembling the next block of data. When a block is received into a buffer, the data are processed before the next block is requested and transferred.

With *single buffering*, one device has to wait for the block to be received before using the data (and the other device has to wait whilst the data are processed). This is inefficient and slow. An improved method is *double buffering*, where two areas of memory are allocated; as one buffer is emptied, the other can be filled up. This reduces the time for which a device has to stop while waiting for the data transfer.

Some peripherals may communicate with single bytes of data, for example keyboard input and musical sounds. The buffer for these peripherals may be organised as a *circular queue* (see page 312), enabling data to be added or removed as required. See also *print buffer* on page 360.

Cycle

including: cycle time, processor cycle time, machine cycle time, millions of instructions per second (MIPS), program loop time
is the sequence of actions to perform a particular hardware operation, which is either repeated continuously or performed whenever it is required. In many cases, the time taken for an operation is constant and is known as the *cycle time*. Cycle time is useful when calculating the speed of a particular computer task.

The *processor cycle time* or *machine cycle time* is the cycle time for one *fetch–execute cycle* (see page 349) and is governed by the speed of access to the immediate-access store. Processor cycle time gives a rough guide to the speed of a computer, although other factors, such as word length, are also important. Processing speed is sometimes expressed in *millions of instructions per second* (*MIPS*), which is also only a rough guide and is normally based on the average number of machine-code instructions executed.

The *program loop time* is the time taken by a single repetition of a *loop* (see page 255) and is useful for calculating the expected speed of a routine.

Arithmetic logic unit (ALU)

including: arithmetic unit, accumulator, arithmetic register
is the part of the central processing unit where data are processed and manipulated. It is also called the *arithmetic unit*. The processing and manipulation of data normally consists of arithmetic operations or logical comparisons allowing a program to take decisions.

Most operations involve the *accumulator*, a special storage register within the arithmetic logic unit. It is used to hold the data currently being processed by the central processor. Any data to be processed are stored temporarily in the accumulator, the results ending up in the accumulator before being stored in the memory unit.

Most computer calculations are based on addition methods, and so the accumulator is where the computer does its additions. A computer performs subtraction by two's complement addition and multiplication by combining addition with shifts for column alignment. See also *two's complement*, page 320, and *shift*, page 357.

The ALU usually includes *arithmetic registers* (see *register*, page 349), which are special store locations used to hold operands and results temporarily during calculation.

Adder

including: full adder, half adder, sum bit, carry bit
is the part of the arithmetic logic unit (ALU) that has the specialised job of addition within the central processor. Its proper name is *full adder*, a logic design that takes two binary numbers and adds the equivalent bits, adding in any carrys. Full adders are made from smaller components called *half adders*, which simply take two bits and add them together, producing the answer (called the *sum bit*) and a *carry bit* if the result is greater than one. See also *standard logic networks*, page 390, for *half adder* and *full adder*.

Only some very specialised computers, such as *super-computers* (see page 168) and computers using *floating-point units* (see page 352), have specific components to do any arithmetic other than addition. The arithmetic unit can do subtraction by adding complements, but it has to do multiplication and division using a special program (often written in *micro-code*, see page 356) that uses combinations of addition and subtraction.

PART D

Interface

is the hardware and associated software needed for communication between processors and peripheral devices to compensate for the difference in their operating characteristics (e.g. speeds, voltage and power levels, codes, etc.). A number of internationally accepted standard interfaces (and their associated protocols) have been defined; these include RS232, IEEE 488, SCSI and Centronics (see D3 Interfaces and Buses, page 361).

Micro-code

including: micro-program, micro-instruction
is machine-code instructions that are executed by calling small programs held elsewhere in the computer. To the user, a micro-code instruction behaves like a machine-code instruction, but the control unit implements it by passing control to the micro-code routine. The micro-code is stored within the central processor for speed of access. Micro-code enables the instruction set of a computer to be expanded without the addition of hardware components, but it will be slower than a machine-code instruction.

Each micro-code routine is a *micro-program* consisting of a sequence of *micro-instructions*, typically defining a machine-code instruction.

Interrupt

including: timer
is a signal generated by a source such as an input or output device or a systems software routine that causes a break in the execution of the current routine. Control passes to another routine in such a way that the original routine can be resumed after the interrupt.

This enables peripherals to operate independently, indicating to the operating system, with an interrupt, when they need to communicate with the central processor. An example is a keyboard, which sends data to the central processor only when a key is pressed. The central processor continues with other tasks until, on receiving an interrupt, it *polls* (see *polling*, page 359) the various peripherals to establish the reason for the interrupt. If the interrupt is from the keyboard, the central processor collects the data, the code for the key that has been pressed, and stores it in the keyboard *buffer* (see page 354) before continuing. Timing circuits, called *timers*, are also used to generate interrupts at fixed intervals, for example to refresh the screen display.

Shift

including: shift register, arithmetic shift, logical shift, cyclic shift, rotation
is an operation that moves the bits held in a register, called the *shift register*, either to the left or to the right.

There are three different types of shift: arithmetic shift, logical shift and cyclic shift (also called a rotation). They are distinguished by what happens to the bits that are shifted out of the register at one end and what is moved in to fill the vacant space at the other end.

Arithmetic shift to the right causes a bit at the right-hand end of the register to be lost at each shift, and a copy of the sign bit is moved in at the left-hand end. This operation preserves the sign of a number and has the effect of dividing a binary number by two at each shift, regardless of the representation system and regardless of whether the number is negative or positive. The division will be inaccurate because of the truncation caused by the loss of a digit at each shift.

Arithmetic shift to the left causes the bit at the left-hand end of the register, the sign bit, to be lost at each shift. A zero bit is moved in at the right-hand end. If the bit to be moved into the sign bit position is different from the one that was there before the shift, then an overflow flag is set.

The use of two's complement representation ensures that shifting left gives correct results for multiplication by two until an overflow is flagged, because the number is too large to be represented in this size of register. See also *two's complement*, page 320.

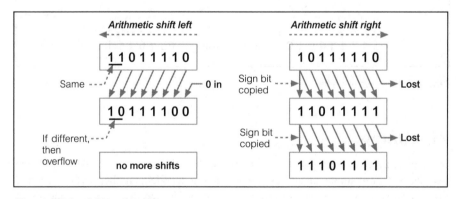

Figure D2.1 Arithmetic shifts

Logical shift is where the bits shifted from the end of the register are lost and zeros are shifted in at the opposite end. It is called a logical shift because it is suitable for *logical operations* (see page 248) rather than for arithmetic. See Figure D2.2.

PART D

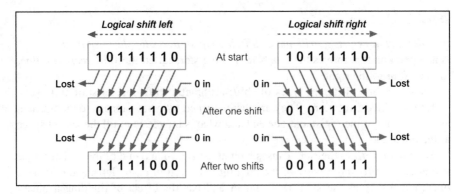

Figure D2.2 Logical shifts

Cyclic shift or *rotation* is where the bits shifted out at one end of the register are reinserted at the opposite end.

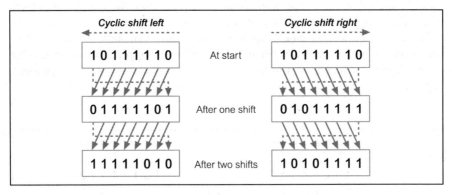

Figure D2.3 Cyclic shifts

Pipelining

is the concurrent decoding of two or more machine instructions. While part of one instruction (for example, an address field) is being decoded, another part of a second instruction (for example, an operation code) may also be decoded, as a means of increasing the speed of execution of a program.

Wait state

is an interval built into some *machine-code instructions* (see page 249) to enable other parts of the computer to complete their actions before the processor moves on to the next instruction. For example, because the processor runs much faster than the RAM, it has to wait for some memory operations to be completed.

Masking

is an operation that selects some of the bits in a register for subsequent processing. Usually, another register of equal length holds a bit pattern called a mask with each bit set to 1 where a corresponding bit is to be selected, and set to 0 otherwise. For example, if a 16-bit register holds a machine-code instruction divided as follows:

Operation code							Address								
1	0	0	0	1	0	1	0	0	1	1	0	1	0	1	1

then the operation code can be selected by constructing the following mask:

1	1	1	1	1	1	1	0	0	0	0	0	0	0	0	0

Using the *AND operation* (see page 248) gives a result of:

1	0	0	0	1	0	1	0	0	0	0	0	0	0	0	0

If necessary, the result can then be *shifted* (see *shift*, page 357) to the right by 9 bit places to put the operation code at the right-hand end of the register.

The idea of using a mask in this way is so fundamental that the same words are used to describe similar selections at a much higher level, such as in using a *data-manipulation language* (see page 298).

Polling

is the sequential checking of a range of possibilities to identify which should be dealt with next. This allows the operating system to manage a range of choices, such as determining what has caused an *interrupt* (see page 356) or which terminal in a multiuser system is waiting for processing. Usually, a message is sent to each routine in turn and the routine has to respond positively to claim the attention of the operating system. The routines are polled one after another so that each routine can claim (if required) its full share of the processor.

Vectoring

is the technique for passing control in a computer program through an intermediate address or vector. For example, on detecting an interrupt, instead of the computer passing control directly to a service routine, it may first jump to a location which in turn hands control to the routine. By altering the contents of this intermediate location, alternative service routines may be introduced without affecting programs that have already been written for that system.

Von Neumann architecture

also known as: Von Neumann concept or machine
is the name given to traditional computer architecture that forms the basis of most digital computer systems. A single control unit manages program control following a linear sequence of fetch–decode–execute–output.

John von Neumann (1903–57), who was a member of a team working on first-generation computers, is credited with the idea that programs and data were indistinguishable and, hence, could be stored in the same memory unit. In early computers, programs and data were stored in separate memories, and the process of entering or altering programs was very tedious. Treating programs as just one form of data made changing programs easier and opened the way for compilers, whose input was text and whose output was a program in binary code.

Von Neumann is also credited with the introduction of the flowchart and with the concept of assertion boxes. These say *what should be true* before or after a step in a program as opposed to *what should be done* at that point in the program.

Print buffer

is an area of computer memory where data to be printed is held until the printer is ready to print it. It enables a program to continue operating without waiting for each character to be printed, as it can send its data to the buffer. The buffer is normally managed by the operating system. When a printer, which works much slower than a computer, is ready to print the next data, it can signal this by means of an *interrupt* (see page 356) to the operating system. The operating system will remove the data from the buffer and send it to the printer. See also *buffer*, page 354.

Interfaces and Buses

Related terms can be found in D2 Machine Architecture, D4 Physical Components and D5 Communications Technology.

What goes on inside a computer is of little interest to most users. For those who are interested in the basic concepts of the internal workings, machine architecture is covered in the preceding section. It is when they connect peripherals to a micro-computer that most users are affected by the computer's architecture.

All peripherals are connected to a computer through an **interface**, but each type of computer may have to be fitted with slightly different interfaces depending on the computer's internal design. Some peripherals require their own dedicated interface, but in situations where a variety of peripherals may be connected, the interface may provide an **expansion bus**. The expansion bus allows several peripherals (of a suit-able type) to be linked in a chain to one computer interface.

Inside a microcomputer, all the components are connected together by a bus. Any peripherals have to be connected to this bus. An **interface board** plugs into a special socket connected to the bus. The electronics on this interface board need to be tailored to fit the electrical connections used by that particular computer's bus; therefore, each design of bus requires its own particular interface boards.

Each peripheral is provided with an interface and is connected, generally through a cable, to the equivalent type of interface on the computer. For the computer and the peripheral to communicate with each other, the interface in the peripheral and the interface in the computer need to be of the same type.

Some peripherals use a **bus interface**. Several peripherals attached to the same bus can share one computer interface, making it easy to use many different peripherals and change peripherals as needed. The computer can identify each peripheral by an address, which is set when the peripheral is first installed.

Interfaces may be plugged into the main printed circuit board of the computer, called the **motherboard**, or into an extension of the motherboard. The degree to which a microcomputer can be expanded depends on the physical space available in its case, which limits the size of the interface board, and the number of sockets avail-able; these are normally called **slots**.

Motherboard

including: mainboard, daughterboard, carrier board
is the printed circuit board (PCB) that holds the principal components in a micro-computer system. The motherboard contains at least the main bus. The other com-ponents, such as the microprocessor and clock chips, will be either plugged into the motherboard or soldered to it. The motherboard is also known as the *mainboard*.

Some components may be mounted on their own printed circuit board, called a *daughterboard*, which will be plugged into the motherboard. Components attached using daughterboards can easily be replaced or upgraded and are not limited by the sockets or circuitry provided by the motherboard. Daughterboards are sometimes called *carrier boards*.

Expansion slot

including: slot, expansion card, card, memory card, PCMCIA card
is a socket which is provided in a computer to allow additional components, such as additional disk drives and network interfaces, to be added to the computer later. These sockets are also called *slots*. The more slots that are provided, the greater the number of extra components that can be added.

Expansion slots allow *expansion cards* (or *cards*) to be added. These expansion cards are usually *interface boards* (see page 363), but they can also provide extra facilit-ies such as a small hard disk drive or a co-processor. Similarly, many computers can accept *memory cards*, which allow the computer's main memory to be increased.

In most microcomputers, the expansion slots are connected directly to the main bus. This means that the expansion board must be designed for that particular bus design (or architecture). One important agreed standard is the *PCMCIA (Personal Computer Memory Card International Association) card*, which is the size of a credit card, for fitting into the expansion slots of small portable computers. Although intended originally for memory expansion cards, a variety of peripheral cards, includ-ing modems and hard disk drives, are now available.

Bus interface

also known as: expansion bus
including: IEEE bus, SCSI (Small Computer Systems Interface) bus
is an *interface* (see page 196) that provides an additional *bus* (see page 353) external to the computer to which several peripheral devices can be connected. This makes it easy to use a range of peripherals or to change the peripherals being used. Each device has an address, which is set on installation, so that the microcomputer can distinguish between the various peripherals. The most common bus interfaces are the SCSI (Small Computer Systems Interface) and the IEEE interface, which are internationally defined standards. Peripherals fitted with one of these interfaces can be connected to any microcomputer fitted with the same type of bus interface; this means that peripherals do not have to be designed for one model of microcomputer

but can be interfaced with many different types of computer. Many different pieces of equipment can be connected to the computer at the same time via the same bus.

IEEE bus conforms to standards defined by the Institute of Electrical and Electronic Engineers (USA). It is used outside the computer to connect scientific equipment to a computer. The computer will have an IEEE interface to convert signals on the IEEE bus into signals suitable for the main computer bus. As it is a common standard, many types of equipment are manufactured with the logic and connections needed for the IEEE bus. These pieces of equipment can easily be connected to computers with an IEEE bus.

SCSI (Small Computer Systems Interface) bus was designed to connect a wide range of devices to microcomputers at minimum cost, in particular disk drives and scanners, which need a high data-transfer rate. It is used widely in general micro-computing. Each SCSI interface can connect up to seven peripheral devices.

Interface board

also known as: interface card
including: parallel port, serial port, Centronics interface, RS232 interface, V.24 interface, RS432 interface, IDE (intelligent device electronics or integrated drive electronics) interface
is the necessary hardware (see *interface*, page 196), mounted on a small printed circuit board (PCB), needed for a microcomputer to communicate with a peripheral device (or another computer). Appropriate *interface cards* can easily be plugged into the *expansion slots* (see above) of the microcomputer.

Some international standard interfaces are used by microcomputers. These include a *parallel port* and a *serial port*. Although these are general terms, when referring to microcomputers they refer to particular international standards. The parallel port is often a Centronics interface and the serial port frequently uses the RS232 interface. The wide range of interface standards include the following:

Centronics interface, an interface designed initially for use with printers, is a form of parallel port. The latest versions have been developed to allow the interface to be used for both input and output, enabling it to be used for data transfer between computers or for the easy attachment of a range of peripherals; this is sometimes called 'the PIO' (parallel input/output) interface.

RS232 interface is a widely used international standard serial interface. The serial port is often referred to as 'the RS232 port'.

The *V.24 interface* and the *RS432 interface* are almost identical to the RS232 interface.

IDE (integrated device electronics or intelligent device electronics) interface is another common standard, which is used to control hard disks in a micro-computer. The IDE interface is built into the hard disk that it is controlling, which reduces the cost of adding hard disks to microcomputers. In high-performance applications, other interfaces such as the *SCSI bus* (see above) are more likely to be used.

PART D

One particular type of interface board is the *expansion bus* (see page 362). Another important standard interface is the *MIDI interface* (see page 50) for sound. See also *Modem*, page 207.

Docking station

is a device containing a range of peripherals and interfaces for use by a portable computer. For lightness and to reduce power consumption, *portable computers* (see page 167) have few peripherals other than disk drives and use a small LCD screen rather than a large monitor. One solution to this lack of peripherals is a docking station, which may be part of a network. When plugged into the docking station, the portable computer has access to a large monitor, printer, extra disk drives and other peripherals, such as modems. The portable computer can be disconnected quickly and used elsewhere.

 Physical Components

Related terms can be found in D2 Machine Architecture.

The computer industry has produced a range of electronic components to perform specific functions within a computer system. Some of these components, such as the clock, simply provide the controlling electronics needed by a computer, whilst others allow a particular type of computer to be designed for a specific role.

Many of these components are integrated circuits and are designed to a standard size, which makes them easy to incorporate into computer designs.

The development of standardised components means that they can be mass-produced rather than being constructed individually. This has the advantage that components are much cheaper and that it becomes economical to design a variety of computers with particular characteristics.

Although computer systems are usually viewed conceptually as a 'black box', it is useful to appreciate the functions of some of the individual components.

Clock

including: clock rate
is the electronic unit that synchronises related components by generating pulses at a constant rate. Clock pulses are used to trigger components to take their next step, so keeping all components in time with each other. The *clock rate* is the frequency at which the clock generates pulses. The higher the clock rate, the faster the computer may work. One limiting factor for machine speed is the manufactured tolerance of the slowest component.

Hard-wired logic

is a function permanently built into the circuitry. Often, this is an integrated circuit designed to control the function. Such functions are immediately available when switched on and cannot be altered by the user. This ensures that the device will always be in the same initial state when switched on.

Integrated circuit (IC)

including: chip, Small-Scale Integration (SSI), Medium-Scale Integration (MSI), Large-Scale Integration (LSI), Very-Large-Scale Integration (VLSI)
is a solid state micro-circuit in which all the components (such as transistors and capacitors) are formed within a very thin slice of silicon. The popular name for an integrated circuit is a '(silicon) *chip*'.

Most integrated circuits used in computers are produced using Large-Scale Integration (LSI) or Very-Large-Scale Integration (VLSI), which are techniques for producing integrated circuits of very high density. These have large numbers of components (transistors, diodes, etc.) and circuits (decoders, flip-flops, etc.) combined as a single integrated circuit.

Small-Scale Integration (*SSI*) has up to 20 logic gates on a chip. Typically they are used for (hard) wired logic circuits.

Medium-Scale Integration (*MSI*) has 20–100 logic gates or less than 1000 memory bits on a chip. These are also used for (hard) wired logic.

Large-Scale Integration (*LSI*) has 100–10 000 logic gates or up to 16 000 memory bits on a chip. These are used for computer logic or memory.

Very-Large-Scale Integration (*VLSI*) has more than 10 000 logic gates or more than 16 000 memory bits on a chip. These are used as standard for computer manufacture.

Bistable

including: flip-flop
is a device that has two stable states. Since each state is stable, the device effectively forms a memory that can differentiate between two pieces of data. Whatever the technology, which could be electronic, magnetic, liquid or pneumatic, the two states are used to represent the binary digits 0 and 1. This means that mathematical manipulation can be performed on data held in binary form.

The bistable in the integrated circuits used for the main memory of computers is a *flip-flop*, a logic circuit designed to store a single data bit. The receipt of an electrical pulse by the flip-flop will reverse its state, and a series of pulses causes it to flip successively between the two stable states.

Latency

including: propagation delay, access time
is the time delay before a component in the computer responds to an instruction, for example the time between data being requested from a memory device and the time when the answer is returned.

Even a single logic gate has a latency (or *propagation delay*), which will be very small (a fraction of a microsecond); with a large number of gates involved, these delays can be significant. The computer cannot work any faster than the limit imposed by latency.

A special case of latency is *access time*, which is the time delay in retrieving data stored either in main memory or on backing store. Access time is relevant when deciding which backing store should be used in any particular context to produce an acceptably fast computer system.

Logic element

including: logic circuit
is a *gate* (see page 380) or combination of gates needed to perform a logical function as part of the circuitry of a computer. It may be a single *AND gate* (see page 384) or a more complex component such as an *adder* (see page 355). Hardware system designers can produce complex circuits using logic elements as modules in the construction of their designs.

A *logic circuit* is designed to perform a more complex function, perhaps specific to the system being built, producing a required set of outputs from a given set of inputs.

Programmable Logic Array (PLA)

also known as: Uncommitted Logic Array (ULA)
is an array of standard logic gates in which each element is identical, manufactured on a single LSI (large-scale integration) chip. The logic circuits required for a particular application are created by 'burning out' unwanted connections.

Real-time clock

is an electronic unit that maintains the time of day in a special register that may be accessed by suitable instructions in a computer program. It is powered by internal batteries and continues to function even when the computer is switched off. For example, the computer can use this time information to label files with the time and date at which they were created, or to trigger timed events such as collecting a weather satellite broadcast.

PART D

ZIF socket

also known as: zero insertion force socket
is a socket on a printed circuit board in the computer into which an *integrated circuit* (see page 366) is plugged. The socket is designed so that no pressure is needed on the component to plug it in (*zero insertion force*) or to remove it. This means that an integrated circuit can be removed and replaced without damage. It also means that a computer can be upgraded easily by having an obsolescent integrated circuit replaced by a new one without risk of damage to the integrated circuits or to the computer itself.

Dual In-Line (DIL) socket

including: Dual In-Line Package (DIP)

is a socket that accepts most standard *integrated circuits* (see page 366). These integrated circuits are constructed with two parallel lines of pins, one at each side of the integrated circuit package. This form of package is known as a *Dual In-Line Package* (*DIP*). There are a number of standard sizes of dual in-line packages, which enable flexible design and interchange of components.

DIN socket

is a plug/socket design adopted by Deutsche Industrienorm (the German standards organisation) but that is used widely internationally. There are a variety of types of DIN socket, with various numbers of pins and layouts. The most common is the 'five-pin DIN', which is also used widely in audio systems.

Communications Technology

This section is concerned with the principles involved in achieving communication between computer systems and the conventions that determine how such systems communicate with each other. Related terms can be found in A13 Communications, A14 Networking and B5 Communications Components.

Ways of communicating data between distant places using electrical energy have been in use for over 100 years, of which the telegraph was the first. Very quickly, machines replaced people and automatic communications became typical. Telephones, tele-printers, radio and television were all well developed before computers were combined with them to produce the range of global communications that is now available.

Global communications require the same standards to be used for equipment worldwide. Some of these standards have been set by those countries that initially developed the systems, but most have been worked out and agreed by international bodies, sometimes with the direct authority of the United Nations. Each industrial country has a national organisation that sets standards for all kinds of products. These organisations have been setting standards, and revising them, throughout the last 100 years. Thus, there are international standards defined by ISO (the International Standards Organisation) and by ITU (International Telecommunications Union), formerly the CCITT (Committée Consultatif International Téléphonique et Télégraphique) of the United Nations, and other standards of a national origin are accepted through organisations like the General Agreement on Tariffs and Trade (GATT).

The specification of standards is a complex and expensive process. The implications of a particular choice can be very far-reaching, both for the industries that make products to those standards and for the consumers of those products. As far as the consumer is concerned, the acceptance of a single manufacturer's standards for some device or system can have limiting effects, particularly when there is severe competition for sales of the product. However, in a situation of rapid technical development, the consumer is likely to benefit from clearly defined standards, which help to ensure some measure of compatibility between hardware and software originating from different sources. The most important areas of standards definition for the computer and information technology industries are those of input/output specifications and external communications.

Transmission

Data transmission

including: duplex, full duplex, half duplex, simplex, synchronous transmission, asynchronous transmission, start bit, stop bit, parallel data transmission, serial data transmission, echo
is the passing of data from one device to another. This may be between parts of a computer system or between computers in a network.

Data transmission may have a number of distinct characteristics:

- it may be synchronised or unsynchronised;
- it may be serial or parallel;
- it may be in both directions at the same time, called *duplex* or *full duplex*; in only one direction at a time, called *half duplex*; or in one direction only, called *simplex*;
- checks may be made on the accuracy of transmission (*parity checks*, see page 80, or by using *echo* processes);
- data may be *packeted* (see *packet switching system*, page 371) with the addresses of destinations.

Synchronous transmission is a method of transmitting data between two devices in which all the data transfers are timed to coincide with a clock pulse. Within a computer, the timing is provided by the computer's clock. Between computers, the clock in one computer acts as the master clock for the system.

Asynchronous transmission is a method of data transmission in which a character is sent as soon as it becomes available rather than waiting for a synchronisation signal or a clock pulse. A *start bit* marks the beginning of a character and one or two *stop bits* mark the end of a character.

Parallel data transmission sends the bits for a character simultaneously along separated data lines. This means that an 8-bit code will require a minimum of nine *channels* (see page 8) for parallel transmission (eight data channels and at least one ground, return channel).

Serial data transmission sends the bits for a character, one after another, along the same data line. This means that serial transmission requires only two wires (a data line and the ground, return line), although more may be provided.

Echo is a feature of data transmission in which the data received are returned to the point of origin for comparison with the original data in order to check them.

Signal routing

including: circuit switching, message switching, message queuing
is the choice of route for a particular message through a network. In *ring* and *star networks* (see page 120), there is little choice of route. More complex network

topologies provide many possible routes for any message. If the direct connection between two nodes is unavailable, perhaps because of some fault or because the connection is busy, then the intelligence in the *routers* (see page 124) at the nodes sends the message forward in a direction that is available. Since the time for a message to travel between nodes is often nearly the same, regardless of the distance apart, this is more efficient than waiting for the direct link to become available. For example, it is possible that a message from London to Manchester may be routed via a satellite to Los Angeles and then on to Manchester. The computer in London that sent the message, and the receiving computer in Manchester, have no control over the route used, nor has the computer in Los Angeles through which it may have passed. The next part of the message may go by some completely different route. See also Figure A12.1, page 99.

Circuit switching is a method of communication in which a path is set up from sender to receiver immediately before the start of transmission and kept open until the transmission is completed. After the transmission is completed, all parts of the path are released and can be used for other transmissions. See also *packet switching*, below.

Message switching is a method of batching, organising and storing sections of data, so that they can be transmitted economically in a network; it is usually applicable to networks with many computers. Each section of a message is sent from node to node, with each node responsible for the choice of route for the next part of the journey. This requires that the nodes are intelligent. A message will be accepted at a node and, if necessary, stored until it can be transmitted onwards. Finally, all the sections of the data are assembled, in the correct order, at their destination.

Message queuing is a method of passing messages in a network in which a host computer stores a message for a terminal until it is ready to receive the message. This is a system appropriate to *star networks* (see page 120).

Packet Switching system (PSS)

including: packet, datagram, IP datagram
is a method of sending data over a *wide area network* (see page 119). Packet-switching networks are available for general use in most countries.

A *packet* is a group of bits, made up of control signals, error control bits, coded information and the destination address for the data. In a given situation, the size of a packet may be fixed. These packets of information are sometimes called *datagrams*. An *IP datagram* is the basic unit of information that is transferred under TCP/IP.

Since each packet occupies a channel for only a short time, this arrangement provides for very efficient use of the system. Error checking should ensure that errors are detected and that appropriate recovery procedures are started automatically. If there is an error, it will be in only a small part of the data, and this can be retransmitted quickly. See also *TCP/IP*, page 110.

PART D

Message fragmentation

is the breaking down of *IP datagrams* (see above) into smaller units so that they can be passed to, or through, a particular processor. See also *maximum transmission unit*, below.

Maximum transmission unit (MTU)

is the largest unit of data that can be transferred by a particular communications system. See also *message fragmentation*, above.

Protocols

Open system

including: Open Systems Interconnection (OSI), ISO 7
is a set of protocols allowing computers of different origins to be linked together. The standards relating to open systems are called *Open Systems Interconnection (OSI)*.

ISO 7 is the seven-layer design for the OSI protocols established by the International Standards Organisation (ISO). It enables manufacturers to design equipment and software for a particular layer. These systems will interconnect with equipment designed for the layer above and the layer below. A brief summary of some of the aspects covered by ISO 7 is given in Table D5.1, below.

Table D5.1 Seven-layer network organisation model (ISO 7)

Level	Level name	Some functions specified within the level descriptions
7	Applications	Specific applications, for example data transfer, messaging, distributed databases; operating system functions and end-user interface
6	Presentation	Data transformation, syntax adjustments and formatting for output devices; data encryption and compression
5	Session	Establishes and maintains session dialogues; synchronises data exchange; provides access control and protection of higher levels from low-level functions
4	Transport	Establishes and maintains communications between users; levels out the data flow; provides greater flow control than the data link layer
3	Network	Routing/addressing between open systems; preventing packets from getting lost when crossing networks; multiplexing and physical network access
2	Data link	Error-free connections to networks; error recognition and correction; creating and synchronising data blocks
1	Physical	How bit sequences are to be sent; there is no error correction

The relations between the levels of the TCP/IP (transmission control protocol/ Internet protocol) network protocol 'family' and ISO 7 are shown in very simple form in Table D5.2. See also *TCP/IP*, page 374.

Table D5.2 Relationship between OSI and TCP/IP protocols

OSI	TCP/IP
Application Presentation	FTP TELNET
Session	SMTP
Transport	TCP
Network	IP
Data Link Physical	Ethernet

Key:
OSI — Open Systems Interconnection
TCP/IP — Transmission Control Protocol/Internet Protocol
FTP — File Transfer Protocol
TELNET — TELetype NETwork
SMTP — Simple Mail Transfer Protocol

Bandwidth

including: broadband, narrow band
is a measure of the capacity of a *communications channel* (see page 18). It is the range of frequencies that a channel can handle. Bandwidth may be given as a frequency (range), such as 3 kHz, or as a transmission rate in bits per second (bps), such as 63 kbps. Transmission rate is often referred to as *line speed* (see page 375). For example, channels might be described as having line speeds of 56 K or 64 K, meaning 56 kbps or 64 kbps.

Broadband is used to describe a transmission channel having a bandwidth in excess of 3 kHz. However, for practical network applications, it probably needs to exceed 300 MHz.

Narrow band is used to describe bandwidths less than the smallest recognised broadband bandwidth. The term is used frequently to mean fractions of a broadband, since a broadband channel is often divided into a number of narrow band channels.

Communications protocol

including: Z modem, Kermit, X.25, X.400, V.22bis, V.32bis, V.34, ARQ (Automatic Repeat Request), TCP (Transmission Control Protocol), MNP (Microcom Network Protocol)
is a standard set of rules used to ensure the proper transfer of data between devices. Protocols exist that specify the format of the data and the signals to start, control and end the transfer. Many current protocols have been specified by the United Nations communications committee, the ITU (International Telecommunications Union), formerly the CCITT (Committée Consultatif International Téléphonique et Télégraphique). See also *ITU*, page 108, *Internet protocol*, page 110, and *Open Systems Interconnection (OSI)*, page 372.

Z modem is a file transfer protocol for networks, in general, but principally on the Internet.

Kermit is an early file transfer protocol for networks in general, which is simple to implement and is still often used.

X.25 is the ITU standard for public *packet switching system (PSS)* networks (see page 371).

X.400 is the ITU standard for *e-mail* (see page 103).

V.22bis is the ITU standard for 2400-bps modems.

V.32bis is the ITU standard for 14 400-bps modems.

V.34 is the ITU standard for 28 800-bps modems, formerly called V-fast.

ARQ (*Automatic Repeat Request*) is an error control protocol used by some modems.

TCP (*Transmission Control Protocol*) is a data transmission protocol defined for high-speed communications within networks.

MNP (*Microcom Network Protocol*) is a set of protocols for error correction and data compression.

ISDN (Integrated Services Digital Network)

including: B-channel, D-channel, ISDN service rates (basic, primary, broadband)
is an ITU definition for (global) digital data communications. Its purpose is to ensure that people, computers and other devices can communicate over standardised connection facilities. The criteria include the setting of standards in such a way that users will have access through a limited set of multipurpose interfaces. This really amounts to the establishment of worldwide digital communications for speech and other data with the simplicity of access that current telephone dialling systems provide. ISDN has definitions for the data transmission speeds, or capacities, of channels and the number of channels in each service.

The capacity of channels is set as follows:

B-channel is a 64-kbit/s channel that can carry pulse code modulation speech, fax and synchronous or asynchronous data up to a maximum of 64 kbit/s.

D-channel is a 16-kbit/s channel that carries the control signals to manage B-channels.

See *Pulse Code Modulation*, page 377.

Table D5.3 ISDN service rates

Rate name	Number of channels	Total capacity
Basic	2 B and 1 D	$2 \times 64 + 16 = 144$ kbps
Primary	30 B and 1 D	$30 \times 64 + 16 = 1936$ kbps
Broadband		More than 34 Mbps

The proposed broadband rates are 150 Mbps and 600 Mbps.

Line speed

including: high-speed links
is the measure of the data capacity of a communications link.

High-speed links are available to provide the opportunities to take advantage of the information available on large networked systems. Transmission capabilities need to be fast enough to handle the large data flows involved. Among the more common transmission capabilities are:

DS0 (digital signal level 0):   64 kbps;

DS1 (digital signal level 1) or **T1**: 1.544 Mbps (that is, 24 DS0s);

DS3 (digital signal level 3) or **T3**: 44.736 Mbps (that is, 28 T1s);

FT1 (fractional T1):   uses less than 24 DS0s, which is less than 1.536 Mbps.

Frame

is a block of data together with the relevant *header* and *trailer* (see page 116).

Signals

Signal

including: carrier signal, carrier wave
is electrical or electromagnetic energy transmitted from one point in a circuit to another along the *channels* (see page 18) connecting them. A signal can carry data of either analogue or digital origin. A basic *carrier signal* consists of a constant-frequency electromagnetic wave. This wave, the *carrier wave*, is modified by combining it with a representation of the data in a way that can be reversed to extract the data after transmission. This process is called *modulation* (see page 376).

Noise

including: signal-to-noise ratio
is electrical disturbances affecting the transmission of intended signals. The existence of noise generally has the same effect on the accurate transmission of signals that people experience when listening to a person talking in a room with other people who are also talking. This is the basic origin of the term. When the noise level is too high, effective transmission ceases. The comparison of the strength of the signal with the level of noise is called the *signal-to-noise ratio*.

PART D

Modulation

including: Amplitude Modulation (AM), Frequency Modulation (FM), phase modulation, Pulse Code Modulation (PCM), demodulation
is the process of introducing variations into the shape (the waveform) of a *carrier wave* (see *signal*, above). The modulation is used to superimpose data on to the carrier wave.

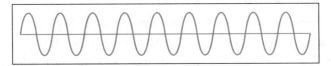

Figure D5.1   Unmodulated carrier wave

Three forms of modulation are used for the transmission of digital data: amplitude modulation, frequency modulation and phase modulation.

In *Amplitude Modulation (AM)*, the amplitude (that is, the height) of the carrier wave is used to represent 0 and 1. The simplest form of amplitude modulation is to switch the carrier wave on for a 1 and off for a 0.

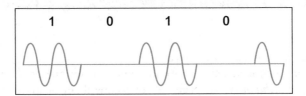

Figure D5.2   Modulation by switching off the wave

Other forms involve increasing above a chosen height and decreasing below a chosen height to represent 1 and 0.

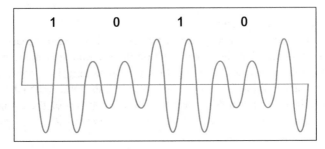

Figure D5.3   Modulation by changing the amplitude

Frequency Modulation (FM) combines two different frequencies with the carrier wave to produce a waveform that is made up of high- and low-frequency parts. This is a very common form of modulation for lower speeds of transmission.

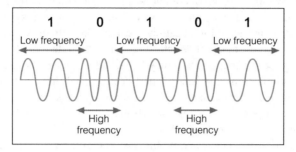

Figure D5.4   Modulation by changing the frequency

Phase modulation combines the carrier wave with an identical wave that is out of phase with it. Two-phase modulation combines two waveforms to provide patterns that are used to represent 0 and 1, as shown in Figure D5.5. Four-phase modulation combines four waveforms to provide patterns that are used to represent 00, 01, 10 and 11. Four-phase modulation transmits two data bits for each element of the wave, and thus sends data at twice the bit rate of two-phase modulation. Eight-phase modulation provides for three bits (000 to 111) for each wave pattern and sends data at three times the bit rate of two-phase modulation.

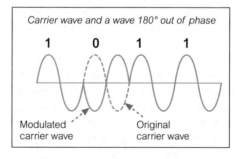

Figure D5.5   Phase modulation

Pulse Code Modulation (PCM) is a method of sampling analogue signals to produce an acceptable digital signal that contains sufficient data to allow an acceptable analogue reproduction of the original signal. It requires three stages: sampling, quantisation and encoding. It was developed for sound transmission and is used principally for voice transmission.

Demodulation is the extraction of the modulating data from the modulated carrier wave signal. The circuits used to do this are similar to those used in radio receivers to convert the received signals into sound signals.

PART D

Interference

including: Electromagnetic Interference (EMI), Radio-Frequency Interference (RFI)
is the introduction of unwanted variations into a transmitted signal. These variations may be caused by faulty design of communications equipment or by external energy sources. Interference can sometimes occur inside a computer system, but more usually it affects external communications. At any place there is a large variety of electromagnetic signals, many of which are generated unintentionally by equipment such as electric motors. These signals may be picked up by wire conductors carrying electronic communications and become part of the signal that reaches the receiver. In addition, there is an increasingly high density of intentionally transmitted signals (for example, from portable phones), which may cause interference on equipment for which these signals are not intended.

Electromagnetic Interference (*EMI*) is the general term for interference caused by electromagnetic radiation at any frequency, whether continuous or intermittent.

Radio-Frequency Interference (*RFI*) is interference generated at typical radio frequencies, in the range 10 kHz to 100 000 MHz. Radio frequencies are at the lower end of the electromagnetic frequency spectrum and are more prone to interference than the higher-frequency radiations, such as infra-red and light.

Collision detection

including: Carrier Sense Multiple Access/Collision Detection (CSMA/CD)
is a method of managing data traffic on a *local-area network* (see page 118). Individual computers are responsible for waiting for the network to be free before sending a message. If two messages are sent at the same time, then a collision occurs. This is detected, and the messages have to be retransmitted when the network is free.

The network interface in each computer is watching all the messages being sent over the network and waits if it detects a message being transmitted. When no traffic is detected by the computer, any message awaiting transmission can then be sent. As it is likely that several computers are waiting to transmit messages and that they will do so at the same time, message corruption will result. The network interfaces detect this corruption (or collision) and are designed to wait for a short time before trying again. This staggers the load on the network.

Carrier Sense Multiple Access/Collision Detection (*CSMA/CD*) is a protocol for implementing this process used on Ethernet local-area networks. See also *token ring network*, page 122.

ACK (acknowledge) signal

is a signal sent back to the sender to confirm that a message has been received by the next point in the communications link. It normally contains the sequence number from the header of the message. See *sequence number*, below, and *header*, page 116.

Sequence number

including: Initial Sequence Number (ISN)
is a number attached to each part of a multipart message to ensure that after transmission, the message is assembled in the correct order.

Initial sequence number (*ISN*) is the first number used in a particular *TCP* connection (see *communications protocol*, page 377).

Public telephone operator (PTO)

is any provider of a publicly available telephone service, such as BT, cable companies and cellular telephone companies.

Public switched telephone network (PSTN)

is the traditional analogue telephone network. It is being replaced by digital services, which are elements of *ISDN* (*integrated services digital network*) (see page 374).

Very-small-aperture terminal (VSAT)

is a satellite communication system using dishes less than 3 m in diameter. It is primarily for down-linking (receiving satellite transmissions), but it can be used for up-linking (transmission to satellites).

High-definition television (HDTV)

is a proposed form of television transmission that will provide a wider picture of much clearer quality than present standards. HDTV transmission will require much greater bandwidth, but data-compression techniques will be possible. For the decompression of picture data, considerable computer processing power will be needed in HDTV receivers.

PART D

Truth Tables and Logic Gates

Binary logic is important in computing because the truth values, True and False, can be represented as the binary digits 1 and 0. All integrated circuits are designed using Boolean logic. They respond to the binary patterns they receive and produce the required outputs as binary patterns. Binary logic influences not only the design of hardware but also the design of algorithms and programming languages, for example the way a test such as 'If the month is February *and* if it is a leap year' is programmed in a high-level language.

Binary Logic

Boolean algebra

including: George Boole
is named after mathematician *George Boole* (1815–64). It is a set of rules for manipulating truth values according to truth tables.

Gate

is an electronic device to control the flow of signals. The output of a gate will depend on the input signal(s) and the type of gate. The components of a computer system can all be seen as combinations of a number of gates, each with a number of possible inputs and a single output. For details of gates see *logic gates*, page 383.

Truth value

also known as: Boolean value
including: true, false
The truth values in Boolean algebra are *True* and *False* (abbreviated to **T** and **F**), often represented by the binary digits 1 and 0. In electronics, these are usually represented by different voltages.

Truth table

is a notation used in Boolean algebra for defining the output of a logic gate or logic circuit for all possible combinations of inputs. For examples, see *logic gates*, page 383, and *logical equivalence and combination of gates*, page 387.

Logical equivalence

exists when two logic circuits have the same output(s) for given inputs. Two equivalent circuits will do the same thing, even though their designs are different. One result of this is that it is possible to construct all logic circuits using only NAND gates or only NOR gates. This is very useful because it allows the use of a single form of component for a variety of purposes. See also *programmable logic array*, page 367. Some examples of logical equivalence are given in *logical equivalence and combination of gates*, page 387.

Karnaugh map

is a method of displaying and manipulating the relationships between Boolean operations. Karnaugh maps are used mainly to reduce logic expressions to their simplest form. They make use of the fact that all logic can be expressed as the 'AND' of 'ORs' or the 'OR' of 'ANDs'.

Input (A)	Input (B)	Input (C)	Output (P)
1	1	1	1
1	1	0	1
1	0	1	0
1	0	0	0
0	1	1	0
0	1	0	1
0	0	1	0
0	0	0	1

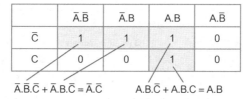

$$\bar{A}.\bar{B}.\bar{C} + \bar{A}.B.\bar{C} = \bar{A}.\bar{C} \qquad A.B.\bar{C} + A.B.C = A.B$$

The shaded areas represent 1 (or true). These are combined in suitable pairs to make the simplified form.

Hence, $A.B.\bar{C} + \bar{A}.B.\bar{C} + \bar{A}.\bar{B}.\bar{C} + A.B.C = \bar{A}.\bar{C} + A.B$

In the three-input logic table, the rows for which the output is 1 represent the logic expression $A.B.C + A.B.\bar{C} + \bar{A}.B.\bar{C} + \bar{A}.\bar{B}.\bar{C}$ The Karnaugh map contains those elements for which the output is 1.

Figure D6.1 Karnaugh map

Logic symbol

is a symbol used to represent a logical operation. In addition to circles with words in them, there are standard symbols which are conventionally used to denote logic operations. These symbols are shown in *logic gates*, page 383.

Venn diagram

is a way of representing the relationships between sets in diagrammatic form. There is a close connection between set operations and logic operations. For example, in Figure D6.2a, the hatched area represents the set operation corresponding to 'XOR'. When the rules for manipulating Venn diagrams are known, it can be seen that this diagram also establishes the logical equivalence:

```
A XOR B = (A OR B) AND NOT (A AND B).
```

Figures D6.2b and c illustrate the same relationships between the two sets.

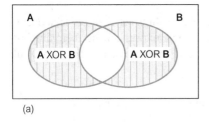

(a)

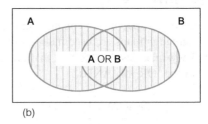

(b)

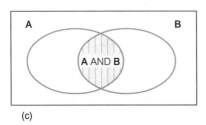

(c)

(a) The hatched area is: A XOR B.
(b) The hatched area is: A OR B.
(c) The hatched area is: A AND B.

Hence, A XOR B   (A OR B) AND NOT (A AND B).

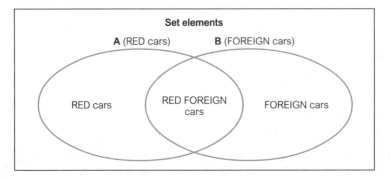

Set elements

A (RED cars)   **B** (FOREIGN cars)

RED cars   RED FOREIGN cars   FOREIGN cars

Figure D6.2   Venn diagrams

Gates

Logic gates

are the components used in making logic circuits. Each gate has one or more inputs and produces a single output that depends upon the input(s). Some important simple logic gates are described below. For each, the following information is given:

- name of the gate;
- brief description of its function;
- how it may be written (there are several notations in common use);
- its truth table (showing how the output changes with different inputs);
- how it may be represented in diagrams (there are several methods, some using different-shaped boxes for different gates).

NOT gate

including: inverse, inverter

The output of a NOT gate is the *inverse* of its input. If the input is TRUE, then the output is FALSE; if the input is FALSE, then the output is TRUE.

NOT gates have only one input and one output.

A NOT gate is also known as an *inverter*.

It may be written as: P = NOT A
Other notations express this as: P = Ā or P = ˜A

Input (A)	Output (P)
0	1
1	0

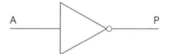

Figure D6.3 NOT gate

OR gate

The output of an OR gate is TRUE if any input is TRUE, otherwise the output is FALSE.

OR gates have two or more inputs and one output.

It may be written as: P = A OR B
Other notations express this as: P = A + B   or   P = A ∨ B

Input (A)	Input (B)	Output (P)
0	0	0
0	1	1
1	0	1
1	1	1

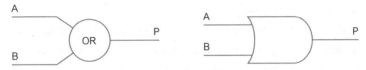

Figure D6.4   OR gate

AND gate

The output of an AND gate is TRUE if all inputs are TRUE, otherwise the output is FALSE.
AND gates have two or more inputs and one output.

It may be written as: P = A AND B
Other notations express this as: P = A.B   or   P = A ∧ B

Input (A)	Input (B)	Output (P)
0	0	0
0	1	0
1	0	0
1	1	1

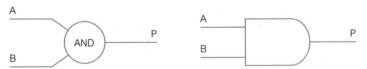

Figure D6.5   AND gate

NOR gate

The output of a NOR gate is TRUE only if all inputs are FALSE, otherwise the output is FALSE.
NOR gates have two or more inputs and one output. They are important because all logic circuits can be constructed from NOR gates alone.

It may be written as: P = A NOR B
Other notations express this as: P = NOT (A + B)   or   P = $\overline{A + B}$
It is equivalent to: P = NOT (A OR B)

Input (A)	Input (B)	Output (P)
0	0	1
0	1	0
1	0	0
1	1	0

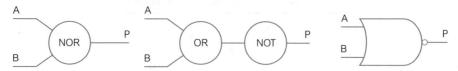

Figure D6.6 NOR gate

NAND gate

The output of a NAND gate is FALSE only if all inputs are TRUE, otherwise the output is TRUE.

NAND gates have two or more inputs and one output. They are important because all logic circuits can be constructed from NAND gates alone.

It may be written as: $P = A \text{ NAND } B$

Other notations express this as: $P = \text{NOT } (A.B) \quad \text{or} \quad P = \overline{A.B}$

It is equivalent to: $P = \text{NOT } (A \text{ AND } B)$

Input (A)	Input (B)	Output (P)
0	0	1
0	1	1
1	0	1
1	1	0

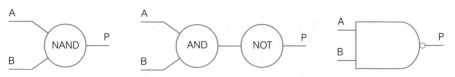

Figure D6.7 NAND gate

XOR (exclusive OR) gate

also known as: EOR gate, NEQ gate, non-equivalence gate

The output of an Exclusive-OR gate is TRUE if the two inputs are different; the output is false if the inputs are alike.

XOR gates have only two inputs and one output.

The Exclusive-OR gate is also known as the EOR gate or NEQ (Non-Equivalence) gate.

It is written as:
P = A XOR B   or   P = A EOR B
P = A NEQ B   or   P = A $\oplus$ B

Input (A)	Input (B)	Output (P)
0	0	0
0	1	1
1	0	1
1	1	0

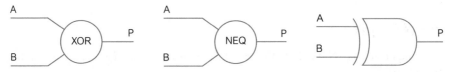

Figure D6.8   XOR or NEQ gate

XNOR (Exclusive NOR) gate

also known as: EQ gate, equivalence gate
The output of an Exclusive-NOR gate is TRUE if the two inputs are the same; the output is FALSE if the inputs are different.
XNOR gates have only two inputs and one output.
The Exclusive-NOR gate is also known as the EQ (Equivalence) gate.

It is written as:
P = A XNOR B   or   P = A EQ B
P = $\overline{A \oplus B}$

Input (A)	Input (B)	Output (P)
0	0	1
0	1	0
1	0	0
1	1	1

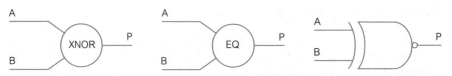

Figure D6.9   XNOR or EQ gate

Gate Combinations

Logical equivalence and combination of gates

All logic circuits can be constructed in many different ways, using different combinations of gate circuits. In particular, all logic circuits can be constructed using only NAND gates, or only NOR gates. Choosing the easiest, or cheapest, to make can influence the manufacture of computer circuits. The following examples are only a small set.

Equivalence for NOT logic

A NOT gate can be made by connecting together both inputs of a NAND gate:

Input (A)	A NAND A	NOT A
0	1	1
1	0	0

$$P = \overline{A \cdot A} = \overline{A}$$

Figure D6.10   A NAND A = NOT A

A NOT gate can also be made by connecting together both inputs of a NOR gate:

Input (A)	A NOR A	NOT A
0	1	1
1	0	0

$$P = \overline{A + A} = \overline{A}$$

Figure D6.11   A NOR A = NOT A

Equivalence for AND logic

A AND B is equivalent to NOT (A NAND B):

Input (A)	Input (B)	A NAND B	NOT (A NAND B)	A AND B
0	0	1	0	0
0	1	1	0	0
1	0	1	0	0
1	1	0	1	1

$$P = A.B = \overline{\overline{A.B}}$$

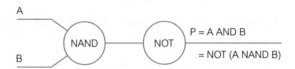

Figure D6.12   A AND B = NOT (A NAND B)

Equivalence for NOR logic

A NOR B is equivalent to (NOT A) AND (NOT B):

Input (A)	Input (B)	NOT A	NOT B	(NOT A) AND (NOT B)	A NOR B
1	1	0	0	0	0
1	0	0	1	0	0
0	1	1	0	0	0
0	0	1	1	1	1

$$P = \overline{A + B} = \bar{A} \cdot \bar{B}$$

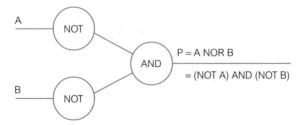

Figure D6.13   A NOR B = (NOT A) AND (NOT B)

Equivalence for XOR logic

A XOR B is equivalent to (A OR B) AND NOT (A AND B):

A	B	A OR B	A AND B	NOT (A AND B)	(A OR B) AND NOT (A AND B)	A XOR B
1	1	1	1	0	0	0
1	0	1	0	1	1	1
0	1	1	0	1	1	1
0	0	0	0	1	0	0

$$P = A \text{ XOR } B = (A + B).\overline{(A.B)}$$

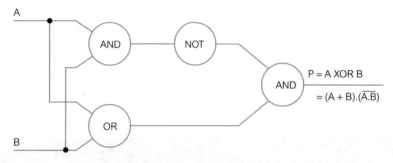

Figure D6.14   A XOR B = (A OR B) AND NOT (A AND B)

A XOR B is equivalent to (A AND NOT B) OR (B AND NOT A):

A	B	NOT A	NOT B	A AND NOT B	B AND NOT A	(A AND NOT B) OR (B AND NOT A)	A XOR B
1	1	0	0	0	0	0	0
1	0	0	1	1	0	1	1
0	1	1	0	0	1	1	1
0	0	1	1	0	0	0	0

$$P = A \text{ XOR } B = (A.\overline{B}) + (\overline{A}.B)$$

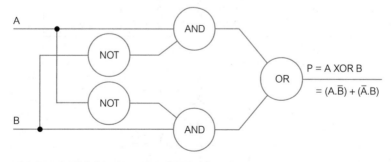

Figure D6.15   A XOR B = (A AND NOT B) OR (NOT A AND B)

PART D

A XOR B can be constructed entirely from NAND gates:

A	B	A NAND B (Q)	A NAND Q (R)	Q NAND B (S)	R NAND S (P)	A XOR B
1	1	0	1	1	0	0
1	0	1	0	1	1	1
0	1	1	1	0	1	1
0	0	1	1	1	0	0

$$P = A \text{ XOR } B = \overline{R.S} = \overline{\overline{A.Q}.\overline{Q.B}} = \overline{\overline{A.\overline{A.B}}.\overline{A.B.B}}$$

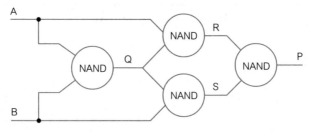

Figure D6.16   XOR circuit constructed from NAND gates

Logic Networks

Half adder

The half adder can add together two bits to produce a sum output (SUM) and a carry output (C_{out}). See also *adder*, page 355.

These are defined as:

```
SUM  = A XOR B
Cout = A AND B
```

bit A	bit B	C_{out}	SUM
1	1	1	0
1	0	0	1
0	1	0	1
0	0	0	0

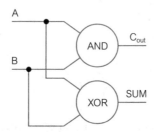

Figure D6.17   Half adder logic circuit

Full adder

The full adder can add together two bits and a carry input (C_{in}) to produce a sum output (SUM) and a carry output (C_{out}). See also *adder*, page 355.
These are defined as:

```
SUM  = (A XOR B) XOR Cin
Cout = (A AND B) OR (A AND Cin) OR (B AND Cin)
```

A	B	C_{in}	C_{out}	SUM
1	1	1	1	1
1	1	0	1	0
1	0	1	1	0
1	0	0	0	1
0	1	1	1	0
0	1	0	0	1
0	0	1	0	1
0	0	0	0	0

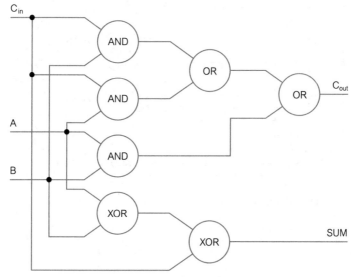

(a) Constructed from individual gates.

More helpfully, a full adder can be seen as a combination of two half adders.

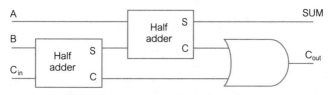

(b) Made up from two half adders and an OR gate.

Figure D6.18 Full adder logic circuit

PART D

Decoder

A decoder circuit is used to select one of several inputs. Address lines are used to indicate the source to be selected. n address lines can handle 2^n sources (e.g. two address lines for four sources, three address lines for eight sources).

$$P = \bar{A}.\bar{B}.S_0 + \bar{A}.B.S_1 + A.\bar{B}.S_2 + A.B.S_3$$

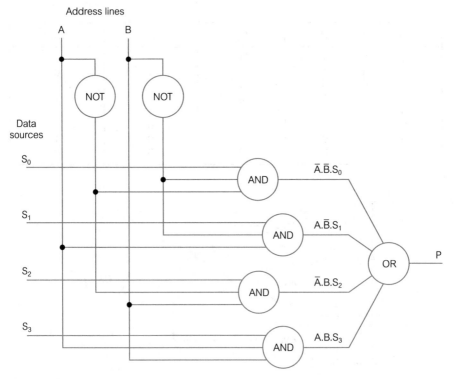

Figure D6.19 Decoder logic circuit

Address switching

A single source can be switched to one of several destinations by a logic network, using address lines to indicate the destination.

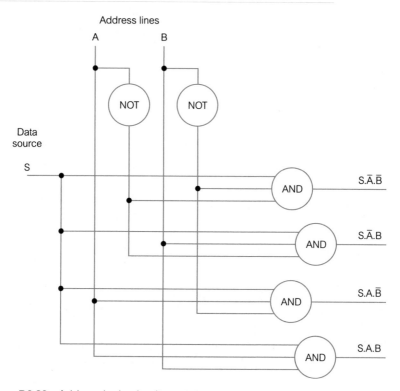

Figure D6.20   Address logic circuit

Part
E
Appendices

One characteristic of modern life, and particularly any form of technological activity, is the use of abbreviations, acronyms and other jargon by those who are involved in any specialised activity. This use of words and terms when writing for or talking to others involved in the same activity can be a way of economically passing information between like-minded people, but it can also be a barrier to understanding for those who do not know the meanings of the strange new words. Computer users have always made great use of a vocabulary containing many abbreviations and acronyms. Over time, this vocabulary has changed as new ideas are developed and old ones are no longer appropriate.

No list would ever be complete or up to date, but in Section E1 there is an extensive list of acronyms and abbreviations whose use is either commonplace throughout most computing activities or is specific to a particular aspect of computing. The list is organised alphabetically and includes many terms that are treated in the main body of the glossary; for these terms, the appropriate page references are given. For terms that have no page reference, the only information provided is the expansion of the abbreviation or acronym and, for some, an indication of the context in which they may be met.

PART E

Acronyms and Abbreviations

Where a page number is given, it indicates where additional information can be found. Brackets are used to indicate the context in which the acronym or abbreviation may be met.

PART E

AT	advanced technology (bus)	
ATM	asynchronous transfer mode	
ATM	automatic teller machine	78
AUP	acceptable use policy	
BA	bus available	
BABT	British Approvals Board for Telecommunications	
BASIC	Beginners All-purpose Symbolic Instruction Code	301
BBC	British Broadcasting Corporation	
BBS	bulletin-board system	115
BCC	block check character	
BCD	binary-coded decimal	320
BCS	British Computer Society	140
BDOS	basic disk operating system	
BEAB	British Electrical Appliances Board	
BEL	bell (buzzer) (ASCII character)	415
BiMOS	bipolar MOS	
BIND	Berkeley Internet Name Domain (software)	
BIOS	basic input/output system	338
bit	binary digit	11
BNF	Backus–Naur form	302
bpi	bits per inch	184
BPP	bits per pixel	
bps	bits per second	210
BS	back space (ASCII character)	415
BSI	British Standards Institution	
BTW	by the way	105
CAD	computer-aided design	157
CAD	computer-aided draughting	157
CAD/CAM	computer-aided design and computer-aided manufacture	157
CAI	computer-assisted instruction	
CAL	computer-aided learning	157
CAM	computer-aided manufacturing	157
CAN	cancel (ASCII character)	415
CASE	computer-aided software engineering	229
CBT	computer-based training	157
CCA	Central Computing Agency	
CCD	charge-coupled device	
CCITT	Committée Consultatif International Téléphonique et Télégraphique	108
CCP	console command processor	
CCR	condition code register	
CD	compact disk	186
CD-I	compact disk interactive	
CD-R	compact disk recordable	186
CD-RW	compact disk rewritable	186
CD-ROM	compact disk read-only memory	186

CDI	collector diffusion isolator	
CEG	Computer Education Group	
CEPIS	Confederation of European Professional Informatics Societies	
CGA	colour graphics adapter	
CIR	current instruction register	
CISC	complex instruction set computer	348
CIX	commercial internet exchange	
CMI	computer-managed instruction	157
CML	computer-managed learning	157
CMOS	complementary MOS	184
CMS	colour management system	193
CMYK	cyan, magenta, yellow, key (black)	193
CNC	computer numeric control	131
COBOL	COmmon Business Oriented Language	300
COM	computer output on microfilm	198
COMAL	COMmon Algorithmic Language	
CP gate	comparator gate (=XOR)	385
CP/M	control program for microcomputers	
CPM	control program monitor	
CPE	central processing element	
cps	characters per second	210
CPU	central processing unit	347
CR	carriage return (ASCII character)	415
CRC	cyclic redundancy check	79
CR/LF	carriage return/line feed	
CROM	control ROM	
CRT	cathode ray tube	196
CSCD	carrier sense collision detection	378
CSCW	computer supported cooperative work	
CSMA/CD	carrier sense multiple access collision detection	378
CSV	comma separated variables (file)	12
CTRL or Ctrl	control (ASCII character)	
CTS	clear to send	
CUA	common user access	345
CUG	closed user group	
CWP	communicating word processors	
CYMK	cyan, yellow, magenta, key (black)	193
DAC	data acquisition and control	
DAC	digital-to-analogue converter	210
DAT	digital audio tape	
DBA	database administrator	138
DBMS	database management system	89
DBS	direct broadcast by satellite	
DCD	data carrier detect (communications)	
DCE	data communications equipment	
DCS	telephone data carrier system	

PART E

DD	double density	184
DDE	direct data entry	75
DDL	data description language	
DDN	Defense Data Network	
DEL	delete (ASCII character)	415
DES	Data Encryption Standard	150
DFD	data flow diagram	240
DFS	disk filing system	
DHTML	Dynamic HyperText Mark-up Language	303
DIB	data input bus	
DIL	dual in-line	368
dil	dual in-line	368
DIN	Deutsche Industrie Norm	368
DIP	dual in-line package	72
DLE	data link escape (ASCII character)	415
DLT	digital linear technology	
DMA	direct memory access	351
DML	data-manipulation language	298
DNS	domain name system	107
DoD	Department of Defense (USA)	
DOS	disk operating system	336
DP	data processing	
dpi	dots per inch	194
DRAM	dynamic random-access memory	184
DSA	digital signature algorithm	145
DSR	data set ready	
DSS	decision-support system	159
DSW	device status word	
DTE	data terminal equipment	
DTL	diode-transistor logic	
D-to-A	digital-to-analog	210
DTP	desktop publishing	160
DTR	data terminal ready	
DV	digital video	37
DVD	digital versatile disk	186
EA	extended addressing	
EAN	European article number	75
EAROM	electronically alterable read-only memory	185
EB disk	electronic book disk	
EBCDIC	Extended Binary-coded Decimal Interchange Code	307
EBR	electron beam recording	
ECD	electrochromeric display	
ECL	emitter-coupled logic	
ECMA	European Computer Manufacturers' Association	274
EDP	electronic data processing	
EDS	exchangeable disk storage	

EEPROM	electrically erasable PROM	185
EFT	electronic funds transfer	78
EFTPOS	electronic funds transfer at point of sale	78
EGA	enhanced graphics adapter	
EIA	Electrical Industries Association (USA)	
EISA	extended industry standard architecture	
EM	end of message (ASCII character)	415
EM character	end-of-medium character (ASCII character)	
Email, e-mail	electronic mail	103
EMI	electromagnetic interference	378
ENQ	enquiry (ASCII character)	415
EOF	end of file	313
EOM	end of message	
EOR	exclusive OR	385
EOT	end of transmission (ASCII character)	415
EPOS	electronic point of sale	
EPROM	erasable programmable read-only memory	185
EPS	encapsulated postscript	
EQ	equal	
EQ	equivalence	386
ESC	escape (ASCII character)	415
ESDI	enhanced systems drive interface	
ETB	end of text block (ASCII character)	415
ETX	end of text (= end of last block) (ASCII character)	415
EULA	end-user licence agreement	154
FAM	fast-access memory	
FAQ	frequently asked question	105
FAST	Federation Against Software Theft	
FAT	file-allocation table	188
FAX	facsimile	6
FD	floppy disk	179
FDD	floppy-disk drive	179
FDDI	fibre-distributed data interface	119
FDM	frequency-division multiplexor (communications)	207
FEP	front-end processor	168
FET	field-effect transistor	
FETMOS	field-effect transistor metal-oxide-semiconductor	
FF	form feed (ASCII character)	415
FFT	fast Fourier transform	
FIFO	first in, first out	312
FM	frequency modulation (sound, communications)	48
FORTRAN	FORmula TRANslation	301
FPA	floating-point accelerator	352
FPU	floating-point unit	
FROM	fusible ROM	
FS	file separator (ASCII character)	415

PART E

FSK	frequency shift keying	
FSM	frequency shift modulation	
FTP	file transfer protocol	102
G	giga	409
Gb	gigabyte	409
GDU	graphical display unit	198
GIF	graphics interchange format	
GIGO	garbage in, garbage out	
GIS	geographical information system	158
GND	ground (connection)	
GPIB	general-purpose interface bus	
GPR	general-purpose register	
GPS	global positioning system	158
GS	group separator (ASCII character)	415
GUI	graphical user interface	59
HCI	human-computer interaction/interface	59
HD	high density or hard disc	184
HDD	high-density disk or hard disc drive	180
HDTV	high-definition television	379
HEX	hexadecimal	321
HMOS	high-performance metal-oxide-semiconductor	
HRG	high-resolution graphics	194
HT	horizontal tabulation (ASCII character)	415
HTML	HyperText Mark-up Language	303
HTTP	HyperText Transfer Protocol	110
Hz	hertz	41
I/O	input/output	5
IAB	Internet Architecture Board	108
IAM	immediate-access memory	
IAR	instruction address register	349
IAS	immediate-access store	178
IC	integrated circuit	366
ICMP	Internet control message protocol	110
ICT	information and communications technology	3
ID	identification	148
IDE	integrated (or intelligent) device electronics	363
IDS	intrusion detection system	148
IEE	Institution of Electrical Engineers (UK)	
IEEE	Institute of Electronic and Electrical Engineers (USA)	362
IFIP	International Federation for Information Processing	
IGFET	insulated gate field-effect transistor	
IIL	integrated injection logic	
IKBS	Intelligent Knowledge-Based System	134
ILS	integrated learning system or international language support	157
IMHO	in my humble opinion	105
IO	input/output	5

PART E

m	milli	409
MAR	memory address register	349
Mb	megabyte	409
MBR	memory buffer register	349
MCA	microchannel architecture	
MDA	monochrome display adapter	198
MDR	memory data register	349
MHS	message-handling system	
MICR	magnetic ink character recognition	77
MIDI	musical instrument digital interface	50
MIME	multi-purpose Internet mail extender	103
MIPS	millions of instructions per second	354
MIS	management information system	159
MMI	man-machine interface/interaction	59
MMU	memory management unit	351
MNP	Microcom Network Protocol	373
modem	modulator-demodulator	207
MOS	machine operating system	336
MOS	metal-oxide-semiconductor	184
MOSFET	metal-oxide-semiconductor field-effect transistor	
MPEG	Motion Picture Expert Group	26
MPS	microprocessor system	
MPU	microprocessor unit	
MPX	multiplex	
MREQ	memory request	
ms	millisecond	
MS-DOS	Microsoft DOS	336
MSB	most significant bit	
MSD	most significant digit	
MSI	medium-scale integration	366
MTBF	mean time between failures	
MTF	mean time to failure	
MTU	maximum transmission unit	372
MUG	multi-user game	108
MUX	multiplexor	207
n	nano	409
NAK	negative acknowledgement (ASCII character)	415
NAND	not AND	385
NEQ	not equivalent	385
NFS	network file system	
NLQ	near-letter-quality	
NMI	non-maskable interrupt	
NMOS	n-channel metal-oxide-semiconductor	
NOR	not OR	384
ns	nanosecond	409
NSFNET	National Science Foundation Network (USA)	100

NTSC	National Television Standards Committee (USA)	
NUL	null (do nothing)	
OCR	optical character recognition	77
OEM	original equipment manufacturer	169
OLE	object linking and embedding	17
OLR	off-line reader	107
OMR	optical mark reader	76
OOD	object-oriented design	227
OOL	object-oriented language	
OOP	object-oriented program(ming)	242
OS	operating system	336
OSI	open systems interconnection	372
OV	overflow	331
p	pico	409
PABX	private automatic branch exchange	207
PAL	phase-alternating line	199
PBX	private branch exchange	207
PC	personal computer (IBM-PC-compatible)	9
PC	program counter	
PC-DOS	personal computer disk operating system	336
PCB	printed circuit board	362
PCI	peripheral component interconnect	353
PCI	programmable communications interface	
PCM	pulse code modulation	376
PCMCIA	Personal Computer Memory Card International Association	362
PD	phase distortion (sound)	48
PDA	personal digital assistant	167
PDM	pulse duration modulation	
PIA	peripheral interface adapter	
PID	personal identification device	148
PILOT	Programmed Inquiry, Learning Or Teaching (language)	
PIN	personal identification number	148
PING	packet internet groper	112
PIO	parallel input/output	363
PIXEL	picture element	197
PL/1	Programming Language 1	300
PLA	programmable logic array	367
PLC	programmable logic circuit	
PMOS	p-channel metal-oxide-semiconductor	
PNG	portable network graphics	
PoP	point of presence	111
POP3	Post Office Protocol 3	110
POS	point of sale	126
ppm	pages per minute	
PPP	point-to-point protocol	110
PRN	printer	200

PART E

PROLOG	PROgramming in LOGic	299
PROM	programmable read-only memory	185
PRR	pulse-repetition rate	
PRT	program reference table	
PSN	packet switching network	
PSS	packet switching system	371
PSTN	public switched telephone network	379
PSU	power supply unit	
PSU	program storage unit	
PSW	program/processor status word	
PTO	public telephone operator	379
QBE	Query By Example	298
QD	quad density (disks)	184
QIC	quarter-inch cartridge	
QWERTY	conventional typewriter keyboard	171
RAID	redundant array of independent (or inexpensive) disks	180
RAM	random-access memory	184
RD	read	
RDBMS	relational database management system	91
REM	remark(s)	
REN	ring equivalent number	
RF	radio frequency	
RFC	request for comment	
RFI	radio-frequency interference	378
RFID	radio-frequency interference device	174
RGB	red, green, blue	193
RI	ring in	
RISC	reduced instruction set computer	348
RJE	remote job entry	344
ROM	read-only memory	185
RPG	report program generator	298
RS	record separator (ASCII character)	415
RSA	Rivest, Shamir, Adleman (algorithm)	151
RTF	revisable or rich text format (file)	
RTL	resistor-transistor logic	
RTS	request to send	
R/W	read/write	186
SAA	systems applications architecture	345
SAR	store address register	
SBC	single-board computer	
SCR	sequence control register	349
SCSI	small computer systems interface	362
SDR	store data register	
SET	secure electronic transaction	146
SHF	super-high frequency	
SI	shift in (ASCII character)	415
SIC	silicon integrated circuit	

SID	standard interchangeable data (file)	
SIMM	single in-line memory module	
SIMS	Schools Information Management System	
Simula	Simulation Language	300
SIO	serial input/output (controller)	
SLIP	serial line Internet protocol	101
SLSI	super-large-scale integration	
SMPTE	Society of Motion Picture and TV Engineers (USA)	46
SMTP	simple mail transport protocol	110
SNA	systems network architecture	345
SNOBOL	String-oriented Symbolic Language	300
SO	shift out (ASCII character)	415
SOH	start of header (ASCII character)	415
SOS	silicon on sapphire	
SP	stack pointer	
SQA	software-quality assurance	
SQL	Structured Query Language	298
SSADM	structured systems analysis and design method	218
SSI	small-scale integration	366
SSL	secure socket layer	146
STD	subscriber trunk dialling	
STX	start of text (ASCII character)	415
SUB	substitute (ASCII character)	415
SVGA	super video graphics array	191
SWR	status word register	
SYLK	symbolic link	
SYN	synchronisation character (ASCII character)	415
sysop	system operator	115
TCP	transmission control protocol	373
TCP/IP	transmission control protocol/Internet protocol	110
TDM	time-division multiplexor (communications)	207
TEMP	temporary	
TLA	three-letter acronym	105
TP	tele-processing	17
TP	transaction processing	17
TP	twisted pair	209
TPA	transient program area	
TPI	tracks per inch	
TRL	transistor-resistor logic	
TSV	tab-separated variables (file)	12
TTL	transistor-transistor logic	
TTP	trusted third party	145
UART	universal asynchronous receiver/transmitter	
UDP/IP	user datagram protocol/Internet protocol	110
UHF	ultra-high frequency	
UJT	uni-junction transistor	
ULA	uncommitted logic array	367

PART E

UML	Unified Modelling Language	
UPC	universal product code	75
UPS	uninterruptable power supply	
URL	uniform resource locator	106
US	unit separator (ASCII character)	415
USART	universal synchronous/asynchronous receiver/transmitter	
USB	universal serial bus	
USRT	universal synchronous receiver/transmitter	
UTP	unshielded twisted pair	209
UUCP	UNIX-to-UNIX copy protocol	110
UV	ultraviolet	
VAN	value-added network	128
VANS	value-added network service	128
VDG	video display generator	
VDT	video display terminal	
VDU	visual display unit	196
VESA	Video Electronics Standards Association	353
VGA	video graphics array	
VHF	very high frequency	
VLSI	very-large-scale integration	366
VM	virtual memory	351
VMOS	vertical-current-flow metal-oxide semiconductor	
VPN	virtual private networking	123
VR	virtual reality	56
VRAM	video RAM	198
VRML	Virtual Reality Mark-up Language	110
VRR	vertical refresh rate	
VSAT	very-small-aperture terminal	379
VT	vertical tabulation (ASCII character)	415
WAIS	wide-area information service	109
WAN	wide-area network	119
WIMP	windows icons mouse pointer	60
WMA	windows, media, audio	
WORM	write-once, read-many	186
WP	word processing	22
WR	write	
WS	working store	188
WWW	World Wide Web	101
WYSIWYG	what you see is what you get	20
XGA	extended graphics array	
XML	extensible modelling language or extensible mark-up language	303
XNOR	exclusive NOR	386
XOR	exclusive OR	385
ZIF	zero insertion force (socket)	367
3GL	third-generation language	293
4GL	fourth-generation language	293

Units

Symbol	Prefix	Meaning	Decimal	Powers
T	tera	one million million	1 000 000 000 000	10^{12}
G	giga	one thousand million	1 000 000 000	10^{9}
M	mega	one million	1 000 000	10^{6}
	kibi		1024	2^{10}
K	kilo	one thousand	1000	10^{3}
		one	1	10^{0}
M	milli	one-thousandth (1/1000)	0.001	$10^{-3} = 1/10^{3}$
μ	micro	one-millionth (1/1 000 000)	0.000 001	$10^{-6} = 1/10^{6}$
n	nano	one-thousand-millionth (1/1 000 000 000)	0.000 000 001	$10^{-9} = 1/10^{9}$
p	pico	one-million-millionth (1/1 000 000 000 000)	0.000 000 000 001	$10^{-12} = 1/10^{12}$

In computer-storage terms, the symbols k, M, G and T have particular values related to the powers of 2, not to the powers of 10:

k is $2^{10} = 1024$ (known as kibi), thus 8 kbytes of store is $8 \times 2^{10} = 8192$ bytes.
M is $2^{20} = 1\ 048\ 576$, thus 4 Mbytes (4 Mb) is $4 \times 2^{20} = 4\ 194\ 304$ bytes.
G is $2^{30} = 1\ 073\ 741\ 824$, thus 60 gigabytes (60 Gb) is $60 \times 2^{30} = 64\ 424\ 509\ 440$ bytes.
T is $2^{40} = 1\ 099\ 511\ 627\ 776$, thus 2 terabytes (2 Tb) is $2 \times 2^{40} = 2\ 199\ 023\ 255\ 552$ bytes.

One nanosecond is the time interval in which a photon or electron will travel 299.7 mm.

Filenames and Filename Extensions

Each computer-stored file needs to have a unique name (a **filename**) in order that it can be saved, located or retrieved by the computer's file management system.

Different operating systems treat files in different ways. Consequently, filenames associated with different operating systems may have different structures or may be displayed differently. Nevertheless, most operating systems associated with personal computers have similar filename conventions where, generally, full filenames such as glossary.doc consist of two parts separated by a dot (.).

The first part is chosen by the person who creates the file and is the name by which the file is recognised. The second part – usually known as the **filename extension** – is determined according to a set of rules (illustrated below) and enables the computer system to determine what action it may need to take in order to enable the file to be processed.

To be valid, filenames must not include certain characters that have specific roles in the command expressions of the operating system (such as * ? "\ /< >: | ~). There may also be a restriction on the length of the filename.

The following is a selection of the more commonly used filename extensions that may typically be seen in directory listings.

Filename extensions designating files used in the set-up configuration of a computer system or denoting files with specific links to operational aspects of the system:

.bat   Batch file: file containing several commands that are operated in sequence.

.cfg   Configuration file: file containing information on the way in which the computer is set up.

.com   Command file: small program that launches executable programs or system commands.

.dll   Dynamic link library file: application extension file.

.drv   Driver file: program file that sets communication parameters for printers, monitors, etc.

.exe   Executable file: file that calls a specific program.

.fnt   Font file: file containing the specification of a particular type font.

.ini   Initialisation file: file containing reference data relating to the first running of a program.

.sys   System file: file containing instructions controlling aspects of the operating system.

Filename extensions that usually identify files as being of a particular type:

.bak   Back-up file: copy of an original file, written by the system, when the original is changed and the changed version is saved by the user using the original filename.

.bmk   Bookmark file.

.bmp   Bitmap file: used to store characters or graphics for displaying data as a series of pixels.

.clp   Clipboard file: temporary file used to store data for later use in the same computer session.

.dat   Datafile.

.gif   Graphics interchange format file: developed to compress and store graphics image data.

.hlp   Help file.

.jpg   Graphics file: standard compression format developed for photographic images.

.log   Log file.

.old   Archive file: created by install programs to preserve previous versions of system files.

.ovr   Overlay file: file, which can be displayed superimposed over another file.

.pat   Pattern file.

.rtf   Rich text format file: word-processed file that saves formatting as text – used in file transfer.

.scr   Screen file: format for many screen savers.

.tif   Graphics file: compressed file containing bitmap graphics.

.tmp   Temporary file: file used by some programs to store data while waiting for further instructions.

.txt   Text file: unformatted (ASCII) file that can be opened in any word processor.

.wav   Wave format file: Sound file.

.$$$ Temporary file: used within a program and normally discarded by that program when no longer required.

PART E

Filename extensions that usually identify files as belonging to, and associate the files with, particular application programs:

.bas   BASIC program file.

.cdr   CorelDraw file: drawing package application file.

.doc   Document file: word-processor application file.

.mdb   Microsoft Access file: database application file.

.pdf   Portable Document Format: Adobe Acrobat file.

.pm   Pagemaker file: desktop publishing application file.

.wmf   MetaFile: clipart file.

.xls   Excel file: spreadsheet file.

.ppt   PowerPoint file: presentation file.

.html   HTML: Web page.

.htm   HTML: Web page.

Geographical Domain Extensions

am	Armenia
aq	Antarctica
ar	Argentina
at	Austria
au	Australia
be	Belgium
bg	Bulgaria
br	Brazil
cl	Chile
ca	Canada
ch	Switzerland
cn	China
co	Colombia
cz	Czech Republic
de	Germany
dk	Denmark
dz	Algeria
ee	Estonia
eg	Egypt
es	Spain
fi	Finland
fr	France
gb	Great Britain (alternative to UK)
gr	Greece
hk	Hong Kong
hr	Croatia
hu	Hungary
id	Indonesia
ie	Ireland
il	Israel
in	India
is	Iceland
it	Italy
jp	Japan

kr	South Korea
li	Liechtenstein
lt	Lithuania
lu	Luxembourg
lv	Latvia
ma	Morocco
mx	Mexico
my	Malaysia
nl	Holland
no	Norway
nz	New Zealand
pe	Peru
pl	Poland
pt	Portugal
ro	Romania
ru	Russia
se	Sweden
sg	Singapore
si	Slovenia
sk	Slovak Republic
su	ex-Soviet Union (Russia)
th	Thailand
tr	Turkey
tw	Taiwan
ua	Ukraine
uk	UK
us	USA (relatively little-used)
ve	Venezuela
za	South Africa

See also Electronic mail, page 103

ASCII Character Codes

Decimal value	ASCII character	Notes	Decimal value	ASCII character	Notes	Decimal value	ASCII character	Notes
0	NULL	Fill character	43	+		86	V	
1	SOH		44	,	Comma	87	W	
2	STX		45	-		88	X	
3	ETX	CTRL-C	46	.		89	Y	
4	EOT		47	/		90	Z	
5	ENQ		48	0		91	[	
6	ACK		49	1		92	\	Backslash
7	BEL	BELL	50	2		93	]	
8	BS		51	3		94	^	
9	HT	Horizontal tab	52	4		95	-	
10	LF	Line feed	53	5		96	`	Grave accent
11	VT	Vertical tab	54	6		97	a	
12	FF	Form feed	55	7		98	b	
13	CR	Carriage return	56	8		99	c	
14	SO		57	9		100	d	
15	SI	CTRL-O	58	:		101	e	
16	DLE		59	;		102	f	
17	DCI		60	<		103	g	
18	DC2		61	=		104	h	
19	DC3		62	>		105	i	
20	DC4		63	?		106	j	
21	NAK	CTRL-U	64	@		107	k	
22	SYN		65	A		108	l	
23	ETB		66	B		109	m	
24	CAN		67	C		110	n	
25	EM		68	D		111	o	
26	SUB	CTRL-Z	69	E		112	p	
27	ESC	Escape	70	F		113	q	
28	FS		71	G		114	r	
29	GS		72	H		115	s	
30	RS		73	I		116	t	
31	US		74	J		117	u	
32	SP	Space	75	K		118	v	
33	!		76	L		119	w	
34	"		77	M		120	x	
35	≠	Hash	78	N		121	y	
36	$		79	O		122	z	
37	%		80	P		123	{	
38	&		81	Q		124			Vertical line
39	'	Apostrophe	82	R		125	}	
40	(		83	S		126	~	Tilde
41	)		84	T		127	DEL	Rubout
42	*		85	U				

Index

Syntax error 286
  program 285
  statement 285
Synthesis
  additive 49
  sound 48
  speech 161
  subtractive 49
Synthesiser 51
  analog 51
  digital 51
  multi-timbral 51
  music 51
  speech 161
  voice 161
Sysop (system operator) 115
System
  computer 4
  customised 223
  decision support (DSS) 159
  domain name 107
  embedded 4
  multiprocessor 168
  real-time 17
  run-time 288
  turnkey 224
System crash 289
System cycle 216
System development cycle 217
System diagram 230
System flowchart 230
  using British Standard alternative
    symbols 236
  using British Standard symbols 234
  using simplified symbols 234
System flowchart symbol 231
System life cycle 216
System operator (sysop) 115
System prompt 337
Systems analysis 219
Systems analyst 138
Systems application architecture (SAA)
  345
Systems design 220
Systems designer 138
Systems development personnel 137
Systems documentation 222
Systems engineer 138
Systems implementation 220
Systems network architecture (SNA) 345

Systems program 336
Systems programmer 138
Systems software 336
Systems specification 217, 227
Systems support personnel 139
Systems testing 220

Tab Separated Variable file (TSV file) 5
Table
  decision 274
  file allocation 188
  hash 329
  lookup 248
  name 341
  symbol 341
  trace 284
  truth 381
Table (data structure) 310
Table (database) 91
Tablet, graphics 31
Tag 303
Tape
  magnetic 182
  scratch 188
Tape cartridge 182
Tape cassette 182
Tape drive 181
Tape file symbol 233
Tape reader 131
Tape reel 182
Tape spool 182
Tape streamer 184
Tape track 182
TDM (Time Division Multiplexor)
  208
Technical documentation 221
Technical support staff 139
Tele-conferencing 116
Tele-processing 17
Tele-working 116
Telecommunications 4
Telemetry 132, 160
Teletext 161
Teletext character set 308
Telnet 111
Template 24
Terabyte 14
Terminal 126
  network 126
  point-of-sale 127